THE MEDIAEVAL ACADEMY OF AMERICA
PUBLICATION NO. 25

THE GOTHS IN THE CRIMEA

THE GOTHS IN THE CRIMEA

ALEXANDER ALEXANDROVICH VASILIEV

Professor of History
University of Wisconsin

THE MEDIAEVAL ACADEMY OF AMERICA

CAMBRIDGE, MASSACHUSETTS

1936

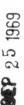

The publication of this book was made possible by grants of funds to the Academy from the Carnegie Corporation of New York and the American Council of Learned Societies

PREFACE

THIS book is not a history of the Goths in the Crimea. Our scattered and fragmentary sources do not permit such a history to be written. I have done my best to collect and use all available material, but I am sure that some related data have escaped my attention. Nor does the title of this book entirely correspond to its subject. The Goths as a remnant of the large Germanic branch which remained in the Crimea and was cut off from the main Gothic stock did not survive the Middle Ages. A minority in the Peninsula, they gradually lost their nationality and their Germanic tongue and were first hellenized and later tartarized. The evidence given by some writers late in the Middle Ages that Gothic was at that time spoken in the Crimea does not change the general picture. Some of these writers are not very reliable, since they drew their information from hearsay, never visiting Gothia themselves; others are more reliable, but their statements may be taken only as proof that in their time some individuals in Gothia, perhaps newcomers from Western Europe, could speak a Germanic dialect. The name *Gothia* finally lost its ethnographic meaning and was given to a Greek principality, in whose name alone the Germanic origin and old Germanic tradition survived. This example is not unique during the Middle Ages. Late in the Middle Ages Italian documents call the Crimea Ghazaria, which reminds us of the past power of the Khazars, who towards the tenth century lost all political significance. The Slavonic country of modern Bulgaria preserves in its name its Hunno-Turkish origin, just as the Slavonic state of Russia by its name goes back to its Scandinavian origin.

No doubt many of my statements in this book will be modified, corrected, or even rejected on the basis of new material. The Genoese, Venetian, and Italian archives in general still retain many secrets of Italian (especially Genoese and Venetian) political and economic activities in the Crimea, and the publication of their documents will throw new light on the history of Gothia in the second half of the Middle Ages. And it is not only archival documents that are extremely important for our subject. Archaeological expeditions to the territory of former Gothia are also of the greatest significance to the Gothic problem in the Crimea. The recent excavations undertaken by the Russian State Academy for the History of Material Culture concentrated on Eski-Kermen have already yielded brilliant results. The Russian archaeologists claim to have shown that the original stronghold of the Goths, Dory or Doros (Doras), which was so effectively described by Procopius, was located not on Mankup but on the plateau of Eski-Kermen. Others besides Russians are interested in the archaeological investigation of Gothia. In 1933 a joint Russo-American expedition (sponsored in part by the University of Pennsylvania) worked there. In 1929 a German scholar, Joseph Sauer, visited Gothia and ended his very interesting article on Christian monuments in the Gothic region in the Crimea with the following words: 'It would be an alluring problem, especially for us Germans, to undertake a thorough and systematic investigation of the whole region from the archaeological and ethnographic standpoints, and to give a concrete and vivid meaning to the term *Gothia* which has been so often discussed in old literature.'[1]

From the standpoint of the general background of political, social, and economic relations in the basin of the Black Sea during the Middle Ages, Gothia may be regarded and studied as one of the essential elements in the process of the development of European civilization in the Near East in general, and in the Crimea in particular.

Professor N. Bănescu of the University of Cluj (in Roumania) is at present particularly interested in the problem of the Crimean Goths. He announced a paper to be read at the Fourth International Congress of Byzantine Studies, which was held at Sofia in Bulgaria 9–16 September, 1934, with the title, 'Contribution to the History of the Principality of Theodoro-Mangup in the Crimea.' Bănescu did not personally attend the Congress, and for a while I had at my disposal only a brief summary of his paper, which runs as follows: 'Analysis of the information on the Goths of the Tauric Chersonesus, from Procopius down to their disappearance. The life of St John of Gothia and the Martyrdom of St Abo of Tiflis. In the fourteenth century Greek rulers replace the Gothic chiefs of the country; they reside in Doros, the same city as that of the former Gothic chiefs. Historical data which permit the identification of χώρα τὸ Δόρυ in Procopius with Doros, Theodoro, Mangup. Explanation of the enigmatic name of "Theodoro" of the Greek princes of Mangup.' In 1935 Bănescu printed his interesting study under the title given above.[2]

The first three sections of this book appeared in Russian, in the *Publications (Izvestiya) of the Academy for the History of Material Culture*, I (1921), 1–80 (pagination of an offprint) and v (1927), 179–282. For this book these three sections have been corrected, revised, and augmented. The last three sections (IV–VI) embracing the period from the year 1204 to the end of the eighteenth century have never before been printed. The manuscript of their original text is in the Archives of the Academy for

---

[1] J. Sauer, 'Die christlichen Denkmäler im Gotengebiet der Krim,' *Oriens Christianus*, 3rd Series, VII (Leipzig, 1932), 202. See also L. Schmidt, 'Zur Geschichte der Krimgoten,' *Schumacher-Festschrift* (Mainz, 1930), p. 336.

[2] N. Bănescu, 'Contribution à l'histoire de la seigneurie de Théodoro-Mangoup en Crimée,' *Byzantinische Zeitschrift*, XXXV (1935), 20–37. The author is not acquainted with the results of the recent Russian expedition to Eski-Kermen.

the History of Material Culture; but in spite of all my efforts the authorities of the Academy have refused to send me my manuscript, so that I have rewritten these sections on a much larger scale.

Working on a subject the references to which are scattered in many publications of different countries, in many languages, I have not been able to obtain access to all this material in the United States. Much of it I used during my stay in Paris in the summer of 1932; but for many questions connected with my work I have been forced to resort to the competence and kindness of my colleagues both in Europe and in this country. Their most liberal help, always offered with good will, spontaneity, and sincerity, has been very useful and comforting to me in the process of writing this book. I take pleasure in expressing my deep gratitude to many of my colleagues: in Czecho-Slovakia, Dr (Miss) M. A. Andreeva, of Prague; in England, Professor V. Minorski, of London; in France, Mr G. Lozinski, of Paris; in Germany, Professor Dr Franz Babinger, of Berlin; in Poland, Professor K. Chylinski, of Lwow (Lemberg); in Roumania, Professors N. Bănescu, of Cluj, N. Iorga, of Bucarest, and O. Tafrali, of Jassy; in Russia, Professor S. A. Zhebelev, of Leningrad, and Mr D. S. Spiridonov, of Simferopol; in the United States of America, Professors R. P. Blake, of Harvard, and N. N. Martinovich, of New York. And last but not least, I acknowledge my indebtedness to Mrs C. W. Thomas, who has conscientiously revised my manuscript and corrected the inadequacies of my English.

A. A. VASILIEV

Madison, Wisconsin
3 June 1935

CONTENTS

THE GOTHS IN THE CRIMEA

CHAPTER I

THE EARLY PERIOD OF CHRISTIANITY
AND THE EPOCH OF THE MIGRATIONS

1. THE APPEARANCE OF THE GOTHS IN THE CRIMEA
AND THE INTRODUCTION OF CHRISTIANITY

BY the middle of the third century A.D. the Goths had migrated from
the shores of the Baltic Sea and settled in the territory known today
as Southern Russia, particularly along the northern and western shores
of the Black Sea. As a natural result, they penetrated into the Tauric
peninsula, where at that time the Bosporan Kingdom was predominant.
The Goths established their suzerainty over the greater part of that kingdom and took possession of its fleet, an important economic achievement.
With the fleet they carried out several bold and far-reaching sea raids.
These raids, as well as those of their compatriots from the mouths of the
Dnieper and the Dniester, not only terrorized the eastern, western, and
southern shores of the Black Sea, but were even felt on the coast of the
Propontis (the Sea of Marmora), and in the islands and on the coasts of
the Aegean and Mediterranean.

The original source for information concerning Gothic raids and invasions before Constantine the Great, and the foundation of all subsequent
sources, is the works of a contemporary Athenian, Herennius Dexippus,
whom Photius calls a second Thucydides;[1] most unfortunately this source
has not come down to us. In the twelve books of his Chronicle (Χρονικά)
Dexippus gave a brief chronological account of events down to the reign of
Emperor Claudius Gothicus (268–270). His Scythian History (Σκυθικά)
described the struggle of the Romans with the peoples north of the lower
Danube and along the northern shore of the Euxine, especially the Goths;
as far as we can judge from the fragments which have reached us, this
covered the years from 238 to 271. Dexippus was largely used by the
so-called Scriptores historiae Augustae, whose compilation is now attributed by most scholars to the fourth century, as well as by Zosimus, an
historian of the fifth century, and by George Syncellus, a chronicler of
the ninth century.

The sources just mentioned give us a fairly clear idea of the sea raids
of the Goths and cause us to wonder at their boldness and enterprise.
After falling upon Pityus (now Pitzunda), on the eastern shore of the
Black Sea, and Trebizond, in the south, the Goths raided Nicomedia,

---

[1] *Photii Bibliotheca*, LXXXII: 'ὡς ἄν τις εἴποι, ἄλλος μετά τινος σαφηνείας Θουκυδίδης, μάλιστά γε ἐν ταῖς
Σκυθικαῖς ἱστορίαις' (Migne, *Patrologia Graeca*, CIII, col. 281).

3

Nicaea, and Prusa in the basin of the Sea of Marmora, the famous Temple of Artemis of Ephesus on the littoral of Asia Minor, and the islands of the Aegean. They besieged Thessalonica and attacked Greece, but were driven back from Athens by the above-mentioned historian, Dexippus, who headed the Athenians. At the same time they invaded the western shore of the Black Sea and the Balkan peninsula as far as the cities of Serdica (Sofia) and Naissus (Nish). Even such distant islands as Crete, Rhodes, and Cyprus failed to escape Gothic incursions. We must bear in mind that the sources dealing with Gothic raids frequently call the Goths Scythians; and both names are used not only for the Goths, but also for other peoples who acted with them, especially the Heruli.

2. The Introduction of Christianity among the Goths

The Gothic invasions of the third century into the territory of the Roman Empire suggest the problem of the origin of Christianity among the Goths. Many sources[1] definitely state that it was introduced by Christian captives from Asia Minor, especially from Cappadocia. In the sources which have survived it is extremely difficult to distinguish the accounts which refer especially to the Crimean Goths. But since we know that they used Bosporan vessels to take an active part in incursions, we may feel certain that they brought back some Christian captives into the Crimea; and for the existence of Christianity in the Crimea in general, and in Panticapaea (Bosporus) in particular, we have corroborative evidence dating from the very beginning of the fourth century, of which I shall speak later.

One of the sources usually referred to for the Gothic invasions of the third century and the carrying away of Christian captives is the Canonical Epistle of the Bishop of Neocaesarea, St Gregory the Thaumaturge, who died not earlier than 270.[2] His epistle was written under the vivid impression of a recent invasion into the province of Pontus by the Goths and a mysterious people, the Boradi (Βοράδοι καὶ Γότθοι), who had terribly devastated the country, murdered and captured its inhabitants, violated women, and indulged in shameless pillaging. This invasion had a bad moral effect on some of the local population; according to the epistle, forgetting that 'they are of Pontus and Christians'[3] they joined the bar-

---

[1] V. Vasilievski, *Works*, II, ii (St Petersburg, 1912), 365–370; D. Belikov, *Christianity among the Goths*, I (Kazan, 1887), 25–36. Both in Russian.

[2] S. N. Sagarda, *Saint Gregory the Thaumaturge, Bishop of Neocaesarea, His Life, Works, and Theology* (Petrograd, 1916), p. 198 (in Russian).

[3] Ἐπιστολὴ κανονικὴ τοῦ ἁγίου Γρηγορίου, Κανὼν Ζ': 'ἐπιλαθομένους ὅτι ἦσαν Ποντικοὶ καὶ Χριστιανοί,' Rhallis and Potlis, Σύνταγμα τῶν θείων καὶ ἱερῶν κανόνων, IV (Athens, 1854), 60; Migne, *Patr. Gr.*, x, col. 1040; Sagarda's Russian translation: *The Works of Saint Gregory the Thaumaturge, Bishop of Neocaesarea* (Petrograd, 1916), p. 61 (§ 7).

barians in plundering and showed them the paths through the mountains.
After the departure of the Goths these men even attacked their own compatriots and seized their property under the pretext that during the invasion they had lost their own; to sum up, according to the epistle, 'since
the Boradi and Goths had treated them as enemies, they became themselves Boradi and Goths towards others.'[1]

I have dwelt on the Canonical Epistle of Gregory, because it has been
the cause of misunderstanding in some historical works, though not in recent ones.   In 1863 Pallmann published a work on the question of the
orthodox ('katholische') Goths in the Crimea and of the origin of Christianity there at an early period; he concludes: 'From an epistle of Gregory,
Bishop of Neocaesarea, and from another reference in his writings we may
suppose that the Crimean Goths were already Christians in 258.'[2]   Ph.
Bruun took over this statement: 'From an epistle of the Bishop of Neocaesarea, Gregory, and from another reference in his writings we learn
that in 258 the Crimean Goths professed the Christian faith, namely the
orthodox, for about the middle of the third century the question of Arianism had not arisen.'[3]   As I have indicated in footnotes, both Pallmann
and Bruun — the latter not directly but through Pallmann — referred
to an old German work by Mascou.   But Mascou, although he refers in
the indicated place to the epistle of Gregory of Neocaesarea, uses it as a
source for the Gothic attack under Emperor Valerian, and not as a proof
of Christianity among the Goths at that time.   In another section, where
he is discussing the conversion of the Goths to Christianity, Mascou does
not mention Gregory of Neocaesarea.[4]

The foundation for the statement given above is the opening lines of
the Canonical Epistle, which run as follows: 'For all say with one voice
that the barbarians who invaded our country offered no sacrifices to
idols.'[5]   But these words do not, in my opinion, necessarily mean that
the Goths were already Christians before their invasion into the Pontus,
that is, in the middle of the third century A.D.; had this been the fact,

---

[1] Κανὼν Ε': 'ἵνα ἐπειδὴ αὐτοὺς Βοράδοι καὶ Γότθοι τὰ τῶν πολεμίων εἰργάσαντο, αὐτοὶ ἄλλοις Βοράδοι καὶ Γότθοι γίνωνται,' Rhallis and Potlis, Σύνταγμα, ιν, 58; Migne, *Patr. Gr.*, x, col. 1037; Sagarda, *Saint Gregory*, p. 60 (§ 5). See Vasilievski, *Works*, ιι, ii, 361–362; Sagarda, *Saint Gregory*, pp. 189–190 (on this same Canonic epistle see pp. 284 ff.).   Both in Russian.

[2] R. Pallmann, *Die Geschichte der Völkerwanderung von der Gothenbekehrung bis zum Tode Alarichs* (Gotha, 1863), p. 65, n. 2, where there is added: 'Cf. Mascou, *Gesch. d. Deutschen*, i, 173.'

[3] Ph. Bruun, 'The Goths of the Black Sea and the Traces of Their Long Stay in Southern Russia,' *Chernomorye*, ιι (Odessa, 1880), 195 (in Russian), with the following reference: 'Mascou, *Gesch. d. Deutschen*, i, 173,' which had already been given by Pallmann (see preceding note).

[4] I. J. Mascou, *Geschichte der Deutschen bis zum Anfang der fränkischen Monarchie* (Leipzig, 1726), pp. 172–173, 317–319.

[5] ''Επειδὴ εἰς λόγος παρὰ πάντων τοὺς καταδραμόντας τὰ ἡμέτερα μέρη βαρβάρους εἰδώλοις μὴ τεθυκέναι,' Rhallis and Potlis, Σύνταγμα, ιν, 45; *Patr. Gr.*, x, col. 1020.

Gregory would have said so more precisely.[1] In that case he would not have found it necessary to answer the question which he does answer at the beginning of the epistle, as to the food of the Christian captives, whether eating with the barbarians was regarded by the Christians as pollution, etc. This question would have been superfluous if Gregory had considered the Goths Christians.

Though our historical evidence positively states that Christianity penetrated among the Goths through the captive Greeks of Asia Minor, there is, on the other hand, a tradition that Christianity in the Crimea, particularly in Chersonesus, appeared from Palestine under Constantine the Great. This tradition has been preserved in the Greek *Lives of the Sainted Bishops of Chersonesus*, as well as in the Slavonic and Georgian versions,[2] and is briefly to the following effect. In the reign of the impious emperor Diocletian, 'the wise Hermon who adorned the throne of the church of Jerusalem' ordained bishops and sent them all over the country to convert the unbelievers to Christianity; among these two bishops were sent to the northern shore of the Black Sea, Basileas to Tauric Chersonesus and Ephraim to Scythia. Basileas paved the way for Christianity in Chersonesus and suffered there a martyr's death. Afterwards three bishops, also sent by Hermon, Eugenius, Agathodorus, and Elpidius, arrived from the province of Hellespont; they also earned the martyr's crown from the pagans and Jews who lived there. Many years later, a fifth bishop, Aetherius, was sent from Jerusalem to Chersonesus; but he did not reach the end of his mission, for his ship drifted to one of the islands at the mouth of the Dnieper and he died there. In the tenth century Constantine Porphyrogenitus speaks of the island of St Aetherius at the mouth of the Dnieper, which shows that the memory of the Saint was preserved in that region during the Middle Ages.[3] After these early attempts Christianity was definitely established among the Chersonesians under Constantine the Great; in the year of the Council of Nicaea, 325, the Cher-

---

[1] S. Vasilievski, *Works*, II, ii, 361–362 and n. 1 (in Russian). An inaccuracy must be mentioned in his note, which runs as follows: 'Hence it is still less apparent that the barbarians who are spoken of here were Christians, as Pallmann, following old Mascou, repeats; Pallmann himself was evidently not acquainted with the contents of the fragment.' As we have seen, Mascou does not speak of it.

[2] V. Latyshev, 'The Lives of the Sainted Bishops of Chersonesus, Study and texts,' *Zapiski* of the Academy of Sciences, VIII, No. 3 (St Petersburg, 1906). In this edition are collected Greek and Slavonic texts. Later this text was re-edited by Latyshev in the *Menologii Anonymi Byzantini saeculi x quae supersunt*, I (St Petersburg, 1911), 197–202. The same text, along with several Slavonic versions, was reprinted by P. Lavrov, *The Lives of the Saints of Chersonesus in Greco-Slavonic Literature, Monuments of the Christian Chersonesus*, II (Moscow, 1911), 154–171. A version of a Georgian text is given by K. Kekelidze in the *Izvestiya* of the Archaeological Commission, No. 49 (St Petersburg, 1913), 83–88.

[3] Constantine Porphyrogenitus, *De administrando imperio*, p. 78 (Bonn ed.). See J. Zeiller, *Les origines chrétiennes dans les provinces danubiennes de l'empire romain* (Paris, 1918), p. 411, n. 3.

sonesian Christians received a bishop, Kapiton, who, like his predecessors, suffered there a martyr's death.

The editor and investigator of the *Lives*, V. Latyshev, considers it 'at first sight very strange and even puzzling that the bishop of Jerusalem, at the very beginning of the fourth century, sent missionaries to far-off Scythia'; but he believes the nucleus of this story is a fact, and he admits that seven bishops of Jerusalem, ordained by Hermon, appeared as missionaries in remote Chersonesus.[1]

Many scholars, however, fail to agree with his opinion. In a work which came out before Latyshev's edition, Franko, after studying and making use of many Greek and Slavonic versions of the *Lives*, came to the conclusion that the tale of seven Chersonesian martyrs was a fabrication which appeared in Chersonesus in the middle of the fifth century. It reflected the ecclesiastical relations of that time, that is, the struggle of the Chersonesian bishops for their independence from the Constantinopolitan patriarch, who endeavored to bring under his jurisdiction the eparchies of the northern shore of the Black Sea. According to Franko, the legend of the mission of Jerusalem was first invented to show the independence of the Chersonesian church from Constantinople. At the Council of Chalcedon in 451, however, the Chersonesian church lost its independence and submitted to the patriarchate of Constantinople. The influence of Constantinople changed the legend to show that the mission of Jerusalem had been fruitless, and that only with the support of Constantinople had Christianity been established in Chersonesus. Franko concludes that the legend possesses no 'real reminiscence from the times of Diocletian and Constantine.'[2]

E. Golubinski also denies the historical truth of the *Lives* and thinks their statements inadmissible; he assumes that the story of the Chersonesian martyrs may have originated from the Christians who were captured by the Goths during their raids on the shores of the Black Sea, and believes that with them is connected the origin of Christianity in the Crimea. The legend of missionaries sent by the bishop of Jerusalem might have been due to the desire of endowing this first establishment of Christianity on the far off border with the special glory of Jerusalem. But Golubinski considers it possible that the Chersonesian Christians asked Constantine the Great for a bishop, and that he granted their request.[3]

[1] Latyshev, *The Lives*, pp. 35, 37.

[2] Franko, 'St. Clement in Korsun,' *Zapiski* of the Learned Society of the Name of Shevchenko, VI (T. LVI), 1903, 163–164 (in Ukrainian). Latyshev became acquainted with this study during the printing of his own texts and referred to Franko's work only in the additions to his own. He denied the scholarly importance of Franko's conclusions (pp. 77–79).

[3] E. Golubinski, 'Chersonian Martyrs Whose Saints' Day is March 7,' *Izvestiya Otdeleniya Russkago Yazika i Slovesnosti*, XII, i (1907), 263–272 (in Russian).

In a long essay on Latyshev's edition, K. Kharlampovich also comes to
the conclusion that Latyshev 'has not succeeded in proving the historical
significance of the tale of seven Chersonesian martyrs.'[1]

E. Ivanov, summarizing these texts, also reaches a negative conclusion
as to their reliability.   'In these texts,' he writes, 'the kernel of historical
truth is always wrapped in a thick layer of apocryphal tales, and it is very
difficult to penetrate this layer and reach the truth. . . .   Giving extracts from the Lives of Chersonesian saints, we do not consider them at
all authentic facts but regard them as apocrypha.'   Ivanov acknowledges
historical significance in the missionary deeds of Bishop Kapiton.[2]

But S. P. Shestakov agrees with Latyshev's view.   After a detailed discussion of Franko's and Latyshev's opinions, Shestakov states that 'even
after the criticism of Franko we are inclined to see in the Chersonesian
legend concerning the first bishops of the city . . . a repercussion of real
events.'[3]

It is very interesting to note here an observation of M. Rostovtzeff on the
decorative paintings of Chersonesian graves.   'The system of decorative
painting of Christian graves in Chersonesus finds its closest parallel either
in the Syro-Palestinian East or among monuments whose connection with
Syria and Palestine seems very probable.   It is quite possible, therefore,
that in the fourth and fifth centuries, along with the establishment of
Christianity in Chersonesus, some Christian graves were painted in the
feeling and style used at an earlier date, as well as at the same time, in
the Syro-Palestinian South.   This, no doubt, indicates a close connection
of the first Christians in Chersonesus, not with Byzantium or the Balkan
peninsula, but with the more distant Syro-Palestinian church, which one
would think might have seemed foreign to them, and with which Christianity in the Caucasus was also connected.'[4]   Thereupon, after a study
of the *Lives* of the Chersonesian martyrs, he comes to the conclusion that
the text which has come down to us is a compilation consisting of three
parts, which belong to three different authors (an account of Basileas and
his companions, the tale of Kapiton, and the legend of St Aetherius).
Rostovtzeff decides that 'the analysis of Chersonesian graves shows that
the first part of the *Life* — that of Jerusalem — goes back to that nucleus
of the Christian community of Chersonesus, which, as the graves de-

[1] K. Kharlampovich, in the *Zapiski* of the University of Kazan, LXXV, ii (1908), 22, criticism and
bibliography (in Russian).

[2] E. Ivanov, 'The Tauric Chersonesus, an Historico-archaeological sketch,' *Izvestiya* of the Tauric
Learned Archive Commission, XLVI (Simferopol, 1912), 54.

[3] S. Shestakov, *Outlines on the History of Chersonesus in the Sixth–Tenth Centuries A.D., Monuments
of the Christian Chersonesus*, III (Moscow, 1908), 25 (in Russian).

[4] M. Rostovtzeff, *Ancient Decorative Painting in South Russia* (St Petersburg, 1914), p. 503 (in
Russian).

scribed have shown, was closely connected with Syria and Palestine, but in no wise with Constantinople; and the clergy of that ancient community was probably not local, but foreigners who had come from the south.'[1] Rostovtzeff's conclusions based on archaeological material serve, certainly, as a justification of the historical value of the Jerusalem tradition of the *Lives* of the Chersonesian martyrs.

But we have some other information which definitely bears on the relations in the fourth century of the shore of the Black Sea (that is, Danubian Gothia) with Syria. I refer to the stay among the Goths of the missionary Audius and his followers (Audians), on which Epiphanius of Cyprus gives us some interesting but rather obscure information. Audius, a contemporary of Arius, came from Mesopotamia, where he distinguished himself by the austerity of his life and his zealous worship of God. But he required the same austerity from others, and therefore vigorously denounced all — no matter whether they were representatives of the clergy, even bishops, or laymen — who in any way deviated from his religious and moral requirements, and in his denunciation he was so inexorable and rigid that he created a great number of personal enemies. These enemies laughed at Audius and his followers, insulted and beat them, and drove them out. Driven to despair, Audius broke with the official church; thereupon his followers abandoned cities and villages and lived in monasteries which they constructed for themselves.[2] From the further account of Epiphanius we see that Audius, in his reference to the passage from Genesis (I, 26), 'Let us make man in our image, after our likeness,' deviated in his doctrine from the Catholic Church and rejected the decree of the Council of Nicaea concerning the time of the celebration of Easter. For us, however, the religious side of the question is of secondary importance, the more so as we have not enough evidence for its complete interpretation.[3] For our purposes it is sufficient to point out that Constantine the Great sent Audius into exile because of his doctrine and deported him to Scythia, where Audius stayed many years among the Goths and converted many of them to Christianity. 'Then in Gothia there came into being monasteries, holy life, purity, and asceticism, which had not existed before.'[4] Epiphanius, author of the story, notes with horrified disgust that Audius called his followers not Christians but Audians.

[1] Rostovtzeff, *op. cit.*, pp. 503–505.

[2] S. *Epiphanii Adversus haereses*, III, i, 1; *Patr. Gr.*, XLII, col. 340. See Belikov, *Christianity among the Goths*, I (Kazan, 1887), 42–44.

[3] See J. Mansion, 'Les origines du christianisme chez les Gots,' in the *Analecta Bollandiana*, XXXIII (1914), 7; J. Zeiller, *Les origines chrétiennes dans les provinces danubiennes* (Paris, 1918), pp. 419–420.

[4] 'Εἰς τὰ πρόσω βαίνων καὶ εἰς τὰ ἐσώτατα τῆς Γοτθίας, πολλοὺς τῶν Γότθων κατήχησεν. ἀφ' οὗπερ καὶ μοναστήρια ἐν τῇ αὐτῇ Γοτθίᾳ ἐγένετο καὶ πολιτεία καὶ παρθενία τε καὶ ἄσκησις οὐχ ἡ τυχοῦσα,' *Patr. Gr.*, XLII, col. 372.

After Audius' death his doctrine was widely adopted not only in Gothia but also in Mesopotamia, where Bishop Uranius received several men from Gothia and ordained them as bishops.[1] This indicates the existence of relations in the fourth century between the western shore of the Black Sea and Mesopotamia. In Antioch and in the region of the Euphrates there were Audian communities. Later, when a local persecution of the Christians in general broke out in Gothia, many Audians left Gothia for the East, and for a time their monasteries existed in Palestine and Arabia.[2] In other words, the story of Audius and the Audians in the fourth century serves to corroborate the historical tradition about the relations of the western shores of the Black Sea with Palestine and Syria. Therefore, from Rostovtzeff's analogies and from the history of the Audian mission, we are inclined to see in the Jerusalem tradition of the *Lives* of the Chersonesian martyrs the nucleus of an historical truth obscured by later local pious inventions.

To my knowledge, the earliest dated evidence for Christianity in the Crimea occurs in the epitaph of a certain Eutropius, which was found in Kerch and is preserved in the Melék Chesmé tumulus (*kurgan*). The stone is a round broken slab in the center of which is cut a cross with widening crosspieces. Above the cross is the following inscription: 'Here rests Eutropius, 601.' This epitaph is particularly interesting on account of the exact date, 601, which, given according to the Bosporan era, corresponds to the year 304 of the Christian era. Hence it proves that in the Bosporus a Christian community must already have been in existence towards the end of the third century.[3]

According to epigraphic indications some other undated Christian epitaphs may be referred to the fourth century, for instance, three epitaphs with the names of Lavnika, Euprepius, and Maria respectively, the last on a stone in the shape of a trapezium. Finally, another epitaph with the name of Plato, on a stone shaped like a cross, has been found in Tamán.[4]

Apparently the first evidence of Christianity among the Goths in general is the oration of Athanasius the Great 'On the Incarnation of the Word,' which was written between 319 and 321. The author refers to

---

[1] ''Από τῆς Γοτθίας δὲ ἔσχε τινὰς, καὶ κατέστησεν αὐτοὺς ἐπισκόπους,' *ibid.*, col. 372.

[2] *Ibid.*, col. 373.

[3] V. Shkorpil, 'Three Christian Epitaphs Found in Kerch in 1898,' *Zapiski* of the Odessa Society of History and Antiquities, xxii (1900), Minutes, p. 59; Y. Marti, 'Description of the Melék Chesmé Tumulus in Connection with the History of the Bosporan Kingdom,' *Prilozheniya* (Supplements) to the *Zapiski* of the Odessa Society, xxxi (1913), 19, 50 (on p. 19 an epitaph is reproduced). Both articles in Russian.

[4] *Prilozheniye* (Supplement) to the *Zapiski* of the Odessa Society, xxviii (1907), 134; Marti, *op. cit.*, p. 66 (Nos. 141, 142, 142a, and 144). In Russian.

superstitions, savage customs, and idolatry occurring among supposedly Christian peoples, the Scythians, Ethiopians, Persians, Armenians, Goths, certain dwellers beyond the Ocean (τοὺς ἐπέκεινα τοῦ Ὠκεανοῦ λεγομένους), Egyptians, and Chaldaeans, and then writes that 'the Lord of all, the Power of God, our Lord Jesus Christ not only preached by means of His own disciples, but also carried persuasion to men's minds, to lay aside the fierceness of their manners, and no longer to serve their ancestral gods, but to learn to know Him, and through Him to worship the Father.'[1] In this passage the Goths, as we see, occur only as one among many other peoples. But it is important for us to note that Athanasius considers them a Christian people.

We have more information on Christianity among the Goths for the epoch of the First Oecumenical Council of Nicaea in 325. At this council some bishops were present and gave their signatures whose eparchies are connected with the Crimea, namely: Cadmus of Bosporus (Κάδμος, Ἄμνος, Βάδμνος), Philippus of Chersonesus, and Theophilus, Metropolitan of Gothia. The first two sees cause no doubt as to location; but there is some discrepancy concerning Theophilus. In the Acts of the Council of Nicaea the signature of the Gothic bishop is read in two different ways. According to the *Colbertinus* version we have:

De Gothis
Theophilus Bosphoritanus
Domnus Bosphorensis

According to some other versions:

Provinciae Gothiae
Theophilus Gothiae metropolis.
Provinciae Bosphori
Domnus Bosphorensis. Cathirius Bosphori.[2]

It is usually thought that in the *Colbertinus* version there is a lacuna, which has given us the idea that there are in it two Bosporan bishops, Theophilus and Domnus; accordingly some scholars assume that the version should be read as follows:

Theophilus Gothiae metropolis
Provinciae Bosphori
Domnus Bosphorensis.[3]

But in my opinion there is no need to assume a lacuna. In the lists of signatures the name of the place which a bishop represents usually stands before his name. Therefore, if we put the words in this order:

De Gothis Theophilus

---

[1] *S. Athanasii Oratio de incarnatione Verbi*, 51; *Patr. Gr.*, xxv, col. 188.

[2] Mansi, *Sacrorum conciliorum nova et amplissima collectio*, ii, 696, 702.

[3] See Vasilievski, *Works*, ii, ii, 369 (in Russian).

Bosphoritanus

Domnus Bosphorensis,

we shall have exactly the same arrangement as in the other versions, that
is: Theophilus represents the Goths, Domnus of Bosphorus represents
Bosporus.   The lack of the name 'Gothia' may indicate the early origin
of the signature, when the name Gothia for the country was less common
than the mere designation 'from the Goths.'

In 1898 many versions of the list of the Fathers of the Nicene Council
were published: four Latin versions, two Greek, one Coptic, two Syriac,
one Arabic, and one Armenian.[1]   In the same year O. Braun edited the
Syriac list of Maruta of Maipherkat, but only in a German translation.[2]
In 1899 C. H. Turner republished the Latin versions of the list.[3]   In 1908
V. Beneshevich published a new list of the Fathers of this Council, based
on a Greek Sinaitic manuscript of the fourteenth century.[4]   Beneshevich
has two other complete Greek lists of 318 names which he discovered in
Jerusalem manuscripts (*Cod. Metoch.* and *Cod. Patr.*) and which he has
not yet published; but he has carefully compared them with the Sinaitic
list and has given the results of his comparison to D. Lebedev, who has
made use of them in his essay on the list of the Bishops of the First
Oecumenical Council.   It has been found that the two Jerusalem lists go
back, evidently, to the same prototype as the Sinaitic.[5]

Theophilus, Bishop of Gothia, is mentioned in almost all lists of the
signatures of the Acts of the Council.   Out of four Latin versions published by Gelzer the name of Theophilus is given in three: (1) 216.   'Theophilus Gutthias'; (2) 216.   'Theofilus Gutthiae'; and (3) 219.   'Theofilus
Gotiae.'[6]   Theophilus is mentioned in all four lists published by Turner:
(1) 'Theophilus Gutthias,' (2) 'Theophilus Gutthiae,' (3) 'Theoilus
Gotiae,' and (4) 'Theophilus Gottiae.'[7]   The name of Theophilus is
found in all five Greek versions: *Cod. Marc. 211*, 'Γοτθίας Θεόφιλος'; *Cod.
Vatic. 88*, 'Θεόφιλος Γοτθίας'; *Cod. Sin. 66*. 'Θεόφιλος Γοτθίας'; *Cod. Hier.
Metoch.* and *Cod. Hieros. Patr. 67*, Θεόφιλος Γοτθίας.'[8]

[1] *Patrum Nicaenorum nomina latine graece coptice syriace arabice armeniace*, ed. H. Gelzer, H.
Hilgenfeld, O. Cuntz, *Scriptores sacri et profani*, II (Leipzig, 1898).   For the sake of brevity, I shall
refer to this edition as Gelzer's.

[2] *De Sancta Nicaena Synodo, Syrische Texte des Maruta von Maipherkat*, translated by O. Braun,
Kirchengeschichtliche Studien, IV, 3 (Münster, 1898), 29–34.

[3] *Ecclesiae Occidentalis Monumenta Juris Antiquissima*, ed. C. H. Turner, I, i (Oxford, 1899),
35–96; II (1904), 97–102.

[4] V. Beneshevich, 'A Sinaitic List of the Fathers of the First Oecumenical Council,' *Izvestiya* of the
Academy of Sciences (St Petersburg, 1908), pp. 281–306.

[5] See D. Lebedev, 'The List of the Bishops of the First Oecumenical Council of 318 Names: On the
Problem of Its Origin and Significance for the Reconstruction of the Genuine List of the Nicene
Fathers,' *Zapiski* of the Academy of Sciences, 8th Series, XIII, 1 (Petrograd, 1916), 4.   In Russian.

[6] Gelzer, pp. 56–57.

[7] Turner, *op. cit.*, I, i, 90–91; see another list, I, ii, 101: '217, Theofilus de Gottia.'

[8] Gelzer, pp. 70 and 73; Beneshevich, p. 290; Lebedev, p. 42.

The Coptic list published by Gelzer is incomplete (162 names in all); therefore we can not be sure whether or not Theophilus was mentioned in it; but since the Coptic list is only a translation of a Greek text, and, according to the table of different lists given by Beneshevich, is particularly related to *Cod. Marc.*, we may assume that the name of Theophilus occurs there also.   In the two Syriac lists published by Gelzer Theophilus is mentioned: (1) 217. 'Theophilus Gothiae'; (2) 220. 'Theophilus Gothorum.'[1]   A bishop at the Nicene Council from Gothia but without a name is also mentioned in the Syriac list of Maruta, Bishop of Maipherkat (died about 420), a contemporary of Arcadius and Theodosius II.[2] In the Arabic list occurs 156, 'Theophilus Gotthopolis'[3] (I shall discuss this form a little later).   In the Armenian list we read 210.   'Theophilus e Gothis.'[4]

It is interesting to point out that in three Greek lists, the Sinaitic and the two from Jerusalem, all of which, as has been noted above, go back to one prototype, there occurs, along with 'Θεόφιλος Γοτθίας,' 'Θεόφιλος Γουτθοπόλεως' (Theophilus of Guthopolis);[5] from these this reading has evidently passed into the Arabic list mentioned above.   As it is improbable that there were two Theophili from the country of the Goths, and as the name 'Guthopolis' is found only in a few later lists, it would be natural to explain the appearance of 'Theophilus of Guthopolis' as a mere mistake in writing.

It may be noticed here that the Russian Voskresenskaya Chronicle (*Letopis*) gives several names of bishops who took part in the Council of Nicaea; among them is 'Ivan, episcop Godskiy' (John, Gothic bishop).[6]

But it is absolutely unexpected for the history of early Christianity in the Crimea to find in the Sinaitic and Jerusalem lists, among other signatures, that of Philippus, Bishop of Chersonesus: in the Sinaitic list 'Φίλιππος Χερσῶνος,' in the Jerusalem 'Φίλιππος Χερσεῶνος.'[7]   From here this signature has passed into the Arabic list, where, in Gelzer's edition, the name of the city from which Philippus comes is given as 'Sirianus'; but the forms of the Arabic letters permit us to read 'Cherson.'[8]   It is difficult to come to a definite conclusion merely on the hypothesis of one Greek prototype of the list of the Fathers of the Council of Nicaea; but if this were justified, it would be, for the question of the origin of Christianity, a new and most important fact that at the Council of 325, along with the Bishop of Bosporus, there was also present the Bishop of Cher-

[1] Gelzer, pp. 117 and 141.   [2] O. Braun, *De Sancta Nicaena Synodo*, p. 34.
[3] Gelzer, pp. 162–163.   [4] Gelzer, pp. 214–215.
[5] Beneshevich, p. 296 (154); Lebedev, p. 40 (155).
[6] *Complete Collection of Russian Chronicles*, VII, 248 (in Old Russian).
[7] Beneshevich, p. 295 (145); Lebedev, p. 27.   [8] Gelzer, pp. 160–161 (117); Lebedev, p. 27, n. 6.

sonesus; in other words, we could conclude that at the outset of the fourth century there existed in the Crimea not only numerous Christians, but also a large church organization.

Some discrepancy has arisen as to Theophilus of Gothia.   Some scholars believe Gothia to have been an eparchy lying within the territory of the Crimea; others, and we must admit the majority, are inclined to place this eparchy in the west, on the western shore of the Black Sea, among those Goths who settled in the northern region of the Balkan peninsula, on the Lower Danube, and whose possessions in the fourth century extended north-eastwards as far as the Dniester and Dnieper.[1]

About 1870 the Archbishop of Kharkov, Macarius, mentions among other signatures of the Acts of the First Oecumenical Council that of the bishop of the Goths, Theophilus, as a Metropolitan of Gothia, or, as is given in other lists, Theophilus *Bosphoritanus* from Gothia, and concludes, 'It shows that the residence of the Gothic bishop was first situated not in the Crimea, where it was established later, but in the country extending from the Danube to the Dniester and the Black Sea, which was then beginning to be called Gothia, in ancient Dacia, that is, in a district of present-day Wallachia; and, still more precisely, the residence was found near Bosporus[2] on the Black Sea — undisputedly, on present-day Russian soil.'[3]   In complete agreement with Macarius, Bishop Hermogenes calls Theophilus Metropolitan of Bosporus from Gothia.[4]   The Archimandrite Arsenius, who explains the origin of Christianity among the Crimean Goths by the influence of Christian captives from Cappadocia, also associates with these Goths the bishop Theophilus.   He gives the two versions of Theophilus' signature and remarks, 'As the Bishop of Bosporus, Domnus (Domnus Bosporitanus), was present and wrote his signature at the same council with Theophilus, it seems probable that Theophilus was called *Bosporitanus* not after the name of the city but as the metropolitan of all the Goths who lived near the Cimmerian Bosporus.'[5]

On this question Vasilievski seems to be rather at a loss.   In one place he writes, 'At the First Oecumenical Council a bishop of Gothia is already present who has his residence in the district of Bosporus, that is, certainly in the Crimea.'   In another place he observes that according to some

[1] The old statement of Koeppen that Theophilus of Gothia is 'doubtless the same person as the translator of the Scriptures into the Gothic, Ulfila,' certainly can not be accepted as valid, P. Koeppen, *Krymsky Sbornik* (St Petersburg, 1837), p. 65 (in Russian).

[2] Obviously the Cimmerian Bosporus.

[3] Macarius, *A History of Christianity in Russia before the Isoapostolic Prince Vladimir* (St Petersburg, 1868), pp. 54–55 (in Russian).

[4] Bishop Hermogenes, *The Tauric Eparchy* (Pskov, 1887), pp. 146–147 (in Russian).

[5] Arsenius, 'The Gothic Eparchy in the Crimea,' *Journal of the Ministry of Public Instruction*, CLXV (1873), 61–62 (in Russian).

scholars Theophilus was the bishop of the Tauric Goths, but according to others, only of the Bosporan Goths; on certain grounds he then comes to the conclusion that 'in the person of Theophilus we do not yet have a real and special Taurico-Gothic bishop.'[1] He is inclined to locate the eparchy of Gothia in the metropolitan city of Tomi (near modern Kustendji) on the western shore of the Black Sea, in the territory of the Scythian eparchy, which, according to the statement of the church historian Sozomenos,[2] was the only orthodox eparchy among the Goths.

Bruun places Theophilus in the Crimea and believes that the orthodoxy of the Crimean Goths is shown by the fact that to the members who signed the Acts of the Council of Nicaea belonged the Gothic bishop Theophilus, Theophilus Bosporitanus.[3] V. N. Belikov, who has done special work on the origin of Christianity among the Goths, relying on an old German book by Krafft,[4] thinks that the Gothic metropole of Theophilus is to be placed, most probably, 'near the Danube, that is to say, not far away from the border of the Empire.'[5] In his very interesting but rather brief book on the later history of the Crimean Goths, F. A. Braun also places the Gothic metropole, not in the Crimea, but on the Lower Danube.[6] Taking into consideration Theophilus' signature to the Acts of the Council, E. Golubinski writes that his see 'was located in the city of Bosporus, modern Kerch,' and thinks that Christianity began to spread among the Western Goths a little later, 'about thirty years before the appearance of the Huns in Europe and before the departure of the Goths away from the Huns westwards.'[7] In confirmation of the theory that 'the appearance of the Goths in the Crimean peninsula, first in its eastern part, near Kerch, may have occurred in the first half of the fourth century A.D.,' S. Shestakov refers to Theophilus of Bosporus de Gothis.[8] We may recall that the famous Russian scholar, V. V. Bolotov, thought that Theophilus of Gothia came to the Council from the western regions.[9] In 1928, C. Patsch placed his metropolitan see on the Danube.[10]

[1] Vasilievski, *Works*, II, ii, 367, 369–370 (in Russian).

[2] Sozomenos, VI, 21: 'Σκύθας . . . ἐπὶ τῆς αὐτῆς μεῖναι πίστεως . . . Μητρόπολις δέ ἐστι Τόμις,' *Patr. Gr.*, LXI, col. 1344; VII, 26 (*ibid.*, col. 1500).　　　[3] Bruun, *Chernomoryé*, II, ii, 195, 310 (in Russian).

[4] W. Krafft, *Die Kirchengeschichte der germanischen Völker* (Berlin, 1854), p. 216.

[5] V. N. Belikov, *Christianity among the Goths* (Kazan, 1887), pp. 34–35 (in Russian).

[6] F. A. Braun, *Die letzten Schicksale der Krimgoten* (St Petersburg, 1890), p. 8 (*Jahresberichte der reformierten Kirchenschule*).

[7] E. Golubinski, *History of the Russian Church*, I, i, (2nd. ed., Moscow, 1901), 7, note (based on an old German book on Ulfila, by Bessel). In Russian.

[8] S. Shestakov, *Outlines on the History of Chersonesus*, p. 8.

[9] V. V. Bolotov, *Lectures on the History of Ancient Church*, IV (Petrograd, 1918), 25 (in Russian).

[10] C. Patsch, 'Beiträge zur Völkerkunde von Südosteuropa, III: Die Völkerbewegung an der unteren Donau in der Zeit von Diokletian bis Heraklios,' *Sitzungsberichte der Akademie der Wissenschaften in Wien, Phil.-hist. Classe*, CCVIII, 2. Abhandlung (Vienna, 1928), 25–26.

The author of a very fine monograph on the Goths in the Tauris (Crimea), W. Tomaschek, writes that the residence 'of the Gothic Bishop whom we find at the Council of Nicaea, Theophilus Gothiae metropolis,' was probably ('wohl') in the Tauric peninsula.[1] Bruno Rappaport, who has given especial attention to the question of Gothic attacks upon the Roman Empire, holds the same opinion.[2]   L. Schmidt,[3] J. Mansion,[4] and J. Zeiller[5] also consider Theophilus the bishop of the Crimean Goths. A. Harnack, after mentioning that at the Council of Nicaea were present Theophilus, Bishop of Gothia, and Cadmus, Bishop of Bosporus, remarks: 'These two eparchies are, certainly, to be sought in the Tauric peninsula,' but he adds, 'It is, however, possible that Gothia is the eparchy of Tomi.'[6]

R. Loewe alone fails to hold any of these views. He points out that the name of the Goths in the third and fourth centuries is used in our sources collectively to signify not only the Goths but also the tribe of the Heruli; and he attributes to the latter the chief participation in the sea raids of the third century mentioned above.   'Soon after the predatory raids of the Heruli Catholic Christianity was to be spread among them.' He gives Theophilus' signature with its variants quoted above and after mentioning the opinions of Tomaschek and Braun continues: 'But even if we admit that "Theophilus Bosphoritanus" is a deterioration in the text and is to be explained by the following name of Domnus Bosphorensis, another reason makes us locate this Gothia near the Bosporus (Kerch). Among the 318 signatures, Theophilus occupies the last place but one, while in the last place occur the words "Provinciae Bosphor.   Domnus Bosphorensis Cathirius Bosphori."   As the list of provinces, at least in general, follows geographic order, and Gothia of the Danubian Goths in all likelihood should have been given among the provinces of the Balkan peninsula, Dacia, Moesia, Macedonia, Achaia, Thessaly, which are given above in order, this Gothia probably lay close to the Bosporus.   If this is correct, it in no wise follows that this Gothia, totally or partially, co-incided with the Gothia of the Heruli who remained in the Crimea; it might as well have been the region of the Tetraxites or Eudusians or of

---

[1] W. Tomaschek, *Die Goten in Taurien* (Vienna, 1881), p. 10 (*Ethnologische Forschungen über Ost-Europa und Nord-Asien*, i).

[2] B. Rappaport, *Die Einfälle der Goten in das Römische Reich bis auf Constantin* (Leipzig, 1899), p. 65.

[3] L. Schmidt, *Geschichte der deutschen Stämme bis zum Ausgange der Völkerwanderung*, i, i (Berlin, 1904), 69.   *Idem*, in his review of Patsch's Book, *Historische Zeitschrift*, cxl (1929), 662–663.

[4] J. Mansion, 'Les origines du Christianisme chez les Gots,' *Analecta Bollandiana*, xxxiii (1914), 10.

[5] J. Zeiller, *Les origines chrétiennes dans les provinces danubiennes de l'empire romain* (Paris, 1918), pp. 409, 414, 428.

[6] A. Harnack, *Mission und Ausbreitung des Christentums in den ersten drei Jahrhunderten* (Leipzig, 1906), p. 203.

both together.'[1]   Thus Loewe considers it possible to transfer the see of
Theophilus to the eastern shore of the Cimmerian Bosporus (the Strait
of Kerch), i.e., into the Tamán peninsula, and the adjoining region where
the Tetraxite Goths and the mysterious Eudusians lived.   But it must
be said that Loewe's opinion contradicts the obvious statement of Procopius.   From him we learn that the so-called Tetraxite Goths formerly
lived on the western shore of Maeotis (the Sea of Azov) and the Straits
of Kerch; only later, along with a branch of the Utigur (Uturgur) — Huns
who were at that time returning home to their own land — did they cross
the Straits of Kerch in order 'to establish themselves on the opposite
mainland (ἐν τῇ ἀντιπέρας ἠπείρῳ) principally along the bank of the outlet,
where they still live now.'[2]

From what I have said above it is clear that opinions, with the exception of Loewe's, may be divided into two groups; the smaller group places
the see of Theophilus in the Crimea, the other and the larger, in the Danubian region, on the lower course of the Danube.

Let us now go on to our other sources, putting aside for the moment the
signatures of the Fathers of the Council of Nicaea.

Eusebius of Caesarea, a contemporary of Constantine the Great, in his
Life of.the Emperor Constantine, lists the members of the Council of
Nicaea, who were the representatives 'of all the churches which filled
all Europe, Libya, and Asia,' and remarks: 'Already a Persian bishop
was present at the Council, and a Scythian (bishop) attended their meeting.'[3]   This statement was later literally transcribed by the Church historians of the fifth century, Socrates the Scholasticus, and the author of
a history of the Council of Nicaea and of the origin of the Arian controversy, Gelasius of Cyzicus.[4]   The same Socrates, in narrating the
events of the time of Emperor Constantius, writes of Ulfila: 'Formerly
he had acknowledged the Nicaean creed, following Theophilus, who, a
bishop of the Goths attending the Council of Nicaea, had signed (the
Nicaean profession).'[5]

---

[1] R. Loewe, *Die Reste der Germanen am Schwarzen Meere* (Halle, 1896), p. 210. *Idem*, 'Die Krim-
gotenfrage,' *Indogermanische Forschungen*, xiii (1902–1903), 1–84.   Max Ebert follows Loewe's
Heruli theory, Max Ebert, *Südrussland im Altertum* (Bonn and Leipzig, 1921), p. 377.   But cf.
Idem, *Reallexikon der Vorgeschichte*, xiii (Berlin, 1929), 114 (no mention of the Heruli).

[2] *Procopii De bello gothico*, iv, 5 (ed. Haury, ii, 506).   See K. Zeuss, *Die Deutschen und die Nachbarstämme* (Munich, 1837), pp. 430–431; Vasilievski, *Works*, ii, ii, 374–375 (in Russian).

[3] *Eusebii Vita Constantini*, iii, 7 (ed. Heikel, p. 80): 'ἤδη καὶ πέρσης ἐπίσκοπος τῇ συνόδῳ παρῆν,
οὐδὲ Σκύθης ἀπελιμπάνετο τῆς χορείας.'

[4] *Socratis Historia Ecclesiastica*, i, 8 (*Patr. Gr.*, lxvii, col. 61), *Gelasii Cyziceni Historia Concilii
Nicaeni*, ii, 5 (*Patr. Gr.*, lxxxv, col. 1229).

[5] Socrates, ii, 41: '(Οὐλφίλας) . . . τὸν γὰρ ἔμπροσθεν χρόνον τὴν ἐν Νικαίᾳ πίστιν ἠσπάζετο, ἑπόμενος
Θεοφίλῳ, ὃς τῶν Γότθων ἐπίσκοπος ὢν τῇ ἐν Νικαίᾳ συνόδῳ παρὼν καθυπέγραψε' (*Patr. Gr.* lxvii, coll.
349–350.)

This text in my opinion helps us to settle the question. As Ulfila is definitely known to have lived and worked among the Western Goths, his predecessor Theophilus, whom he followed in acknowledging the Nicaean creed, may also be referred to the Western Goths. As has been said above, the Scythian eparchy was situated on the western shore of the Black Sea with the metropole in the city of Tomi. It is from the latter eparchy that the 'Scythian' Bishop Theophilus, as Eusebius of Caesarea and his copyists, Socrates and Gelasius, call him, would have arrived at the Council of Nicaea.

But the text that, in my opinion, finally settles the allocation of Theophilus to the Western Goths is to be found in the *Life* of Nicetas of Gothia, who suffered martyrdom among the Goths some time after 370. The *Life* of Nicetas in a compilation of Metaphrastes has been known for a long time,[1] and in connection with the history of Christianity among the Goths has been used by many scholars. But not until 1912 appeared the edition of an older version of the *Life*, which deals more plainly with its sources.[2] In the Lives, *Menologia*, and *Synaxaria* the memory of Nicetas of Gothia is honored on September 15, the date on which his remains were transported from the banks of the Danube to Asia Minor and solemnly placed in the basilica of the Cilician city of Mopsuestia.[3] For our discussion it is of secondary significance that most scholars do not consider the *Acts of Nicetas* authentic, but a mere compilation of the data of Socrates.[4] In the first place, the martyrdom of Nicetas is an historical fact; and, secondly, the anonymous compiler of the *Life* gives his opinion about Theophilus in conjunction with his narrative about Nicetas, a fact of great importance to us. True, the first part of the *Life* (§§2–5, according to Delehaye's edition) is for the most part made up of extracts from Socrates slightly changed; but in connection with the text of the *Life* as a whole, they give interesting material for our question.

The data of the *Life* which are of importance for us are as follows. St Nicetas was a barbarian from the Goths, who lived beyond the river Ister, which is called Danubius; he learned his faith in Christ and the orthodox doctrine from Theophilus, Bishop of the Goths, who attended the Holy Council in Nicaea and gave his signature to the Symbol of Faith.[5] This *Life* of Nicetas gives also the extract from Socrates already quoted above about Ulfila and Theophilus.[6]

---

[1] *Acta Sanctorum*, Sept., v, 40–43; *Patr. Gr.*, cxv, coll. 704–712.

[2] H. Delehaye, 'Saints de Thrace et de Mésie, 7, Passio S. Nicetae (Μαρτύριον τοῦ ἁγίου μεγαλομάρτυρος Νικήτα),' *Analecta Bollandiana*, xxxi (1912), 209–215.　　　　[3] Delehaye, pp. 214 and 281.

[4] See, for instance, H. Achelis, 'Der älteste deutsche Kalender,' *Zeitschrift für die neutestamentliche Wissenschaft*, i (1900), 320; L. Schmidt, *op. cit.*, i, 93, n. 4; J. Zeiller, *op. cit.*, p. 428.

[5] Delehaye, p. 210 (§ 2). Cf. Socrates, ii, 41. See also *Acta Sanctorum*, v, 40; *Patr. Gr.*, cxv, col. 705.

[6] Delehaye, p. 211 (§ 4). See also *Acta Sanctorum*, v, 41; *Patr. Gr.*, cxv, coll. 705–708.

From the data of the *Life* of Nicetas, no matter whether we consider its text genuine or spurious, it is clear that in the imagination of the people of the earlier Middle Ages Theophilus of Gothia, whose signature is preserved in the Acts of the Council of Nicaea, was a bishop of the Western Danubian Goths; therefore any further attempts to refer him to the Crimean Goths or to the so-called Tetraxite Goths are to be discarded, and the question must be considered solved.

The memorial of the Gothic martyr Nicetas is also included in the Great Russian *Menologion* of Macarius, where in the opening brief eulogy of the Saint we read the following (in old Russian): 'The sainted martyr of Christ, Nicetas, lived in the reign of the Great Tsar Constantine; he was a Goth by origin, from those who lived on the river Danube. Being pious and fearing God, and living in the city of Gatan, he was instructed in the Christian faith by Theophilus, the reverend bishop of Gothia.'[1] Besides this brief eulogy, the *Menologion* of Macarius also includes 'a martyrdom of the great sainted martyr Nicetas' the text of which, for the most part, corresponds to the Greek text of Metaphrastes.

As an example I will give here two passages which may be of interest.

Acta Sanctorum, v, 40; *Patr. Gr.*, cxv, col. 705:	*Velikiye Minei Chetii* of Macarius, p. 1204:

Θεοφίλου δὲ ἦν οὗτος ἐπὶ νεαζούσῃ τῇ ἡλικίᾳ τῶν ἱερῶν τῆς διδασκαλίας ἀπερυσάμενος ῥευμάτων. Ὅπερ δὴ Θεόφιλος, τὴν ἀρχιερατικὴν ἐφορείαν τῶν Γότθων πεπιστευμένων, καὶ τῇ ἐν Νικαίᾳ οἰκουμενικῇ καὶ πρώτῃ συνόδῳ ἐμάθομεν ἐνεπιστῆναι καὶ τὰ τῆς εὐσεβείας χειρί τε καὶ γλώσσῃ παρὰ πᾶσι κρατῦναι δόγματα.

Феофила же бѣ сей о младеньствующи возрастѣ свящ̃енныхъ источникъ ученіа исчерпавъ; ему же убо Феофилу архиерейское достоиньство готфовъ въвѣрено, иже в Никеи первомъ соборѣ разумѣхомъ бывша, и яже благочестіа рукою и языкомъ предъ всѣми утвердиша догматы.

ASS., 41 = *PG*, 705–708:	*Ibid.*:

Οὐρφιλος (*i.e.* Ulfilas) δὲ διάδοχος μὲν τῶν ἀρχιερατικῶν θεσμῶν ἐχρημάτιζε Θεοφίλου. συμπαρὼν δὲ αὐτῷ πάλαι κατὰ τὴν Νίκαιαν καὶ τὰ ἴσα φρονῶν . . .

Африлъ же наслѣдникъ убо архиерейска сана бѣ Феофилъ. вкупѣ же с нимъ бывъ в Никеи древле и равная мудроствуя . . .

In the brief eulogy of Nicetas in the *Menologion* of Macarius it is interesting to note the mention of the city of Gatan where Nicetas and Theophilus lived, and to compare this city with 'Γουτθόπολις' mentioned in the lists of the names of the Fathers of the Council of Nicaea (the Sinaitic and the two Jerusalem lists); from here this name has passed into

---

[1] *Velikiye Minei Chetii*, September, Days 14–24 (St Petersburg, 1869), p. 1200. See Arch. Sergius, *The Complete Liturgical Calendar (Menologion) of the Orient*, 2nd ed. (Vladimir, 1901), II, i, 283; II, 376.

an Arabic list. As has been noted above, the Bishop of Guthopolis was apparently the same Theophilus. I do not know of any Greek version of the *Life* containing the name 'Γουτθόπολις.' It is not aside from the point to notice that in a Greek version of the *Life* of Nicetas his teacher is called not Theophilus, but Macarius, 'archbishop of that place.'[1]

Thus at the beginning of the fourth century in the Crimea there was, we may state with certainty, only one Bishop of Bosporus, whose name in the lists of the Council of Nicaea is given in different forms (Camdos, Cathmus, Cathirius, Cadamnus, Κάδιος, Κάδμος, Βάδμνος, Cadmus, Marcus). Philip of Chersonesus, whose name is found only in one group of later Greek lists, from which it has passed into an Arabic version, is subject to doubt. And, finally, Theophilus of Gothia must be definitely removed from the Crimea and referred to the Western Danubian Goths.[2]

It is usually stated that from the fourth century, i.e., from the epoch of the Arian troubles, the Visigoths, and also, later, the other Germanic tribes of the early Middle Ages except the Franks, adopted Arianism and therefore created for long a serious barrier against an understanding with their new subjects of the West-European provinces, who were Orthodox. But as far as the Goths are concerned, such a statement must be considerably limited. The Crimean Goths, who had already received the first principles of Christianity in the third century, that is to say, before the appearance of Arianism, always remained Orthodox; and later no Arian missionaries came into the Crimea. As to the Danubian Goths, i.e., the Visigoths, throughout the third century they, like the Crimean Goths, remained Orthodox; but in the fourth century, owing to Audius and the Audians, and then to the famous Ulfila, who was an Arian, they also turned to Arianism. Perhaps the Hunnic invasion which in the second half of the fourth century befell present-day Southern Russia, prevented Arianism from penetrating into the Crimea from the Western Goths. But on the Danube, even after the conversion of the Goths to Arianism, there remained the Audians and the Orthodox Goths, who are often mentioned in our sources and who had several martyrs.[3] At that time the Ortho-

---

[1] ''Εμαθε δὲ τὴν εὐσεβῆ πίστιν παιδιόθεν ἀπὸ τὸν Μακάριον τὸν 'Αρχιερέα τοῦ τόπου ἐκείνου,' K. Dukakis, Μέγας Συναξαριστης, ΙΧ (Athens, 1894), 191. The word 'τόπος' is to be taken here as meaning the country, 'πέραν ἀπὸ τὸν ποταμὸν "Ιστρον,' where the Goths dwelt.

[2] A remark of Golubinski is rather puzzling. He places in the Crimea two eparchies—the Crimean Gothic eparchy and the Gothic Bosphoritan or Bosphoran eparchy, *Izvestiya Otdeleniya Russkago Yazika i Slovesnosti*, XI, i, (1907), 269 and n. 2 (in Russian). This confusion is probably to be explained by the *Colbertinus* list of the Fathers of the Council of Nicaea, which has been published by Mansi (see above).

[3] See Belikov, *op. cit.*, pp. 63–64 (in Russian); Schmidt, *Geschichte der deutschen Stämme*, I, i, 92; Delehaye, in *Analecta Bollandiana*, XXXI (1912), 283.

doxy or Arianism of the Goths depended on the conditions of local Christian preaching, and in the fourth century the Goths could not clearly distinguish all the subtleties of the religious controversy of the epoch; according to a source,[1] they embraced Christianity 'with great simplicity of mind,' in proportion to the presence of more or less active and skillful preachers, no matter whether they were Arian or Orthodox. The Audians apparently disappeared among the Arians, and concerning them the sources are silent. In the second half of the fourth century, when the Goths were in a state of continuous migration and permanent wars, there could be no question, even after the preaching of Ulfila, of any regular church organization which might comprise the masses of the Goths; there existed only separate centers of Christianity, often without any intercourse between them, and with different religious doctrines, as has been said. According to a recent study of the origins of Christianity among the Goths, 'it would be too simple to imagine the whole of Gothia Arian, because Ulfila, Bishop of the Goths, was Arian.'[2] Only in the early fifth century, when after Alaric's death the Visigoths left Italy and settled in southern France, did they begin to recognize their political and national as well as ecclesiastical unity. Just at this time, at the beginning of his rule, Ataulf, Alaric's successor, was very anxious 'to wipe out the Roman name and to make and call the whole of the Roman Empire the single Empire of the Goths, so that Gothia might become what Romania had been before, and Ataulf become now what Caesar Augustus had formerly been.'[3] Nothing like this feeling of unity existed in the time of Ulfila.

3. The Fall of the Bosporan Kingdom in the Fourth Century A.D.

Very scanty evidence has survived concerning the position of the Goths in the Crimea in the fourth century; but we know at least that at that time the larger part of the peninsula was in their hands. Under the Gothic power also was the Bosporan Kingdom, except its eastern region with its capital, Panticapaeum, which, in the first half of the fourth century at least, still had its own kings, for coins with the name of the Bosporan king of the fourth century, Rhescuporis (VI or VII), have come down to us; the latest coin of his time, according to some numismatists, may be attributed to A.D. 341–342.[4] On the other hand, according to M.

---

[1] *Socratis Historia ecclesiastica*, IV, 33, 9: 'οἱ δὲ βάρβαροι [the Goths] ἁπλότητι τὸν χριστιανισμὸν δεξάμενοι.' Hence this statement passed into the *Life* of Nicetas: 'οἱ πολλοὶ δὲ τῶν βαρβάρων ἁπλῇ τῇ πίστει τὸν χριστιανισμὸν δεξάμενοι,' Delehaye, *op. cit.*, pp. 211 (§ 3) and 283.

[2] Mansion, *op. cit.*, pp. 6, 8.   [3] *P. Orosii Historiae adversum paganos*, VII, 43, 5.

[4] See *Inscriptiones oris septentrionalis Ponti Euxini*, I, 2nd ed. (Petrograd, 1916), lii; Latyshev, Ποντικά (St Petersburg, 1909), pp. 121–122. In this is given the opinion of A. V. Oreshnikov, who is doubtful about the dating of the coin noted above.

Rostovtzeff, Panticapaeum may have been a vassal city of the Goths. He writes: 'The Goths probably used Panticapaeum, their vassal, as they used Olbia and Tyras, both as a starting-point for their expeditions against the Roman Empire, and as a harbour which allowed them to receive goods not only from the Orient through the Sarmatians, but also from the eastern provinces of the Roman Empire.'[1] Twenty years later, i.e., in 362, according to Ammianus Marcellinus, the fame of Emperor Julian had reached the remotest peoples, and among other embassies sent to him with presents, 'from the north, and also from those hot climates through which the Phasis passes on its way to the sea, and from the people of the Bosporus, and from other unknown tribes came ambassadors entreating that on the payment of annual duties they might be allowed to live in peace within their native countries.'[2]

Besides these data we have also an indication of the independence of Bosporus at this time in the legendary tales about the relations between Chersonesus and Bosporus which are found in the work of Constantine Prophyrogenitus *On the Administration of the Empire*. I must admit that his account is confused and completely unreliable;[3] none the less I can not help seeing at least some reflection of historical truth concerning the position of the Peninsula in the fourth century. Writing of the time of Diocletian, i.e., about the end of the third century and the very beginning of the fourth (284–305), Constantine says that Bosporus had a ruler of its own, Sauromates,[4] who collected the Sarmatians [Sauromatians] who dwelt by the Maeotis, and made war on the Romans; in this war Chersonesus was later involved, taking the side of the Romans.[5] Beside the indication of the independence of Bosporus, it is interesting to notice that the Sarmatians or Sauromatians, by whom in my opinion the Crimean Goths are meant, acted with the Bosporans. An historian of the fifth and early sixth century, Zosimus, also mentions 'the Sauromatians [Sarmatians] who dwelt by the Maeotis' and attacked the Empire in 322.[6] In spite of considerable ethnographic confusion in Zosimus, (as well as in some other authors among our sources)[7] who in other places calls the

---

[1] M. Rostovtzeff, *Iranians and Greeks in South Russia* (Oxford, 1922), p. 217.

[2] *Ammiani Marcellini Res gestae*, XXII, 7, 10: 'ab aquilone et regionibus solis, per quas in mare Fasis accipitur, Bosporanis aliisque antehac ignotis legationes vehentibus supplices ut annua conplentes sollemnia, intra terrarum genitalium terminos otiose vivere sinerentur.'

[3] See, for instance, Mommsen's opinion on this question: 'The Chersonese legends in the work of the later Constantine Porphyrogenitus, of course, must not be taken into account,' Mommsen, *Römische Geschichte*, v (Berlin, 1885), 291; see also Shestakov, *Outlines on the History of Chersonesus*, p. 5 (in Russian).   [4] In Constantine's treatise all personal names for this epoch are fictitious.

[5] Constantine Porphyrogenitus, *De administrando imperio*, Ch. 53 (pp. 244 f.).

[6] Zosimus, II, 21 (ed. Mendelssohn, p. 77).   Cf. his statement with *De adm. imp.*, p. 244: 'Σαρμάτας τὴν Μαιῶτιδα Λίμνην οἰκοῦντας.'

[7] See Wietersheim-Dahn, *Geschichte der Völkerwanderung*, I (Leipzig, 1880), 375 ff.

Goths Scythians, nevertheless in the reference given the general sense indicates that the Sauromatians (Sarmatians) are the Goths.[1]

Chersonesus also remained independent of the Goths; in fact, apparently with a view to the possibility of Gothic attacks, the Roman government fortified Chersonesus, and provided it with a garrison and weapons.[2] According to M. Rostovtzeff, Chersonesus was the last stronghold of Roman power in the Crimea.[3] An inscription from Chersonesus in which the names of three emperors are mentioned, Gratian, Valentinian, and Valens, and which may have been set up between A.D. 370 and 375, illustrates the efforts of the Roman Empire to protect the city from Gothic attacks, so that after a temporary interval Chersonesus was again taken care of by the imperial power.[4]

However, we may assume in all likelihood that at the end of the fourth century, at any rate after A.D. 362, Bosporus passed into the hands of the Goths. This was but quite natural, for the eastern plain section of the Peninsula was already under their power, so that their establishment on the banks of the Cimmerian Bosporus was but the consummation of the Gothic movement eastwards in the Peninsula. Our sources are silent about the actual fall of Bosporus. But that towards A.D. 400 Bosporus did already belong to the Goths, is testified by a letter of John Chrysostom, of which we shall speak below.

In the eighth decade of the fourth century the Tauric peninsula fell under the Hunnic invasion, which, rushing from east to west through the steppes of present-day South Russia, overwhelmed the Crimea on the south. We will now pass on to the consideration of this invasion.

4. The Invasion of the Huns in the Crimea in the Fourth Century, and the Legend of the Doe and the Cow

Our sources give us fairly exact information concerning the invasion of the Huns about 370 into the territory of present-day southern Russia, as well as concerning the subjugation of the Ostrogoths and the conflicts of the Huns with the Visigoths. But we have exceedingly poor data about this Hunnic invasion in the Crimean peninsula. However, the passage of the Huns through the Peninsula is to be considered an historical fact which in the first half of the fifth century had already received legendary

---

[1] See Vasilievski, *Works*, ii, i, 54 (in Russian). Schmidt thinks it possible that these Sarmatians (Sauromatians) were the Heruli or the Crimean Goths (L. Schmidt, *Geschichte der deutschen Stämme*, i, i, 81, n. 2). [2] See Shestakov, *op. cit.*, p. 5.

[3] M. Rostovtzeff, *Iranians and Greeks in South Russia* (Oxford, 1922), p. 217.

[4] M. Rostovtzeff, 'New Latin Inscriptions from Chersonesus,' *Izvestiya* of the Imperial Archaeological Commission, xxiii (1907), 5–18 (in Russian). The same inscription, with brief notes, is reprinted in *Insc iptiones orae septentrionalis Ponti Euxini*, i, 2nd ed. (Petrograd, 1916), No. 449 (pp. 408–410). See also Rostovtzeff, *Iranians and Greeks*, p. 217.

color. The main mass of the Huns evidently rushed from the eastern steppes straight westwards into the South Russian steppes, where in their onset they caught the Ostrogoths who dwelt there, and drove away from their abodes the Visigoths, who were forced to seek new settlements within the Roman Empire. The other and, of course, considerably smaller wave of Huns, went south, crossed the Cimmerian Bosporus (the Straits of Kerch) into the Crimean Peninsula and passed through its steppes in a northwesterly direction; on their way they vanquished the Goths and probably drove them, at least in part, into the mountains; then through the Isthmus they proceeded to the South Russian steppes and joined the chief mass of their countrymen. Perhaps a small group of the Huns even remained in the Peninsula. In any case there is no information about the real subjugation of the Crimean Goths, even of those in the steppes, to the Huns late in the fourth century and early in the fifth.

The writers of the second half of the fourth and of the fifth century are unsatisfactorily informed concerning the original history of the Huns; therefore very early this took on legendary color. The historical work of Eunapius, a pagan writer of the second half of the fourth and of the beginning of the fifth century, which dealt with the events of the Empire from A.D. 270 to 404, has not survived in its entirety; we may judge it only from the extracts which have been preserved in Photius, Suidas, and Constantine Porphyrogenitus.

From a fragment of Eunapius, which has come down to us, in which he tells of the Huns, we may conclude that he drew his information from two sorts of sources: first, he had at his disposal the information about the Huns given by ancient writers from whom he borrowed data, in his opinion, reliable; then later he added some new data from other sources, which, as he thought, would bring him nearer to the truth. Here is his text:

Although no one has told anything plainly of whence the Huns came and by which way they invaded the whole of Europe and exterminated [drove out][1] the Scythian people,[2] at the beginning of my work, after collecting the accounts of ancient writers, I have told the facts as seemed to me reliable; I have considered the accounts from the point of view of their exactness, so that my writing should not depend merely on probable statements and my work should not deviate from the truth. We do not resemble those who from their childhood live in a small and poor house, and late in time, by a stroke of good fortune, acquire vast and magnificent buildings, and none the less by custom love the old things and take care of them. ... But we rather [resemble those] who first using one medicine for the treatment of their body, in the hope of help, and then through their ex-

---

[1] In new editions 'ἔτριψαν,' in old 'ἔρριψαν.'   [2] Eunapius calls the Goths Scythians.

perience finding a better [medicine], turn and incline towards the latter, not in order to neutralize [the effect] of the first one by the second but in order to introduce the truth into erroneous judgment, and, so to speak, to destroy and enfeeble the light of a lamp by a ray of the sun. In like manner we will add the more correct [evidence] to the aforesaid, considering it possible to keep the former [material] as an historical point of view, and using and adding the latter [material] for [the establishment] of the truth.[1]

From this fragment of Eunapius' history, which shows him to be a very conscientious and serious historian, it is clear that already at the end of the fourth century and early in the fifth the question of the first appearance of the Huns in eastern Europe had been dealt with in different ways, and that at that time there already existed such accounts of it as to raise doubts about their reliability. Eunapius' history became the foundation for several later historians who have written about the Hunnic invasion; since in their works the legend of the cow or doe occurs, we may say almost with certainty that this legend had already found its place in Eunapius' work and was exactly that earlier material about which he later became doubtful.

As early as the first half of the fifth century the church historian, Sozomenos, gives this legend. After mentioning that the Goths who had been driven away from their settlements by the Huns passed over into the Roman territory, he writes:

This [Hunnic] people is said to have been formerly unknown both to the Thracians of the Ister and to the Goths; for though they were dwelling secretly near to one another, a lake of vast extent was between them, and the inhabitants on each side [of the lake] respectively imagined that their own country was situated at the extremity of the earth, and that there was nothing beyond them but the sea and water. It so happened, however, that a cow stung by a gadfly crossed over the lake, and was pursued by the herdsman, who perceiving for the first time that the opposite bank was inhabited, made known the circumstance to his fellow-tribesmen. Some, however, relate that a doe fleeing from Hunnic hunters showed them the way, which was concealed superficially by the water. On arriving at the opposite bank, the hunters were struck with the beauty of the country, the serenity of the air, and the suitability of the land for cultivation; and they reported what they had seen to their king. The Huns then made an attempt to attack the Goths with a few soliders; but they afterwards raised a powerful army, conquered the Goths in battle, and took possession of their country.[2]

---

[1] *Eunapii Excerpta de Sententiis*, ed. U. P. Boissevain, *Excerpta historica jussu imp. Constantini Porphyrogeniti confecta*, IV (Berlin 1906), 84–85 (Fr. 39). Among older editions see *Eunapii Excerpta*, in the *Corpus scr. hist. byz.* (Bonn, 1829), pp. 75–76 (Fr. 34).

[2] *Sozomeni Historia ecclesiastica*, VI, 37; *Patr. Gr.*, LXVII, col. 1404; an English version in *A Select Library of Nicene and Post-Nicene Fathers of the Christian Church*, 2nd Series, II (New York, 1890), 373.

A pagan historian of the second half of the fifth century and of the beginning of the sixth, Zosimus, gives a somewhat different account of this story. Writing of the epoch of Emperor Valens, about A.D. 370, Zosimus says:

Under these circumstances, a barbarian people formerly unknown suddenly appeared and rose against the Scythians [that is, Goths[1]] dwelling beyond the Ister. They were called Huns: perhaps it would be more fitting to call them Royal Scythians, or as Herodotus says, the blunt-nosed and weak people who dwelt near the Ister,[2] or who had passed from Asia to Europe. I have found an account that the Cimmerian Bosporus was converted into earth by deposits from the (river) of Tanais, which enabled them to pass on foot from Asia to Europe. Travelling with their horses, wives, children, and chattels, they attacked the Scythians who dwelt beyond the Ister; being absolutely inexperienced and unable to carry on any pitched battle (spending their lives on horseback and even sleeping on their horses, they could not stand firmly on the ground), they killed an enormous number of Scythians by their ridings about, raids, and timely retreats, shooting arrows from horseback.[3]

Then Zosimus tells the very well-known story of how the Goths were forced to cede their lands to the Huns, how they crossed the Danube and sought permission of Valens to settle on Roman territory.

First of all is to be noted Zosimus' mention of the river Tanais, i.e., the Don, the mouth of which lies far away from the Cimmerian Bosporus; some scholars therefore have been rather puzzled as to how the distant Tanais could have filled the Straits with deposits, so that the Huns crossed as if on land. The Tanais of the editions of Zosimus may be either the result of an inaccurate reading of the name of the river in the manuscript of Zosimus, or want of attention of the author in using his sources — if, of course, the correct name was given in his source.[4] It goes without saying that it would be more natural to find here the river Hypanis ('Υπάνιος), the present-day Kuban, which empties quite close to the Cimmerian Straits. But, like other writers of that time, Zosimus might have considered the whole of Maeotis as the mouth of the Don, of which we shall speak later.

As to the sources of Sozomenos and Zosimus, this question is sufficiently clear. For both writers the source is Eunapius, who, according to his own statement, made use of several versions on the passage of the Huns to Europe; some of them he considered less reliable, others more; but he included both versions in his work. We find both these versions

---

[1] In Zosimus the Scythians are Goths.   [2] See Herodotus, v, 9.

[3] *Zosimi Historia*, IV, 20.

[4] On the writing of the name of the river in a manuscript of Zosimus see Mendelssohn's edition of Zosimus, p. 174. The editor is doubtful on this point.

reflected in the accounts of Sozomenos and Zosimus.[1]　In his *Bibliotheca* the Patriarch Photius remarks with some exaggeration, 'It may be said that [Zosimus] wrote no history, but copied the history of Eunapius, which he merely abridged.'[2]

Let us postpone for the moment the interpretation of the passage of the Huns across the Cimmerian Straits; we shall now follow the development of its tradition in subsequent literature.

In the *Gothic History* of Jordanes, written in Constantinople in the middle of the sixth century, we find the same tale.　In describing the Hunnic invasion into Europe Jordanes refers to Orosius and Priscus.　The passage in which we are interested follows:

This cruel tribe, as Priscus the historian relates, settled on the farther bank of the Maeotic swamp.　They were fond of hunting and had no skill in any other art.　After they had grown to a nation, they disturbed the peace of neighboring races by theft and rapine.　At one time, while hunters of their tribe were as usual seeking for game on the farthest edge of Maeotis, they saw a doe unexpectedly appear to their sight and enter the swamp, acting as guide of the way, now advancing and again standing still.　The hunters followed and crossed on foot the Maeotic swamp, which they had supposed was impassable as the sea. Presently the unknown land of Scythia disclosed itself and the doe disappeared. Now in my opinion the evil spirits, from whom the Huns are descended, did this from envy of the Scythians.[3]　And the Huns, who had been wholly ignorant that there was another world beyond Maeotis, were now filled with admiration for the Scythian land.　As they were quick of mind, they believed that this path, utterly unknown to any age of the past, had been divinely revealed to them. They returned to their tribe, told them what had happened, praised Scythia, and persuaded the people to hasten thither along the way they had found by the guidance of the doe.　As many as they captured when they thus entered Scythia for the first time they sacrificed to Victory.　The remainder they conquered and made subject to themselves.　Like a whirlwind of nations they swept across the great swamp and at once fell upon the Alpidzuri, Alcidzuri, Itimari, Juncarsi, and Boisci,[4] who bordered on that part of Scythia.[5]

In his *Gothic War* Procopius of Caesarea, a Greek historian of the sixth

---

[1] See G. Schoo, *Die Quellen des Kirchenhistorikers Sozomenos* (Berlin, 1911), pp. 83 and 150; Schmidt, *op. cit.*, i, ii, 106; Franz Dölger, in his review of my Russian version, *Byz. Zeitschrift*, xxv (1925), 449.

[2] *Photii Bibliotheca*, cod. 98; *Patr. Gr.*, ciii, col. 365 (ed. I. Bekker, Berlin, 1824), p. 84.　See also the *Praefatio* to the edition of Zosimus by Mendelssohn, pp. xiv and xxxv.

[3] Jordanes speaks a little above of the descent of the Huns from evil spirits, *Getica*, xxiv, 121–122 (ed. Mommsen, p. 89).

[4] A series of mysterious peoples whose names are differently written in manuscripts.　See Mommsen ed., p. 90.

[5] *Jordanis Getica*, xxiv, 123–126 (ed. Mommsen, pp. 89–90); *The Gothic History of Jordanes*, English version with an introduction and a commentary by C. C. Mierow (Princeton, 1915), pp. 85–86.

century, gives a similar account.   After mentioning that the Huns, then
called the Cimmerians, dwelt on the eastern bank of Lake Maeotis, Procopius writes:

All these now continued to live in this region, associating freely in all the business of life, but not mingling with the people who were settled on the other side
of the [Maeotis] Lake and its outlet; for they never crossed these waters nor did
they suspect that they could be crossed, being fearful of that which was really
easy, simply because they had never even attempted to cross them, and they
remained utterly ignorant of the possibility.   . . . But as time went on they say
— if, indeed, the story is sound — some youths of the Cimmerians were engaged in hunting, and a doe which was fleeing before them leaped into these
waters.   And the youths, either moved by a thirst for glory or in some sort of
competition, or constrained by some deity, followed after this doe and refused
absolutely to let her go, until they came with her to the opposite shore.   And
then the quarry, whatever it was, immediately disappeared from sight; for in
my opinion it appeared there for no other purpose than that evil might befall
the barbarians who lived in that region.   Thus, while the youths did fail in their
hunt, they found an incentive to battle and plunder.   For they returned as fast
as they could to their own land, and thus made it clear to all the Cimmerians
that these waters could be crossed by them.   Accordingly they immediately took
up arms as a nation, and making the crossing with no delay got on the opposite
mainland.   . . . So they suddenly fell upon the Goths who inhabited these plains
and slew many of them and turned the rest to flight.[1]

The most definite account of the passage of the Huns across the Cimmerian Bosporus is that of another historian of the sixth century,
Agathias of Myrina.   After mentioning that the Huns of old dwelt east
of Lake Maeotis and north of the river Tanais, he writes:

Many generations later [the Huns] crossed to Europe; either, indeed, as the story
tells, a doe showed them the way [thither] for the first time, or using another
opportunity, then they crossed, in some way, the mouth of the [Maeotis] Lake
which flows into the Euxine; till then [this lake] seemed impassable.   Wandering
round about the foreign country they, by their sudden attack, inflicted a terrible
damage to the natives, so that they drove away the former inhabitants and took
possession of their land.[2]

This literary tradition found its reflection in the Byzantine chronicle
of the debatable and puzzling writer of the tenth century, Simeon the
Logothete.   It is known that the original text of Simeon the Logothete
has survived in a Slavonic translation, where in the account of Valens
we read the following brief statement: 'Under him [i.e., Valens] the Goths

---

[1] *Procopii De bello gothico*, IV, 3 (ed. Haury, II, 503–505); *Procopius*, with an English translation by
H. B. Dewing, V, Loeb Classical Library (London-New York, 1928), 88–91.

[2] *Agathiae Historiae*, V, 11.

guided by a doe[1] crossed Lake Maeotis and came into Thrace.'[2] In the Greek versions of the chronicle of the Logothete, in the works of the so-called Leo the Grammarian (Grammaticus) and of Theodosius of Melitene, this passage has been preserved in Greek.[3] From the Logothete this statement passed word for word into the chronicle of a writer of the end of the eleventh century and the beginning of the twelfth, George Cedrenus.[4] This abridgment of the well-known story of the doe erroneously calls the Huns Goths. Finally, Sozomenos' account with its two variants, that of the cow stung by a gadfly and that of the doe, in a rather abridged form was included in the *Ecclesiastical History* of a writer of the beginning of the fourteenth century, Nicephorus Callistus Xanthopulos.[5]

We have followed the development of the legend of the cow and the doe in the sources; now let us turn to its analysis and evaluation. First, this legend reflects the undoubted historical fact that under Emperor Valens (A.D. 364–378) a group of Huns crossed the Cimmerian Bosporus into the Crimea. This event is connected with the general movement of the Huns westward to Europe through the steppes of South Russia which occurred in the eighth decade of the fourth century. Thus the appearance of the Huns in the Crimea is also to be referred to that time.

If we turn now to the original subject of the legend, we shall see in it a survival of the ancient myth of Io, whom Zeus loved and whom Hera changed into a heifer. The myth relates that Hera sent a gadfly to this heifer which drove her over various lands and seas. It is interesting to notice that the first mention of this myth, which we find in Aeschylus' tragedy *Prometheus Bound*, is connected with the Cimmerian Bosporus. Prometheus speaks to Io as follows: 'Next, just at the narrow portals of the lake, thou shalt reach the Cimmerian isthmus. This thou must leave with stout heart and pass through the channel of Maeotis; and ever after among mankind there shall be great mention of thy passing, and it shall be called after thee Bosporus. Then, leaving the soil of Europe, thou

---

[1] In Slavonic *elafom vodimi* is a translation of ἐλάφου ἡγησαμένης. *Elaf*=ἔλαφος= doe.

[2] *Simeona Metafrasta i Logotheta Spisanie mira ot bytiya i letovnik sobran ot razlichnykh letopisetz*, edd. A. A. Kunik, V. G. Vasilievski, V. I. Sreznevski (St Petersburg, 1905), p. 45. A Slavonic version of the *Chronicle* of Simeon the Logothete with additions.

[3] *Leonis Grammatici Chronographia*, ed. Bonn, pp. 98–99: 'ἐπὶ αὐτοῦ (i.e., under Valens) οἱ Γότθοι περάσαντες τὴν Μαιῶτιν λίμνην ἐλάφου ἡγησαμένης ἦλθον εἰς τὴν Θράκην'; *Theodosii Meliteni qui fertur Chronographia*, ed. T. L. T. Tafel, *Monumenta saecularia* (Munich, 1859), p. 70. See a very important article on the mutual relations between the Slavonic text of Simeon Logothete and the different Greek versions by G. Ostrogorski, 'The Slavonic Version of the Chronicle of Simeon Logothete,' *Seminarium Kondakovianum*, v (Prague, 1932), 17–37 (in Russian); cf. also M. Weingart, *Byzantské Kroniky V Literatuři Církevněslovanské*, i (Bratislava, 1922), 63–83.

[4] *Georgii Cecreni Historiarum compendium*, ed. Bonn, i, 547.

[5] *Nicephori Callisti Historia ecclesiastica*, xi, 48; *Patr. Gr.*, cxlvi, coll. 736–737.

shalt come to the Asian continent. . . .[1] We may note that the compound adjective 'οἰστροπλήξ' ('stung by a gadfly'), which Aeschylus uses for the story of Io in another part of the same tragedy, passed through many intermediaries to Sozomenos. Io says in Aeschylus, 'I, still stung by a gadfly, am driven on from land to land by the heaven-sent scourge.'[2] Sozomenos writes, 'It so happened that a cow stung by a gadfly crossed the lake.'[3] We must not forget that a tragedy of Euripides, *Iphigenia in Tauris*, also deals with a legend of a doe.

If we wish to combine the historical part of the legend, that is, the actual fact of the passing of the Huns through the Cimmerian Bosporus, with the mythical passage of a cow or doe, the only explanation, in my opinion, is to attribute the crossing of the Huns to the winter, when the channel was covered with ice over which they could pass into the Crimea.

Some ancient writers tell us of the freezing over of the Cimmerian Bosporus. In the fifth century B.C. Herodotus, dealing with the severe climate of Scythia, writes, 'The sea freezes and all the Cimmerian Bosporus; and the Scythians dwelling this side of the fosse[4] lead armies over the ice, and drive their wains across to the Sindi.'[5] The geographer Strabo gives very similar information about the Cimmerian Bosporus. Mentioning the solidity of the ice at the mouth of Lake Maeotis, i.e., in the Cimmerian Bosporus, he remarks that 'the passage from Panticapaeum across to Phanagoria is at times performed in waggons, thus being both a sea passage and an overland route.'[6] A few lines below we read, 'It is related that Neoptolemus, the general of Mithradates, defeated the barbarians during summer-time in a naval engagement in this very strait, and during the winter in a cavalry action.'[7] In another place Strabo writes of the same strait, 'The ice extends as far as this, the Maeotis being so frozen at the time of frosts that it can be crossed on foot.'[8]

---

[1] Aeschylus, *Prometheus Bound*, vv. 729–735. An English translation by H. W. Smyth, Loeb Classical Library, I (London-New York, 1922), 279–281.

[2] 'Οἰστροπλὴξ δ'ἐγὼ μάστιγι θείᾳ γῆν πρὸ γῆς ἐλαύνομαι,' Aeschylus, *Prometheus*, vv. 681–682.

[3] 'Συμβὰν δὲ βοῦν οἰστροπλῆγα διαδραμεῖν τὴν λίμνην,' Sozomeni Hist. eccl., VI, 37; *Patr. Gr.*, LXVII, col. 1404.

[4] On this rather obscure word 'fosse' (wide trench) in the Tauric peninsula Herodotus writes a little above (Herodotus, IV, 3). Perhaps this word 'τάφρος' ('fosse, pit') means the Putrid Sea (Sivash)?

[5] Herodotus, IV, 28: 'ἡ δὲ θάλασσα πήγνυται καὶ ὁ Βόσπορος πᾶς ὁ Κιμμέριος, καὶ ἐπὶ τοῦ κρυστάλλου οἱ ἐντὸς τάφρου Σκίθαι κατοικημένοι στρατεύονται καὶ τὰς ἁμάξας ἐπελαύνουσι πέρην ἐς τοὺς Σίνδους.'

[6] Strabo, VII, 307: 'τῶν δὲ πάγων ἡ σφοδρότης . . . περὶ τὸ στόμα τῆς Μαιώτιδος δῆλός ἐστιν. ἁμαξεύεται γὰρ ὁ διάπλους ὁ εἰς Φαναγόρειαν ἐκ τοῦ Παντικαπαίου, ὥστε καὶ πλοῦν εἶναι καὶ ὁδόν.'

[7] Strabo, *ibid.*: 'Νεοπτόλεμον δέ φασι, τὸν τοῦ Μιθριδάτου στρατηγὸν, ἐν τῷ αὐτῷ πόρῳ θέρους μὲν ναυμαχίᾳ περιγενέσθαι τῶν βαρβάρων, χειμῶνος δ' ἱππομαχίᾳ.'

[8] Strabo, XI, 494: 'μέχρι γὰρ δεῦρο καὶ ὁ κρύσταλλος διατείνει, πηττομένης τῆς Μαιώτιδος κατὰ τοὺς κρυμνοὺς ὥστε πεζεύεσθαι.'

Pallas, who travelled in this region at the close of the eighteenth century, wrote that the Strait of Kerch, near the northern bank, is so narrow because of the adjacent islands as to be not quite three versts in extent (about two miles). This shallow surface barely covered with water serves as a resting place for cattle and is very convenient for driving them to the European shore.[1] In the middle of the nineteenth century elderly inhabitants of Tamán assured Goerz that the Tartars used to ride over from the northern bank to Kerch on camels.[2] Goerz asserted that the jutting out of the northern and southern promontories, particularly the latter, makes the Strait as narrow as three or four versts (about two miles or slightly more).[3] Pallas, the traveller mentioned above, wrote that in spite of the current the strait freezes, even with moderate frosts, along with the greater part of the Azov Sea.[4]

Various peoples who during the Middle Ages wandered through South Russia chose for their movements the winter season, when the rivers which lay in their way were frozen. A Syriac chronicler of the twelfth century, Michael the Syrian, gives us interesting information on this subject; it is very probable that the passage I am about to quote refers to that crossing of the Huns over the Cimmerian Bosporus which we are now considering. Speaking of the epoch of Emperor Maurice, i.e., the close of the sixth century, Michael the Syrian relates, 'At that time three brothers [came] from the interior of Scythia at the head of 30,000 Scythians and took a journey of sixty-five days from the mountain of Imaion.[5] They travelled during the winter, *because (then) the water which lay in their way [was frozen]* and reached the river of Tanais which goes from Lake Maeotis and discharges itself into the sea of Pontus.'[6] Sometimes ancient writers considered the mouth of the Tanais the whole of Lake Maeotis, which empties into the Pontus through the Cimmerian Bosporus. According to Arrian, a contemporary of Hadrian (the second century A.D.) and the author of the *Periplus of the Euxine Sea* (Voyage

---

[1] P. S. Pallas, *Bemerkungen auf einer Reise in die südlichen Statthalterschaften des Russischen Reichs*, II (Leipzig, 1801), 284.

[2] K. K. Goerz, *Works*, I (St Petersburg, 1898), 17.

[3] *Ibid.* See the map appended to the first volume of the works of Goerz.

[4] Pallas, *op. cit.* (at the close of the eighteenth century).

[5] Cf. on these mountains Agathias, v, 11: '[The Huns] καὶ τὰ ἄλλα βάρβαρα ἔθνη ὁπόσα ἐντὸς 'Ιμαίου ὄρους ἀνὰ τὴν 'Ασίαν ἐτύγχανον ἱδρυμένα.'

[6] Since I am not acquainted with the Syriac language, I asked Professor M. N. Sokolov to make a literal translation of this passage and to interpret it; I hereby express my sincere gratitude to him. See J. Marquart, *Osteuropäische und ostasiatische Streifzüge* (Leipzig, 1903), p. 484; he translates the underlined words, 'wegen des Auffindens von Wasser.' In the translation of Chabot these words are not very clear — 'afin de trouver de l'eau,' *Chronique de Michel le Syrien*, ed. J.-B. Chabot, II (Paris, 1904), 363 (1). See also *Gregorii Abulpharagii sive Bar-Hebraei Chronicon Syriacum*, ed. Bruns et Kirsch (Leipzig, 1789), p. 95.

Around the Euxine Sea), 'Tanais starts from Lake Maeotis and empties into the Euxine Sea.'[1] Procopius writes that 'the inhabitants indeed give the name Tanais also to this outlet which starts from Lake Maeotis and extends to the Euxine Sea.'[2] Hence we may conclude that both Lake Maeotis, which some writers take for the mouth of the river Tanais, and the Strait of Kerch froze to such an extent that large migrations of various peoples, with their wagons, could cross them like land. One winter shortly before 378, when Valens fell at the battle of Hadrianople, the Huns crossed the frozen Cimmerian Bosporus into the Tauric Peninsula. For some reason not clear to me this historical fact, of great importance for the history of the peninsula, is reflected in the sources in the shape of the legend dealt with above, which is deeply rooted in Greek tradition.

As far as we may judge from the later course of events, the probably small group of Huns who crossed into the Crimea then went westward with the chief mass of their tribesmen, and took part in the creation of the short-lived Hunnic Empire. The Goths retained their power in the peninsula, and Orthodoxy remained the form of their religious faith.

5. The Origin of the Gothic Eparchy in the Crimea

Our first information about the bishopric among the Crimean Goths assigns it to the very close of the fourth century.

The Gothic Church in the Crimea was under the supervision of the Constantinopolitan Patriarchs, who ordained bishops there. The famous father of the early Christian church, John Chrysostom, was particularly interested in the Orthodox Goths. When Bishop of Constantinople, he assigned to them a church outside the city, where they worshipped and preached in the Gothic tongue; sometimes John Chrysostom himself visited them and through interpreters engaged with them in pious discussions.[3] A sermon delivered by John in 398 or 399 at the church of St Paul in Constantinople has come down to us. It was given after the Goths had read in their own tongue a chapter of the gospel and the Gothic presbyter had delivered a sermon. In his sermon John Chrysostom

---

[1] *Arriani Periplus Ponti Euxini*, 19: 'καὶ ὁρμᾶται μὲν (Tanais) ἀπὸ λίμνης τῆς Μαιώτιδος, ἐσβάλλει δὲ ἐς θάλασσαν τὴν τοῦ Εὐξείνου Πόντου.'

[2] *Procopii De bello gothico*, iv, 4 (ed. Haury, ii, 502). On this text of Procopius see Marquart, *op. cit.*, p. 530.

[3] *Theodoreti Historia ecclesiastica*, v, 30 (ed. Parmentier, p. 330). Theodoret calls the Goths here Scythians. It is interesting to note that a Western historian of the sixth century, Cassiodorus, in his *Historia tripartita*, summarizing the passage of Theodoret cited above, gives the Celts instead of the Scythians (*Cassiodori Historia tripartita*, x, 5; *Patr. Lat.*, LXIX, col. 1168). Cf. a rather serious misunderstanding in this connection in Th. Uspenski, who sees here the Arian Goths, Th. Uspenski, 'Constantinople in the Last Years of the Fourth Century,' *Isvestiya* of the Russian Archaeological Institute in Constantinople, iv (1899), 162–163; idem, *History of the Byzantine Empire*, i (St Petersburg, 1914), 200–201.

wishes he might see that day in church many Hellenes, i.e., pagan scholars, in order that they might realize the triumph of Christianity. 'Where
is the doctrine of Plato, Pythagoras, and those who taught in Athens?
It has been forgotten. Where is the teaching of fishermen and tent-
makers? It shines brighter than the sun, not only in Judaea but also,
as you have heard today, in the tongue of the barbarians.'[1] Apparently
to the cultured men of Constantinople the Goths who came there were
utter barbarians. A little later in the same sermon John Chrysostom
says: 'And you have seen today the men who are most barbarian of all
men standing with the sheep of the Church; the pasture is common, the
enclosure is the same, and the same food is offered to all of them.'[2] Baur,
in his recent work on John Chrysostom, comments on this sermon:
'Chrysostom became the founder of a "German" national church in Constantinople, the oldest known to history.'[3] A priest and missionary of
broad education and wide horizons, John Chrysostom was interested in
the state of Christianity not only in the Empire but also beyond its
limits, for instance in Persia. John also took great care of the Crimean
Goths. During his patriarchate (398–404) he ordained as their bishop
Unila, who probably died in 404, i.e., in the year of John's exile to a far-
away city of Armenia, Cucusus. In a letter from Cucusus to the dea-
coness Olympias, a favorite correspondent to whom he wrote seventeen
letters, we read as follows:

The Marsian monks, the Goths,[4] notified me . . . that the deacon Maduarius had
come with the news that the excellent bishop Unila whom I had previously
ordained and sent to Gothia, after performing many great achievements had
passed away; he [Maduarius] came with a letter from the prince [king] of the
Goths[5] who begs that a bishop be sent to them. Since I see no other means to
avert the threatening catastrophe but delay and postponement (for it is impossible now for them to sail to Bosporus or to those general regions),[6] do make them
for the time being adjourn their departure on account of the winter.[7]

In the same letter John fears lest the future bishop for the Goths should
be ordained by his enemies, ordination by whom he considers illegal. It
would be best, in his opinion, for Maduarius silently and secretly to flee
to him at Cucusus. 'But if this is impossible, let it be as circumstances
allow.'

[1] *S. Joannis Chrysostomi VIII Homilia*, 1; *Patr. Gr.*, LXIII, col. 501.

[2] *Patr. Gr.*, LXIII, col. 502. Theodoret erroneously thinks that these were the Arian Goths, *Theodoreti Historia ecclesiastica*, v, 30 (ed. Parmentier, p. 330).

[3] P. Chrysostomus Baur, *Der heilige Johannes Chrysostomus und seine Zeit*, II (Munich, 1930), 70.

[4] *Joannis Chrysostomi Epistola XIV Olympiadi diaconissae*: 'ἐδήλωσάν μοι οἱ μονάζοντες οἱ Μαρσεῖς,
οἱ Γότθοι . . . ,' *Patr. Gr.*, LII, col. 618. On the interpretation of the adjective 'οἱ Μαρσεῖς' see below.

[5] 'Τοῦ ῥηγὸς τῶν Γότθων' (*ibid.*).

[6] 'Οὐδὲ γὰρ δυνατὸν αὐτοῖς πλεῦσαι εἰς τὸν Βόσπορον νῦν, οὐδὲ εἰς τὰ μέρη ἐκεῖνα' (*ibid.*). [7] *Ibid.*

Fears for the future destinies of the Gothic Church continued to alarm John, and in another letter of the year 404, from the same remote place, Cucusus, he wrote to the deacon Theodulus, 'Although the storm is severe and has risen violently to its height, and those who wish to stain the churches in Gothia are active and exert themselves to the utmost, do not cease to do your duty.'[1] He begs Theodulus to do his best to prevent troubles from arising there and urges him to pray fervently that God may cause misfortunes to cease and give peace to the Church. 'For the time being, as I have previously written, try to do everything in your power to postpone this affair in one way or another.'[2] In these last words John apparently has in view the matter of which he wrote in his letter to Olympias, the postponement of sending a bishop to Gothia.

John Chrysostom's keen interest in this question was entirely natural. The party hostile to him, with the Empress Eudoxia at its head and supported by many eminent members of the Church who were discontented with the straightforward and uncompromising policy of John Chrysostom as Patriarch of Constantinople, had triumphed and obtained from the Emperor the order of his deportation to Cucusus. Arsacius was made Patriarch of the capital, and he pursued a policy differing from John's and no doubt hostile to him. To John the arrangements of Arsacius and other bishops who had seceded from himself were illegal. But one of John's cherished works had passed into the hands of Arsacius, the care of the Gothic eparchy. This is why this letters show such strong alarm lest the Gothic Church be stained by the ordinations and deeds of unworthy persons; he hopes accordingly for delay in the appointment of a bishop to Gothia. Another letter of John Chrysostom, from Cucusus in the same year, 404, to 'the Gothic monks who lived on the estate of Promotus,'[3] has come down to us. Promotus was the deceased husband of Marsa, whose attitude to John was hostile.[4] The monks were the Orthodox Gothic monks with whom John, as we have said above, had very close relations. As John's followers were closely connected with him by ties of love and devotion, after his exile they were persecuted and harassed by the new church authorities; John's friends wrote to him in Cucusus about the matter. His letter to the Gothic monks begins thus: 'Before I received your letter, I had learned what affliction, plots, temptations, and insults you have endured; I therefore consider you blessed, having in my mind the crowns, reparations, and rewards which are prepared for

---

[1] *Joannis Chrysostomi Epistola* CCVI: 'εἰ καὶ χαλεπὸς ὁ χειμὼν καὶ πρὸς ὕψος ἐγήγερται, καὶ οἱ βουλόμενοι λυμαίνεσθαι ταῖς Ἐκκλησίαις ταῖς εἰς Γοτθίαν πολλὴν ποιοῦνται σπουδὴν πανταχοῦ περιτρέχοντες, ἀλλ' ὑμεῖς μὴ διαλίπητε τὰ παρ' ἑαυτῶν εἰσφέροντες,' *Patr. Gr.*, LII, col. 726.   [2] *Ibid.*

[3] 'Τοῖς μονάζουσι Γότθοις τοῖς ἐν τοῖς Προμώτου,' *Patr. Gr.*, LII, coll. 726–727.

[4] On this see below.

you for this. . . . Your patience, courage, endurance, your sincere and ardent love, your firm unshakable, and steadfast spirit, are well known to me. For this I express much gratitude to you.' He also seems to refer to his letter to Olympias, i.e., to the postponement of sending a new bishop to Gothia. 'I thank you for the zeal that you have manifested in keeping troubles from the Gothic church, and in supporting the delay of the matter. Not only do I refrain from blaming you for having sent no one, but I praise you and admire; for it is particularly laudable that you are unanimously engaged in this matter. So do not cease to do your best, both through yourselves and through others whom you may find, to postpone the matter. Whether you succeed in this or not, you will earn full reward for your intention and zeal.'

Thus on the basis of our evidence of John Chrysostom's activities we may come to the following conclusions. About 400 John ordained and sent to the Crimean Goths Bishop Unila, who stayed in the Crimea only a short while, dying probably in 404; in this year John wrote a letter to Olympias from which we learn of Unila's death. We do not know where Unila's residence was. It may have been located in Bosporus, which at that time belonged to the Goths, since the new Gothic bishop had to proceed thither. Less probably, according to some scholars, Unila's residence was in the region of Dory,[1] i.e., in the mountainous region which in the second half of the fifth century became and for a long time remained the centre of the Gothic power in the Crimea. The Goths were driven thither by the Huns on their return eastwards after the dismemberment of the empire of Attila, which will be discussed below. At the close of the fourth century, when Unila was ordained, there were no grounds whatever for the formation of a centre, political or religious, in such a mountainous and inaccessible region as Dory.[2]

On the basis of the title of the king (prince) of the Goths ($\tau o \hat{v}$ $\dot{\rho} \eta \gamma \dot{o} s$ $\tau \hat{\omega} \nu$ $\Gamma \dot{o} \tau \theta \omega \nu$) who asked for a new bishop, mentioned in John Chrysostom's letter, Tomaschek supposed that here John referred not to the Crimean Goths, but to the Gothic Church on the Lower Danube.[3] But this opinion can hardly be correct. First, the Crimean Goths of course had a ruler who according to the terminology of that time, and especially among those who did not live in the Crimea, might very easily have been called 'king' or 'prince' ($\dot{\rho} \dot{\eta} \xi$ –rex). Secondly, at the outset of the fifth century the Goths, with their king, were not on the Lower Danube. At that time the Visigoths had already lived through the period of their penetration into the Empire during the germanophile policy of Theodosius the Great, and at the close of the fourth century, under the command of

---

[1] Hermogenes, *op. cit.*, p. 147 (in Russian). [2] On Dory see below. [3] Tomaschek, *op. cit.*, p. 10.

their famous chief Alaric, had already devastated Greece in their movement westwards. The Ostrogoths, on the other hand, had been driven
to the West by the Hunnic hordes as early as the seventies of the fourth
century. Holding his unconfirmed hypothesis that the Crimean Goths
mean for the most part the Heruli, who at the outset of the fifth century
were still pagan, Loewe refers the statement of John Chrysostom quoted
above to the Caucasian Germans, i.e., to the mysterious Goths — Tetraxites and Eudusians — who supposedly dwelt on the eastern side of the
Cimmerian Bosporus, in the Tamán Peninsula and the adjoining regions.[1]
But the unreliability and arbitrariness of Loewe's theory have already
been noted above. In my opinion, there is no doubt that the data of
John Chrysostom referred to the Crimean Goths. His writings, therefore, are an important and contemporary source for the history of present-
day South Russia at the close of the fourth century and the outset of
the fifth.

It now remains to explain whom John Chrysostom meant in his letter
to Olympias by the 'Marsian Goths' (οἱ Μαρσεῖς οἱ Γότθοι). In the life
of John Chrysostom written in the form of a dialogue by his contemporary
and ardent admirer and friend, Palladius of Helenopolis, who is particularly well known for his *Historia Lausiaca* and is the main authority for
the history of Egyptian monasticism in the fourth century, we find mentioned three noble widows who were admitted to the court and were
hostile to John because he ridiculed some of their foibles. Palladius
writes,[2] '(These three women were) widows left wealthy by their husbands, possessing money made by extortion to the loss of their own salva-
tion, husband-baiters and disturbers of the peace:[3] Marsa, Promotus'
wife (Μάρσα Προμότου γυνή), Castricia, Satorninus' wife, and Eugraphia,
an absolute maniac. I am ashamed to speak of other things.[4] (The

---

[1] Archbishop Macarius erroneously refers all these data of John Chrysostom to the Danubian
Goths, Macarius, *History of Christianity in Russia before Vladimir* (St Petersburg, 1868), pp. 59–60
(in Russian).

[2] *Palladii Dialogus de Vita S. Joannis Chrysostomi*, Patr. *Gr.*, XLVII, col. 16. A new edition of this
Dialogus with revised text, introduction, notes, indices, and appendices, by P. R. Coleman-Norton
(Cambridge, 1928), p. 25. An English translation of the *Dialogus* by the Reverend Herbert Moore,
The Dialogue of Palladius concerning the Life of Chrysostom, in *Translations of Christian Literature:
Greek Texts* (London-New York, 1921), pp. 32–33.

[3] 'Ταραξάνδριαι καὶ ἀνασείστριαι.' In his translation of the *Dialogus* Herbert Moore remarks, 'Two
curious words apparently of the author's own coinage' (p. 32, n. 4).

[4] Marsa, Castricia, and Eugraphia are unknown outside the *Dialogus*. On Saturninus see a note
of P. R. Coleman-Norton, p. 159. He says wrongly that Promotus is unknown outside the *Dialogus*
(p. 159); we have already noted that the name of Promotus appears in one of Chrysostom's letters.
See also R. Janin, 'Les sanctuaires byzantins de Saint Michel (Constantinople et environs),' *Echos
d'Orient*, XXXVII (1934), 40–42: in one of the European suburbs of Constantinople there was the
shrine of Saint Michael τῶν Προμότου. In his historical sketch of Promotus' estate Janin does not refer
to our sources quoted above. According to Janin, Promotus was a consul in 389. I believe that
our Promotus is the same person.

widows and their late husbands) being sluggard-hearted in the matter of the faith, like a throng (φάλαγξ) of drunken people, united in their hatred of Christian teaching have organized a flood of ruin against the peace of the Church.'   Besides this, we know that John's third letter cited above was addressed 'To the Marsian monks, on an estate of Promotus' (ἐν τοῖς Προμώτου).   Hence we may conclude that the Goths who were in Constantinople and with whom John was on friendly terms dwelt on an estate which after Promotus' death came into the possession of his wife Marsa.   Her name explains the name of 'the Marsian Goths,' i.e., the Goths who in 404, when John's letter was written, were living on an estate belonging to her.[1]   At any rate, Loewe's opinion concerning this name must be decisively rejected; he wrote that the 'Marsians' in all likelihood meant some tribe of the Caucasian Germans, perhaps that of the Tetraxite Goths.[2]   As the adherents of John Chrysostom, the Goths who dwelt on Marsa's estate after his deposition and exile endured many persecutions, which explain the allusions in his letters and his care for them.

One question remains obscure: when and under what circumstances the Gothic bishop made his appearance in the Crimea.   The bishops of the Danubian Goths in the fourth century are known: Theophilus, a contemporary of the Nicaean Council; his successor, the famous Gothic missionary, Ulfila, who died in 388; his successor Selina.   This list brings us to the very close of the fourth century.   It is difficult to suppose that at that time, with the permanently military and migratory life of the Goths, any well-organized and fixed eparchy, and consequently any definite residence for the Gothic bishop, could have existed.   Being preachers of Christianity, the bishops also spent a rather nomadic life and journeyed from one place to another.   In this respect it is worth while to recollect Ulfila's life.   At the close of the fourth century the main mass of the Goths receded from the Balkan Peninsula and went to Greece, and later to Italy.   In the Peninsula there remained a small number of the Goths, the so-called 'Lesser Goths' (Gothi minores), who dwelt in Lesser Scythia, i.e., in present-day Dobrudja, along the shore of the Black Sea, south of the mouths of the Danube.   In the sixth century, according to Jordanes, 'they are poor and unaggressive, rich in nothing save flocks of various kinds, pasture-lands for cattle, and forests for wood; their country is not fruitful in wheat or other sorts of grain; some of the Goths, though buying wine from neighbouring countries, do not even know that vineyards exist elsewhere; but most of them drink milk.'[3]   In the ninth century a West-

---

[1] See P. Chrysostomus Baur, *Der heilige Johannes Chrysostomus und seine Zeit*, ɪɪ (Munich, 1930), 33 and n. 15; also p. 164.

[2] Loewe, *Die Reste der Germanen am schwarzen Meere* (Halle, 1896), pp. 71–72.

[3] *Jordanis Getica*, ʟɪ, 267; ed. Mommsen, p. 127.   Cf. the *Gothic History* of Jordanes in an English version by C. C. Mierow (Princeton, 1915), p. 128

ern Frankish writer and poet, Walafrid Strabo, a contemporary of Lewis the Pious, mentions these Goths, who spoke in the Teuton (i.e. German) tongue and as late as his time used the Gothic translation of the Bible.[1] Afterwards the 'Lesser Goths' disappeared; they apparently assimilated with the Slavs and Bulgarians who filled the Peninsula in the ninth century.   This comparatively small group of 'Lesser Goths' did not have a Gothic bishop of their own.   But since the maritime city of Tomi (Τόμης or Τόμις), the residence of the Scythian bishop, of whose eparchy from the sixth century we know almost nothing, was situated in the territory of the Lesser Goths, it is very natural to suppose that their pastor, who at that time already bore the title of Scythian Bishop, resided in this city.   At any rate, in the distribution of metropoles made under Leo the Philosopher (886–911), the Scythian eparchy is given as subject to the jurisdiction of the Constantinopolitan Patriarch.[2]   Let us note by the way that Theotimus was a Scythian bishop contemporary with John Chrysostom.[3]

Thus, after the departure of the Goths from the Balkan Peninsula at the close of the fourth century, the Gothic bishops there disappeared. The Crimean Goths who had entirely broken away from the main mass of their countrymen remained in the Tauric Peninsula and were Orthodox. According to our sources John Chrysostom, carrying out his vast missionary plans, about 400 appointed there the first bishop, Unila.   From this time on some scattered information about the bishops of Crimean Gothia and the eparchy of Gothia, though with many intervals of silence, begins to reach us.

6. THE HUNNIC PREDOMINANCE IN THE FIFTH CENTURY

We have no information on the life of the Crimean Goths during most of the fifth century.   Only at its close, in connection with the end of Attila's Hunnic empire, can we draw from our sources information about the Tauric Peninsula.

After the sudden death of Attila in 453 his huge empire broke up.   The peoples who had been under his power scattered in different directions. As Jordanes writes, 'Kingdoms with their peoples are divided, and out of one body are made many members.'[4]   According to the same writer,

---

[1] *Walafridi Strabonis Liber de exordiis et incrementis quarundam in observationibus ecclesiasticis rerum*, VII, *Patr. Lat.*, CXIV, col. 927; ed. A. Knoepfler (Munich, 1899), p. 20.

[2] See *Hieroclis Synecdemus et notitiae graecae episcopatuum*, rec. G. Parthey (Berlin, 1866), p. 57 (No. 43); ed. A. Burckhardt (Leipzig, 1893), p. 3 (No. 636, 9).   Cf. E. Gerland, *Corpus notitiarum episcopatuum*, I, i, (Kadiköy-Istanbul, 1931), Introduction, 47.

[3] On the Scythian eparchy see Macarius, *op. cit.*, pp. 38–47 (in Russian).

[4] *Jordanis Getica*, 261; ed. Mommsen, p. 125: 'dividuntur regna cum populis, fiuntque ex uno corpore membra diversa.'

after the heroic death in battle of Attila's oldest and favorite son, Ellac, 'his remaining brothers are put to flight near the shore of the Sea of Pontus, where we have said the Goths first settled';[1] in other words, the Huns again reached the shore of the Black Sea. One of the Hunnic tribes, the Utigurs, returning homeward with their leader to the place of their former settlement in the east, proceeded through the Tauric Peninsula and in its eastern section, near Lake Maeotis, chanced upon the Goths who are called (in my opinion erroneously) Tetraxites, of whom we shall speak later at length. These Goths Procopius calls 'the most stalwart of all the barbarians of that region';[2] trusting both in their own strength and the advantage of their position, they formed a barrier with their shields and at first made a stubborn stand against their assailants, but finally could not resist superior numbers. Procopius' description of the place of the conflict is rather obscure; but he mentions only one not very wide approach which was open to the Huns who attacked the Goths. This allows us to assume that he refers here to the narrow place in the eastern region of the Peninsula between the gulfs of Arabat and Theodosia,[3] i.e., that the battle took place in the Peninsula of Kerch.

The belligerents opened negotiations and came to an understanding, agreeing that the Tetraxite Goths should join forces with the Huns, make the crossing in common, and on the opposite mainland should be thereafter friends and allies of the Utigurs and live forever on terms of complete equality with them. This portion of the Crimean Goths crossed the Strait and settled in the Tamán Peninsula and the neighboring regions.[4]

This second irruption of the Huns into the Tauric Peninsula had evidently much greater significance than the first: it separated the Goths who dwelt in the Peninsula. The Goths who dwelt in the eastern plain of the Crimea, after fruitless resistance, left the Peninsula and crossed to the opposite bank of the Strait; but the Goths who dwelt in the south in the mountains and along the coast were out of danger from the Huns, who, being particularly an equestrian people accustomed to live and fight in the plains, could not undertake serious measures against the inaccessible heights of the Crimea. Of course at the threat of the Hunnic passage many of the Goths of the plain rushed to seek safety in the mountains

[1] *Ibid.*, 263; ed. Mommsen, pp. 125–126: 'reliqui vero germani ejus eo occiso fugantur juxta litus Pontici maris, ubi prius Gothos sedisse descripsimus.' See also *Getica*, 28; ed. Mommsen, pp. 60–61.

[2] *Procopii De bello gothico*, IV, 5; ed. Haury, II, 506; ed. H. B. Dewing, V (London-New York, 1928), 92–93.

[3] *Procopii De bello gothico*, IV, 5; ed. Haury, II, 506; ed. Dewing, V, 92–95: 'ἡ πρώτη τῆς Μαιώτιδος ἐκροὴ οὗ δὴ τότε οἱ Τετραξῖται Γότθοι ἵδρυντο ἐν κόλπῳ ξυνιοῦσα μηνοειδεῖ, περιβαλοῦσά τε αὐτοὺς ἐκ τοῦ ἐπὶ πλεῖστον, μίαν ἐπ' αὐτοὺς εἴσοδον οὐ λίαν εὐρεῖαν τοῖς ἐπιοῦσι παρείχετο.'

[4] *Procopii De bello gothico*, IV, 5; ed. Haury, II, 506–507; ed. Dewing, V, 94–95.

with their countrymen.　From that time on, i.e., from the second half
of the fifth century, the Huns who crossed with the eastern Crimean
Goths to the opposite shore of the Strait became the masters of the steppe
region of the Peninsula.

In connection with the events just dealt with it is important to examine
the well-known passage of Procopius concerning the region of Dory.
Speaking of the fortifications erected by Justinian in the Crimea he writes:

There is a region on the sea coast, called Dory (Δόρυ), where the Goths dwelt
from of old; they did not follow Theoderic who proceeded to Italy, but voluntarily remained there and still in my day are allies of the Romans; along with
them they go to war on their enemies, when the Emperor pleases.　Their number is about three thousand; they are excellent warriors as well as able cultivators
of their own land; they are the most hospitable of all men.　The region of Dory
itself lies high; however, it is neither rugged nor arid but fertile and abundant in
the best fruits.　In this country the Emperor built nowhere city or fort, for the
inhabitants of that place would not tolerate to be shut within any walls, but
they always liked best to dwell in a plain.[1]

This interesting account of the sixth-century writer depicts the situation which the mountain Goths in the Crimea inherited from the preceding century.　As far as we may judge from this text, Procopius means by
Dory the whole region (χώρα) occupied by the Goths, and not merely
their chief centre, which occurs in the sources either by the name of Dory
or by its variants, Doros, Doras, Daras, and, finally, Theodoro, while
the whole region is called Gothia or the Gothic Climates (*Climata* —
Κλίματα).　Procopius connects the formation of the Gothic region Dory
with the departure of Theoderic to Italy, i.e., chronologically with the
time of the Hunnic invasion in the Crimea in the second half of the fifth
century, for Theoderic entered Italy, which allured him so much, in 488.
We must point out a rather considerable oversight of Procopius.　He
thought that at the close of the fifth century the Ostrogoths of Theoderic
and the Crimean Goths were still living a common life and were in close
touch with each other.　In reality, at the close of the fifth century the
Ostrogoths of the Balkan Peninsula and the Tauric Goths were already
living absolutely separate lives, without any contact, for the Hunnic
hordes who had come out of Attila's disintegrated empire were wandering between them and separated them completely.　But this oversight
of Procopius, in my opinion, does not weaken his first chronological dating
of the division of the Crimean Goths into two sections and the increase
of the Gothic mountain element in connection with the Hunnic invasion

---

[1] *Procopii De aedificiis*, III 7; ed. Haury, III, ii 101; Vasilievski, II, ii, 371 (in Russian); N. Bănescu,
'Contribution à l'histoire de la seigneurie de Théodoro-Mangoup en Crimée,' *Byz. Zeitschrift*, xxxv
(1935), 24.

in the Peninsula.   From the same text of Procopius we may draw another
interesting conclusion, that the Hunnic danger in the Crimea which was
felt both by the Goths and by the peoples belonging to the Roman Empire
and first of all by Chersonesus, induced both sides to seek an alliance
with each other.   The initiative probably came from the Goths, since
they were most threatened and less organized.   The number of three
thousand Goths recorded by Procopius presents some difficulty.   We can
hardly suppose that here Procopius meant the total number of the mountain Goths with their families.   It seems to me this rather means the
auxiliary body of troops, which, according to reciprocal obligations, the
Goths in case of need were bound to put at the disposal of the Romans.
Furthermore, Procopius gives us some idea of the location of the region
of the mountain Goths; it extended along the southern coast of the Peninsula[1] and went northwards into the interior, where it was bounded by the
Crimean mountains, i.e., Chatyrdagh, the massif of Mankup, and so on.
Procopius' statement that the Goths liked best to live in the plains is in
perfect accordance with all their previous history on the great east-Euro-
pean plain; even when they came into the Crimea they remained for some
time at least in its steppes.

Thus Procopius meant by Dory the region of the Crimean mountain
Goths.   In this case he made use of the name of a definite city for that
of the country.   On this point we have exact information from Priscian,
Procopius' contemporary and a famous grammarian who lived in Constantinople in the time of Emperor Anastasius I (491–518) and his immediate successors.   Priscian wrote in Latin an excellent detailed manual
for the study of the Latin language (*Institutiones grammaticae*) which became one of the most popular books of the Middle Ages and which because
of its collection of material from ancient writings is not devoid of interest
even today.   Two passages in Priscian's manual are important for us.

In one place we read, 'There are fourteen final letters for names used
in the Latin language . . . among the Greek letters there is also *y*, as
Dory, the name of a Pontic city, and Aepy.'[2]   In another part of the

---

[1] The terminating points of the Gothic possessions along the coast can be approximately fixed.
In the west they were apparently not far away from the Roman Chersonesus; see Procopius,
'χώρα κατὰ τὴν παραλίαν, Δόρυ ὄνομα' (*ibid.*), and 'παραθαλασσία' in an inscription of the year 1427 on
the construction of a temple at Theodoro, Latyshev, *Collection of Greek Inscriptions of Christian Times
from South Russia* (St Petersburg, 1896), pp. 51–52 (in Greek and Russian).   If in the statement of
the Geographer of Ravenna given below (IV, 5) 'Getho Githorum patria' means the region of the
Crimean Goths, as is most probable, and since the next region in the Geographer of Ravenna is that
of Sugdaia (Sugdabon), i.e., not a Gothic region, we may conclude that the Gothic coastland was
situated between Chersonesus in the west and Sugdaia (now Sudak) in the east.   See note below.

[2] *Prisciani Grammatici Caesariensis Institutionum Grammaticarum libri XVIII*, VI, 1: 'Quattuor-
decim sunt literae terminales nominum, quibus Latinus utitur sermo . . . in Graecis autem invenitur
etiam y, ut "Dory," nomen oppidi Pontici, et "Aepy",' ed. M. Hertz, I (Leipzig, 1855), 195 (*Gram-*

same manual Priscian writes, 'There are also Greek names which end
with *y*: *hoc Dory, hoc Aepy*, names of cities.'[1]

A passage is worth mention from the so-called Geographer of Ravenna
or Anonymus of Ravenna, the author of a rather unreliable and confused
cosmography which was originally written late in the seventh century
in the Greek language at Ravenna, and at a later date, not earlier than
the ninth century, translated into Latin; only the Latin version has come
down to us.[2] The passage is as follows: 'We have read that in the Bosforian country there were very many cities, out of which we wish to designate some, i.e., . . . Boristenida, Olbiapolis, Capolis, Dori, Chersona,
Thesiopolis, Careon, Trapezus.'[3] It is true that this text, particularly
in reference to the name of Dory, arouses doubt, for in the corresponding
passage of Jordanes, who is here the source of *Anonymus*, the name of
Dory is lacking. The editor of Jordanes, Mommsen, remarks that in
the text of *Anonymus* 'Capolis, Dori' *dori* is nothing but a distorted
syllable *da* from the preceding name of the city Callipolida, as this name
occurs in Jordanes.[4] This is very probable, because in another place in
Anonymus, where the same names are given, the name of the city of
Dory is lacking.[5]

But Priscian testifies with absolute certainty that late in the fifth century the city of Dory already existed, and that it was one of the 'Pontic
cities' (*oppidum Ponticum*), i.e., one of those which lay near the Euxine
Pontus. In some manuscripts of Priscian's work this name is even written in Greek, Δόρυ, as with Procopius, though the latter used the name
of the city for the whole region. The question whether towards the sixth
century the Gothic region in the Crimea already had a special regional
name has been definitely answered in John Chrysostom's letter to Olym-

---

matici latini ex recensione H. Keilii, II). For the name 'Dory' there are given variants: 'Dopy,'
'doroy.'

[1] *Ibid.*, VII, 1: 'inveniuntur etiam in y desinentia Graeca: "hoc Dory," "hoc Aepy," nomina
civitatium' (ed. Hertz, I, 283). Variants for 'hoc Dory': 'hordory,' 'doroy.'

[2] On the Geographer of Ravenna see Mommsen, in the *Prooemium* to his edition of Jordanes, p.
xlv; W. S. Teuffel, *Geschichte der römischen Litteratur* (Leipzig, 1913), pp. 544–546.

[3] *Ravennatis Anonymi Cosmographia*, IV, 3: 'in qua Bosforiana patria plurimas fuisse civitates legimus, ex quibus aliquantas designare volumus, id est . . . Boristenida, Olbiapolis, Capolis, Dori,
Chersona, Theosiopolis, Careon, Trapezus,' ed. M. Pinder and G. Parthey (Berlin, 1860), p. 172–174.

[4] See *Jordanis Getica*, 32, ed. Mommsen, p. 62.

[5] *Ravennatis Anonymi Cosmographia*, V, 11: 'Porestenida, Calipolis, Cersona, Theodosia, Dosiopolis, Careon, Trapezus' (ed. Pinder-Parthey, p. 370). I think that in one more place *Anonymus* deals
with the Crimean Goths, namely IV, 5: 'item ad frontem Roxolanorum regionis sunt patriae, id est
Sithotrogorum, item patria Campi Campanidon, nec non Getho Githorum, Sugdabon, Fanaguron,
paludis Maeotidon' (ed. Pinder-Parthey, p. 176). Here the geographical names are distorted (some
of them doubled) for example, the obscure 'Campi Campanidon' and 'Getho Githorum'; the latter
must mean the region of the Crimean Goths; then follow 'Sugdea,' 'Phanagoria,' and 'Lake Maeotis.'
Is the first part of the name 'Sithotrogorum' a form of 'Scytho'?

pias quoted above, which states that Bishop Unila had been ordained by him and sent to Gothia.   Hence we may definitely conclude that at the close of the fifth century Dory was already the centre of so-called Gothia. We know that Chersonesus belonged to the Roman Empire and we have the place list of the Geographer of Ravenna, Getho Githorum and Sugdabon; by combining these two pieces of information we may determine, for the early period of Crimean Gothia, at least from the close of the fifth century, the extent of its littoral possessions: they began a little east of Chersonesus, or perhaps it is better to say, of Balaklava, and ended not far west of Sugdaia.   These limits are entirely suitable for those of the mountain Goths, for along the coast the mountains rise to a considerable height only from a little east of Balaklava (ancient Symbolon, Italian Cembalo), and become much lower not far west of Sugdaia.   Whether the hilly territory on the seashore was assigned to the Goths by Emperor Zeno, in the eighties of the fifth century, as S. P. Shestakov states, using as authority an inscription of the year 488,[1] of which we shall speak a little later, or whether they previously possessed the littoral, is not yet entirely clear to me.

7. ZENO'S INSCRIPTION (A.D. 488)

In my opinion the Chersonesian inscription of Emperor Zeno of the year 488 is to be interpreted in connection with the invasion of the Huns into the Crimea at the close of the fifth century.   The question of the original location of this inscription has been long disputed; only late in the nineteenth century did Bertier Delagarde prove that it undoubtedly belonged to Chersonesus.[2]

The inscription runs as follows:

Autocrator Caesar Zeno, pious, victorious, triumphant, supreme, venerable.   His reverence taking care both of all cities in general and of this city of his own in particular has granted an amount of money, namely [that] collected from the treasury of the *vicaratus* of the devoted *ballistarii* of this place.   Restoring by means of this the walls for the safety of this city and expressing our gratitude, we have set up our inscription in eternal memory of his reign.   This tower has been restored by the care of the magnificent *comes* Diogenes, in the year 512, indiction 11.[3]

---

[1] Shestakov, *Outlines on the History of Chersonesus*, p. 8; he notes on the same page, 'The Goths — agriculturists — were settled by Zeno,' etc.

[2] Bertier Delagarde, 'An Inscription from the Time of Emperor Zeno, in Connection with the Fragments from the History of Chersonesus,' *Zapiski* of the Odessa Society of History and Antiquities, XVI (1893), 45–88 (in Russian).   On the history of the inscription itself see *ibid.* and Latyshev, *Collection of Christian Inscriptions*, pp. 7–10.

[3] The inscription itself and its Russian translation in Latyshev, *Collection of Christian Inscriptions*, pp. 10–11.

We shall put aside the complicated and debatable questions concerning the Greek text of the inscription and its interpretation, which have aroused contradictory arguments.[1]   To us it is the dating of the inscription which is important.   After careful study the date has been definitely established as the eleventh indiction, not the fourteenth, as had been previously thought; and the eleventh indiction falls during the reign of Zeno (474–491) within the year 488, or, to be exact, between the first of September 487 and the first of September 488.   At that time, apparently, danger was threatening, because the walls were restored 'for the safety of the city.'   As far as we may judge from the rather obscure statement of the inscription, the *ballistarii*, i.e., the military force of this distant frontier city, which was defended by *ballistae*, a sort of artillery, had to give money for the restoration of the walls.   From Constantine Porphyrogenitus, who drew his information from earlier sources, we learn that at least in the fourth century, during the period of Constantine the Great, the *ballistarii* played a very important rôle in the struggle of Chersonesus against the barbarian enemies of the Empire.[2]   This important aspect of the military technique of Chersonesus, which the barbarians inexperienced in military training could not withstand, evidently continued to flourish there also throughout the whole fifth century.[3]   According to the inscription, in the time of Zeno the *comes* Diogenes was sent to Chersonesus, where he restored the tower.   Diogenes was not unknown at that epoch; he may almost certainly be identified with the *comes scholarum* Diogenes, who at the outset of the reign of Zeno's successor, Anastasius I, was appointed commander-in-chief to make war on the Isaurians.[4]   An inscription from Megara of the same epoch reports that 'the most magnificent *comes* Diogenes, a son of Archelaus, taking care of Hellenic cities as of his own home and considering nothing more noble than to benefit the Hellenes and to restore their cities, gave the Megarians 250 gold coins for the construction of towers and 2200 feet of marble for the restoration of a bath.'[5]

All these energetic measures for the security of Chersonesus were undertaken because of serious danger.   Some scholars suppose that it was

---

[1] Information on this argument is to be found in Shestakov, *Outlines on the History of Chersonesus*, pp. 95–103, 142.

[2] *Const. Porphyrogeniti De administrando imperio*, Ch. 53 (ed. Bonn, pp. 250–251).

[3] In the inscription the *ballistarii* are entitled 'devoted — καθωσιωμένοι — devoti — devotissimi.' This example may be added to the chapter on 'devotus, devotissimus' (καθωσιωμένος) in P. Koch's book, *Die byzantinischen Beamtentitel von 400 bis 700* (Jena, 1903), pp. 78–81.

[4] *Theophanis Chronographia*, ed. de Boor, p. 138.   See A. Rose, *Kaiser Anastasius I, Erster Teil: Die äussere Politik des Kaisers* (Halle a. S., 1882), p. 22; Latyshev, *Collection of Christian Inscriptions*, p. 15 (in Russian).

[5] Boeck, *Corpus inscriptionum graecarum*, IV. No. 8622 (pp. 292–293).   See Latyshev, *Collection of Christian Inscriptions*, p. 15 .

necessary to restore the walls of Chersonesus on account of a violent earthquake which occurred in September, 480, and lasted forty days. 'Much damage was done, possibly not only in Constantinople but also in other cities; thus the mission of the *comes* Diogenes might have been part of a general measure which dealt with many cities; therefore in the inscription of 488 it is noted, probably not without reason, that the favor was conferred on Chersonesus equally with other cities.'[1] It seems to me that this theory has insufficient grounds. The earthquake referred to here occurred, according to some sources, in 480, and according to others, in 477. The source closest in time, namely the *Chronicle of Marcellinus*, of the sixth century, gives under the year 480 the following reference: 'The imperial city having been shaken forty days in succession by a violent earthquake, [the people] were greatly depressed and lamented. Both Troadian porticos fell down; several churches either broke asunder or collapsed; the statue of Theodosius the Great in the *forum* of Taurus, which stood on the top of the spiral column, fell down because its two supporting arches collapsed. The Byzantines keep this dreadful day on September 24.'[2] A chronicler of the ninth century, Theophanes, gives a similar account and adds that the interior walls of the city collapsed to a considerable extent and countless numbers of people were buried under them; in addition Theophanes gives the date of the earthquake — September 25, indiction one.[3]

But possibly under Zeno there was also another earthquake, which, without the exact date, is noted by a chronicler of the sixth century, John Malalas, as follows: 'In the reign of Zeno, by the wrath of God Constantinople suffered a second earthquake to a small extent, as far as [the *forum*] of Taurus. Nicomedia, the metropole of Bithynia, suffered for the sixth time, as well as Helenopolis, a city of the same eparchy. And Zeno helped them in many respects'.[4] We see from this that this earthquake covered a part of Asia Minor and perhaps was felt also in the Cyclades.[5] If we combine the account of John Malalas with the chron-

---

[1] Bertier Delagarde, in the *Zapiski* of the Odessa Society of History and Antiquities, XVI, 82. Latyshev follows him, Latyshev, *op. cit.*, p. 15. Both in Russian.

[2] *Marcellini Comitis Chronicon*, s. a. 480, ed. Mommsen, *Mon. Germ. Hist., Chronica Minora*, II (1894), 92.

[3] *Theophanis Chronographia*, ed. de Boor, pp. 125–126. 25 September of the first indiction corresponds to 25 September 477. From Theophanes in Georgius Cedrenus, I, 618.

[4] *Joannis Malalae Chronographia*, p. 385. From here the first portion of this account, up to the words 'as far as the Taurus,' has passed into the Easter Chronicle, which refers the earthquake to 26 September, indiction 10, i.e., 26 September 486, *Chronicon Paschale*, I, 605. Some scholars believe the Easter Chronicle confuses this account with the earthquake of 480. See note in *Chronicon Paschale*, II, 438.

[5] See Al. Perrey, 'Mémoire sur les tremblements de terre ressentis dans la péninsule turco-hellénique et en Syrie,' *Mémoires couronnés et mémoires des savants étrangers publiés par L'Académie Royale des sciences, des lettres et des beaux-arts de Belgique*, XXIII (1850), 8.

ological indication of the Easter Chronicle, we should have for the beginning of the second earthquake 26 September 486.

But I believe it is probable that we are dealing here with only one earthquake, which occurred in the autumn of 480 and was felt in some provinces of Asia Minor as well as in Constantinople. In its early portions the chronology of the Easter Chronicle is not very exact, and is not to be relied on. The nearest chronicler in time, Marcellinus, reports the disaster only in Constantinople, but an earthquake so violent could not have been confined to the capital. Other sources also note additional places affected by the earthquake, though with confused chronology. In the Slavonic version of the Chronicle of Simeon Metaphrastes and Logothete (the complete Greek text is yet unknown), we read: 'In the time of [Zeno] a formidable earthquake occurred in Constantinople, and many churches and houses collapsed; the metropolitan see of Nicomedia also suffered.'[1] This information may confirm our belief that the 'formidable earthquake' of 480 also affected Asia Minor. There is also a Syriac source for the earthquake under Zeno, i.e., Michael the Syrian. True, he is a late writer, of the twelfth century, but he made use of ancient texts. As far as I know, no one has used this source for our question. He writes of the earthquake in two places. In the first place we read: 'At that time an earthquake occurred in Thrace, and many regions were destroyed. Fear seized all those who saw the misfortunes which befell the people, and everyone thought that the end of the world was at hand.'[2] This passage mentions Thrace, a region adjoining Constantinople. In the other reference Michael gives the account already known from other sources: a violent earthquake occurred, and the major part of the Imperial city was destroyed as far as the Taurus.[3]

Thus, in 480 a violent earthquake occurred in the Empire: it particularly affected Constantinople and Thrace, and devastated a portion of Asia Minor and perhaps the Cyclades. According to John Malalas, Zeno brought active aid to the suffering regions.[4]

Of course, in spite of the complete silence of the sources, it is possible

---

[1] *Simeona Metafrasta i Logotheta Spisanie mira* (St Petersburg, 1905), p. 53 (in Old Slavonic). From him Leo Grammaticus, pp. 116–117. A chronicler, probably of the seventh century, John of Antioch, also mentions an earthquake in the time of Zeno, Joannes Antiochenus, Fragment 211, 2 (the text has deteriorated at the end), C. Müller, *Fragmenta historicum graecorum*, IV, 619.

[2] *Chronique de Michel le Syrien*, II (Paris, 1901), 147.   [3] *Ibid.*, p. 149.

[4] See Clinton, *Fasti Romani*, I (Oxford, 1843), 692, 708; E. Muralt, *Essai de chronographie byzantine*, I (St Petersburg, 1855), 96, 104; Perrey, *op. cit.*, p. 8. They note two earthquakes: Clinton in 480 and 487, Muralt in 480 and 488, Perrey in 477 (478; 480) and 487. See W. Barth, *Kaiser Zeno* (Basel, 1894), p. 78 and n. 3 (Sept., 478; two earthquakes under Zeno.) Recently, on the basis of the indiction given, September of 479 has been considered more correct; see *The Cambridge Medieval History*, I (Cambridge, 1911), 476, n. 1.

that the earthquake of 480 affected the Crimea; it is quite natural that an earthquake in such a distant country as Chersonesus might easily have been overlooked in the sources. Malalas' reference to Zeno's support of the regions affected may be correlated with the words of the Chersonesian inscription of 488: '(Zeno) took care both of all cities in general and of this city of his own.' None the less I can not consider this earthquake the chief cause of the restoration of the walls and towers of Chersonesus; for eight years elapsed between the earthquake in 480 and the restoration of the walls in 488.

However, why the walls of Chersonesus were in a state of decay is a question of secondary importance to us; our main interest is to know why at the close of the eighties decisive measures were undertaken for their restoration. And when we raise this question we cannot avoid pointing out the coincidence in time of the Hunnic invasion and the restoration of the Chersonesian walls and towers. Under pressure of the Hunnic danger the Imperial government undertook speedy measures for the fortification of its chief stronghold in the Peninsula. This danger, common both to the Empire and to the Crimean Goths, led to the conclusion of an alliance between them. It was owing to this alliance, as we have already learned from Procopius' account given above, that the mountain Goths at the Emperor's desire participated in his wars with the enemies of the Empire. Thus, beginning with the close of the fifth century, the history of the Crimean Goths is closely connected with their obligations towards the Empire, and it goes without saying that in this Gotho-Roman alliance the Goths played the rôle of a vassal state. At that time, in view of the Hunnic danger, the Roman Empire was intensely interested in supporting the Goths on its border. It is also probable that, when the Goths escaped into the mountains and begged aid from the Emperor, Zeno allotted them the southern coast line of the Peninsula; or perhaps, to be more exact, he officially confirmed them in the possession of land a part of which, at least, they already held.[1]

8. THE SITE OF DORY AND THEODORO-MANKUP

Let us now turn to the question of the site of Dory, later Doros, Doras, and finally Theodoro. Till 1866 it was generally thought that Theodoro was on the site of present-day Inkerman, near Sebastopol.[2] In 1866 Ph. Bruun, who has worked a great deal on the history of the Crimea, proved that Theodoro must be identified, not with Inkerman, but with the almost inaccessible massif of Mankup (Mangub) or Mankup-Kalé on the

---

[1] On this point see above.

[2] The identification of Theodoro with Inkerman sometimes occurs in later works. See for instance *Atti della Società Ligure di Storia Patria*, VII, 2 (1879), 981.

top of which a number of remains of mediaeval buildings have been pre-served.[1] In the early seventies, after the discovery of the ruins of a *basilica* at Parthenite on the seashore close to the promontory of Ayudagh, the opinion was expressed that the former city of Theodoro was on the site of Parthenite; but this view has been thoroughly refuted.[2]

The idea has often been advanced that Theodoro is identical with Man-kup, with more or less debatable proofs. But the identification has been absolutely proved by the collation of the Italian and Russian sources of the fifteenth century. A Genoese charter of 26 April 1471 is addressed to 'our magnificent and dearest friend, Lord Saichus, master of Tedori' (Magnifico amico nostro carissimo, domino Saicho, domino Tedori). In this document the Genoese authorities persuade Saichus to enter into close relations with Kaffa (Caffa — Theodosia) to fight their common enemy the Turks.[3] Another Genoese document of 10 February 1475 also speaks of friendly relations with 'Lord Saichus, master of Theodori and Gothia' (domini saici domini theodori et Gottie).[4] Thus from these docu-ments we may conclude that in 1471 and 1475 a certain Saichus was the ruler of Theodoro.

Let us turn to the Russian sources. In 1475 the Russian Grand Prince Ivan III Vasilyevich (John III) sent an embassy to the Tartar Khan Mengli-Girei with a *boyar* (noble), Aleksei (Alexis) Ivanovich Starkov, at its head. At the end of the instructions received by Starkov from the Grand Prince we find 'a note to Oleksei (i.e. Starkov) on the Mankup affair,' from which we learn of Starkov's relations with the Prince of Mankup, Isaiko. We read that a year earlier (in 1474) an ambassador from the Russian Grand Prince, the *boyar* (noble) Nikita Vasilyevich Beklemishev, had also visited Isaiko, who offered friendship to the Rus-sian Grand Prince and expressed the wish to marry his own daughter to the son of the Russian ruler. We read in this document, 'My *boyar* Mikita visited Prince Isaiko and saw the girl.' The Russian Prince wished to know, 'Of how many thousand gold coins is the dowry of the girl?' Starkov also was entrusted with a commission to carry on similar friendly negotiations with Isaiko.[5] Therefore from the Russian sources

---

[1] Ph. Bruun, *Notices historiques et topographiques concernant les colonies italiennes en Gazarie* (St Petersburg, 1866), pp. 72–73 (*Mémoires de l'Académie Impériale des sciences de St Pétersbourg*).

[2] On the history of the question of the site of Theodoro see Latyshev, *Collection of Greek Inscriptions of Christian Times in the South of Russia*, pp. 48–50 (in Russian).

[3] *Codice diplomatico delle Colonie Tauro-Liguri durante la signoria dell'Ufficio di S. Giorgio*, ed. P. A. Vigna, II (Genoa, 1874), p. 769 (*Atti della Società Ligure*, VII, 1).

[4] *Atti della Società Ligure*, VII, 2 (Genova, 1879), 194–195.

[5] *Documents (Pamyatniki) of Diplomatic Relations of the State of Moscow with the Crimean and Nogai Hordes and Turkey*, I (St Petersburg, 1884), 12–13 (*Sbornik* of the Imperial Russian Historical Society, Vol. XLI). In Russian. Bruun knew these data from the *History of Russia* by Karamzin, who used

we know that in 1474 and 1475 in the Crimea the Prince of Mankup was Isaiko, who of course is identical with Saichus of the Genoese documents of 1471 and 1475, in which he is called the master of Theodoro.   Hence it is clear that Theodoro was built on Mankup.

In addition, in the ruins of Mankup have been found two inscriptions dealing with the fort and city of Theodoro.   The first inscription, discovered in 1889 by F. Braun, copied in 1895 by J. A. Kulakovski and published by Latyshev, mentions the Theodorites, i.e., the inhabitants of Theodoro, and the 'God-guarded fortress of Theodoro,' and is seemingly to be assigned to the fourteenth century.[1]   Its text is rather obscure.   The second inscription, which was found by R. Ch. Loeper in 1913 during his excavations on Mankup, refers to the year 1363.   It deals with the construction of a tower of 'the upper city of the venerable Poiki(?)' and with a restoration of the city of Theodoro.[2]

All these data leave no doubt as to the identification of Theodoro with Mankup.

Mankup or Mankup-Kalé is an almost inaccessible massif which reaches nineteen hundred feet above sea level and has rocky cliffs on almost all sides; it lies about eleven miles from the city of Baghchesarai and about ten miles from the railroad station Belbek.   'The mountain looks like the wrist of a human hand with four short outspread fingers.'[3]   The massif of Mankup has made a striking impression on foreign travellers of all times.   An English traveller who saw Mankup in 1800, E.D. Clarke, wrote, 'There is nothing in any part of Europe to surpass the tremendous grandeur of the place.'[4]   About 1835 Dubois de Montpéreux wrote of Mankup that 'this enormous rock, precipitous on all sides, rises like a

---

the manuscript of these documents. See also V. I. Ogorodnikov, 'Ivan III and the Jews Living Abroad (Khozya Kokos and Zacharias Gooil-Goorsis),' in *Essays Presented to D. A. Korsakov* (*Mélanges Korsakoff*) (Kazan, 1913), pp. 59–62 (in Russian).

[1] See *Otchety* (*Reports*) of the Archaeological Commission (St Petersburg, 1890), pp. 19–20; Latyshev, *Sbornik* (*Collection*) *of Christian Inscriptions*, pp. 56–57 (No. 47). Both in Russian.

[2] See *Izvestiya* of the Tauric Learned Archive Commission, LI (Simferopol, 1914), 298; A. L. Bertier-Delagarde, *Kalamita and Theodoro, ibid.*, LV (1918), 6, n. 1, 32. Both in Russian. These writings contain only a Russian translation of the inscription. Its original Greek text was published by N. Malitzki in 1933. See below.

[3] See *Crimea, Guidebook*, by K. T. Bumber and others (Simferopol, 1914), p. 258 (in Russian). Among the plans of Mankup see the plan in Bertier-Delagarde, *Izvestiya* of the Tauric Commission, LV (1918), between pp. 10 and 11; also in Loeper, *Izvestiya* of the Archaeological Commission, XLVII (1913), 74; another plan of the year 1833, in P. Köppen, *Krymsky Sbornik*, p. 278; an inaccurate plan in Dubois de Montpéreux, *Altas*, 1st Series, XVII, 6. Some unpublished plans of Theodoro-Mankup were drawn up by topographers in the late eighteenth century and used to be kept in the Archives of the Main Staff of the Army, see *Izvestiya* of the Tauric Commission, LV (1918), 10.

[4] E. D. Clarke, *Travels in Various Countries of Europe, Asia, and Africa*, I, *Russia, Tartary, and Turkey;* see American edition (New York, 1813), p. 367, also London edition: *Travels in Russia, Tartary, and Turkey* (London, 1839), p. 478.

single caisson of a bridge.   No position in Crimea could be stronger; there
was none more important.'[1]   In 1837 Köppen declared the position of
Mankup extraordinary; located, so to speak, between heaven and earth,
on an inaccessible rock, it seemed able to resist all mutations of this
world.[2]   Mankup also produced the same powerful impression on travellers of the late nineteenth and the twentieth century.   Mankup is surrounded by mediaeval walls, up to now well preserved, in one place in
two rows, with towers and inscriptions.   The area of the mountain is
covered with many ruins which are still waiting for systematic and sci-
entific investigations.   The excavations of Christian basilicas have not
yet been completed.   In a word, the territory of Mankup, the chief center
of Crimean Gothia, has been unsatisfactorily studied.[3]

The mediaeval name of Theodoro has, in all likelihood, survived up
to our day in the name of the village of Ai-Todor which lies not far south
of Mankup.   But according to Köppen no remains of antiquity are to
be found.[4]   According to contemporary records, the village of Ai-Todor
(Saint Theodore) lies on the stream of the same name about two miles
(three versts) from the village of Shulu and two miles and a half (four
versts) from Mankup.   In this village in 1897 there were registered 487
persons of both sexes, 481 of them Muslims.[5]

The question has hardly been raised as to what name in antiquity was
given to such a remarkable stronghold as Dory-Theodoro-Mankup; perhaps the ancient writers did not know of this natural fortress.   I have
found only one statement on this point in the book of an English traveller, Maria Guthrie, who visited the Crimea at the close of the eighteenth
century.   'Mankup or Mangup, the Tabane of Ptolemy and the Kastron
Gothias, or Goths' citadel, of the Middle Ages.'[6]   It is true that among
fourteen cities in the interior of the Tauric Peninsula given by Ptolemy

[1] Dubois de Montpéreux, *Voyage autour du Caucase*, vi (Paris, 1843), p. 272.

[2] Köppen, *Krymsky Sbornik*, p. 269.

[3] See a curious misunderstanding in Lebeau, *Histoire du Bas-Empire*, ed. by Saint Martin et M.
Brosset, xxi (Paris, 1836), 421: 'Mahomet ii, pour mieux s'assurer de la Crimée et en interdire l'accès
aux étrangers, fit élever sur l'isthme de la presqu île une forteresse à la quelle on donna le nom de
Mantzup [*sic*].'

[4] Köppen, *op. cit.*, p. 221 (in Russian).   But up to recent times some false identifications of Theodoro have been made.   For instance, in 1907 Golubinski and following him in 1908 Kharlampovich
placed the city of Theodoro, which does not now exist, on the Promontory of Ai-Todor, about six
miles (eight versts) south of Yalta.   Golubinski, 'Chersonesian Martyrs Whose Saints' Day Is March
7,' *Izvestiya Russkago Yazika i Slovesnosti*, xii (1907), 269; Kharlampovich, in the *Zapiski* of the
University of Kazan, lxxx (1908), 19.   Both in Russian.

[5] *A Complete Geographic Description of Our Fatherland*, ed. P. P. Semenov-Tyan-Shanski, xiv,
Novorossiya and the Crimea (St Petersburg, 1910), 710 (in Russian).

[6] Maria Guthrie, *A Tour, Performed in the Years* 1795–96, *through the Tauride or Crimea* (London,
1802), p. 86 (Letter xxv).

the last is called 'Tabana' (τάβανα) and placed at 62°20′–47°15′.[1]   I think Miss Guthrie makes this identification on the ground that one of the northern ravines of Mankup is now called Tabana-deré.   But both this name and the names of other ravines and high points on Mankup are Turko-Tartar words.   'Tabana-deré' is usually translated as the 'leather ravine' (*taban*, the heel of the foot or of a shoe).[2]   The question therefore of what Mankup was called in antiquity remains unsolved.

Several recent archaeological expeditions have been undertaken in the territory of former Gothia; these investigations have been made either by individuals, such as N. L. Ernst of Simferopol (in the Crimea) or Joseph Sauer of Germany, or by institutions, like the State Academy for the History of Material Culture in Leningrad or the University of Pennsylvania Museum coöperating with the Academy for the History of Material Culture.   The chief attention of modern archaeologists has been concentrated on Eski-Kermen, about twelve kilometers southeast of Baghchesarai.   Eski-Kermen has been the least explored and studied of any of the Crimean centers such as Mankup, Inkerman, Chufut-Kale, etc.   Work has been difficult because the many ruins of various buildings on this mountain are overgrown with almost impenetrable shrubs and heath; but the recent excavations have thrown a new light on Eski-Kermen and shown that it played an important part in the history of the Crimea.   Eski-Kermen is one of a number of enigmatic 'cave-cities' in the Crimean Peninsula which may have originated and flourished in the twelfth, thirteenth, and fourteenth centuries.   Eski-Kermen alone has four hundred to four hundred and fifty caves.[3]

The result of these recent archaeological investigations is very important and unexpected.   According to Russian scientists, Eski-Kermen, a fortified town, was built during the fifth century A.D. on a high plateau with steeply sloping sides.   The site has been partially excavated by the State Academy during the past five years (1929–33), and the results so far obtained indicate that Eski-Kermen, not Theodoro-Mankup, was the old capital of the Goths in the Crimea, called Dory, Doros, Doras, which was attacked by the Khazars about A.D. 962.   At that time the flourishing town was transformed into a mere village and later it was altogether

[1] *Ptolemaei Geographia*, III, 6; V. Latyshev, *Scythica et Caucasica e veteribus scriptoribus Graecis et Latinis collegit et cum versione Bossica*, ed. V. L., I, *Auctores Graeci*, 234 (published in the *Transactions* of the Russian Archaeological Society of St Petersburg, XI).

[2] Köppen wrote that according to the tales of the local Tartars this name was given the ravine on account of a leather factory which stood there, Köppen, *Krymsky Sbornik*, p. 258 (in Russian).

[3] See N. L. Ernst, 'Eski-Kermen and the Cave-Cities in the Crimea,' in the *Izvestiya* of the Tauric Society of History, Archaeology, and Ethnography, III (Simferopol, 1929), 31 pages (I use an off-print.)   A very conscientious and interesting study (in Russian).

abandoned.[1]　From these investigations we come to an absolutely new and very important conclusion, that Dory or Doros (Doras) cannot be identified with Theodoro-Mankup.　Dory-Doros, which was described by Procopius, must have been located on the plateau of Eski-Kermen; and only later — we do not know exactly when — was the administrative center of Gothia, Theodoro, established on Mankup.[2]

9. The Etymology of the Name 'Dory-Doros-Doras-Daras'

The question of the etymological origin of the Gothic center in the Crimea, Dory-Doros-Doras-Daras-Theodoro, has not yet been satisfactorily solved.

Dubois de Montpéreux recognized in Procopius' name Dory (Δόρυ) a Greek word δόρυ, 'which signifies a *forest* or *wood*, a meaning which perfectly suits the northern slope of the Tauric mountain chain, in contradiction to the woodless steppe.'[3]　But the Greek meaning of Dory given by Dubois, though very alluring at first sight, seems inadmissible in the light of the later changes of the name; therefore his interpretation has not been adopted.　Since Dory was the main center of the Gothic settlement in the Crimea, it is quite possible that a Gothic root may occur in this name. Kunik admits that the relation of the various forms in which the names of the land and city of the Goths are given in the sources is still obscure, but he assumes that in the Gothic tongue one of these forms must have been *Dôrant*; though he adds in a note, 'It is possible the name Dory is not of Gothic origin.'[4]　Tomaschek definitely connects this name with a Gothic root; he writes, 'This name, whatever Greek form it has, must nevertheless be explained from the Gothic tongue; Kunik assumes the form *daurant*; we indicate the Gothic plural form *daurôns*, from a Swedish word of feminine gender *daurô*, *gates*, and the form *thurn*, *porta*, given by Busbecq, the latter of course distorted in its initial sound.　This would show that this place overlooked the ravine or was situated not far away from the fortified gorge which led from the interior of the Peninsula to the southern coast.'[5]　Braun considers Tomaschek's Gothic etymology most acceptable.[6]

---

[1] See *Bulletin of the University of Pennsylvania Museum*, iv, 5 (October, 1933), 142–143.　See also Joseph Sauer, 'Die christlichen Denkmäler im Gotengebiet der Krim,' *Oriens Christianus*, 3rd Series, vii (Leipzig, 1932), 195, 198.　Sauer visited the Crimea in 1929.　See also F. Shmit, 'Report on the Expedition to Eski-Kermen,' in the *Soobscheniya* of the Academy for the History of Material Culture, vii (1931), 25–29.

[2] In his recent article N. Bănescu seems not to have known of the results of those expeditions in the Crimea, 'Contribution à l'histoire de la seigneurie de Théodoro-Mangoup en Crimée,' *Byz. Zeitschrift*, xxxv (1935), 20–37.　　[3] Dubois de Montpéreux, *Voyage autour du Caucase*, vi (Paris, 1843), 224.

[4] A. Kunik, 'On the Report of a Toparch of Gothia,' *Zapiski* of the Academy of Sciences of St Petersburg, xxiv (1874), 77 and n. 1 (in Russian).　　[5] Tomaschek, *Die Goten in Taurien*, p. 15.

[6] Braun, *Die letzten Schicksale der Krimgoten*, p. 11.

But several scholars attempt to identify Dory with the Gothic pronunciation of the name Tauris. Such a thought seems also to have crossed Kunik's mind,[1] although in another place, in his additional notes to Bruun's article on the Crimean Goths,[2] without mention either of the Gothic etymology or of the Gothic pronunciation of Tauris, he poses the question, 'As far as the Crimean Δόρυ is concerned, it is necessary to examine whether it is not a shortened form. There have even been attempts to connect this name with that of θεοδωρώ (genitive -οῦς) which very often occurs in later times and among other places even in inscriptions.[3] Perhaps some place has received its name from that of the Chersonesian martyr 'Αγαθόδωρος?'[4] Hence it is obvious that Kunik was doubtful in the end regarding the connection of the early name of the place with Theodoro, and in passing threw out the rather unexpected idea of the origin of the name of some place from one of the Chersonesian martyrs, Agathodorus, of whom we have spoken above. But in my opinion this idea cannot be supported by any source at our disposal. In addition, the Archimandrite Arsenius and Vasilievski both regard 'Dory' as the Gothic pronunciation of the name 'Tauris.'[5]

Besides the opinions just given, an attempt has been made to explain this puzzling name by Caucasian elements. Bruun assumed that Procopius, without knowing it, meant by the name Dory the ancient region of the Taurians which his contemporary Armenians might easily have named Dory, for they call the Taurus of Asia Minor Doros.[6] Some years later, however, Bruun wrote that although he had formerly believed the

---

[1] Kunik, *op. cit.*, p. 77, n. 1 (in Russian).

[2] Bruun, *Chernomorye*, II (Odessa, 1880). In Russian.

[3] See, for example, L. Schmidt, *Geschichte der deutschen Stämme bis zum Ausgang der Völkerwanderung*, 2nd ed. (Munich, 1934), p. 400: 'Doros — Abkürzung für Theodoros.' In the appendix to his book, *The Goths in the Crimea* (pp. 398–400), the author gives a very brief outline of the history of the Crimean Goths. *Idem*, 'Zur Geschichte der Krimgoten,' *Schumacher-Festschrift* (Mainz, 1930), pp. 332–336 (very brief outline); on p. 336 the author writes: 'Doros-Doras ist natürlich nur Abkürzung von Theodoro(s).'

[4] Kunik, *op. cit.*, p. 134.

[5] Arsenius, 'The Gothic Eparchy in the Crimea,' *Journal of the Ministry of Public Instruction*, CLXV (1873), 64; Vasilievski, *Works*, II ii, 372. Both in Russian. In two lists of 'the cities which later changed their names' we find 'Δάρες τὸ νῦν Ταῦρες' or 'Δάρας τὸ νῦν Ταῦρες.' See the Bonn edition of Constantine Porphyrogenitus, III, 281, 282 (from Banduri's *Imperium Orientale*); *Hieroclis Synecdemus*, ed. Parthey (Berlin, 1866), App. I, p. 312 (22), App. II, p. 315 (78); ed. Burckhardt (Leipzig, 1893), pp. 62 (22), 67 (78); Tafel, *Constantinus Porphyrogenitus, De provinciis regni Byzantini* (Tübingen, 1847), pp. 21, 22. But these two names refer to Dara, built by Anastasius I, in the east, northwest of Nisibis. See H. Gelzer, 'Ungedruckte und wenig bekannte Bistümerverzeichnisse der orientalischen Kirche,' *Byz. Zeitschrift*, I (1892), 269; J. Ebersolt, 'Un itinéraire de Chypre en Perse d'après le Parisinus 1712,' *ibid.*, XV (1906), 224. Cf. my mistake in the Russian text of this book, *Izvestiya* of the Academy of the History of Material Culture, I (1921) p. 324, 60 (reprint).

[6] Ph. Bruun, *Notices historiques et topographiques concernant les colonies italiennes en Gazarie* (St Petersburg, 1866), pp. 65–66.

name of the region a reflection of the Armenian word for Tauris, i.e., Doros, he had later been obliged to relinquish his hypothesis, because Procopius made a clear distinction between Dory and Tauris; like Herodotus, by Tauris he meant the whole mountain region of the Peninsula. 'The old name of this region was doubtless known to the Goths; but because of their peculiar pronunciation of the word Tauris they substituted for it *daur, daura, porta, janua,* which induced Procopius to call their whole region Dory.'[1]

It is obvious that the question of the etymology of the name Dory remains unsolved. Loewe considers all attempts futile, so that we are at a complete loss as to whether the origin of this word is Crimeo-Gothic, Greek, Scythian, or Tauric.[2]

Since, however, so much and such various linguistic material has already been considered, I feel justified in my turn in calling attention to some other possibilities. These, particularly the first, may not solve the question; but they will once more emphasize the complex ethnographic composition of the Peninsula and will perhaps induce linguists to study seriously the geographic nomenclature of Tauris.

First I wish to say a few words on the possibility of Celtic influence in the Crimea. We must always remember that, in all the sources in general and in the Greek mediaeval sources in particular, the term 'Celt' is very often hazily and indefinitely used; sometimes, like other similar names, it is a collective noun designating a group of several nationalities. Bearing this in mind, I venture none the less to hazard some conjectures.

It is very probable that in their movement from the north of Europe to the south in the third century A.D. the Goths met the Celts and forcibly carried along part of them.[3] The Celts had lived in the Carpathian Mountains from time immemorial. According to Braun, the Goths and the Gepidae found them still there. 'Although their history does not mention conflicts with the Celts, none the less in their language a trace of their close neighborhood in those regions has been preserved.' Philological comparisons show 'the presence of more or less considerable Celtic settlements in the neighborhood of the Gothic region of the second period, i.e., in the South Russian steppes.'[4] In another place the same author

---

[1] Ph. Bruun, *Chernomorye,* II, 210–211 (in Russian).

[2] Loewe, *Die Reste der Germanen am Schwarzen Meere* (Halle, 1896), p. 215. Unfortunately, I have not seen the popular sketch of W. T. Raudonikas, 'Doros-Feodoro, die Hauptstadt der Goten,' *Die Umschau, Wochenschrift über die Fortschritte in Wissenschaft und Technik,* XXX (Frankfurt, 1929), 435 ff.

[3] On the ancient Celts see the old but still very useful book of K. Zeuss, *Die Deutschen und die Nachbarstämme* (Munich, 1837), pp. 172 ff.

[4] F. Braun, *Studies in the Domain of Gotho-Slavonic Relations,* I (St Petersburg, 1899), 165 (in Russian).

remarks that many Celtic words passed into the Gothic language in the prehistoric period.[1]   Shakhmatov writes that the trend of the Germans southwards induced the Celts to occupy the region along the Vistula abandoned by the Germans; he continues, 'This circumstance does not exclude some other movements of the Celts south or southeast; in the second century B.C. we see the Galatians (Celts) allied with the Germanic Scirians in South Russia, where they threatened the Greek colonies.'[2]

We are definitely informed that the Celts participated in the Gothic attacks on the Empire in the third century A.D.   In his biography of the Emperor Claudius Gothicus (268–270) the historian Trebellius Pollio names the Celts among the peoples who invaded the Roman territory together with the Goths; a little below, telling of the victory of Claudius over the Goths, he exclaims, 'What a number of the famous Celtic mares our ancestors saw.'[3]

We notice also the confusion of the Goths with the Celts in later writers. I shall give some little-known examples.   A Western writer of the sixth century, Cassiodorus, in paraphrasing the account cited above of Theodoret of Cyrus on John Chrysostom's relations with the Orthodox Goths, calls the latter Celts.[4]   Simeon Metaphrastes in his *Life of John Chrysostom* compiled in the tenth century also calls the Goths (Scythians) Celts in recording the same episode.[5]

Recently, speaking of the Slavonic tribe of the Antes, Shakhmatov admits the Celtic origin of this name, though this point is still a matter of dispute.   He recalls that a large votive tablet of the second century A.D. has been found at Kerch, in which, among many barbarian names of various origins, occurs the name of Ἄντας Παππί(ου).[6]

All these examples, although not definite proof, none the less justify our hypothesis that the Celtic element, in one form or another, penetrated into the Crimean Peninsula.

If we turn now to the well-proved Celtic geographic nomenclature in

[1] *Ibid.*, p. 304.

[2] A. Shakhmatov, 'On Finno-Celtic and Finno-Slavonic Relations,' *Izvestiya* of the Academy of Sciences (St Petersburg, 1911), p. 722 (in Russian).

[3] *Trebelii Pollionis Claudius*, 6 and 9, *Scriptores historiae Augustae*, rec. H. Peter, II, 127, 129; ed. E. Hohl, II (Leipzig, 1927), 137–138, 140.   Vasilievski without solid grounds wished to see here the Slavs, *Works*, II, ii, 358, 364 (in Russian).

[4] *Cassiodori Historia tripartita*, x, 5; *Patr. Lat.*, LXIX, col. 1168 ('populus Celticorum'; 'interpres Celticus').   Let us recall that in this place Theodoret calls the Goths Scythians.

[5] *Symeonis Logothetae, cognomento Metaphrastae, Vita S. Joannis Chrysostomi*, 20: 'πρὸς δὲ καὶ Κελτοὺς ἀκούσας τῆς Ἀρειανικῆς εἴσω θήρας κειμένους . . . ,' *Patr. Gr.*, CXIV, coll. 1096–1097.

[6] A. Shakhmatov, *The Earliest Fortunes of the Russian Nation* (Petrograd, 1919), p. 11, n. 2 (in Russian); the tablet in *Inscriptiones oris septentrionalis Ponti Euxini*, II, 29 (30).   A. L. Pogodin takes this Antas of Kerch for a Slav, Pogodin, *Collection of Articles on Archaeology and Ethnography* (St Petersburg, 1902), pp. 163–164 (in Russian).

Western Europe, we shall see that cities with Celtic names extend from
the far West almost to the shores of the Black Sea. It is very well
known, for example, that a great many Celtic town names end in *dunum*.
In the Balkan Peninsula, besides *Singidunum* (now Belgrad), we find
Noviodunum (Νουϊόδουνον in Ptolemy, on the site of the present-day city
Isakchi), at the very mouth of the Danube, on its right bank, i.e., quite
close to the coast of the Black Sea.   There were many towns in Western
Europe with the name *Noviodunum*, and most of them have preserved
their original name up to today, though in a changed form.[1]

Another Celtic word exists which has often been used as a component
part of geographic names, *duros, durus*.   This word is sometimes found
in the second part of a compound geographic name, of which one of the
oldest is *Octo-durus*, now Martigny, in Switzerland.[2]   But this Celtic word
often occurs also in the first part of compound geographic names, in Great
Britain, Ireland, France, and Bulgaria.   In Bulgaria, on the Lower Danube stood the city *Durostorum* (now Silistria), Dorostero, Durostero,
Durosterus, Δορόστολος in Theophanes, Δορύστολον in Leo the Deacon;
Derester, Derstr, Derster in Russian annals, etc.[3]

The Celtic word *dūro-s, dūron* signifies 'fortress, castle.'[4]   Perhaps the
name of the Gothic center in the Crimea, Dory-Doros-Doras, in this
Celtic word 'fortress, castle,' which would peculiarly fit its topographic
location.   For my part, this is only a suggestion thrown out to help explain the puzzling name, and of course I am unable to insist on the correctness or reliability of my hypothesis.   I should like to see the Celtolo-
gists turn their attention to the geographic names of the Crimea, for they
might solve the not uninteresting question of whether or not Celtic elements exist there.

Moreover, it would be very useful for the linguists in the domain of the
Oriental languages, particularly the Caucasian or in a still larger form,
the Japhetic, to examine the Crimean geographic names.   Perhaps some
of the names might thus be explained.   For instance, we have at our disposal two names in their old 'Tauric' form.   In the treatise of Pseudo-
Plutarch *Concerning the Names of Rivers and Mountains, and their Contents* we read the following statement: 'Near it (i.e., Tanais) lies a mountain called in the tongue of the local inhabitants Brixaba (Βριξάβα) which
means in translation the *Ram's Forehead* (Κριοῦ μέτωπον).'   This name

---

[1] See F. Braun, *Studies in the Domain of Gotho-Slavonic Relations*, ɪ (St Petersburg, 1899), 127–128.

[2] In the first century B.C. See Caesar, *De bello gallico*, ɪɪɪ, 1.

[3] On the Celtic word *dūros, dūrus*, see D'Arbois de Jubainville, *Les premiers habitants de l'Europe*,
2nd ed., ɪɪ (Paris, 1894), 266–268.   Bruun once found in the name 'Δορόστολος' or 'Δορύστολον' the
Gothic *daura* in connection with another word *stuls*, 'throne,' Bruun, *Chernomorye*, ɪɪ, 211 (in Russian).   On several variants of *Durostor* in the sources see A. Holder, *Alt-celtischer Sprachschatz*, ɪ
(Leipzig, 1896), 1386.   [4] A. Holder, *op. cit.*, ɪ, 1383.

comes from the myth of Phrixus, his sister Helle, and the ram with the golden fleece who brought Phrixus to Colchis.[1]   Then in the anonymous *Periplus Ponti Euxini*, of the fifth century A.D., we find that the former name of the modern city Theodosia in the Alan or Tauric language was Ardabda, i.e., 'of seven gods.'[2]   At present these names, as well as several others, need a new linguistic examination.

If we turn to the name 'Dory-Doros-Doras,' we can indicate some similar words in Caucasian languages: for instance, the Ossetian *dor*, 'stone,' or *duar* 'door, gate';[3] the Armenian *duïʼn* (genitive *dʼran*), 'door, gate, entrance' (cf. the Greek form of the name 'Δώρας' (genitive 'Δώραντος').

In collecting some notes on the etymological origin of the name Dory I have had neither the wish nor the power to solve the question.   I have only attempted modestly to call to the attention of specialists in various branches of linguistics the geographic nomenclature of the Crimea, in the hope that they might examine and solve not only the origin of the name of the main Gothic center, but also the names of other regions of the Peninsula.

Before we take up the later history of the Crimean Goths we must consider the question of the so-called 'Tetraxite Goths' who, as has been said before, yielded to the Huns, crossed with them the Cimmerian Straits, and settled in the Tamán Peninsula and the adjoining regions.

10. The Tetraxite Goths

In the history of the Goths in general and of the Crimean Goths in particular the name of one branch has up to now presented a riddle to scholars.   It is that of the Tetraxite Goths, who are known only through Procopius of Caesarea.   Here is his account of them, contained in his work on the Gothic war.

He first gives a geographic outline of the eastern coast of the Black Sea and characterizes the peoples who dwelt there, the Abasgi (Abkhaz), the Zechi, and the Saginae, and then continues:

Above the Saginae are settled numerous Hunnic tribes.   And from there onward the country has received the name of Eulysia, and barbarian peoples hold both

[1] *Pseudo-Plutarchi Libellus de fluviis*, xiv, 4, C. Müller, *Geographi Graeci Minores*, ii (Paris, 1882), 653; Latyshev, *Scythica et Caucasica*, i, 502.   In the first part of the name 'Βριξάβα' we have, in all likelihood, a reflection of the proper name Phrixus.   But cf. Celtic names with the syllable 'Βριξ' in F. Braun, *Studies*, i, 128 (in Russian).

[2] 'Νῦν δὲ λέγεται ἡ Θεοδοσία τῇ Ἀλανικῇ ἤτοι τῇ Ταυρικῇ διαλέκτῳ Ἀρδάβδα τουτέστιν ἑπτάθεος,' *Periplus Ponti Euxini*, C. Müller, *Geographi Graeci Minores*, i (Paris, 1855), 415 (51); on the author see p. cxviii.   For an attempt to explain this name through Iranian languages, see V. Th. Miller, *Ossetian Studies*, iii (Moscow, 1887), 76–77 (in Russian); Tomaschek, in *Pauly-Wissowa*, i, 22 (s.v. *Abdarda*); Vasilievski, *Works*, ii, ii, 377, n. 1 (in Russian).

[3] See V. Miller, *op. cit.*, iii, 8; *Idem*, 'Concerning the Iranian Element in Greek Inscriptions of the Pontus,' *Izvestiya* of the Archaeological Commission, xlvii, 83 (13).

the coast and the interior of this land, as far as the so-called Lake Maeotis and the Tanais River which empties into the lake. And this lake has its outlet at the coast of the Euxine Sea. The people who are settled there were named in ancient times Cimmerians, but now they are called Utigurs. And above them to the north the countless tribes of the Antes are settled. But beside the point where the outlet of the lake commences dwell the Goths who are called Tetraxites, a people who are not very numerous, but they reverence and observe the rites of the Christians as carefully as any people do . . . As to whether these Goths were once of the Arian belief, as the other Gothic nations are, or whether the faith as practised by them has shown some other peculiarity, I am unable to say, for they themselves are entirely ignorant on this subject, but at the present time they honor the faith in a spirit of complete simplicity and with no vain questionings. This people a short time ago (that is, when Emperor Justinian was in the twenty-first year of his reign) sent four envoys to Byzantium, begging him to give them a bishop; for the one who had been their priest had died not long before and they had learned that the Emperor had actually sent a priest to the Abasgi; and Emperor Justinian, very willingly complying with their request, dismissed them. These envoys were moved by fear of the Utiger Huns in making the public declaration of the object of their coming — for there were many who heard their speeches — and so they made no statement whatever to the Emperor openly except regarding the matter of the priest, but meeting him with the greatest possible secrecy, they declared everything, showing how it would benefit the Roman Empire if the barbarians who were their neighbors should be always on hostile terms with one another. Now as to the manner in which the Tetraxites settled there and whence they migrated, I shall proceed to tell.

In ancient times a vast throng of the Huns who were then called Cimmerians ranged over this region which I have just mentioned, and one king had authority over them all. And at one time the power was secured by a certain man to whom two sons were born, one of whom was named Utigur (Utugur, Uturgur) and the other Kutrigur (Kuturgur). These two sons, when their father came to the end of his life, divided the power between them, and each gave his own name to his subjects; for the one group has been called Utigurs (Uturgurs) and the other Kutrigurs (Kuturgurs) even to my time. All these continued to live in this region, associating freely in all the business of life, but not mingling with the people who were settled on the other side of the Lake and its outlet; for they never crossed these waters at any time nor did they suspect that they could be crossed, being fearful of that which was really easy, simply because they had never even attempted to cross them, and they remained utterly ignorant of the possibility. Beyond Lake Maeotis and the outlet flowing from it the first people were the Goths called Tetraxites, whom I have just mentioned, who in ancient times lived close along the shore of this strait; but the Goths (i.e. Ostrogoths) and the Visigoths and Vandals were located far away from them as were other Gothic nations.

Then Procopius gives the well-known story of the doe who showed the Huns the way to cross the Strait into the Crimea; after this the Huns crossed the Strait and 'suddenly fell upon the Goths who inhabited these plains and slew many of them and turned the rest to flight. . . .' Some lines beyond we read:

The Huns, after killing some of them and driving out the others, as stated, took possession of the land. And the Kutrigurs summoned their children and wives and settled there in the very place where they have dwelt even to my time. And although they receive from the emperor many gifts every year, they still cross the Ister River continually and overrun the emperor's land, being both at peace and at war with the Romans. The Utigurs, however, departed homeward with their leader, in order to live alone in that land thereafter. When these Huns came near Lake Maeotis, they chanced upon the Goths there who are called Tetraxites. At first the Goths formed a barrier with their shields and made a stand against their assailants in their own defence, trusting both in their own strength and the advantage of their position; for they are the most stalwart of all the barbarians of that region. The head of Lake Maeotis, where the Tetraxite Goths were then settled, forms a crescent-shaped bay by which they were almost completely surrounded, so that only one approach, and that not a very wide one, was open to those who attacked them. But afterwards, seeing that the Huns were unwilling to waste any time there and the Goths were quite hopeless of holding out for a long time against the throng of their enemy, they came to an understanding with each other, agreeing that they should join forces and make the crossing in common, and that the Goths should settle on the opposite mainland, principally along the bank of the outlet (where they are actually settled at the present time), and that they should continue to be thereafter friends and allies of the Utigurs and live for ever on terms of complete equality with them. Thus it was that these Goths settled here.[1]

This is Procopius' account, the only source of information about the Tetraxite Goths. It should be added that in another passage of the same work on the Gothic war, after relating that by money and gifts Justinian induced the Utigurs (Uturgurs) to make a rear attack upon the Kutrigurs (Kuturgurs) who at that time were invading the Roman territory, Procopius remarks, 'They first drew into alliance with them two thousand of the Goths called Tetraxites, who are their neighbors, and then crossed the Tanais River in full force. They were commanded by Sandil.'[2]

From the account just given we learn that before the Hunnic invasion,

---

[1] *Procopii De bello gothico,* iv, 4–5; ed. Haury, ii, 501–507; ed. H. Dewing, v (London-New York, 1928), 84–95. A Russian translation of this account is given by Vasilievski, *Works,* ii, ii, 372–374. See K. Zeuss, *Die Deutschen und die Nachbarstämme* (Munich, 1837), pp. 430–431; Loewe, *Die Resten der Germanen,* pp. 25–26; J. Kulakovski, 'An Inscription with the Name of Emperor Justinian,' *Vizantiysky Vremennik,* ii, 192–193 (in Russian).

[2] *Procopii De bello gothico,* iv, 18; ed. Haury, ii, 583–584; ed. Dewing, v, 240–241. Cf. G. L. Oderico, *Lettere ligustiche* (Bassano, 1792), p. 138: 'If I am not mistaken, Procopius speaks of them (the Crimean Goths) in two places; he calls them *Tetraxitae;* they dwelt close to the sea, in a place called Doris, near the straits.'

in other words, before the seventies of the fourth century, the Tetraxite
Goths dwelt on the western side of the Sea of Azov and the Strait of
Kerch, i.e., in the eastern region of the Crimean Peninsula, where they
had settled in connection with the general movement of the Goths southwards in the third century.   Then, later, in all probability after the
breakup of the Hunnic Empire of Attila in the second half of the fifth
century, a branch of the Huns, the Utigurs, on their way back to the
place of their original settlement, were passing through the Crimea, where
they chanced upon the Tetraxite Goths; according to a friendly agreement the Goths crossed with the Huns 'to the opposite mainland' (ἐν τῇ
ἀντιπέρας ἠπείρῳ) i.e., to the eastern side of the Strait of Kerch, to the
Tamán Peninsula, and, generally speaking to the eastern coast of the Sea
of Azov, where they lived in Procopius' time, in the sixth century.[1]

That the Gothic language was spoken in this region in the fifth century
is proved by the anonymous *Periplus Ponti Euxini*, which was compiled
by that time.   In it we read the following: '[In the region from the
Sindian bay to the bay of Pagrae there formerly lived the nations called
Kerketae (Circassians) or Toritae; now the so-called Eudusians dwell
there who use the Gothic and Tauric languages.'[2]   The Sindian bay mentioned in the *Periplus* is now the city Anapa with its port, Pagrae-
Guelendjik, south of Novorossisk.   The Eudusians probably mean the
inhabitants of Eulysia mentioned above by Procopius, which lay on the
eastern coast of the Sea of Azov.

Thus as late as the second half of the fifth century the Tetraxite Goths
lived in the Crimea and belonged to the so-called Crimean or Tauric
Goths.   Not all the Goths left the Crimea with the Utigur Huns for the
eastern coast of the Strait of Kerch and the Sea of Azov.   Part of them
remained in the Peninsula and lived there all through the Middle
Ages.

Procopius in his work *On Buildings* gives a well-known account of those
Goths who remained in the Crimea.   According to him, Justinian built

---

[1] This text of Procopius has sometimes been incorrectly interpreted by Russian scholars. See
Zabelin, *History of Russian Life*, I (Moscow, 1876), 326–327: '[After the Hunnic invasion] the Goths
(Tetraxite) will dwell there where they dwelt, close to the Strait, probably in the city of Bosporus,
present-day Kerch.   Thus, these (Tauric) Goths became friends and allies of the Uturgurs; according
to the treaty the Huns left the Goths in their place in Bosporus, but it is unknown where they themselves settled.'

[2] *Anonymi Periplus Ponti Euxini*, C. Müller, *Fragmenta historicorum graecorum*, v, ii, 182, §22:
'ἀπὸ οὖν Σινδικοῦ λιμένος ἕως Πάγρας λιμένος πρώην ᾤκουν ἔθνη οἱ λεγόμενοι Κερκέται ἤτοι Τορῖται, νῦν δὲ
οἰκοῦσιν Εὐδουσιανοὶ λεγόμενοι, τῇ Γοτθικῇ καὶ Ταυρικῇ χρώμενοι γλώττῃ.'   Concerning the dates of the
anonymous compiler of this *Periplus* see C. Müller, *Geographi Graeci Minores*, I (Paris, 1855), cxviii.
This *Periplus* has been printed also in the latter edition, but the passage just given is there lacking;
it should have been inserted in *Geographi Graeci Minores*, p. 412, after § 42.   See Bruun, *Chernomorye*, II, 207 (in Russian).

forts in Alusta (Alushta) and Gorzuvitae (Gurzuf) and with especial care fortified Bosporus; then he turned his attention to

a region on the seacoast, called Dory, where the Goths dwelt from of old; they did not follow Theoderic, who proceeded to Italy, but voluntarily remained there and still in my day are allies of the Romans. . . . Their number is about three thousand; they are excellent warriors as well as able cultivators of their own land; they are the most hospitable of all men. The region of Dory itself lies high; however it is neither rugged nor arid but fertile and abundant in the best fruits. In this country the Emperor built nowhere city or fort, for the inhabitants of that place would not tolerate to be shut within any walls, but they always liked best to dwell in a plain; only in points which seemed accessible to enemies he barred these entrances by long walls and freed the Goths from the danger of invasion.[1]

As we have already pointed out, the region of Dory, later Doros, Doras, Theodoro, Gothia, the Gothic *Climata*, probably extended along the south coast of the Crimea from Balaklava to Sudak (Surozh, Sugdaia), and in the interior of the Peninsula was bounded by Chatyrdagh and other mountains.[2] The three thousand Goths mentioned by Procopius were once united with the Tetraxite Goths, but the Hunnic irruption separated them into two parts. Those just mentioned remained in the mountains, which saved them from the Hunnic assault, while the others, who were in the steppe region of the Peninsula, fell a prey to the Huns, submitted to their power, and finally with the Hunnic branch of the Utigurs migrated to the eastern coast of the Strait of Kerch and the Sea of Azov. I am very much inclined to believe that the so-called Tetraxite Goths, if we admit such a name, must mean the Crimean Goths in general, both those who in the fifth century crossed the Strait and those who escaped the Hunnic assault in the Crimean mountains. Such an identification seemed natural to some scholars of the eighteenth century.[3] In the nineteenth century several Russian scholars who attempted to throw light on the first pages of the history of Russia, and therefore approached the question of the Tetraxite Goths, were also inclined to identify the latter with the Tauric Goths in general. N. P. Lambin wrote, 'The region of Dory, with its inhabitants the Tetraxite Goths, the ancient kinsmen of the Varangian Russes of Oleg.'[4] In another article by the same author we read, 'The Tetraxite Goths who inhabited the eastern region of the Tauris, the ancestors of the famous Goths of the Black Sea, the ancient

---

[1] *Procopii De aedificiis*, III, 7; ed. Haury, III, ii, 101. A Russian translation by Vasilievski, II, ii, 371; a French version by Bănescu, *Byz. Zeitschrift*, XXXV (1935), 24–25.

[2] Vasilievski, II, ii, 372. But cf. Bruun, *Chernomorye*, II, 210. Both in Russian.

[3] See Stritter, *Memoriae populorum*, I (St Petersburg, 1771), 245 ff. (§ 374 ff.).

[4] N. P. Lambin, 'Is the Campaign of Oleg on Tsargrad a Fairy Tale?' *Journal of the Ministry of Public Instruction*, CLXVIII (1873), 127 (in Russian).

kinsmen of Norman Russia . . . .'[1]   D. I. Ilovaiski wrote: 'In the south, besides the Chersonesian Greeks, there bordered upon the latter the small remnant of the Tetraxite Goths, who occupied the mountainous region of the southern Crimea called Dory.   Owing to the mountains, these Goths succeeded in protecting themselves against complete extermination by the Bulgarians-Uturgurs.'[2]   I believe the scholars who find these Russian historians at fault for such an identification are themselves at fault.[3]

The etymology of the name *Tetraxite* has already long occupied scholars, and no little time and labor has been devoted to its interpretation. I shall recall some of the attempts.

At the beginning of the eighteenth century, in the index of Gothic, Vandal, and Lombard proper names appended to the Latin version of Procopius' *Gothic War* which was published in the first volume of the well-known collection of Muratori, we find an attempt to interpret *Tetraxitae* by *Tetraug sitten*, which in Latin meant *sub induciis sedentes*, in Greek ἐκεχειριεῖς, 'Gothica gens quietis amans ad Pontum Euxinum.'[4]   In the Gothic tongue *Tetraug sitten* might represent *du* = *zu*; *triggua* = *treuga* (truce); *sitan* = *sitzen*.   As F. A. Braun and S. C. Boyanus have kindly informed me, each of these three identifications taken separately is in complete accordance with the laws of the Gothic language.   But, as Braun points out, their combination into the name of a nation in the form *Tetraug sitten* is from the morphological point of view absolutely impossible.

Siestrzencewicz de Bohusz is the author of a book on the history of the Tauric Peninsula from ancient times to the annexation of the Crimea by Russia.   This book was published in French in 1800 and translated into Russian in 1806.   He wrote: 'The Goths of the Bosporan state were called Traxites[5] or Tetraxites probably for the reason that they were divided into four settlements.   For the same reason the Galilean princes

---

[1] Lambin, 'Concerning Tmutarakan Russia,' *ibid.*, CLXXI (1874), 71 (in Russian).

[2] D. Ilovaiski, *Studies on the Origin of Russia* (Moscow, 1882), p. 229; see also p. 233 (in Russian).

[3] See Bruun, *Chernomorye*, II, 210; Vasilievski, II, ii, 370–371.   More recently, J. B. Bury has written on the Tetraxite Goths in the Crimea in the eighth century and their subjugation to the Khazars (Chazars), J. B. Bury, *A History of the Eastern Roman Empire* (London, 1912), p. 409.

[4] Muratori, *Rerum italicarum scriptores*, I (1723), 377: 'Tetraxitae.   Tetraug sitten.   Sub induciis sedentes, quod nomen graeca voce ἐκεχειριεῖς reddidit addidque Scylaci, ut multa alia, exscriptor aliquis.'   Vasilievski has apparently incorrectly attributed this interpretation to Hugo Grotius.   True, this volume of Muratori contains *Hugonis Grotii Explicatio nominum et verborum Gothicorum, Vandalicorum ac Langobardicorum* (pp. 370–372), but in this *Explicatio* there is no mention of the Tetraxites.   The index which follows, and in which the name of the Tetraxites is found, does not belong to Hugo Grotius.   Besides this, Vasilievski says that the explicative glossary of Hugo Grotius was appended to the edition of Jornandes (Jordanes); but actually it was appended to Procopius' *Gothic War*. See Vasilievski, *Works*, II, ii, 379.   [5] On this form see below.

were called Tetrarchs, and the Seleucid Syrians Tetrapolites.'[1]   The close relation of *Tetraxite* to the Greek numeral τετράκις has been frequently emphasized; Procopius' report given above of the sending of *four* envoys by the Tetraxite Goths to Justinian to ask for a bishop has usually been adduced to support this thesis.   An old German writer on Ulfila, H. Massman, observed: 'The Greeks called them Tetraxite Goths probably after some division (nach einer Vergliederung), for they represented four small tribes or communities; at least, later, they sent to Emperor Justinian an embassy which consisted of four of their countrymen.'[2]   The Archimandrite Arsenius also believes that the Goths were called Tetraxites probably according to the number of their communities, and mentions the embassy to Justinian.[3]   Kunik, who wrote an additional note to the work of Bruun concerning the Crimean Goths, is at a loss when he raises the question of the origin of the name Tetraxite.   He writes:

If the word Τετραξῖται is not distorted, on account of its ending (-ίτης) it would seem most natural to interpret it as the name of the inhabitants of a region which is called Tetrax.   The adjective τετράξοος has been used as the name of a peculiar sort of wood the closer definition of which is unknown.   Has it something in common with the word τέτραξ related to the Russian *teterev* (black grouse, heath grouse)?   Might the derivation of the name of the Tetraxites be philologically admitted from the Greek word τετράκις (four times)?   At any rate one might advance some historical data in support of this derivation.   In 548 the Tetraxite Goths sent four envoys to Justinian . . . Among the (Celtic) Galatians of Asia Minor each tribe was divided into four regions, at the head of which stood four tetrarchs who were in charge of military matters.[4]

Cassel alone fails to hold any of these views: in Tetraxite he sees a deteriorated form of 'tetrarchites,' because after their conversion to Christianity in the Crimea they divided their possessions, like Palestine at that time, into four provinces governed by tetrarchs, in order to distinguish themselves from their Tauric kinsmen who had not yet adopted baptism.[5] Finding the previous attempts at interpretation of the name Tetraxite doubtful both philologically and historically, Vasilievski sets forth the theory of the identification of the land of the Tetraxites with later Tmutarakan — in other words, he suggests that the name of Tmutarakan

---

[1] Siestrzencewicz de Bohusz, *History of the Tauris*, I (St Petersburg, 1806), 270–271 (in Russian); *Idem, Histoire du royaume de la Chersonèse Taurique*, 2nd ed. revised (St Petersburg, 1824), pp. 154–155.   [2] H. Massman, *Ulfilas* (Stuttgart, 1857), p. xxvii.

[3] Arsenius, 'The Gothic Eparchy in the Crimea,' *Journal of the Ministry of Public Instruction*, CLXV (1873), 60 (in Russian).

[4] Kunik, 'On the Report of a Gothic Toparch,' *Zapiski* of the Academy of Sciences, XXIV (1874) 134 (in Russian).

[5] P. Cassel, *Der Chazarische Königsbrief aus dem 10. Jahrhundert* (Berlin, 1877), p. 21.

is derived from the Tetraxites who dwelt there.[1] But some scholars consider this view more than hazardous.[2] Tomaschek writes that 'the name οἱ Τετραξῖται which the Tauric Goths bear may be best explained if we admit that at their head stood four dukes (in Gothic *fidur-reiks*) who may be compared with the Galatians of Asia Minor; each of them could have commanded a band of a thousand men capable of bearing arms. This division is in accordance with the fact that later the Goths sent four envoys to Byzantium.'[3]

From the examples given above it is obvious that none of the scholars has succeeded in interpreting in any satisfactory way the name *Tetraxite*; up to the present it still remains puzzling and obscure. Its collation with the Greek words τετράκις, τέσσαρες, τέτταρες, which outwardly is very close, continued to raise doubts. It is entirely arbitrary to conjecture that the four envoys sent to Justinian were representatives of four Gothic subdivisions of which we know nothing. More likely the number was entirely fortuitous. It would be strange that such a comparatively small group as the Tauric Goths should fall into four still smaller divisions. Lastly, it would be extremely surprising for the Goths to call themselves by a Greek name.[4] It seems to me that in the study of this question it is now time to turn our serious attention to another side of the matter and to put aside fruitless considerations about the etymological derivation of the name *Tetraxite*.

We know that for a long time there was no satisfactory publication of Procopius' works. Not to mention an uncritical edition of some separate writings in the sixteenth century, neither the Parisian edition by the Jesuit Maltret, of 1662–63, nor the Venetian edition of 1729, which only reproduced the previous edition, nor, finally, the Bonn edition by Dindorf, of 1833–38, which was the most frequently used up to the close of the nineteenth century, was even approximately adequate to the actual requirements of scholarly critical editions of the text.[5] But at the end of the nineteenth century simultaneously in three countries, Italy, Germany, and Russia, scholars set to work on the preparation of a new and critical edition of Procopius' works. A Russian philologist, M. N. Krasheninnikov, published in 1899 the *Secret History* of Procopius, which is of no importance for the question of the Tetraxites. But an Italian scholar, Comparetti, who published in 1895–98 the *History of the Gothic*

---

[1] Vasilievski, ii, ii, 378–390 (in Russian).

[2] See Braun, *Die letzten Schicksale der Krimgoten*, p. 9, n. 1. But cf. Loewe, *op. cit.*, pp. 33–34 (he is inclined to adopt Vasilievski's hypothesis).

[3] Tomaschek, *Die Goten in Taurien*, p. 12.   [4] See Vasilievski, ii, ii, 379.

[5] See Kunik, *op. cit.*, p. 133 (in Russian); Krumbacher, *Geschichte der byzantinischen Litteratur*, 2nd ed. (Munich, 1897), p. 234.

War, and a German philologist, Haury, who issued from 1905 to 1913 a collected edition of Procopius' writings, have done work of very great importance.[1]

First of all we must remember that the manuscript tradition of the name *Tetraxite* is subject to doubt. In the sixteenth century, when some scattered writings of Procopius were published for the first time, the edition of the *Gothic War* omitted, evidently following the manuscript, certain passages which in other manuscripts mentioned the Tetraxite Goths. These omitted passages were later restored and published along with the *History or Chronicle of the Goths, Vandals, and Svevs* compiled by the very well-known bishop of the seventh century, Isidore of Seville. I have used the edition of 1579, which after a preface of four pages without pagination prints the Greek text and a Latin translation of the fragment of Procopius' *De Bello Gothico* IV, 4–5, i.e., the fragment which is the chief source for the question under consideration. Throughout this edition the name *Traxites* is printed for *Tetraxites* — Γότθοι οἵ τε Τραξίται καλούμενοι.[2] Hence the form *Traxites* was taken over by Siestrzencewicz, as has been mentioned above.

But it is particularly interesting that in many manuscripts *Trapezites* — τραπεζίται occurs for *Tetraxites*; this fact has been noted in all editions, from the Parisian on.[3] Comparetti gives variants in particular detail: 'τραπεζίται MC τραπεζῆται D τραπεζίται mf (corr. in marg.), H.'[4]

I do not intend to examine the complicated and very debatable question of the interrelation of Procopius' manuscripts, i.e., the question of the so-called *stemma*.[5] But according to the data given by Comparetti the variant *Trapezitae* occurs in so many manuscripts that it might be better to use *Trapezites* in the text and *Tetraxites* in the notes; the more so as the form *Trapezitae*, in my opinion, in many respects simplifies and explains the question under consideration.

[1] The most recent edition of Procopius' works with an English translation is by H. B. Dewing (Loeb Classical Library) in seven volumes. I have seen six of these, containing the history of Justinian's wars and *Anecdota* (London-New York, 1914–1935). The translation is very valuable, but the Greek text followed in this edition is that of Haury; see I, Introduction, p. xiii.

[2] *Codicis Legum Wisigothorum Libri XII, Isidori Hispalensis episcopi de Gothis Wandalis et Svevis Historia sive Chronicon, ex Bibliotheca Petri Pithoei I. C. Procopii Caesarensis Rhetoris ex lib. VIII Histor. locus de Gothorum origine qui in exemplaribus editis hactenus desiderantur* (Paris, 1579).

[3] See *Procopii Caesariensis Historiarum sui temporis libri VIII*, Interprete C. Maltreto, II (Paris, 1663), 199: 'Boic. Τραπεζίται,' ed. Bonn, II, 474, 17: 'Τραπεζίται H et infra'; ed. Haury, II, 502: 'Τραπεζίαι hic et infra L.'

[4] *Procopii Bellum Gothicum*, ed. Comparetti, III (Rome, 1898), 23, 5; see also pp. 24, 13; 26, 2; 29, 5, 9; 136, 12.

[5] On this subject see M. Krasheninnikov, 'On the Criticism of Part II, Ὑπὲρ τῶν πολέμων by Procopius of Caesarea,' *Vizant. Vremennik*, V (1898), 439–482, and especially 471–482 (in Russian); Haury, I, *Prolegomena*, xl–xlii.

First, the name *Trapezites* indicates a definite geographic name in the Crimea.   Speaking of the Tauric Peninsula, Strabo writes: 'In the mountainous district of the Taurians stands also the mountain Trapezus, which has the same name as the city in the neighborhood of Tibarania and Colchis.'[1]   The mountain Trapezus, i.e. Table Mountain, means the actual Chatyrdagh (in Russian *Shater-gora* or *Palat-gora*, in Italian *Tavola* [table]).   Pallas, who travelled in the Crimea in 1793–94, writes: 'But Chatyrdagh is more visible on the side from the sea, where nothing hides it, for it rises vertically over the valley of Alushta.   Therefore it is not surprising that the Greek navigators in ancient times paid particular attention to it, and that Strabo calls it *Trapezus* (table).'[2]   Besides the mountain Trapezus there was also a city Trapezus in the Crimea.   The well-known author Jordanes who compiled his *Gothic History* at Constantinople in 551 writes: 'In that region where Scythia touches the Pontic coast it is dotted with towns of no mean fame: Borysthenis, Olbia, Callipolis, Cherson, Theodosia, Careon, Myrmicion, and Trapezus.   These towns the wild Scythian tribes allowed the Greeks to build to afford them means of trade.'[3]   At a later date we find this passage of Jordanes repeated in the Geographer or *Anonymus* of Ravenna quoted above. There we read: 'According to Libanius,[4] mentioned above, I have listed the towns of the Bosforian country to be named below; we have read that in this Bosforian country there were very many towns, some of which we wish to designate, i.e., . . . Boristenida, Olbiapolis, Capolis, Dori, Chersona, Thesiopolis, Careon, Trapezus.'[5]   In another place the same Geographer mentions 'Poristenida, Calipolis, Cersona, Theodosia, Dosiopolis (Theodosiopolis?), Careon, Trapezus.'[6]   It is interesting to note that the copy of Jordanes which the Geographer of Ravenna made use of, and which is unknown to us as yet, helps us to correct in the manuscripts of Jordanes which have come down to us the distorted name of Trapezus;

---

[1] Strabo, VII, 4, 3 (c. 309): 'ἐν δὲ τῇ ὀρεινῇ τῶν Ταύρων καὶ τὸ ὅρος ἐστὶν ὁ Τραπεζοῦς, ὁμώνυμος τῇ πόλει τῇ περὶ τὴν Τιβαρανίαν καὶ τὴν Κολχίδα.'

[2] P. S. Pallas, 'A Journey in the Crimea in 1793 and 1794,' translated from the German, *Zapiski* of the Odessa Society of History and Antiquities, XII (1881), 173 (in Russian).

[3] *Jordanis Gethica*, v, 32 (ed. Mommsen, p. 62): 'in eo vero latere, qua Ponticum litus attingit, oppidis haut obscuris involvitur, Boristhenide, Olbia, Callipolida, Chersona, Theodosia, Careon, Myrmicion et Trapezunta, quas indomiti Scytharum nationes Graecis permiserunt condere, sibimet commercia praestaturos,' *The Gothic History of Jordanes*, English version by C. C. Mierow (Princeton, 1915), p. 59.

[4] On this so-called Macedonian philosopher see a note in Teuffel, *Geschichte der römischen Litteratur*, 6th ed., III (1913), 545 (§ 497, 4).

[5] *Ravennatis Anonymi Cosmographia*, IV, 3; ed. Pinder-Parthey (Berlin, 1860), pp. 171–174: 'ego secundum praefatum Livianium inferius dictas civitates Bosforaniae patriae nominavi, in qua Bosforaniae patria plurimas fuisse civitates legimus, ex quibus aliquantas designare volumus, id est, Boristenida, Olbiapolis, Capolis, Dori, Chersona, Thesiopolis, Careon, Trapezus.'

[6] *Idem*, v, 11; ed. Pinder-Parthey, p. 370.

for in the manuscripts on which Jordanes' edition by Mommsen is based Trapezus is given as Trapeiunta, Trapeiuncta, Trepeiunta, Trapeianta, Tarpeianta, so that it is only owing to the Geographer of Ravenna that we have been able to establish the correct reading of this name in Jordanes.[1]   Thus, we know with certainty that in the Crimea there was a geographic center Trapezus — first, a mountain, secondly, a town.   Since this is so, and since in many manuscripts of Procopius we have the 'Trapezite Goths' for the 'Tetraxite Goths,'[2] we must recognize the form *Trapezitae* as historically more correct and simpler than *Tetraxitae*, and we must consider the former Tetraxite Goths as really the Trapezite Goths, i.e., the Goths who dwelt in the region of the mountain Trapezus, modern Chatyrdagh, where in the early Middle Ages was also situated the town Trapezus.

The name *Trapezite* itself is not absolutely new.   Along with the Traxite or Tetraxite Goths Siestrzencewicz speaks also of the *Trapezite or Dorian Goths, the Gotho-Trapezites, the Goths-Trapezite* who differed from the Tetraxites.[3]   He writes:

Another part of the Goths who lived in Tauris from of old and who instead of following King Theoderic remained under the protection of the Huns and Ungurs, were the Gotho-Trapesites.   The Greeks gave them this name on account of their location on the top of the mountain Sinap-dagh, flat like a plant. . . . This region was called Dorye. . . . Misfortunes which at a later day befell them from the invasions of the barbarians compelled the Goths of Dorye and the Gotho-Trapezites to ask for the protection of the Eastern Emperors. . . . The advantageous location of Dorye defended the Gotho-Trapesites much more effectively than the protection of the Emperor.[4]

Of course Siestrzencewicz is wrong in making a distinction between the Tetraxite and the Trapezite Goths.   But in my opinion he does not deserve Loewe's too severe judgment; Loewe gave him no credit whatever, charged him, in connection with the Trapezites, with excessive imagination ('Ausgeburt der Phantasie') and finally remarked, 'There is no such name anywhere as "Trapezites"' ('Nirgends aber steht etwas von einem Namen wie "Trapeziten"').[5]   At present I do not know why Siestrzencewicz spoke with such certainty of the Trapezite Goths, because he always referred to the pages of the Parisian edition of Procopius, in which occurs

[1] *Jordanis Getica*, ed. Mommsen, p. 62; Prooemium, p. xlv.

[2] The variant *Traxite Goths* mentioned above emphasizes once more the unreliability of the reading *Tetraxites*.

[3] Siestrzencewicz de Bogusz, *History of the Tauris*, I (St Petersburg, 1806), 272, 276, 278 (in Russian); the second French edition, p. 155, 157, 158.   On the mountain Trapezus see I, 26 (32).

[4] Siestrzencewicz, I, 276 (157) and 278 (158).

[5] Loewe, *Die Reste der Germanen*, pp. 202–203.

Tetraxites.   What other sources he used for his statement I have not
yet been able to make out.

There is an older German article by Herschel which is specially devoted
to the question of the Tetraxite Goths.   The author gives a brief summary of the sources concerning the Crimean Goths.   By the Tetraxite
Goths he means the Crimean Goths up to recent times.   His conclusion
runs as follows: 'The name "Tetraxites" has not yet been satisfactorily
interpreted.   If the reading of some of Procopius' manuscripts, *trapezitae*,
were correct, the meaning of the name could be easily explained.   Strabo
calls the Table Mountain or Chatyrdagh Trapezus, and in that case by
the Trapezites we ought to mean the inhabitants who dwelt in the neighborhood of this mountain.'[1]   The Archimandrite Arsenius also notes that
the Tauric Goths were called either 'Trapezite Goths after the Table
Mountain (now Chatyrdagh) . . . or Tetraxites, probably according to
the number of their communities.'[2]

The question may be raised why the Crimean city Trapezus has completely disappeared in the history of the Peninsula.   As far as I know, in
the sources there are no definite data for the solution of this question.
In all probability, the city was destroyed by the Huns in the second half
of the fifth century, when they forced one part of the Trapezite Goths to
emigrate to the eastern coast of the Strait of Kerch and the Sea of Azov,
and drove the other part into the mountains of the southern part of the
Peninsula; the Huns for a time were masters of a considerable territory in
the Crimea.   We should not be surprised that the Crimean city Trapezus
was mentioned as if it still existed by Jordanes in the sixth century and
still later by the Anonymous Geographer of Ravenna.   In this case we
are witnessing a rather common phenomenon; authors borrowing their
geographic information from earlier writers incorporate it in their writings
in full, without any change, and without paying any attention to changed
conditions; this is especially natural when, as in this case, the question
is of countries so far off and so little known as the northern coastland of
the Black Sea.   In support of this statement let me adduce a writer of
the tenth century, Emperor Constantine Porphyrogenitus, who in his
treatise on the *Themes* made use of the geographer of the sixth century,
Hierocles, and without changing his data included them in the geography
of the tenth century, thereby causing many difficulties to later investiga-
tors.

As a result of all these considerations, the Tetraxite Goths must dis-

---

[1] Herschel, 'Die tetraxitischen Gothen,' *Anzeiger für Kunde der deutschen Vorzeit*, Neue Folge, VI
(1859), 95.

[2] Arsenius, 'The Gothic Eparchy in the Crimea,' *Journal of the Ministry of Public Instruction*,
CLXV (1873), 60 (in Russian).

appear from history and be replaced by the Trapezite Goths. Before the division of the Goths into two groups owing to the Hunnic irruption in the second half of the fifth century, the Trapezite Goths may have meant the Crimean Goths in general. After the departure of a portion of the Trapezite Goths eastwards, the group of Goths who settled in the Crimean mountains no longer bore this name, evidently because of the disappearance of the city of Trapezus itself. The mountain Trapezus — Table Mountain — still stands under its Turko-Tartar name of Chatyr-dagh — Tent Mountain.

CHAPTER II

THE PERIOD OF BYZANTINE, KHAZAR AND RUSSIAN INFLUENCE

(FROM THE SIXTH CENTURY TO THE BEGINNING OF THE ELEVENTH)

1. The Hunnic Danger in the Sixth Century

AFTER the close of the fifth century the Huns occupied the steppe region of the Peninsula; or, as Procopius states of the sixth century, between Bosporus and Chersonesus 'everything is held by the barbarians, the Hunnic nations.'[1] Bosporus (Panticapaeum), situated on the Strait itself, also became subject to the Huns.[2] There is no ground for speaking, as certain scholars do, of the complete destruction by the Huns of this important center.[3] The Byzantine government, protecting its own interests on the far-off borderland of the Tauris as well as those of its vassals and allies, the mountain Goths, could not submit easily to the domination of the Huns in the steppes of the Peninsula. According to Procopius, under Justin I (518–527) the Bosporites 'decided to become subjects' of the Empire.[4] We do not know the reason of this decision, which was not carried into effect. Justin sent Probus, the nephew of the late Emperor Anastasius, with a great sum of money to Bosporus to bribe an army of Huns and send them as allies to the Iberians, in the Caucasus, who at that time were fighting against the Persians and badly needed Roman support. But Probus was unsuccessful in his mission and departed from Bosporus without accomplishing anything. The Huns, torn by internal strife, were not in a condition to respond to the Emperor's request.[5] As a result Justin's successor, Justinian, took advantage of the Huns' internal strife, sent troops, and captured Bosporus.[6] And since

[1] *Procopii De bello persico*, I, 12, 7; ed. Haury, I, 57; ed. Dewing, I, 96–97. *Idem, De bello gothico*, IV, 5, 27; ed. Haury, II, p. 508; ed. Dewing, V, 96–97.

[2] *Procopii De bello persico*, II, 3, 40; ed. Haury, I, 159–160; ed. Dewing, I, 280–281.

[3] I do not know why Mommsen (*Römische Geschichte*, V, 289, n. 2) speaks of the ruin of Panticapaeum during Hunnic attacks. On other holders of this opinion see J. Kulakovski, 'A Christian Catacomb of the Year 491 at Kerch,' *Materialy* on the Archaeology of Russia, VI, 1891, 24 (in Russian).

[4] *Procopii De bello persico*, I, 12, 8; ed. Haury, I, 57; ed. Dewing, I, 96–97. In the Russian translation of Procopius by G. S. Destunis this passage is incorrectly rendered; hence some misunderstandings occur in his commentary on this text, G. Destunis, *Procopius of Caesarea, The War of the Romans with the Persians*, I, 144 (in Russian).   [5] Procopius, *ibid.*

[6] Procopius, *ibid.*, II, 3, 40 (ed. Haury, I, 160; ed. Dewing, I, 280–281); *De aedificiis*, III, 7, 12 (ed. Haury, III, ii, 101); Malalas, *Chr.*, pp. 431–433; *Theoph.*, de Boor, I, 175–176; (*Landulfi*) *Historia miscellanea*, *Mon. Germ. Hist.*, *Auctores antiquissimi*, II, 369. Cf. Kulakovski, *op. cit.*, pp. 25–27; Latyshev, *Collection of Christian Inscriptions*, pp. 101–102; Vasilievski, II, ii, 382–384. All three in Russian.

that time, as John Malalas remarks, 'Bosporus occupied by the Romans has lived in peace.'[1]   In connection with the expansion of his power in the Peninsula, Justinian, however, realized that the capture of Bosporus did not settle the Hunnic problem there; therefore he set to work both to restore the former fortifications in the Peninsula and to build new ones. He restored the walls of Cherson[2] and built two new forts on the southern coast, one at Aluston (Alushta), the other at Gorzuvitae (τό ἐν Γορζουβίταις — later Gurzuf); but he took special care of Cherson, which he accordingly strongly fortified.[3]   Perhaps those scholars are right who believe the subjugation of Bosporus to the Emperor in the sixth century also meant the restoration of the power of the Bosporan king, who was later, of course, a vassal of the Empire; in that case, a Bosporan inscription with the name of 'the pious king Tiberius Julius Diptunus, a friend of Caesar and of the Romans,' who erected a tower in Bosporus, may with great probability be referred to the epoch of Justinian.[4]   It is very probable that Justinian's constructive and restorative activity extended also over the Tamán Peninsula, where an inscription with his name has been found; this inscription is referred by V. Latyshev to the year 533.[5]

A Greek inscription particularly interesting for our purpose was found by R. Loeper in 1913 during his work on Mankup.   This occurs on a fragment of a limestone plate in a group of graves on the left side of the central nave of the large basilica.   The plate is broken on both sides as well as at the bottom, giving us parts of two and a half lines.   On this fragment we read, 'Of Justinian . . . Emperor . . . Augustus' ("Ιουστινιανοῦ . . . Αὐτοκράτορος . . . Σεβαστοῦ).   The inscription despite its fragmentary text proves that under Justinian Dory (Doros) already was important enough to be considered by the Emperor.[6]   Since this inscription was found in a basilica, the basilica also may probably be connected with the name of Justinian.   *The Guidebook to the Crimea* published in Simferopol in 1914 (p. 264) contains a chapter on Mankup very carefully and fully compiled on the basis of the most recent data, including R. Loeper's

---

[1] *Joannis Malalae Chronographia*, p. 433: 'καὶ γέγονεν ἐν εἰρήνῃ ἡ Βόσπορος, ὑπὸ 'Ρωμαίων οἰκουμένη.'

[2] From this time on the name Cherson for Chersonesus becomes very common; accordingly we shall use both names indiscriminately.   [3] *Procopii De aedificiis*, iii, 7; ed. Haury, iii, ii, 101.

[4] *Inscriptiones oris septentrionalis Ponti Euxini*, ii, 49.   In my opinion, Kulakovski's suggestion ('A Christian Catacomb of 491 at Kerch,' p. 26) that this inscription refers to the period of Justin i is not to be accepted.

[5] Latyshev, *Collection of Christian Inscriptions*, p. 98, and especially pp. 101–103. See some doubts of Latyshev's statements expressed by Kulakovski, in the *Vizant. Vremennik*, ii (1895), 189–198 (in Russian).

[6] Latyshev, *Izvestiya* of the Archaeological Commission, lxv (1918), 18–19.   According to the character of the writing, the inscription is to be referred rather to the period of Justinian i than to that of Justinian ii.   See Loeper's account of his excavations on Mankup, in the *Izvestiya* of the Tauric Learned Archive Commission, li (1914), 298.   Both in Russian.

excavations; the following passage is apparently taken from Loeper's official report: 'We may learn something concerning the date of the construction of the first (i.e., older) temple from an inscription on the cornerstone, placed between the southern and central naves and seen from the southern nave; it indicates the existence of the temple under Justinian the Great .... Such a magnificent temple was in perfect accord with the epoch of this Emperor, the protector of the Goths.' If this information is correct, we have a very interesting example of Justinian's construction of a large church in the Crimean mountains, on Mankup. We shall speak later of the identification of this basilica with the Church of St Constantine, described by the Polish envoy Bronevski, who visited Mankup in the sixteenth century.[1] To confirm this hypothesis indirectly we may give here an interesting analogy from Procopius' work *On Buildings*, where he reports Justinian's constructive activities in a Bithynian city, Helenopolis. Justinian's motive was devotion to Constantine and to Helen, for whom this city was named.[2] His devotion to the founder of the capital on the Bosphorus might have induced him to build a church of St Constantine on Mankup also. The discovery by R. Loeper of Justinian's inscription just mentioned in a basilica on Mankup must be taken into consideration in connection with the recent claims of Russian archaeologists that Dory (Doros, Doras) described by Procopius was located not on Mankup but on the plateau of Eski-Kermen.[3] In my belief, this inscription undermines to some extent the rather sensational results of their archaeological work. In addition, Justinian barred the approach of enemies by means of long walls, so that, according to Procopius, he 'freed the Goths from any danger of invasion.'[4]

Thus for the sixth century we have a fairly definite picture of the position of the Goths in the Crimea. The common danger from the Huns both to the Imperial possessions in the Peninsula and to the mountain Goths forced the threatened parties to combine. The Goths became vassal allies of the Empire, under obligation to furnish auxiliaries. On the other hand Justinian pledged himself to protect his own possessions and the settlements of his allies against Hunnic attacks. Thereupon he erected a line of forts whose terminals were Bosporus in the east and Cherson in the west; and his constructive activities were not confined to the coast, but extended into the Crimean mountains, as proved by the inscription found on Mankup. From the north the passes and the mountain abodes of the Goths were secured by long walls constructed by

---

[1] *Martini Broniovii Russia seu Moscovia itemque Tartaria* (Leyden, 1630), p. 263. A Russian translation by Shershenevich, in the *Zapiski* of the Odessa Society of History and Antiquities, vi (1867), 343. [2] *Procopii De aedificiis*, v, 2, 1–5; ed. Haury, iii, 152.
[3] See the preface of this book. [4] *Ibid.*, iii, 7; ed Haury, iii, 101.

Justinian, the remains of which can still be seen today.[1] In a word, there was a very well fortified *limes Tauricus* which reminds us, of course on a very small scale, of the *limes Romanus* on the Danubian border, the Syrian *limes* in the East against the attacks of the Arabic tribes, and other *limites* organized by Justinian on the various borders of his vast empire.

I wish to mention here that in popular Byzantine speech in the sixth century there existed an expression, evidently proverbial, 'to shout like a Goth.' The *Life* of Saint Dosithaeus, who lived in Palestine and died there about 540, contains the following passage: 'Then he says to him, "Oh, foolish man, you shout like the Goths, for they when enraged become angry and shout. For that reason I said to you, 'Take a piece of bread soaked in wine, because you shout like a Goth' "'.[2]

During the period of Justinian's successor, Justin II (565–578), under the supervision of an Imperial governor — duke (δουκός) another structure was erected in Cherson for the further defence of the city; our record of this is a fragment of a marble slab with some slight remains of an inscription, found in 1905 near the southern wall.[3]

The system of Crimean fortifications created by Justinian was destined to serve as a defence against various barbarian peoples who, one after another, after the Hunnic danger in the fourth, fifth, and sixth centuries, menaced the Crimea for many generations.

At the close of Justinian's reign the Avars, driven by the Turks, had moved westwards from the Caucasian steppes and the regions between the Don and the Volga, and part of them had reached the Cimmerian Bosporus.[4] But by reason of the complete silence of the sources we may conclude that the Avars did not enter the Peninsula; they were probably driven back from the Strait and passed through the South Russian steppes farther west, in order on the one hand to cross the Danube, extend over the Balkan Peninsula, and in 626 threaten Constantinople, and on the other hand to establish themselves in the Middle-Danubian plain. Thus the Avar barbarian wave spared the Tauris.

---

[1] Tomaschek, *Die Goten in Taurien*, pp. 15–16. The remains of Justinian's walls should be studied *in situ*.

[2] Pierre-Marie Brun, 'La vie de Saint Dosithée, texte critique avec introduction, traduction française et notes,' *Orientalia Christiana*, XXVI, 2, 120: 'Τότε λέγει αὐτῷ· Μωρὲ, ἐπειδὴ κράζεις ὥσπερ καὶ οἱ Γότθοι· καὶ γὰρ ἐκεῖνοι, ὅταν ἐκχολοῦνται, χολοῦσιν, καὶ κράζουσιν· καὶ διὰ τοῦτο εἶπόν σοι· λάβε βουκάκρατον, ὅτι καὶ σὺ ὡς Γότθος κράζεις.' I am greatly indebted to Professor H. Grégoire of Brussels, who called my attention to this text.

[3] Latyshev, in the *Izvestiya* of the Archaeological Commission, XVIII (1906), 121–123, No. 37. Kulakovski erroneously refers this structure to Bosporus, Kulakovski, *The Past of the Tauris*, 2nd ed. (Kiev, 1914), 62. Both in Russian.

[4] *Evagrii Historia Ecclesiastica*, v, 1; ed. Bidez and Parmentier, p. 196. Hence this account has passed into the so-called *Chronicle of Monemvasia*, S. Lambros, Ἱστορικὰ μελετήματα (Athens, 1884), p. 98.

But in the seventies of the sixth century a new and serious danger to the Crimea appeared. I refer to the Turko-Khazar hordes who were to play for a considerable time an important rôle in the Peninsula.

In 575 when Tiberius was proclaimed co-emperor with Justin II, who was ill at that time, a *novella* was issued containing various privileges for different regions of the Empire. This *novella* exempted the Caucasian land of the Lazi, Bosporus, and Chersonesus from the naval duty formerly imposed upon them.[1] Hence it is obvious that in 575 Bosporus still belonged to the Empire. But in the following year (576) circumstances changed. Through the Avars the Byzantines first became acquainted with the 'eastern' Turks, as Byzantine sources sometimes call the Khazars;[2] for the Turko-Khazars begged Justin II not to admit the Avars into the Empire.[3] In the sixth century the Turko-Khazars already had considerable strength and by their conquests in the Caucasian steppes and the Caucasus itself menaced the Persian Sassanids. On the other side, their advance from the Caspian Sea westwards drew them nearer to the Cimmerian Bosporus and the South Russian steppes. In 576 they captured the city of Bosporus and in 581 they were already in view of Chersonesus.[4] A serious danger was looming over the Tauric fortified border from the north, and the Gothic possessions were also inevitably affected by the Turko-Khazarian advance.

I shall digress to emphasize a passage in Vasilievski's work which arouses some doubt. Narrating the relations formed between Byzantium and the Turks to make an alliance against the Persians, he wrote: 'One such embassy arrived in 579 from Sinope in the city of Cherson in order to proceed farther towards Bosporus by the south coast and through the city of Phullae, which at that time probably already belonged to the Goths.'[5] But the passage in Menander's fragments on which Vasilievski bases his statement is desperately distorted and obscure:[6] the words 'through the city of Phullae' do not occur in the text but are the result of Vasilievski's conjecture; he replaces the words 'διὰ φύλων,' which occur

---

[1] Zachariae von Lingenthal, *Jus graeco-romanum*, III, 23: 'ὁμοίως δὲ καὶ ἐπὶ τοῖς λεγομένοις τῶν εἰδῶν πλωίμοις, γενομένοις ἐπί τε τῆς Λαζῶν χώρας καὶ Βοσπόρου καὶ Χερσονήσου.'

[2] *Theopanis Chronographia*, ed. de Boor, p. 315.

[3] Theophanes Byzantius, ed. Bonn, Fr. 484; *Historici graeci minores*, ed. Dindorf, I, 447.

[4] *Menandri Fragmenta*, ed. Bonn, p. 404; Fr. 45, *Hist. graeci minores*, ed. Dindorf, II, 90: 'ἡ πόλις ὁ Βόσπορος ἧλω'; ed. Bonn, p. 337; Fr. 64; ed. Dindorf, II, 125; *Excerpta de Legationibus*, ed. C. de Boor, I (Berlin, 1903), 474: 'Τούρκων ἤδη περὶ Χερσῶνα ἐστρατοπεδευομένων.' Cf. Kulakovski, in the *Viz. Vremennik*, III (1896), 12–14; Shestakov, *Outlines on the History of Chersonesus*, p. 11 and n. 2. Both in Russian.

[5] Vasilievski, *Works*, II, ii, 386. Vasilievski's chronology is incorrect.

[6] See Dindorf's note in *Historici graeci minores*, II, 85. Cf. Kulakovski, in the *Viz. Vremennik*, III (1896), 9, n. 5.

in the text, by 'Φούλλων,' which is hardly permissible.[1]   Therefore this embassy, the itinerary of which is unknown, cannot be referred to the Crimean Goths.

In connection with the capture of Bosporus by the Turko-Khazars in 576 and their appearance near Chersonesus in 581 the question arises of the beginning of the Khazar predominance in the Crimea, of which in later times we have positive information.   Was the capture of Bosporus in 576 a transient occurrence of short duration, or from this time on may we speak of actual Khazar domination in the Peninsula?

In 1896 J. Kulakovski wrote: 'After 575 Byzantium had no power whatever in the Cimmerian Bosporus nor made any claim to suzerainty over this region: therefore we must consider the capture of Bosporus in 575 the beginning of the Khazar domination in these regions.'[2]   This opinion would seem to be correct, because the sources do not mention the recapture of Bosporus by the Empire.   But we must consider the so-called inscription of Eupaterius, which was found in the Taman Peninsula early in the nineteenth century.[3]   This inscription deals with the restoration in Bosporus of a Caesarian building (i.e., a palace) through 'the magnificent *stratelates* and *dux* of Chersonesus, Eupaterius,' in the eighth indiction, under 'our most reverend lord, protected by God . . . .'   The name of the Emperor has survived only in its final syllable 'κιc.'   Scholars who have been interested in this inscription have come to different conclusions: while some of them have reconstructed the name of Maurice (Mauricius) (Μαυρίκις for Μαυρίκιος, 582–602), others have recognized here Isaac II Angelus ('Ισαάκις for 'Ισάκης or 'Ισαάκιος, 1185–1195 and 1203–1204).   The Emperors Stauracius (811) and Isaac I Comnenus (1057–1059) are excluded, because the eighth indiction did not fall within their very short reigns.   Choice must be made between the two rulers first mentioned.   Under Maurice, the eighth indiction coincided with the period from 1 September 589, to 1 September 590, and under Isaac Angelus from 1 September 1189, to 1 September 1190.

On palaeographic evidence V. Latyshev attributes the inscription to a period much earlier than the close of the twelfth century or the opening years of the thirteenth.[4]   On historical grounds we have no reason to suppose that Isaac Angelus, who was thoroughly busy in the Balkan penin-

---

[1] The question of the location of Phullae is debatable.   Kulakovski identifies it with the *Stary Krim — Eski-Krim — Solkhat, Journal of the Ministry of Public Instruction*, Feb. 1898, p. 194 ff. See also Shestakov, *Outlines*, p. 37, n. 1.   With good reason Bertier Delagarde ascribes Phullae to Chufut-Kalé (Kyrkoru), *Izvestiya* of the Tauric Learned Archive Commission, LVII (1920), 66–124. All in Russian.   [2] *Viz. Vremennik*, III (1896), 14.

[3] Latyshev, *Collection of Christian Inscriptions*, No. 99, p. 109.

[4] Latyshev, in the *Viz. Vremennik*, I (1894), 667 ff., and in the Ποντικά, p. 206 ff. (in Russian).

sula and in Asia Minor, and occupied with the Crusaders, would have erected buildings in far-off Bosporus, whose connection with the Empire at that time is completely obscure.[1]   In addition, after careful investigation of the original inscription, A. Bertier Delagarde has discovered before the ending 'κιc' the letters 'ΜΑ . . ι' ('ΜΑ . . . ικιc');[2] V. Latyshev also finds the letters 'ι' and 'Μ.'[3] If they are correct, this name is that of Maurice, and the inscription refers to the end of 589 or to 590. If at that time the *stratelates* and *dux* of Chersonesus, Eupaterius, following the will of the Emperor, was reconstructing the Caesarian building in Bosporus, it is clear that the Turko-Khazar capture of Bosporus in 576, which has been spoken of above, is proved to be only of short duration, and that towards 590 the power of the Empire was restored in Bosporus at least, and perhaps in the Crimea in general.

Thus, the Tauric *limes* and along with it the territory of the Tauric Goths were under the menace of the Turko-Khazar danger only for a few years, in the seventies and eighties of the sixth century.

2. The Khazar Predominance from the Close of the Sixth Century to the Beginning of the Eighth

The Khazars appear under their own name in Byzantine sources for the first time in 626, when they concluded an alliance with the Empire for common offense and defence against the Persians.[4]

The seventh century was for the Khazars a period of growing power and of the formation of their state, which at that time lay between the lower course of the Volga and the Don and extended southwards over the Caucasian plain.   For the whole seventh century the sources give no exact information on relations between the Khazars and the Crimea.   But on the basis of the account just mentioned of their alliance with the Empire in 626 we may state with certainty that before 630 the Khazars opened no offensive policy against the Peninsula, which was dependent upon Byzantium and to a certain extent its possession.   But somewhat later circumstances changed.   How and why this happened, we do not know; but we are certain that late in the seventh century the Khazars crossed the Cimmerian Strait, captured Bosporus, set up their governor there, and took possession of a large section of the Peninsula.   As far as we may judge from the sources, which will be discussed below, the Khazars did not conquer the Gothic possessions.

[1] This inscription has been ascribed to Isaac Angelus by Vasilievski, *Works*, iii, clxvi; also by Tolstoi and Kondakov, *Russian Antiquities*, iv (St Petersburg, 1904), 14.   Both in Russian.

[2] A. Bertier Delagarde, in the *Zapiski* of the Odessa Society of History and Antiquities, xvi (1893), 83 (in Russian).

[3] V. Latyshev, *Collection of Christian Inscriptions*, p. 107 ff. (in Russian).

[4] See A. Pernice, *L'imperatore Eraclio* (1905), pp. 152–155.

In the middle of the seventh century Pope Martin I was exiled to Chersonesus.[1] He landed there in May, 654, and, utterly worn out by his privations and sufferings, died in his place of exile, 16 September 655. In two letters from Chersonesus[2] the exiled Pope describes, perhaps, as Vasilievski remarks, with some exaggeration, the desperate economic conditions on this Byzantine frontier.[3] According to the Pope, there was not even bread. 'Bread,' he writes, 'is talked of but never seen.'[4] Even for a trimisium' (i.e., a third of one Byzantine gold solidus) he could not obtain it;[5] only from small ships which came for salt[6] at rare intervals from Romania was he able to get a little bread and other provisions which barely kept him alive. If Martin's letters accurately reflect the situation, Dory, the Gothic region in the Crimea, though, according to Procopius' statement quoted above, 'abundant in the best fruits' and inhabited by 'able cultivators,' was apparently unable to relieve the economic crisis in nearby Chersonesus. This was probably because the mountainous aspect of the Gothic territory in the Crimea was not well suited for raising corn.

In one of Martin's letters we read: 'The inhabitants of this country are all pagans; and those who dwell here have also assumed pagan customs; they manifest not the slightest love for their neighbors, which is usually expressed in human nature, even among the barbarians, in the form of abundant compassion.'[7] In connection with this passage S. Shestakov remarks: 'The pagans mentioned by Martin usually mean the Goths first of all. Such was apparently Vasilievski's opinion; Tomashek and Loewe express themselves more definitely on this subject. They find in Martin's statement a proof of the predominance of the Gothic influence in the south-western coastland of the Crimea in the seventh century.'[8] S. Shestakov seems to me wrong in attributing this view to these scholars. V. Vasilievski writes as follows: 'It is difficult to say whether or not the neighboring Goths are meant here, who still maintained the superstitious worship of sacred trees as at Phullae.'[9] Tomaschek says with regard to the passage under consideration, 'By contact with the barbarians, the people living in the neighborhood [of Cherson] have grown savage.'[10] These statements of Vasilievski and Tomaschek do not support Shesta-

---

[1] See Shestakov, *Outlines*, pp. 115–124; H. K. Mann, *The Lives of the Popes in the Early Middle Ages*, 2nd ed., I, i (London, 1925), 399–400.

[2] Letters XVI and XVII, Mansi, *Conciliorum Sacrorum Amplissima Collectio*, x, coll. 861–863; Migne, *Patr. Lat.*, LXXXVII, coll. 202–203.   [3] Vasilievski, *Works*, II, ii, 388.

[4] Mansi, col. 861; Migne, col. 202.   [5] Mansi, col. 862; Migne, col. 203.

[6] The exporting of salt is an old Chersonesian business known from the times of Strabo to our own day. See Shestakov, *op. cit.*, p. 118; Bertier Delagarde, 'How Did Vladimir Besiege Cherson?,' *Izvestiya Otdeleniya Russkago Yazyka i Slovesnosti*, XIV, i (1909), 17.

[7] Mansi, x, col. 862; Migne, LXXXVII, col. 203. Cf. Shestakov, *Outlines*, p. 116 (in Russian).

[8] Shestakov, *op. cit.*, p. 118.   [9] Vasilievski, *Works*, II, ii, 388; also 425.

[10] Tomaschek, *op. cit.*, p. 19.

kov's conclusions. Only in Loewe's book do we find some indication
that in this case 'barbarians' meant the Goths. Loewe points out that,
because of their remoteness from Byzantium and the regions where the
Greeks dwelt in thickly settled areas, the culture of the Greek cities in
the Tauric coastland was so insignificant that it could exert no powerful
influence upon the Gothic country-folk ('Bauernvolk'); he then observes
that we have information on this point in Martin's letters of complaint.

Martin's letters about the pagans who lived in the neighborhood of
Cherson certainly do not identify them with the Goths; at that time
paganism was not a distinctive feature of the Goths who, as we know,
had long ago adopted Christianity. In my opinion, we must first allow
for Martin's desire to present the living conditions of his exile in the dark-
est possible colors, and admit his exaggeration. On the other hand, it is
hardly possible that these heathens could have been the Khazars, who
in the middle of the seventh century must still have been at some distance
from Chersonesus if indeed they were in the Peninsula at all. Possibly
there is also a reference to the Goths in a scholium on the brief *Life* of
Theodore and Euprepius which has been preserved in the *Collectanea* of
Anastasius Bibliothecarius, in the ninth century; we read here that Euprepius (died about 655) and Theodore (died about 667), who were exiled
to Cherson by Heraclius, were there often separated by force and sent
to forts belonging to neighboring peoples.[1]

But a statement in a letter of Pope Gregory II to Emperor Leo the
Isaurian may refer to the Goths, among other peoples. 'That Martin is
a blessed man, to this testify the city Cherson where he was exiled and
Bosporus as well as all the north and the inhabitants of the north who
hasten to his grave and are healed.'[2] There is good reason to believe
that among those who came to venerate the grave of the distinguished
exile there were Goths.

Late in the seventh century, for the first time after Dory was mentioned
by Procopius, we find this geographic name of the Gothic possession in
the form 'Doras' ('Δόρας,' gen. 'Δόραντος'). I refer to a signature in the
Acts of the so-called Trullan or Quinisextine (*Quinisextum*) Council in
Constantinople, in 692: 'Γεώργιος ἀνάξιος ἐπίσκοπος Χερσῶνος τῆς Δόραντος' ('George the unworthy bishop of Cherson Doras').[3] This somewhat

---

[1] *Patr. Lat.*, cxxix, col. 684: 'Chersonem in exilium missis et illic vi saepius ab invicem separatis
et in castris gentium ibidem adjacentium deputatis.' Should *deputatis* be translated here, as by
Shestakov (*op. cit.*, p. 120) 'sent as envoys'?

[2] *Gregorii II Epistola XIII*, Mansi, *Conciliorum collectio*, xii, col. 2, p. 972; Migne, *Patr. Lat.*,
lxxxix, col. 520. E. Caspar, 'Gregor ii und der Bilderstreit,' *Zeitschrift für Kirchengeschichte*.
Dritte Folge, lii (1933), 83 (a new edition of Pope Gregory's letter). Recently the question of
whether this letter is spurious or genuine has been reconsidered, with the decision in favor of its
authenticity; see G. Ostrogorski, 'Les débuts de la querelle des images,' in *Mélanges Charles Diehl*,
i (Paris, 1930), 235–255, and especially 249–250. Caspar, *op. cit.*, p. 31.

[3] Mansi, *op. cit.*, xi, col. 992.

puzzling signature has been variously interpreted by Scholars. Le Quien did not at all understand the meaning of the name 'Doras'.[1] The Archbishop Macarius thought it possible that this signature showed the recognition by the Tetraxite Goths of the supreme authority of the Chersonesian bishop.[2] The Reverend Innocent of Cherson believed that George's signature might have meant that the region Dory included Cherson.[3] The Archimandrite Arsenius thought that 'τῆς Δόραντος' signified 'in the region Dory. The Gothic settlements bordered upon the territory of this Republic (i.e. Chersonesus); therefore George called himself the Bishop of Tauric Cherson'[4] (as well as Bishop of Dory). Tomaschek offers two hypotheses: either the conjunction 'καί' might have fallen out between 'Χερσῶνος' and 'τῆς Δόραντος,' in which case we should read 'George, bishop of Cherson and Doras'; or, since Cherson and Doras were two different bishoprics, the words 'τῆς Δόραντος' might belong to another proper name omitted in the text.[5] This point of view was adopted by Braun.[6] Loewe, rejecting Arsenius' identification of Dory with Tauris and considering Tomaschek's conjecture superfluous, believes that, since the region Doras or Dory certainly goes beyond the limits of the Bishopric of Gothia and the region of the Crimean Goths, it might have comprised the Greek maritime towns as well; and here Loewe refers to Procopius' statement that Dory 'Χώρα κατὰ τὴν παραλίαν.'[7] It is obvious that Loewe thinks it possible to assign Cherson to the region Dory; in other words, he independently arrives at the conclusion of Innocent of Cherson quoted above.

Perhaps it is not irrelevant to recall that in some versions of the *Life* of the Apostle Andrew, whose missionary activities the legend connects with the Caucasus and the Crimea, Chersonesus is called a city of the Goths. We read, for instance, in a Russian version, 'The Apostle withdrew to the western extremity of the Peninsula, to the city of the Goths, Chersonesus, where savage and pagan people dwelt.'[8] In a Georgian version of the same *Life* which is preserved in the monastery Davidgaredji we find an almost identical statement, 'The Apostle left Theodosia and withdrew to the city of the Goths, Chersonesus, where savage and pagan people dwelt.'[9]

---

[1] Le Quien, *Oriens Christianus*, i (Paris, 1740), 1113.

[2] Macarius, *History of Christianity in Russia before Vladimir* (St Petersburg, 1868), p. 62 (in Russian).　　　　　　　　　　　[3] See Bruun, *Chernomorye*, ii, 211.

[4] Arsenius, 'The Gothic Eparchy in the Crimea,' *Journal of the Ministry of Public Instruction*, (1873), 64 (in Russian).　　　　　　　　[5] Tomaschek, *op. cit.*, p. 20.

[6] Th. Braun, *Die letzten Schicksale der Krimgoten*, p. 51.

[7] Loewe, *Die Reste der Germanen*, pp. 214 ff.

[8] (Muravyev), *The Lives of the Saints of the Russian Church* (St Petersburg, 1856), November, p. 443.

[9] A Russian translation of this Georgian *Life* in the *Christianskoye Chteniye*, ii (1869), 165. See Vasilievski, 'The Journey of the Apostle Andrew in the Country of the Myrmidons,' *Works*, ii, i (St Petersburg, 1909), 282 (in Russian).

In the Georgian synaxarium compiled in the eleventh century by George Mtazmindeli, a translator of Greek books into the Georgian tongue, we have the same passage without the name Chersonesus, 'Hence [i.e., from Theodosia] he came to the city of the Goths where the inhabitants proved to be very wicked and impious.'[1]   It is interesting to note that in later documents Cherson is also sometimes placed in the region of Gothia, as, for instance, in the bull of Pope John xxii issued at Avignon, 16 July 1333, on the appointment of Richard as Bishop of the Chersonesian Church ('Richardus Anglicus ecclesiae Chersonensi in episcopum praeficitur').[2]

It is difficult definitely to explain Bishop George's signature at the Council of 692.   Tomaschek's conjecture seems to me most plausible; he believes that a '*καί*' must be inserted between 'Χερσῶνος' and 'Δόραντος'; in this case we should read 'George, bishop of Cherson and Doras.'   The following consideration may serve to confirm this view.   In the list of the metropoles usually connected with the name of Epiphanius of Cyprus but compiled, in all likelihood, in the seventh century, among autocephalous archbishops are named in the eparchy of Zikhia three: the Archbishops of Cherson, Bosporus, and Nicopsis.[3]   This list gives neither Doras nor Doros nor the eparchy of Gothia.   But on the basis of the *Life* of John of Gothia, of which we will speak below, we know that in the second half of the eighth century the Archbishopric of Gothia, with its center at Doros, already existed.   Combining these data, we may conclude that the eparchy of Gothia with its center at Doros was established in the eighth century.   In this case, in the seventh century Doros or Doras was subject to the Bishop of Cherson, i.e., belonged to the eparchy of Cherson.[4]   It is very possible that John of Gothia was the first Archbishop of Gothia.[5]

---

[1] M. G. Djanashvili, 'Accounts of Iberian Annals and Historians on Chersonesus, Gothia, Osetia, Khazaria, Didoëtia, and Russia,' *Collection of Materials for the Description of the Regions and Tribes of the Caucasus*, xxvi (Tiflis, 1899), 3. Djanashvili thinks he sees here Dory (Mangup).

[2] 'Locum Cersone, situm in terra Gothie consistente in partibus orientis,' A. Theiner, *Vetera monumenta Poloniae et Lithuaniae gentiumque finitimarum historiam illustrantia* (Romae, 1860), p. 348 (No. cdlxi).

[3] See H. Gelzer, 'Ungedruckte und ungenügend veröffentlichte Texte der Notitiae episcopatuum,' *Abh. philos.-philol. Cl., Bayer. Akad.*, xxi (1901), 535; on the dating of the list, p. 545.   Previously Gelzer was inclined to assign the list to the seventh century, or, at the latest, to the outset of the eighth, *Jahrbücher für protest. Theologie*, xii (1886), 556.   See also *Hieroclis Synecdemus et notitiae graecae episcopatuum*, ed. Parthey (Berlin, 1866), 153 (*Not.* 7).

[4] See Bertier Delagarde, *Izvestiya* of the Tauric Learned Archive Commission, lvii (1920), 40, 43 (in Russian).

[5] A list of the early Orthodox bishops of the Crimea, including those of Gothia, is given by J. Zeiller, *Les origines chrétiennes dans les provinces danubiennes de l'Empire Romain* (Paris, 1918), p. 411. Mentioning John, Metropolite of Bosporus in 536, Zeiller (p. 412) believes that he had under his jurisdiction the whole Crimea, and that the Bishops of Cherson and Gothia were subordinate to him.

At the close of the seventh century and the beginning of the eighth, Crimean Gothia took part in the political events of the Empire.

The popular revolt which burst out in Constantinople in 695 proclaimed Leontius Emperor. Justinian II was dethroned, mutilated, and exiled to Cherson. After the revolution in the capital in 698, when Leontius was dethroned and Apsimar-Tiberius raised to the throne, Justinian hoped to regain his power and spoke openly of his eventual restoration. The inhabitants of Cherson, fearing lest his recklessness should bring danger upon them from the ruling Emperor, determined either to kill Justinian or to send him in chains to Apsimar. Learning of this plan, Justinian fled to the fortress Doros or Doras in Gothic territory and thence asked the Khagan of the Khazars for permission to come to him.[1] The Khagan granted permission, and Justinian went to his court; the Khagan received him with honor, married him to his own sister, upon whom, after baptism, the name of Theodora was bestowed, and then assigned to the couple the city Phanagoria which lay on the eastern shore of the Cimmerian Bosporus. Informed of Justinian's friendly relations with the Khagan, Apsimar-Tiberius opened negotiations with the latter: he promised him rich presents if he would deliver up Justinian, living or dead. The Khagan was inclined to comply with the Emperor's overtures: first of all he surrounded Justinian with a Khazar guard under the pretext of protecting him from danger from Byzantium, but in reality to prevent his escape; and then he gave instructions to the governor of Phanagoria, Papatzi, and the governor of Bosporus, Balquitzi, to kill Justinian on the receipt of specific orders.[2] Theodora, informed of her brother's plans by one of the Khagan's slaves, warned Justinian. He sent his wife to Khazaria, and then secretly escaped from Phanagoria. Boarding a ship, he sailed along the southern coast of the Crimea. On his way he stopped at the port Symbolon, near Cherson (later Balaklava) and secretly asked some of his adherents from Cherson to join him; then he rounded the lighthouse of Cherson and passing by the Dnieper and Dniester reached the Danube. There he came to an agreement with the Khan of Bulgaria, Terbel, and, supported by the Bulgarians, advanced upon the capital and in 705 regained the throne.[3] Desirous of revenge for the plots which, during his stay in the Tauris, the inhabitants of Cherson, Bosporus, and the other 'climata'[4] had formed against him,

[1] Theoph. p. 372; Niceph., *Chron.*, p. 40; Cedr., I, 778. Simeon Metaphrastes Logothete (*A Slavonic version*, p. 73) says that Justinian fled from Cherson to Khazaria; see Leo Grammaticus, p. 167. Some scholars place the site of Doros 'on the border of the Gothic region,' which is closer to the text of our sources, but contradicts the real state of things; see Bruun, *Chernomorye*, II, 212, and Shestakov, *Outlines*, p. 32. Both in Russian.   [2] Theoph. p. 373; Niceph., *Chron.*, p. 41.

[3] Theoph., pp. 372–374; Niceph., *Chron.*, pp. 40–41; Cedr., I, 778–779.

[4] Theoph., p. 377; Niceph,, *Chron.*, p. 44, writes: 'τοὺς ἐν Χερσῶνι καὶ Βοσφόρῳ καὶ τοὺς τῶν ἄλλων ἀρχοντιῶν λαούς,' i.e., he gives 'ἀρχοντίαι,' which corresponds to 'κλίματα' in Theophanes.

Justinian sent a huge fleet to Cherson with orders to slay the population of those regions and apparently to send to the capital the members of the chief Chersonesian families. One of these ships carried the *spatharius* Elias, who was appointed governor of Cherson. On arriving, the imperial troops without meeting any resistance captured the fortified cities and put most of the population to the sword. But the Khagan's viceroy at Cherson, whose title was the *Tudun*, as well as Zoilus, the 'first citizen' of Cherson (protopolite — πρωτοπολίτης), and forty other prominent citizens were sent in chains to the capital. A considerable number of other well-known men were cruelly tortured before execution. The Emperor commanded the fleet to return to the capital; on these ships were the children who, in spite of the Emperor's orders, were left alive and reserved for slavery. On its return voyage the fleet was almost entirely destroyed by a storm. The sources give a figure, certainly exaggerated, of those who perished — 73,000 men. This disaster not only did not afflict Justinian, as Theophanes and Nicephorus write, but filled him with great joy. As Bury remarks, the Emperor seems to have become really insane.[1] All this, however, did not satisfy Justinian, who threatened to send another fleet to Cherson with orders to raze all buildings to the ground and to plow the soil left after the destruction. But the inhabitants of the fortified places ('τῶν κάστρων') which had incurred the Emperor's rage appealed to the Khazar Khagan for troops to protect them. At the same time Elias, who had recently been appointed governor of Cherson, and Vardan, who had been exiled there, rose against the Emperor.

On learning of this revolt Justinian sent, in a few military vessels (*dromons*), three hundred armed men, headed by the patrician and logothete (γενικὸς λογοθέτης) George, surnamed the Syrian (a very high official), the eparch (prefect) John, and the turmarch of the Thracesian troops, Christophorus. Along with them were sent back to Cherson the *Tudun* of the Khazar Khagan and the protopolite of Cherson, Zoilus, who have been mentioned above. They had been brought to Justinian from Cherson; now they were sent back to take their former position as governors. A special Imperial envoy was to apologize to the Khagan for what had happened. Justinian wanted Elias and Vardan, who had revolted against him, to be brought to the capital. The Chersonesians, however, would not come to any agreement with the Imperial envoys and disposed of the expedition in the following manner. On the arrival of the Imperial navy the Chersonesians immediately put to death the logothete George and the eparch John, and through the Khazars sent the *Tudun*,

---

[1] J. B. Bury, *A History of the Later Roman Empire*, II (London, 1889), 363.

Zoilus, the turmarch Christophorus, and the three hundred armed men to the Khagan. The *Tudun* died on the way; the rest of the company were killed by the Khazars. Cherson and the other towns of the Peninsula thus seceded from Justinian and proclaimed the above-mentioned Vardan Emperor under the name of Philippicus.

Beside himself with rage, Justinian prepared a new armament under the command of Maurus the patrician, who was abundantly provided with different sorts of siege machinery. Maurus was ordered not only to destroy the walls of Cherson, but also to raze to the ground the whole city and to spare not a soul in it. On arriving at his destination, Maurus laid siege to the town; two towers collapsed under the blows of his engines. But with this the success of the Byzantine arms ceased; the Khazars who had arrived at the town compelled Maurus to suspend hostilities. Then the unsuccessful army, afraid to return, deserted Justinian and embraced the cause of Vardan-Philippicus, who at that time was staying at the Khagan's court. Maurus and his troops asked the Khagan to bring the new Emperor to them; but evidently fearing for Vardan's safety the Khagan surrendered him only after having received from Maurus' troops a large security in money. In 711, with the new Emperor at its head, the army sailed towards Constantinople, where Philippicus was received by the population without a blow being struck. Justinian was assassinated, and the capital proclaimed Vardan-Philippicus Emperor.[1] This was Emperor Philippicus (Vardan, Bardanes) who reigned from 711 to 713.

Now let us draw from this account the data pertaining to the Gothic and Khazar question in the Crimea. We shall begin with the ten years of Justinian's exile, i.e., from 695 to 705.

Cherson at that time belonged to the Empire and as formerly was serving as a place of exile for the most dangerous and prominent enemies of the Empire; hence Justinian's flight from here to Doros or Doras (Dory according to Procopius), i.e., to the chief center of the Gothic settlement in the Tauris, shows that at that time this section of the mountain Crimea had slipped away from the suzerainty of Byzantium and enjoyed independence.[2] As Vasilievski wrote, this was a sort of 'neutral territory, in which Justinian was inaccessible to the direct attempts of the Byzantine authorities, and at the same time was not yet under the power of the Khazar Khagan.'[3] The towns which depended upon the Khazars were

---

[1] Theoph., pp. 372–381; Niceph., *Chron.*, pp. 40–48; Cedr., I, 778–784.

[2] The excessive brevity of the sources produces here some doubt. See Braun, *Die letzten Schicksale der Krimgoten*, p. 13: 'Ob auch Gotien unter der direkten Oberherrschaft eines Tudun stand, lässt sich nicht mit Sicherheit sagen'; Tomaschek, *op. cit.*, p. 19: '[In the seventh century] die Goten, die einen langen, aber fruchtlosen Widerstand leisteten.' [3] Vasilievski, *Works*, II, ii, 388.

governed by the Khagan's vicars, who at that time were Papatzi in Phanagoria and Balquitzi in Bosporus.. Theophanes calls the former 'ὁ ἐκ προσώπου' and the latter 'ὁ ἄρχων,' which enables some scholars to speak of Bosporus as partly independent of the Khazars; but this should not confuse us, for Nicephorus, though he does not give their names, calls both governors 'οἱ ἄρχοντες.' Thus we find here a state administered by means of vicars — governors who were, of course, absolutely dependent upon the Khagan. As has been said above, Justinian appealed to him from Doros for permission to come to his court. It is uncertain where in Khazaria the former Emperor met the Khagan and married his sister. It is hard to believe that Justinian reached the far-off residence of the Khazar Khagans, famous in later days, on the lower course of the Volga, Itil, which is described by Arabian geographers of the tenth century.[1]

Thus in the opening years of the eighth century the eastern and, as we shall see presently, the northern and south-western sections of the peninsula, up to Cherson, i.e., the major part of the Crimean steppe, were in the power of the Khazars. The flight of Justinian has usually been referred to 704.[2] The southern coast — its mountain section at least — seems not to have belonged to the Khazars. For that time we possess reliable evidence concerning the Byzantine power in the south-western section of the Crimea, namely at Symbolon (Balaklava) and Cherson.

The evidence of the *Chronicles* regarding Justinian's punitive expeditions against Cherson shows us the Khazar successes in the Crimea, which evidently took place in the first decade of the eighth century. When about 710 an Imperial army arrived at Cherson, it found in the city a Khazar governor, the *Tudun*, as well as the representative of the city, the protopolite Zoilus. It is very probable that the advance of the Khazars to Cherson occurred in connection with Justinian's flight from there to Doros, his appeal for help to the Khagan, and the strained relations between the Khazars and the Empire which must inevitably have appeared as a result of these political complications.[3]

Tudun is a term often used by various sources in dealing with the Avars and Khazars: Greek writers give the form 'Τουδοῦνος' or 'Τονδοῦνος';

---

[1] Shakhmatov, *The Earliest Fortunes of the Russian People*, p. 53 (in Russian). After mentioning the formation of the large Khazar state in the seventh and eighth centuries, he says that its political center was Itil. Under the form *Astil* Itil is given in the *Notitia episcopatuum* of the period of the first iconoclasts, i.e. in the eighth century; see C. de Boor, *Zeitschrift für Kirchengeschichte*, xii (1891), 531, 533–534: 'ὁ 'Αστὴλ ἐν ᾧ λέγεται ὁ 'Αστὴλ ὁ ποταμὸς τῆς Χαζαρίας, ἔστιν δὲ κάστρον.'

[2] Muralt, *Essai de chronographie byzantine*, i (St Petersburg, 1855), 323 ff.; Bury, *History of the Later Roman Empire*, ii (London, 1889), 360. I do not know why Tomaschek says (p. 20) that Nicephorus ascribes this fact to 698.

[3] Kunik, ('On the report of a Gothic Toparch,' p. 118) believed that the first *tudun* was appointed in Cherson about 705.

Western mediaeval annalists, 'Tudun,' 'Thodanus';[1] Armenian texts, 'tndiyun,' 'tndiun,' 'tndyan';[2] later Italian documents of the fourteenth and fifteenth centuries, 'lo Titano,' 'Titanus.' Some western European writers have considered this title a proper name, as, for instance, a Spanish traveller to the court of Timur (Timurlane, Tamerlane) at the outset of the fifteenth century, Ruy Gonzales de Clavijo.[3]

The etymology of the word *tudun* is debatable. It has been compared with the Gothic word *thiudans* ('rex,' 'dominator'), and a Turkish root *tut* in the verb *tutmak* (' to keep,' 'to hold'). Some scholars derive the term *tudun* from a Chinese word *tudunj* used down to the present to designate a provincial commander; in Chinese annals which deal with the history of the Turco-Mongol tribes in the seventh and eighth centuries we find this term employed of an officer similar to the *tudun* of the Khazars, a sort of viceroy.[4] If this derivation is correct, the Khazars may have assumed this title at that remote time when they were wandering as a nomadic tribe in Central Asia and were in contact with the Chinese. But recently one scholar has rejected the Chinese origin of the term. Another linguist identifies the term *tudun* with the Turco-Bulgarian word *turun*; but he writes that it can not be explained by any Turkish language or dialect.[5] So far, therefore, it is unknown from what foreign linguistic group the title was taken by the Turks.

Thus about 705 a Khazar governor already resided in Phanagoria and Bosporus. He is called by Theophanes and Nicephorus 'ὁ ἐκ προσώπου' and 'ὁ ἄρχων.' These are of course only Greek names for the Khazar word *tudun*.

It is interesting to note that the Khazar system of domination over the conquered regions, which set up governors in their chief centers, sometimes failed to destroy the organs of municipal city administration; for instance in Cherson as well as a *tudun* we find a protopolite, i.e., a sort of mayor of the city. Light has recently been thrown upon the formerly

---

[1] See *Annales Laurissenses*, s.a. 795, 796 (*Mon. Germ. Hist., SS.*, I, 180, 182); *Einhardi Annales* s.a. 811 (*ibid.*, 199); *Chronicon Moissiacense*, s.a. 795 (*ibid.*, 302); *Annales Fuldenses*, s.a. 795–796 (*ibid.*, 351). In some other west European chronicles 'Zotan,' see Shakhmatov, *Sbornik* of the Museum of Anthropology and Ethnography, v (1918), 396 (in Russian).

[2] Moses Kagankatvatzi, *History of the Avghans* (St Petersburg, 1861), p. 337 (in Russian). Cf. the Greek form 'Τονδοῦνος.'

[3] Ruy Gonzales de Clavijo, *A Diary of the Journey to the Court of Timur (Tamerlane), to Samarqand in 1403–1406*, Spanish text with a Russian translation and commentary by J. Sreznevski (St Petersburg, 1881), p. 154; Clavijo, *Embassy to Tamerlane 1403–1406*, transl. from the Spanish by Guy Le Strange (London, 1928), p. 374, Index, under Toktamish (Tetani).

[4] On the *Tuduns* see Kunik, 'On the Report of a Gothic Toparch,' pp. 134 ff., and especially V. D. Smirnov, *The Crimean Khanate under the Supremacy or the Ottoman Porte up to the Beginning of the Eighteenth Century* (St Petersburg, 1887), pp. 38–47. Both in Russian.

[5] Samoilovich, *Sbornik* of the Museum of Anthropology and Ethnography, v (St Petersburg, 1918), 398–400, and Shakhmatov, *ibid.*, pp. 395–397. In Russian.

obscure question of the municipal structure of Byzantine cities by extremely important and fresh material from the data of Byzantine hagiography.   New study of this aspect of the internal life of the Empire is urgently needed.   Our material already justifies us in speaking of the 'extraordinary vitality of the municipal spirit' in Byzantine provinces.[1] Zoilus of Cherson, the protopolite under the power of the Khazars, must have his place among other examples of the vitality of this system in Byzantium.

The punitive expedition sent by Justinian to the Crimea easily obtained the mastery over the rebellious towns.   It is hardly to be supposed that the Imperial troops captured all the cities and regions mentioned in the sources which had revolted against Justinian, i.e., Cherson, Bosporus, and the 'other climata'; the latter apparently comprised the Gothic possessions in the Crimea, which are often given this name.[2]   But some of them, including Cherson, passed into the Emperor's hands, and the captured *Tudun* and protopolite were carried to Constantinople.   On learning that a new expedition was being prepared against Cherson, its governor, Elias, who had been sent there by the Emperor, and Vardan, who had been exiled there, revolted against Justinian, and the regions which had just returned to the Imperial power asked the Khagan for protection.   Justinian determined to bring the rebellion to an end, but he realized that he must come to an agreement with the Khagan.   The Emperor would have been willing to restore the Khazar administration in Cherson, i.e., to reëstablish the *Tudun* and the protopolite Zoilus, and to apologize to the Khazar Khagan for what had happened.   But the Khagan evidently failed to meet these overtures.   As we know, the Chersonesians killed some of the Greek leaders and sent the *Tudun*, Zoilus, and the soldiers to the Khagan.   Shortly after, Vardan, who at that time was at the Khagan's court, was proclaimed Emperor in Cherson and in some other places which belonged to the Empire.

We have thus proof of the very interesting fact that the Khazars were allied with the Greek possessions in the Crimea against the Emperor. This alliance became still stronger when on reaching Cherson the Khazars compelled the new commander Maurus, who had been sent from the capital, to raise the siege of the city and to range himself on Vardan's side.   We have already dealt with the revolution of 711, the dethronement of Justinian, and the proclamation of Vardan (Bardanes)-Philippicus.

From all these facts it is obvious that at the very beginning of the

---

[1] See interesting data and opinions on this subject in A. P. Rudakov, *Outlines on Byzantine Culture Based on Data from Greek Hagiography* (Moscow, 1917), pp. 72, 78–79 (in Russian).   This book is practically unknown to European and American scholars; see G. Ostrogorski, 'Löhne und Preise in Byzanz,' *Byz. Zeitschrift*, XXXII (1932), 293.

[2] On the Gothic *climata* see Kunik, 'On the Report of a Gothic Toparch,' pp. 74–81 (in Russian).

eighth century the Khazars took a most important part in the history of the Crimea. The revolution of 711 was supported by the Khagan, and from that time friendly relations between Byzantium and the Khazars were continued for many years.

Obviously many of these events took place in the territory of Crimean Gothia. About 700, when Justinian fled from Cherson to Doros, to the Goths, the Gothic possessions in the Crimea, the so-called 'Gothic *climata*,' took advantage of the external difficulties of the Empire to free themselves from their allied and vassal relationship with Byzantium, which, as we know, had been established under Justinian the Great, in the sixth century. At the outset of the eighth century, in its relations with Justinian ii, Crimean Gothia was acting with Cherson and the Khazars; according to the sources, the *climata* were hostile to the Emperor. The Khazars occupied the steppe region of the Peninsula early in the eighth century, but they failed to possess mountain Gothia. The conquest of Doros by the Khazars took place later, at the end of the eighth century; we will speak of this below.[1]

The Khagan's friendly relations with the Empire prevented him from further occupation of the Peninsula. These relations are to be explained by the Arabian danger which in the eighth century menaced the vital interests both of the Empire and of the Khaganate. Through all the eighth century these two states were stubbornly fighting against the Muhammedans. While in the far West the Frankish majordomos with Charles Martel at their head were defending Western Europe against the Arabs who were advancing from beyond the Pyrenees, and the Emperors of the Isaurian house were driving them back from the walls of Constantinople and carrying on energetic war against them in Asia Minor, the Khazars at the same time were vigorously fighting with the Muhammedans in the Caucasus, finally preventing them from crossing the Caucasian range and spreading over the Caucasian steppes, north of the mountains.

In 732 the Khazaro-Byzantine alliance was sealed by the marriage of Constantine, son and heir of Leo iii the Isaurian, with the daughter of the Khazar Khagan, who took the Christian name Irene. This son of Leo iii was the future iconoclastic Emperor Constantine v Copronymus.

3. The Iconoclastic Epoch and the Khazar Predominance in the Eighth and Ninth Centuries

The iconoclastic movement of the eighth century in Byzantium vigorously affected the Crimean Peninsula in general and Crimean Gothia in

---

[1] Count Bobrinski states incorrectly, 'In 702 the Khazars definitely conquered the Goths. . . . The Khazar Khagan made his residence in the fort Dory, on the border of the Gothic settlement,' Bobrinski, *The Tauric Chersonesus* (St Petersburg, 1905), p. 97 (in Russian).

particular.   During the reign of Leo III, the iconoclastic tendencies of
the government were only beginning to make themselves felt; but his
successor, Constantine V Copronymus, was a real iconoclastic leader.   Accordingly, many representatives of the clergy determined not to submit
to his policy.   Wishing to preserve intact the dogmas of the Orthodox
iconodulic faith, they preferred voluntary exile and left the regions of the
Empire where iconoclasm was prevalent.   It is known that the iconoclastic tendencies of the Isaurian emperors were not accepted all over the
Empire.   On this subject we have interesting data in the *Life of Stephen
the Younger*, who lived in the eighth century (died 28 November 764).[1]

According to the *Life*, monks and hermits, 'dwellers of caves and inhabitants of mountains,'[2] streamed to the saint, who had fled for refuge
to the mountains of Asia Minor, and begged him to instruct and console
them in their calamity.   Stephen advised them to seek refuge in those
regions of the Empire which were not affected by the iconoclastic movement or, in the words of the *Life*, 'were not under the power of the dragon
and sharing his error.'[3]   Three such regions were: first, the northern
shores of the Euxine, its coast regions towards the eparchy of Zikhia,
and the territory from Bosporus, Cherson, and Nicopsis towards Lower
Gothia;[4] secondly, southern Italy; and thirdly, the south of Asia Minor,
Cyprus, and the coast of Syria and Palestine.   Persecuted monks proceeded to these three asylums.   According to the *Life*, Byzantium was
empty of monks because all of them had been brought into captivity.
'Some sailed on the Euxine, others fled to the island of Cyprus, and others
were planning to go to Rome.'[5]   Therefore, later, at the opening of the
second period of the iconoclastic movement, in 819, Theodore of Studium
(Studion) spoke truly in a letter entitled 'Instruction' ('Κατήχησις') and
addressed 'to the scattered brethren': 'Hear, O heavens, and give ear, O
earth (Isaiah, I, 2)!   Moab, that is to say, Byzantium, has disregarded
[its faith]; it has shaken off the Evangelical bond and is going mad like
a rebellious heifer . . . .   But with us is God, in the east, west, north, and
on the sea!'[6]

The fact of a large emigration of Byzantine monks to Italy is very well
known and has many times been duly estimated in the history of South-
Italian Hellenism in the Middle Ages.   For our purpose, the information
of the *Life* on the analogous emigration of persecuted Byzantine monks
to the Tauric Peninsula, to Cherson, Bosporus, and Gothia, is extremely
important and interesting — a fact which has not been noted by Byzan-

---

[1] *Vita Stephani Junioris, Patr. Gr.*, c, coll. 1069–1186.

[2] 'σπηλοδίαιτοι καὶ ὀρεόμονες,' *Vita*, col. 1113.   [3] *Vita*, col. 1117.

[4] 'Τὰ πρὸς τὴν Γότθιον Κοίλην ἀπαντῶντα'; in another version 'Τοττίαν Κοίλην' (*Vita*, col. 1117).

[5] *Vita*, coll. 1117–1120.   [6] *Theodori Studitae Epistolae, Patr. Gr.*, XCIX, col. 1280.

tine chroniclers. This is, doubtless, a very important cultural phenomenon in the history of the mediaeval Crimea, for it indicates the increase
of the Hellenic element in the Peninsula.[1]

The origin of rock-cut churches and monasteries in various places in the
Crimean mountains, the remains of which have survived down to the
present day, is in all likelihood, to be referred to the epoch of the emigration of the monks in the eighth century. Examples of these cave dwellings can be noted also in the territory of Crimean Gothia. These monuments may be compared with analogous monuments in southern Italy,
and their study in connection with the general epoch of iconoclasm is of
great interest and one of the important problems of the cultural history of
Byzantium in general and of the mediaeval Crimea in particular.

Now we turn to the *Life* of John of Gothia, a prominent figure of the
iconoclastic epoch of the eighth century. This *Life* throws an unusually
clear light on the history of Crimean Gothia, which in general lacks evidence.[2] The *Life*, which gives a great deal of interesting cultural as well
historical material, was compiled by an anonymous author who probably
lived on the Asiatic shore of the Black Sea, during the second period of
iconoclasm, i.e., not earlier than 815, when under Leo v the Armenian the
iconoclastic policy was resumed, and not later than 843, when icon-worship was restored.[3]

The Bishop of Gothia, John's predecessor, whose name is unknown,
participated in the meetings of the iconoclastic Council of 753–754 and
gave his signature to its decrees; in recognition he was transferred by
Constantine v from the Gothic borderland as metropolite to Heraclea of
Thrace, near Constantinople.[4] The Crimean Goths remained faithful to
Orthodoxy and did not wish 'to take part in the novelties of the lawless
Council.' Accordingly they elected John,[5] and the election must have
taken place soon after the Council of 753–754, i.e., about 755.

John's family originally came from the northern coast of Asia Minor,

---

[1] Vasilievski, *Works*, II, ii, 328.

[2] *Acta Sanctorum*, Jun. VII, 167–171. The Greek text of the *Life* with a Russian translation, is
reprinted by A. Nikitski, *Zapiski* of the Odessa Society of History and Antiquities, XIII (1885), 25–34.
A Russian translation of the *Life* is also given by Vasilievski, *Works*, II, ii, 396–400. A brief Georgian
synaxarium in Djanashvili, *Collection of Materials for the Description of the Regions and Tribes of the
Caucasus*, XXVI, 11. A brief Greek synaxarium in *Propylaeum ad Acta Sanctorum Novembris.
Synaxarium Ecclesiae Constantinopolitanae* (Brussels, 1902), coll. 772–774.

[3] Vasilievski, II, ii, 426 ff. Cf. Chr. Loparev, *The Greek Lives of the Saints of the Eighth and Ninth
Centuries* (St Petersburg, 1914), p. 238 (in Russian).

[4] *Vita*, Ch. I (pp. 167–168). See Vasilievski, *op. cit.*, pp. 396, 406–407; A. Lombard, *Constantin
V, empereur des Romains* (Paris, 1902), p. 133. I do not know on what authority some scholars state
that John of Gothia himself took part in the Council of 753–754 and only later renounced the iconoclastic doctrine. See C. Hefele, *Conciliengeschichte*, 2nd ed., III (Freiburg i.B., 1877), 429; Arsenius,
op. cit., p. 65 (in Russian). [5] *Vita*, Ch. II (p. 168).

whence his grandfather, after the completion of his military service, emigrated to the Crimea. John's parents, Leo and Photina, were natives of Gothia. John's birthplace was Parthenitae (the present-day Tartar village Parthenit), a trading place or 'mart' which was subject to the Goths, on the southern coast of the Crimea, at the foot of Ayu-Dagh. From the point of view of the author of the *Life*, who lived, as has been noted above, in Asia Minor, John's birthplace was 'the land of the Tauroscythians situated on the other side (of the sea).'[1]

John proceeded to Jerusalem, where he spent three years, and then after visiting the Holy Places returned to Gothia. Then, since the Patriarch of Constantinople who had adopted the erroneous path of iconoclasm could not ordain an Orthodox bishop, the inhabitants of Gothia sent John to Iberia, i.e., Georgia, to the Archbishop (*Katholikos*) there, who ordained him bishop.[2] An interesting addition to the Greek *Life* is the Georgian Church tradition which has been preserved in the *Life* of Saint George the Hagiorite (the Athonite), the founder of the Iberian monastery (*Lavra*) on Mount Athos. The *Life* gives George's address to the Patriarch of Antioch vindicating the Georgian Church from various accusations. He declares Georgia the firmest foundation of Orthodoxy 'in all Greece' at the iconoclastic epoch and the preserver of the Orthodox faith transmitted by the Apostles. Then comes the following interesting passage: 'At that hard time there was almost no Orthodox temple in the Greek regions for the ordination of Saint John, the Bishop of Gothia; therefore he was ordained in our patriarchal church of the Vivifying and Myrrh-pouring Pillar of Mzkhet, and then he was sent to the see of Gothia, to which testify both our synaxarium and yours.'[3] Thus John was ordained Bishop of Gothia by the Archbishop (*Katholikos*) of Georgia, whose residence at that time was at Mzkhet, near Tiflis.[4] We have stated above that the election of John as Bishop of Gothia took place about 755; taking into consideration his three years' stay in Palestine before his ordination at Mzkhet, we may refer this ordination probably to 759.

John remained as Bishop in Gothia for a long time. According to the

---

[1] *Vita*, Ch. I (pp. 167–168): 'ὁρμώμενος ἐκ τῆς περατικῆς τῶν Ταυροσκυθῶν γῆς, τῆς ὑπὸ τὴν χώραν τῶν Γότθων τελούσης, ἐμπορίου λεγομένου Παρθενιτῶν.'   [2] *Vita*, Ch. II (p. 168).

[3] M. Sabinin, *A Complete Biography of the Saints of the Georgian Church*, II (St Petersburg, 1871), 190. A Georgian synaxarium published by Djanashvili (*op. cit.*) says: 'John went to the Kartvely Katholikos.' Both in Russian. See also P. Peeters, 'Histoires monastiques géorgiennes, vita et mores sancti et beati patris nostri Georgii Hagioritae,' *Analecta Bollandiana*, XXXVI–XXXVII (1917–1919), 117 (§ 51).

[4] N. Marr, 'The Caucasian Cultural World and Armenia,' *Journal of the Ministry of Public Instruction*, LVII (1915), 326. On the church of Mzkhet mentioned in the text see Vasilievski, *Works*, II, ii, 407–408. Both in Russian.

Life, after the death of Emperors Constantine v (775) and Leo iv the Khazar (780), when the latter's son Constantine vi, a minor, and his mother Irene, the future restorer of the veneration of icons, had begun to rule, John sent to Constantinople to Patriarch Paul iv (780–784) a decree of the Council of Jerusalem on the adoration of holy icons and relics, which was sent to Gothia soon after his ordination. Then, with the permission of Irene, he himself arrived in the capital, where he spoke boldly of the recognition of holy icons. He soon afterwards returned to the Crimea.[1] As Vasilievski correctly remarks, the account in the *Life* 'of John's coming to Constantinople and his discussion with spiritual and secular authorities in favor of the restoration of the veneration of icons must be accepted without any demur or reservation.'[2] The time of this visit may be exactly defined by the date of the accession to the throne of Constantine and Irene, in 780, when the government openly favored icon-worship, as well as by the date of the patriarchate of Paul iv (780–784). Since the *Life* asserts that John left Constantinople in Paul's lifetime, his voyage must have taken place early in the eighties of the eighth century. John was not present at the second Council of Nicaea, in 787, which restored icon-worship. Among the signatures of the Acts of this Council we find the name of his representative, the monk Cyril.[3] But in some other places of the Acts we also find a mention of the Bishop of Gothia, Nicetas.[4] This apparent contradiction is to be explained by the political situation in Gothia.

By that time, owing to causes which are not very clear, John had taken part in the political events of Gothia. About 787 (perhaps in 786) the Khagan of the Khazars captured the chief center of Gothia, Doros (Δόρος) and put a garrison there, i.e., made the Gothic ruler his vassal.[5] But evidently Gothia was far from being reconciled to the Khazar domination. A plot was formed with the participation of the ruler of Gothia, his chief officers, and according to the *Life,* 'of all the people,' to shake off the Khazar domination and regain political freedom. For some unknown reason John of Gothia was at the head of this plot. At first the bold undertaking was successful, and John, along with 'his people' drove out the Khazar garrison from Doros and took possession of the mountain passes (*clisurae*) which led there.[6] But soon afterwards, John was delivered up

---

[1] *Vita,* Chs. ii and iii (p. 168).   [2] Vasilievski, *Works,* ii, ii, 411.

[3] Mansi, *Sacrorum Conciliorum Collectio,* xiii, 137: 'Κύριλλος μοναχὸς καὶ ἐκ προσώπου Ἰωάννου ἐπισκόπου Γότθων.'   [4] For these signatures see Vasilievski, ii, ii, 415–416.

[5] *Vita,* Ch. V (p. 169). See Vasilievski, ii, ii, 400, 417–420, 426. In Ch. ix (p. 171) of the *Vita* we find an obscure charge brought against John by one man to the effect that he was guilty of the surrender of the stronghold to the Khagan. On this subject see Vasilievski, ii, ii, 425–426.

[6] In the printed text of the *Life* there is the reading 'τὰς χλησούρας ἐκράτησεν' for 'τὰς κλεισούρας' (Ch. v).

by a group of people[1] to the Khagan, who quickly reëstablished his power in Gothia. The conspirators fell into his hands; he spared the ruler of Gothia but put to death seventeen absolutely innocent slaves. John of Gothia himself was imprisoned in the city Phullae whence, however, he managed to escape across the sea to Amastris, which lay on the northern shore of Asia Minor. There about four years later he died on June 26.[2] Enraged at John's escape, the Khagan seized and threw into prison a number of his disciples, who after confinement and interrogation seem to have been released unharmed.[3] Among the Crimean Goths there was apparently a party devoted to the Khazar interests, who gave up John as the chief leader of the opposition. In my opinion, John being imprisoned by the Khagan in 786 or 787 could not attend the Council of 787 and was represented by the monk Cyril. But shortly after, Nicetas became John's successor on the episcopal throne of Gothia and had time enough to come to Constantinople and attend the Council.

The year of John's death may be determined only approximately, though the *Life* notes that the saint died forty days after having received the news of the Khagan's death.[4] Were the fact of the Khagan's death confirmed by any other chronologically exact source, the date of John's death would be definitely solved. But so far no such source is known. The German historian and orientalist, Gustav Weil, in his *History of the Califs* deals with the Arabo-Khazar relations at the close of the eighth century; on the basis of later Arabic historians, he explains the cause of the Khazar attack on the Muhammedans and under the year 183 of the Hegira (12 February 799–1 February 800) makes the following remark: 'According to other sources, the Khagan was killed by an Arab who wished to avenge his father's death.'[5] But this must be a mistake, because none of the Arabic sources cited by Weil speaks of the Khagan's death.[6] Therefore, since the revolt of the Goths against the Khazars took place probably in 786 or 787, since John's confinement in a Khazar prison before he fled to Amastris is not noted in the *Life* as of long duration, and finally since, according to the *Life*, he stayed at Amastris four years, we may place the death of the Gothic bishop on 26 June 791 or 792.[7]

[1] *Vita*, Ch. v (p. 169). In the *Life* is a rather obscure passage: 'ὑπὸ ἑνὸς χωρίου παραδοθέντα.' What is 'χωρίον'?   [2] *Vita*, Ch. vi (p. 169).

[3] *Vita*, Ch. vii (pp. 170–171).   [4] *Vita*, Ch. v (p. 169).

[5] G. Weil, *Geschichte der Chalifen*, ii (Mannheim, 1848), 158, n. 1.

[6] Weil refers to Ibn-al-Athir (in the thirteenth century), Ibn-Haldun (died in 1406), and al-Yafey (in the fourteenth century). See the Russian translation of these passages, made by Baron Rosen, in Vasilievski, *Works*, ii, ii, 392–393. In 1880 the Arabic text of the historian of the tenth century, Tabari, was published; this work is the source of Ibn-al-Athir's passage, but Tabari does not mention the Khagan's death. See Tabari, ed. de Goeje, ii (Leyden, 1880), 648.

[7] Vasilievski (p. 420) refers John's death to 792–798; Bishop Hermogenes (*The Tauric Eparchy*,

In solemn procession, with George, the Bishop of Amastris, at its head, with censers and candles, the body of the deceased Bishop was transported on board a vessel and sent to the Crimea, to his brithplace, Parthenitae, where it was buried in the monastery of the Holy Apostles, which had been erected there by John's labors.   According to the *Life*, John furnished this monastery 'with the magnificence of buildings, holy vessels, and various books, and placed there a very great number of reverend monks.'[1]   This was one of the large and prosperous Crimean monasteries constructed in the eighth century; it possessed a rich library.   The account in the *Life* of the construction of this monastery by John of Gothia is clearly confirmed by an inscription found in 1871 at the excavations on the modern estate of Parthenitae, which belonged at that time to the painter, D. M. Strukov.   In this inscription of 1427 we read that the church of the Apostles Peter and Paul 'was erected many years ago (πρὸ χρόνων πολλῶν) by our holy father and Archbishop of the city Theodoro and all Gothia, John the Confessor, and restored now,' etc.[2]   The inscription gives the exact name of the monastery erected by John, namely 'the monastery of the Apostles Peter and Paul' (*Petropavlovski monastyr*) and calls John the Archbishop of the city Theodoro, as his former residence was called in the fifteenth century, and of all Gothia.

Excavations in the second half of the nineteenth century and more particularly at the opening of the twentieth have revealed the very foundation of the monastery constructed by John.   The mediaeval name of John's birthplace, Parthenitae, has survived up to our day in the Parthenite valley, by the eastern foot of the mountain Ayu-Dagh, as well as in a small Tartar village, Parthenit, which is situated there, and in the name of the estate of M. G. Rayevski, 'Parthenit.'   Part of the Parthenite monastery was dug out in 1871 by Strukov, who is mentioned above.   The discovery on the floor of the central part of the church of the inscription of 1427 already quoted and an incidental discovery in Parthenit in 1884 of a funeral inscription with the name of the Abbot (Hegumenos) of the Monastery of the Holy Apostles, Nicetas, who died in 906,[3] have added some new data to the account in the *Life*.   This

---

Pskov, 1887, p. 148) to 791; Arsenius ('The Gothic Eparchy in the Crimea,' p. 65) to about 785. All three in Russian.   P. Peeters, 'Les Khazars dans la Passion de S. Abo de Tiflis,' in *Analecta Bollandiana*, LII (1934), 40–41: 'not before 791.'   Peeters does not mention my Russian article on the Goths in the Crimea.   See also N. Bănescu, 'Contribution à l'histoire de la seigneurie de Théodoro-Mangoup en Crimée,' *Byz. Zeitschrift*, XXXV (1935), 28.   [1] *Vita*, Ch. VI (p. 169).

[2] Latyshev, *A Collection of Greek Inscriptions of Christian Times from South Russia* (St Petersburg, 1896), No. 70, p. 78.   [3] *Ibid.*, No. 69, pp. 74–77.

church (the so-called Parthenite *basilica*) was thoroughly excavated by
N. J. Repnikov in 1907.[1] His excavations have shown that the church
has been several times and considerably reconstructed. Three methods
of laying walls clearly indicate three different periods of construction,
which can be easily verified by literary evidence. The foundation portions of the ruins are of the late eighth century, i.e., the epoch of John
of Gothia. Since the epitaph in memory of the Abbot (Hegumenos) Nicetas mentions that the monastery existed early in the tenth century, and
since on the other hand absolutely no traces have been found on the site
of the church pertaining to the eleventh, twelfth, and thirteenth centuries, not even a coin, we may suppose that the church was destroyed
before the eleventh century, most probably, in N. Repnikov's opinion,
at the close of the tenth century. The building seemingly perished in a
fire traces of which can still be seen in some sections of the church and
in its neighborhood; in the layer beneath the burnt layer there have been
found Byzantine copper coins of the ninth and tenth centuries. After
this destruction, according to the inscription of 1427, the church was restored at the outset of the fifteenth century. It was destroyed for the
second time late in the fifteenth century by the Turks, who after captur-
ing Kaffa (Caffa) in 1475 rapidly subdued to their power all Christian
possessions in the Crimea. In the sixteenth century the church probably was restored once more, but on a more modest scale, as hardly more
than a chapel, and by the end of the eighteenth century it was definitely
abandoned by the local Christian population.

The church erected by John of Gothia was a basilica with three naves
and three apses; like most Chersonesian basilicas it was oriented to face
the north-east. On the north-western side of the basilica was a portico
and a closed gallery (narthex). In the side naves are preserved interesting
mosaics.[2] Very interesting also is a marble tomb, No. 18.[3] The method
of laying the stones in the niche, similar to that of the oldest portions of
the ruins, and its location in the wall of the southern nave permit us to
assume that the niche was constructed at the same time as the basilica,
at the close of the eighth century. Many things indicate that for some
special reasons this tomb was particularly highly regarded through all
the existence of the church: for instance, the flagstones which covered

---

[1] N. Repnikov, 'The Parthenite Basilica,' in the *Izvestiya* of the Archaeological Commission, 32
(1909), 91–140 (in Russian). See also Le baron J. de Baye, in the *Bulletin de la Société Nationale des
Antiquaires de France* (1909), p. 276; J. Zeiller, *Les origines chrétiennes dans les provinces danubiennes*
(Paris, 1918), p. 416, n. 7. For the previous epoch see Vasilievski, II, ii, 420–422, and Latyshev,
A Collection of Greek inscriptions, pp. 72–73. Both in Russian. On Repnikov's important discoveries
see also L. Schmidt, 'Zur Geschichte der Krimgoten,' *Schumacher-Festchrift* (Mainz, 1930), p. 336.

[2] Repnikov, *op. cit.*; the plan of the church on p. 123, No. 13.   [3] *Ibid.*, p. 136.

the tomb were found *in situ*; although some of the neighboring tombs contained several skeletons, this tomb was empty. On account of this Repnikov believes that only the founder of the basilica, John of Gothia, could have been buried there. It is to be noted that John's name has survived among the population of the southern coast up to our day, although they adopted Islam.[1] At the pillaging and destruction of the church of the Holy Apostles in the tenth (?) century or in 1475 John's remains might have been carried away or destroyed; but at the restoration of the church the tomb, though empty, was carefully covered again with flagstones and thus has come down to us.[2]

Bishop Nicetas, whose name, as has been noted above, occurs with that of the monk Cyril among the signatures of the Council of 787, was John's successor on the episcopal throne of Gothia.[3]

Besides giving us some records of political events in the Crimea, the *Life* of Gothia also furnishes interesting glimpses of the situation of the Gothic Church in the Crimea under Khazar domination. The Gothic Church did not cease its relations with Jerusalem. We know that John himself, after his election as Bishop, spent three years in the Holy Land. Longinus, one of John's disciples, also made a pilgrimage to Jerusalem.[4] The Gothic trading-place Kurasaïtoi (Κουρασαῖτοι) evidently possessed a large church, for many tombs were placed within it.[5] Recently some scholars have supposed that the modern village Koreiz reflects the undoubtedly somewhat distorted name of Kurasaïtoi.[6]

During John's imprisonment at Phullae, he healed of his wounds by a miracle the son of the ruler of the city.[7] This story testifies to the influence which the Bishop of Gothia exerted over the representatives of the Khazar power in the Peninsula. There is also a tale of another miracle, when John's prayers from Amastris released his disciples, who had been

[1] Repnikov, *op. cit.*, pp. 110 ff.

[2] Some scholars believe it possible to recognize the name of John of Gothia in the name of a modern village, Ayan, on the northern slope of the mountain Chatyr-Dagh, Tomaschek, *Die Goten in Taurien*, p. 23.

[3] Vasilievski, II, ii, 415–416, Hermogenes, *op. cit.*, p. 149, and Arsenius, *op. cit.*, p. 65 without any reservations consider Nicetas John's successor.   [4] *Vita*, Ch. VII.

[5] *Vita*, Ch. VIII, p. 171. Vasilievski (II, ii, 424) conjectures that this is one of the Crimean rock-cut churches. I do not believe this conjecture is justified.

[6] Bertier Delagarde, in the *Izvestiya* of the Tauric Learned Archive Commission, LVII (1920), 15–17. Previously Kurasaïtoi had been identified with Gurzuf. See Vasilievski (II, ii, 424), who also referred to the monastery Kirizu (now Koreiz) in Crimean Khazaria, mentioned in the patriarchal charters of the close of the fourteenth century (1395). See Miklosich and Müller, *Acta et diplomata graeca medii aevi*, II (Vienna, 1862), 249, 258: 'ἡ Κυρίζου σεβασμία μονή, τὸ τῆς Κυρίζου μετόχιον.' Murzakevich, in the *Zapiski* of the Odessa Society (XIII, 31) remarks: 'Perhaps Karasu-bazar, by the stream Kara-su?' But this is a later Tartar name. Kulakovsky, in the Archaeological *Izvestiya* and Notes, IV (1896), 5–6, indicates Karasan-Charasan, a locality between Parthenite and Lambat. All works in Russian.   [7] *Vita*, Ch. XI (p. 171).

imprisoned by the Khagan because of the Bishop's flight. These two
stories perhaps justify us in considering the position of the Christians
in the Crimea under Khazar domination a favorable one. The tolerant
treatment of Christians in the Crimea confirms once more the interesting
fact of the tolerant attitude of Khazar authorities towards Christians all
over the empire of the Khagan.

In connection with the *Life* of John of Gothia it is not irrelevant to
say a few words concerning another document of the same sort. The
Life of St Abo of Tiflis, a Georgian martyr of the second half of the eighth
century (died 6 January 786)[1] relates that a certain Nerses, the ruler of
Kartalinia, which in the eighth century was under the power of the Muhammedans, was falsely accused before the Calif of Bagdad and put in
prison. After three years of confinement he was released and sent as
governor to Kartalinia. An eighteen-year-old youth, Abo, of an Arabic
family, accompanied him. Living among Christians, Abo was convinced
of the truth of the Christian faith and became a deeply sincere convert.
Under the menace of a new Muhammedan irruption into Georgia, Nerses
and Abo proceeded through the Darialan Gates (the Daryal gorge) 'into
a northern country, where is located the residence of the sons of Magog,
who are Khazars, a savage and raging people, who use blood as food and
who have no religion whatever, although recognizing the being of a sole
god.'[2] After this severe criticism of the Khazars, the *Life* continues: 'The
Khazar King received Nerses as a traveller pursued by enemies; he gave
him and all his companions food and drink. The blessed Abo seeing
himself safe from the Muhammedans hastened to join Christ and took
the holy baptism in the name of the Holy Trinity from a pious priest.
In this country there were many cities and villages which peacefully lived
in the faith of Christ' (or, as others translate, 'where Christians safely
served Christ' or 'where [the people] fearlessly confessed the faith of
Christ').[3] Later, the Khazar Khagan allowed Nerses and Abo to go to

---

[1] On this date see Paul Peeters, 'Les Khazars dans la Passion de S. Abo de Tiflis,' *Analecta Bollandi-*
ana, LII (1934), 30.

[2] K. Schultze, 'Das Martyrium des hl. Abo von Tiflis,' *Texte und Untersuchungen* (Leipzig, 1905),
Neue Folge, XIII, IV, 23; M. Sabinin, *A Complete Biography of the Saints of the Georgian Church*, I,
167 (in Russian); Brosset, *Additions et éclaircissements à l'Histoire de la Géorgie* (St Petersburg, 1851),
pp. 132–134; E. K., *Saint Abo, a martyr of Tiflis* (Tiflis, 1899), pp. 3–6 (a popular pamphlet in Russian). Peeters, *op. cit.*, p. 25. Cf. the correspondence of the Katholikos Samuel with John Sabanis-
dze concerning the compilation of St Abo's martyrology, in N. Marr, 'Hagiographic Materials according to the Georgian manuscripts of Iberon,' *Zapiski* of the Oriental Section of the Russian
Archaeological Society, XIII (1900), 51–56 (in Russian); Fr. Dvornik, *Les légendes de Constantin et de*
Méthode vues de Byzance (Prague, 1933), p. 164.

[3] K. Schultze, *op. cit.*, p. 23; M. Sabinin, *op. cit.*, I, 167–168; Brosset, *op. cit.*, p. 134; from Brosset,
T. Marquart, *Osteuropäische und ostasiatische Streifzüge* (Leipzig, 1903), p. 419; E. K., *op. cit.*, p. 7;
Peeters, *op. cit.*, p. 25.

Abkhazia. Thus, on the basis of the text of this *Life*, we see that Nerses and Abo spent some time in Khazar territory; no definite region is noted in the text. Therefore, however interesting it would be, we are not justified in affirming that Nerses and Abo visited the Crimea, as some scholars believe.[1]

In 1891, on the basis of a Parisian manuscript of the fourteenth century, Carl de Boor published a list of bishoprics (*notitia episcopatuum*) under the supervision of the Constantinopolitan Patriarchate. He attributes the list to the epoch of the first iconoclasts, or at any rate to a time before the seventh Oecumenical Council in 787, i.e., to the eighth century; at the same time he admits that his list may be not homogeneous but composed of various portions which may belong to different periods of time.[2] A portion of this list of bishoprics deals with the eparchy of Gothia and gives very interesting and unexpected information regarding the position of the Christian Church in Khazaria in general in the eighth century.

In this list of the eparchies subject to the Patriarchate of Constantinople the eparchy of Gothia (ἐπαρχία Γοτθίας) is found in the thirty-seventh place and ranks as a metropole with its residence at Doros (ὁ Δώρους, and below Δόρος). Then following the general list of metropoles and archbishoprics (οἱ αὐτοκέφαλοι) is given a list in which the bishoprics are named which are under the supervision of each metropolite. In this section in the thirty-eighth place we have the following list of the bishoprics of the Gothic eparchy:

Λη'. 'Επαρχία Γοτθίας.

α'. Δόρος μητρόπολις. β'. ὁ Χοτζήρων. γ'. ὁ 'Αστήλ. δ'. ὁ Χουάλης. ε'. ὁ 'Ονογούρων. ϛ'. ὁ 'Ρετέγ. ζ'. ὁ Οὔννων. η'. ὁ Τυμάταρχα.

From this list we see that the Gothic metropolite had his residence in the chief center of the Crimean Goths, Doros. In addition, the same list brings us beyond the limits of the Tauric Peninsula into the general

---

[1] Brosset, *Histoire de la Géorgie*, i (St Petersburg, 1849), 262: '(Nersé) avec Abo passa dans la Crimée, ou plutôt dans la Khazarie ou la Sarmatie.' Following Brosset, Vasilievski (ii, ii, 394) writes that Abo spent some time in the Crimea, and a little below (p. 395), noting the Khazar tolerance towards Christians, remarks, 'These words seem to refer to the Tauric Peninsula.' Kulakovski does not believe that Nerses and his companions stayed in the Crimea and notes that some hints in the *Life* rather suggest the region of the Volga, J. Kulakovski, 'On the History of the Gothic Eparchy in the Crimea in the Eighth Century,' *Journal of the Ministry of Public Instruction*, February, 1898, p. 184 (in Russian). See also Peeters, *op. cit.*, p. 38.

[2] C. de Boor, 'Nachträge zu den Notitia episcopatuum,' *Zeitschrift für Kirchengeschichte*, xii (1891), 519. C. de Boor published in this German periodical two articles regarding the Parisian *notitia*, xii (1891), 519–534, and xiv (1894), 573–599. The Parisian manuscript contains many brief articles on various church subjects; see Omont, *Inventaire sommaire des manuscrits grecs de la Bibliothèque Nationale*, ii (Paris, 1888), 93–94, No. 1555 (foll. 23v–28).

territory of the Khazarian empire. At the end of this document there is an explanatory note, which says:

Λζ'. 'Επαρχία Γοτθίας.

α'. ὁ Χοτζίρων σύνεγγυς Φούλων καὶ τοῦ Χαρασίου ἐν ᾧ λέγεται τὸ μάβρον ναιρῶν. β'. ὁ 'Αστὴλ ἐν ᾧ λέγεται ὁ 'Αστὴλ ὁ ποταμὸς τῆς Χαζαρίας, ἔστιν δὲ κάστρον.

If we now pass to the bishops under the supervision of the Metropolite of Gothia, we notice first of all that three of them were called after the names of peoples, ὁ Χοτζήρων,' 'ὁ Ονογούρων,' and 'ὁ Οὔννων,' and the other four after the names of places, 'ὁ 'Αστήλ,' 'ὁ Χουάλης,' 'ὁ 'Ρετέγ,' and 'ὁ Τυμάταρχα.' Since the first three bishoprics are designated by the names of peoples in the genitive case, J. Kulakovski believes that the bishops of these three bishoprics were missionaries who must have established and propagated Christianity among a population which still for the most part remained pagan.[1]

Let us examine more closely the data of de Boor's *notitia*.

1. ὁ Χοτζήρων, or, as in the explanatory note, ὁ Χοτζίρων. In this note we read, 'The bishop of the Khotzirs is near Phullae and Kharasiu, which means the Black Water.'[2] In the name Khotzirs (Khozirs) we must almost certainly recognize *Khazar*. In the name Kharasiu we have the Crimean river Karasu, which in Turkish and Tartar means 'the black water'; on this river lies the city Karasubazar. As we have noted, the city of Phullae (Phulae) remains to be identified; the most recent attempt is that of A. Bertier Delagarde (see above), who 'with much probability' has identified this city with Chufut-Kalé (Kyrkoru). In any case, from all these considerations we may conclude that the bishop of the Khozirs (Khazars) lived according to this list in the eastern part of the Crimea, north-east of the Crimean mountains. As we shall see later, the *notitiae* of the tenth century show that the residence of the bishop of the Khozirs was the city Phullae.

2. ὁ 'Αστήλ. The explanatory note to this name runs as follows: 'Astil; by this name is called Astil the river of Khazaria as well as a city (κάστρον).' Astil of course means the Volga, which Byzantine and Arabic writers call Attila, Til, Atil, Atel, Adil, Itil.[3] From Arabic sources we know that the capital of the Khazar empire bore the same name as the river on which the city was located. Here we have new evidence of the

---

[1] J. Kulakovski, 'On the History of the Gothic Eparchy in the Crimea in the Eighth Century,' *Journal of the Ministry of Public Instruction*, Feb. 1898, p. 188 (in Russian).

[2] 'Τὸ μάβρον ναιρῶν = τὸ μαῦρον νερὸν — the black water.' See Vasilievski, 'The Life of Stephen of of Surozh,' *Works*, III (Petrograd, 1915), cclxxxv, n. 1.

[3] See references in Kulakovski, *op. cit.*, p. 182; C. A. Macartney, *The Magyars in the Ninth Century* (Cambridge, 1930), pp. 50–56.

existence of a bishop in the Khazar capital. If we recall that St Abo of Tiflis visited the Khazar Khagan, was baptized in Khazaria by a pious priest, and spent three months on his way back to Abkhazia, we may with much probability assume that Abo was baptized in the capital of the Khagan, Itil (Astil). In other words, the *Life* of Abo gives us indirect evidence that a Christian center existed in the Khazar capital. For a somewhat later period, this fact is recorded by Arabic writers.[1] But this is not decisive proof for the existence of a bishopric in Itil in the eighth century.

3. ὁ Χουάλης. To interpret this somewhat puzzling name we must take into account some interesting observations of J. Kulakovski.[2] He points out the fact that the Greek name Χουάλης (Khualis, Khuali) is similar in sound to the old Russian name of the Caspian Sea, 'Khvalis-skoye,' which still survives in Russian popular songs in the form 'Khvalyn-skoye.' He writes: 'If in the eighth century there was a settlement which bore the name Χουάλης, it is natural to suppose that the Russians, on their first acquaintance with this sea, borrowed hence the name for it, and then that this city lay on the shore of the sea.' Then Kulakovski, from the accounts of the Arabic historians of the campaigns of the Russians against Berdaa at the close of the ninth century and the beginning of the tenth, conjectures that the city Χουάλη lay somewhere near the mouths of the Volga. In my opinion, credit must be given to Kulakovski's suggestions, and we must suppose that the city Khualis did exist, and most probably lay on the Khazar coast of the Caspian Sea.

We may add to Kulakovski's observations the fact that the names of 'the Khvalisskoye Sea' and of the people 'Khvalisi,' who occur in Russian annals,[3] have already long ago been compared with the name of the Khalisians who, according to John Cinnamus,[4] fought with the troops of the Dalmatians against Emperor Manuel Comnenus in the middle of the twelfth century. Up to that time they had 'been governed by the Mosaic laws, though not in their pure form.' In another place the same historian asserts that in his time the Khalisians were under the power of the Hungarian kingdom; but they differed from the Hungarians (whom Cinnamus calls Huns) in their religion, 'being of the same faith as the Persians.' The Khalisians, under the name Caliz, are often mentioned in Hungarian mediaeval sources.[5] In the forties of the nineteenth century a Hun-

---

[1] Kulakovski, *op. cit.*, pp. 184–185.   [2] *Ibid.*, pp. 185 ff.

[3] Shakhmatov, *Povestj vremennikh let*, I (St Petersburg, 1916), 7 (in Old Russian).

[4] *Joannis Cinnami Historiae*, III, 8, and v, 16; Bonn ed., pp. 107 and 247.

[5] Kunik, 'On the Turkish Patzinaks and Polovtzi according to Magyar Sources,' *Zapiski* of the Academy of Sciences, III (1855), 736 ff.; Vasilievski, 'The Alliance of the Two Empires,' *Slaviansky Sbornik*, II (St Petersburg, 1877), 247; reprinted in his *Works*, IV (Leningrad, 1930), 58–59.

garian, Jerney, wrote that the name *Khalisa* (Khalisians in Cinnamus) 'leads directly to the Khvalisi and the Khvalynskoye Sea as well as to the Volga.'[1]   Some other scholars, for example A. Harkavi, believe that the Khalisians in Cinnamus probably are the Khazars whom the Hungarian Duke Taksony in the tenth century invited to settle in his domains in order to make good the losses in population that his country had suffered from the raids of the Hungarians.[2]

4. ὁ Ὀνογούρων.   Topographically the Onogurs can be exactly located. The Onogurs, with other tribes closely related to them, such as the Utigurs, Kutrigurs, etc., are often mentioned by Byzantine writers.   The Onogurs occupied the basin of the river Kuban and the steppes northward, so that they dwelt on the eastern shore of Lake Maeotis as far north as the Don.   Sometimes their country is called in the sources Onoguria.[3]

5. ὁ Ῥετέγ is so far an absolutely unknown name.   J. Kulakovski does not venture to hazard any guess on this subject.[4]   I do not know why the word *Reteg* should remind V. J. Lamanski of the name of Rededya, a Kassogian prince[5] who was vanquished by Svyatoslav.   Lamanski notes: 'Perhaps the tradition has confused a local name with a proper name.'[6] It seems to me there is neither ground nor need for such a conjecture. For my own part I admit this geographic name is so far obscure to me. But if I may venture an hypothesis, let us suppose that the writer of the list under consideration may have transposed the consonants in this barbarian and little known name: that is, perhaps ὁ Ῥετέγ may read ὁ Τερέγ. This name, then, might be that of either the river Terek, or the city Tarku-Tarki, which lay on the western shore of the Caspian Sea[7] and is often mentioned in connection with the Arabo-Khazar conflicts of the eighth century.

6. ὁ Οὕννων.   By the Huns, Byzantine sources meant not only the Huns themselves.   On the one hand they often used this name for the

---

[1] Kunik, *op. cit.*, pp. 732, 737.

[2] See the article *Chalyzians* in the *Jewish Encyclopedia;* this gives the opinion of a Polish historian, A. Bielkowski, that the Khalisians in Cinnamus are the Khvalisi in the Russian annalist Nestor.

[3] On Onoguria see references in Kulakovski, *op. cit.*, p. 188; more recently and with more details and exactness, J. Schnetz, 'Onoguria,' in the *Archiv für slavische Philologie*, 40 (1926), 157–160; J. Moravcsik, 'Zur Geschichte der Onoguren,' *Ungarische Jahrbücher*, x (1930), 65–68.

[4] Kulakovski, *op. cit.*, p. 185.

[5] The Yasians and the Kassogians are two peoples north of the Caucasus who are mentioned in the Russian annals.

[6] V. Lamanski, *The Slavonic Life of St Cyril as a Religious and Epic Work as Well as an Historical Source* (Petrograd, 1915), p. 134, n. 1 (in Russian).

[7] For some considerations on Tarku-Tarki see F. Westberg, 'On the Analysis of Oriental Sources for Eastern Europe,' *Journal of the Ministry of Public Instruction*, March, 1908, pp. 41–43 (in Russian).

nomadic tribes of the South Russian steppes in general; on the other hand, they often applied it to various nomadic tribes, sometimes, doubtless, not Huns at all. In the list under consideration the name of the Huns must of course be used in the latter sense; but what tribe they were and where they dwelt, we are unable to determine. J. Kulakovski is inclined to place these 'Huns' in Crimean territory, perhaps in the Kerch Peninsula.[1] I myself prefer to identify the Huns in the list with some tribe north of the Sea of Azov and west of the Don, for example, the Black Bulgarians or the Magyars.[2]

7. ὁ Τυμάταρχα. The location of this place is definitely fixed: this is Tamatarkha or Tamatrakha in Byzantine sources, Tmutarakan in Russian, Matrega or Matriga in Genoese, in the modern Tamán Peninsula.

Besides the Bishop of Doros and the Khozirian Bishop the list published by de Boor includes the autocephalous Bishops of Cherson, Bosporus, and Sugdaia who were under the jurisdiction of the Archbishop of Zikhia. We know that they actually existed in the eighth century.

This list has aroused considerable interest among scholars, and various opinions have been expressed about it. The editor himself, C. de Boor, has found in it some irreconcilable contradictions. As regards the eparchy of Gothia, he assumed that this document preserved the conditions of the period of Justinian the Great. His reason was that the invasion of the Avars in Justinian's last years widely devastated the South Russian steppes and thoroughly changed political conditions there; therefore the organization described in the list could not possibly have remained intact during the Avar invasion, and could not possibly have reappeared.[3] But in spite of some insertions reflecting earlier conditions, C. de Boor, as has already been noted above, refers this list as a whole to the first iconoclastic period, i.e., to the eighth century, before the Seventh Oecumenical Council, in 787.[4]

The first serious attempt to reconsider de Boor's view of the Gothic eparchy in the Crimea was made by J. Kulakovski. He has successfully shown that no such eparchy could have existed at the time of Justinian the Great.[5] In his opinion, the Crimean Goths who had been driven

---

[1] Kulakovski, *op. cit.*, p. 189.

[2] See J. Bury, *A History of the Eastern Roman Empire* (London, 1912), pp. 410–411; Shestakov, *Outlines on the History of Chersonesus* (Moscow, 1908), p. 130. The Black Bulgarians were remnants of one branch of the Huns, somewhere between the Dnieper and the Don. Their exact seat has not yet been established. See J. Moravcsik, 'Zur Geschichte der Onoguren,' *Ungarische Jahrbücher*, x (1930), 84, n. 3; C. A. Macartney, 'On the black Bulgars, *Byzantinisch-Neugriechische Jahrbücher*, viii (1931), 150–158.   [3] C. de Boor, *op. cit., Zeitschrift für Kirchengeschichte*, xiv (1894), 590.

[4] *Ibid.*, xii (1891), 519; xiv (1894), 573.

[5] J. Kulakovski, 'On the History of the Gothic Eparchy in the Crimea in the Eighth Century,' *Journal of the Ministry of Public Instruction*, Feb., 1898, pp. 173–202 (in Russian).

into the mountains in the fifth century represented in the sixth century, in the period of Justinian, an insignificant force; accordingly it is absolutely impossible that a Gothic eparchy could have existed in the Crimea, especially one which in size and importance would have greatly surpassed the sees of the Bishops of Cherson, Bosporus, and others, on the northern shore of the Black Sea.[1]   Kulakovski concludes that the portion of the list referring to the Gothic eparchy in the Crimea is to be attributed not to the epoch of Justinian, but to the time when the whole *notitia* was compiled, i.e., to the middle of the eighth century.

In 1920, A. Bertier Delagarde after examining the list of the Gothic eparchy concluded that ' not only under Justinian the Great but also up to the outset of the tenth century and even as far as the close of the eleventh there was no period when such a metropole might have existed; hence we may decide that this portion of the list was included on the basis of much later data; it even seemingly represents plans which were only projected and never carried into effect.'[2]   The general result of his study is that since the whole list has not been carefully examined the list can not be used.[3]   In 1927, following Bertier Delagarde, in my Russian version of this book, I was of opinion that the *notitia* was a later modification or forgery, at least in part.   'But why special attention has been paid in it to the Tauric Peninsula is unknown.'[4]   In 1926, in his very important book *The Slavs, Byzantium, and Rome in the Ninth Century*, F. Dvornik casually declared that de Boor's list was compiled in the iconoclastic period.[5]

Now, I think, we may consider the year 1929 the turning point in the study of this fragment on the Gothic eparchy in the Crimea.   In that year a Russian historian now living in Yugo-Slavia, V. Moshin, published a very interesting and convincing article, 'The Eparchy of Gothia in Khazaria in the Eighth Century.'[6]   In his opinion, the ethnographic and geographic data of the fragment entirely correspond to the general setting of the eighth century.   Bertier Delagarde and I had stated that the Gothic eparchy was raised to the rank of metropole only at the close of the thirteenth century.   Referring to this, Moshin correctly remarks: 'It

[1] Kulakovski, *op. cit.*, pp. 177–178.

[2] Bertier Delagarde, in the *Izvestiya* of the Tauric Learned Archive Commission, LVII (1920), 48 (in Russian).   [3] *Ibid.*, p. 48.

[4] A. Vasiliev, 'The Goths in the Crimea,' *Izvestiya* of the Academy of the History of Material Culture, v (Leningrad, 1927), 215, 210 (in Russian).

[5] F. Dvornik, *Les Slaves, Byzance et Rome au IXe siècle* (Paris, 1926), pp. 143–144.   *Idem, Les légendes de Constantin et de Méthode vues de Byzance* (Prague, 1933), p. 160–168 (seem to date from the eighth century).

[6] V. Moshin, "Ἐπαρχία Γοτθίας in Khazaria in the Eighth Century,' in the *Trudy* of the Fourth Meeting of Russian Academic Organizations Abroad, I (Belgrade, 1929), 149–156 (in Russian).

is hardly possible that in the thirteenth century the idea would have occurred to any one of the existence of a Gothic bishopric among the
Khvalisians who, in all likelihood, had emigrated to the Magyars in Hungary in the ninth or tenth century. Likewise the city Tarku, which
played an important part in the eighth century during the seventy years'
Khazaro-Arabic war in later times . . . ceases to be mentioned in the
sources, and all traces of it disappear.' In his article Moshin endeavors
to learn whether the appearance of the Gothic eparchy described in the list
in the territory of Khazaria was possible in the eighth century. In the
middle of the eighth century, on the one hand, the pressure of the iconoclastic policy of the Isaurian emperors caused many Orthodox monks to
emigrate to the north-eastern coast of the Black Sea, among other places,
as I have pointed out above; on the other hand, relations between Byzantium and Khazaria were particularly friendly. This circumstance alone
might have evoked in Constantinople the desire to carry out in Khazaria
a new organization of the Christian Church, in order to prevent there the
formation of an iconodulic front. Besides this, Moshin takes into consideration another fact; between 737 and 763 the conversion of the
Khazars to Judaism took place. But before their official conversion to
Judaism there was a transitory period just at the middle of the eighth
century, when Christianity, Islam, and Judaism were struggling for religious supremacy in Khazaria.[1] Constantinople could not have been in-
different to this fact, which promised to have important political conse-
quences, and it may be assumed that this compelled the Patriarchate to
set to work hastily to organize the Christian Church all over the territory
of Khazaria; for this purpose the Gothic bishopric in Khazaria was to be
transformed into an eparchy with seven subject bishoprics to be established in all regions of this empire. The fragment of de Boor's *notitia* regarding the eparchy of Gothia is a trace of this project which never was
realized, because immediately after the Khazars professed Judaism. At
any rate, their conversion occurred before 759, when the Bishop of the
Goths, John, arrived in Doros; according to his *Life*, he was the pastor
only of the geographic region of Gothia and in no wise the head of the
whole church in Khazaria. Thus this fragment is not a later interpolation but a contemporary unrealized project of the middle of the eighth
century which was included in the general list and testifies to an attempt
to bring Khazaria into the bosom of the Christian faith at the period of
the missionary competition with Judaism and Islam. It is possible that
this measure had another aim: the organization of the state iconoclastic

---

[1] Moshin, *op. cit.*, p. 155. See also Moshin's article, 'Kad su Hazari prešli na židovsku vjeru
(When Did the Khazars Adopt the Judaic Faith?),' *Riječ*, xxvii, 48 (Zagreb, 1931), 9 (in Croatian).

church in Khazaria in order to prevent the agglomeration and organization of iconodulic priests and monks who had emigrated from officially iconoclastic Byzantium. But the attempt failed, and all the proposed bishoprics remained on paper. Thus may be summarized Moshin's interesting and stimulating article.[1]

In connection with this study, a Hungarian scholar, J. Moravcsik, writes that Moshin has convincingly ('in überzeugender Weise') proved that the part of the list in which we are interested was compiled in the middle of the eighth century — at any rate before 759.[2] For my own part, I am now very much inclined to support Moshin's theory of the activities of the Byzantine Church in Khazaria during the transitory period of competition between Christinaity, Islam, and Judaism, before the final conversion of the Khazars to Judaism. His idea is very fresh and illuminating.

Ecclesiastical life in Crimean Gothia apparently did not lack internal dissention and discord. At the opening of the ninth century an Archimandrite of Gothia whose name has not come down to us appealed to Constantinople, to Theodore of Studion, to explain several disputable and obscure questions. Theodore gave him his authoritative interpretation[3] and at the same time sent to the Crimea another epistle to 'Father and Archbishop Philaretus, dearest to God,' who was in all probability the hierarch of the eparchy of Sugdaia (Surozh), adjacent to Gothia.[4] The aim of Theodore's epistle was to establish peace in the Peninsula, 'which is the most useful thing possible and by which the disciples of Christ who are called by Him must distinguish themselves.' Evidently at that time the Church was not enjoying peace in the Crimea. As regards other questions raised by the Archimandrite of Gothia, Theodore recommends the use of the 'book of the Great Basile graven by God which teaches the salutary and beneficial achievements of the monastic and cenobitic life.' From this letter we learn that the monks who committed transgressions were subject to trial by laymen, i.e., 'the door was open to those who have no right to interfere in our affairs.' Some men were tonsured without passing through the required probation; some even renounced their priesthood. 'To withdraw from monastic orders is the same as to renounce baptism. However, there are some who dare to do so; it is horri-

---

[1] Besides Moshin's main article just mentioned see *idem*, 'Les Khazares et les Byzantins d'après l'Anonyme de Cambridge,' *Byzantion*, vi (1931), 317–318.

[2] J. Moravcsik, 'Zur Geschichte der Onoguren,' *Ungarische Jahrbücher*, x (1930), 64–65, 65, n. 1, 74, 81. Moravcsik has studied the actual Parisian manuscript of de Boor's list (*ibid.*, p. 64, n. 2).

[3] *S. Theodori Studitae Epistolae*, ii, No. 164; *Patr. Gr.*, xcix, coll. 1520–1521.

[4] Vasilievski, *Works*, ii ii, 427; iii, cclxvi–cclxvii, cclxxii–cclxxiii; Bruun, *Chernomorye*, ii, 127. Both in Russian.

ble even to hear [of this] . . . . The lightminded who abandon their convents must not be accepted by other brotherhoods; all should live in mutual coöperation and accord and not destroy each others' achievements.' There were also monks who, unwilling to imitate 'the life of Paradise, free from sorrow,' introduced slaves into their monasteries. 'For a monk to have a slave in his monastery is as strange as to have a wife.'

Such occurrences in the domestic life of the Gothic Church in the Crimea manifested themselves at the close of the eighth century and the opening of the ninth. Hence it is obvious that though the Crimean Peninsula was not affected by the iconoclastic movement, none the less at that time the Church there had troubles and problems of its own.

Late in the eighth century some change apparently occurred in the political life of Crimean Gothia. From the *Life* of John of Gothia we learn that about 787 the Khazar Khagan took possession of the main center of Gothia, Doros, and put a garrison there. But in the nineties of the same century, according to one of the sources,[1] there was a Toparch of Gothia, who in another source is called 'the governor of the people' in the Tauric *Climata*.[2]

This fact is connected with the family life of Emperor Constantine VI (780–797), who in 795 to the great scandal of the church and people confined his first wife, Maria, in a monastery and married a *cubicularia* (a maid of honor), Theodota, a relative of Theodore of Studion. As Patriarch Tarasius refused to sanction this marriage, the wedding ceremony was performed by a presbyter and steward (*oeconomus*) of Saint Sophia, Joseph. By this act Constantine violated canonical regulations and aroused strong indignation among the clergy and people. The *Life* of Theodore of Studion describes Constantine's depraved actions and notes that from the capital this evil reached the farthest quarters of the Empire, where local rulers in their behavior thought it possible to follow the Emperor's example. 'The King (ῥήξ) of Lombardy, the Toparch of Gothia, and the Toparch of Bosporus, referring to the violation of this law, indulged themselves in adulterous longings and unbridled desires and found justification for their behavior in the action of the Emperor of the Romans.'[3] Another version of the *Life* says that not only the rulers men-

---

[1] The *Life* of Theodore of Studion. See below.

[2] *Vita Nicephori*, ed. de Boor, p. 160: 'ὁ γὰρ τὴν τότε τοῦ ἔθνους ἡγεμονίαν ἐπανῃρημένος.'

[3] *Vita S. Theodori Studitae a Michaele Monacho conscripta*, 14, *Patr. Gr.*, XCIX, col. 252. In some works 'the Toparch of Gothia' has been incorrectly translated as 'the King of Gothia,' see Ch. Loparev, 'A Description of Some Greek Lives of the Saints,' *Viz. Vremennik*, IV (1897), 349–350; *Idem, The Greek Lives of the Saints of the Eighth and Ninth Centuries* (St Petersburg, 1914), p. 166; A. Vasiliev, 'The Life of Philaretus the Merciful,' *Izvestiya* of the Russian Archaeological Institute in

tioned but also other provincial rulers and governors of cities repudiated their own wives and brought to their homes other women.[1]

The data of the *Life* are very well confirmed by the letter of Theodore of Studion, usually ascribed to 808, 'to the brethren who are at Saccudion,' i.e., a monastery near Saccudion, probably in the neighborhood of the Bithynian Olympus. From this letter we learn that the presbyter Joseph, who married Constantine VI to Theodota and was unfrocked for it, continued in spite of this to perform his offices. Theodore writes that the Imperial conduct induced far-off rulers and governors to imitate the Emperor, as happened in Lombardy, Gothia, and in the Gothic *Climata* ('ἐν τοῖς Κλίμασιν αὐτῆς'), 'while nothing similar occurred among the pagans.'[2] The *Life* of Patriarch Nicephorus speaks of only one ruler of the Tauric *Climata*, i.e., a Gothic ruler, who, 'seized with ignominious passion, tried to divorce his wife, in order to bring [to his home] a lewd woman.' Nicephorus threatened the guilty ruler with severe punishment if he did not give up his plan.[3]

It is difficult to define the attitude of this Gothic Toparch toward the Khazar power. Generally speaking, the Toparch's residence was at Doros. But we know that in 786 or 787 this stronghold was captured by the Khazars, who put a garrison there. How long this was maintained is unknown. As far as we may judge from our fragmentary sources, the southern coast of the Crimea and the major part of mountainous Gothia never belonged to the Khazars. Therefore if at the very close of the eighth century a Khazar *Tudun* was still at Doros, the Gothic Toparch might have existed as a ruler of the section of Gothia which remained independent of the Khazars.

Generally speaking, there is no definite information on the Crimean Goths for the first half of the ninth century, i.e., before 843, when veneration of icons was restored in Byzantium, and normal ecclesiastical relations must have been established between the northern border and the center of the Empire. Some scholars believe that the Crimean Goths

---

Constantinople, v (1900), 61. All in Russian. The King of Lombardy here means not the Duke of Benevento, Arichis, who died in 789, i.e., before Constantine's domestic scandal, as Loparev asserts, but his son and successor, Grimoald, who married a Byzantine princess and later divorced her. See J. Gay, *L'Italie Méridionale et L'Empire Byzantin* (Paris, 1904), p. 39.

[1] *Patr. Gr.*, XCIX, col. 137; A. Dobroklonski, *Saint Theodore, Confessor and Abbot (Hegumenos) of Studion*, I (Odessa, 1913), xlvi; 'Vita S. Theodori Studitae,' ed. B. Latyshev, *Viz. Vremennik*, XXI 268. Both in Russian and Greek. For the dating of the compilation of Theodore's *Life* see N. Grossu, *Saint Theodore of Studion* (Kiev, 1907), pp. xiv, xxii; Dobroklonski, *op. cit.*, pp. 165–218. Both in Russian.

[2] *Theodori Studitae Epistolae*, I, 31; *Patr. Gr.*, XCIX, col. 1013. For the circumstances which induced Theodore to write this letter see Dobroklonski, *op. cit.*, pp. 605 ff. (in Russian).

[3] *Vita Nicephori*, ed. de Boor, p. 160.

took part in the rebellion of Thomas the Slavonian in Asia Minor, at the outset of the reign of Michael II the Stammerer, in 820–823. Thomas collected under his command many varied nationalities. A source contemporary with the event, the letter of Michael II to the Western Emperor Lewis the Pious, lists Saracens, Persians, Iberians, Armenians, Abasgians (Abkhaz), and 'other foreign nations.'[1] An historian of the tenth century, Genesius, who liked to relate miracles and not infrequently inserted in his writing popular tales and rumors, gives a very large number of peoples who participated in the rebellion; some of them are incomprehensible even in the tenth century; we find in his history the Hagarites (Saracens), Indians, Egyptians, Assyrians, Medes, Avasians (Abasgians), Zikhi, Iberians, Kabiri, Slavs, Huns, Vandals, Getae, Manichaeans, Lazi, Alans, Khaldi, Armenians, and 'all other nations.'[2] This lengthy list, which seems intentionally to include some artificial names to increase the effect of the story,[3] interests us because of the mention of the Getae.

A. Kunik accepts Genesius' list as valid, and attempts to define all the peoples given there; of the Getae he asserts, 'As the Getae are put between the Vandals and Manichaeans, no one else may be meant but the Goths of Asia Minor.'[4] As a mere guess Bruun is inclined to identify the Getae in Thomas' troops with the Tetraxite Goths, or, as we call them, the Trapezite Goths.[5] We find the same identification, but in a categorical form, in Loewe's book.[6] Finally, more recently, Bury made a passing remark to the effect that the Getae here may be the Goths of the Crimea.[7] Of course all these identifications are only hypotheses made on the grounds of Genesius' list, which is not reliable. At any rate, it is hard to admit that Thomas' troops formed in Asia Minor included the Crimean Goths. Topographically the Crimea, separated from Asia Minor by the sea, was far from the place of the rebellion, and as we know there were but a very few Goths in the Crimea. It is to be noted that Genesius' list does not mention the Khazars, who were well known in the ninth century and whose interests were closely connected with the Crimea.

---

[1] Baronius, *Annales Ecclesiastici,* XIV (Lucca, 1743), 63 (xix). For Thomas' rebellion see A. Vasiliev, *Political Relations between Byzantium and the Arabs during the Amorian Dynasty* (St Petersburg, 1900), pp. 21–43 (in Russian); Bury, *A History of the Eastern Roman Empire,* (London, 1912), pp. 84–110; A. Vasiliev, *Byzance et les Arabes: Tome I, La dynastie d'Amorium* (Brussels, 1935), 22–49.

[2] Genesius, p. 33. Abridging Genesius' text, *Theophanes Continuatus* (p. 55) omits the Getae.

[3] See F. Hirsch, *Byzantinische Studien* (Leipzig, 1876), p. 131.

[4] Kunik, 'On the Report of a Gothic Toparch,' p. 133 (in Russian). Only by an oversight may we explain the following statement of Tomaschek (*op. cit.,* p. 28): 'Agreeing with Kunik we must consider the Goths who were in the army of the rebel Thomas the Mysian [mysische] Goths.'

[5] Bruun, *Chernomorye,* II, 208.   [6] Loewe, *op. cit.,* pp. 72–74.

[7] Bury, *A History of the Eastern Roman Empire,* p. 89, n. 2.

About 833 the Khazar Khagan sent an embassy to Emperor Theophilus asking him to send engineers to build a fortress on the Lower Don; in support of his request the Khagan referred to danger threatening from some enemies.   Complying with this request, Theophilus sent to the Khazars the *spatharocandidatus* Petronas Kamateros (Camaterus) who reached Khazaria by way of Cherson.   He erected there a fort, Sarkel, which in Russian annals is called Byela Vyezha (the White Tower). Petronas' mission was not confined to this.   On his return to Constantinople he suggested to the Emperor that if he did not wish to lose Cherson he had better appoint there a governor (*strategos*) to head the Chersonesian authorities.   In other words, he suggested the organization of the Chersonesian *theme*.   In accordance with this proposition Theophilus appointed Petronas Kamateros himself the *strategos* of the new theme, as a man very well acquainted with local conditions;[1] the representatives of the local Chersonesian municipal authorities, for example, the *protevon* (πρωτεύων), continued to exist, but under the jurisdiction of the *strategos*. The official title of the *strategos* of the new theme was 'the patrician and *strategos* of the *Climata*' (ὁ πατρίκιος καὶ στρατηγὸς τῶν Κλιμάτων), as he is called in the table of offices compiled under Michael III and his mother Theodora,[2] i.e., between 842 and 856, when Michael forced Theodora to become a nun and exiled her.   But in the table of ranks compiled by Philotheos in 899, and in another table published by V. Beneshevich, as well as on the lead seals (*molybdobulla*) of the tenth and eleventh centuries described by G. Schlumberger, the governor of the reorganized region of Cherson is called 'the *strategos* of Cherson,' 'the *anthypatos* patrician and *strategos* of Cherson,' or 'the *protospatharios* and *strategos* of Cherson.'[3]

The facts mentioned above show that in the ninth century the same friendly relations between Byzantium and Khazaria continued to exist as in the eighth century.   Then, from the fact that on the one hand Sarkel was built and on the other hand Cherson and the surrounding region were turned into a theme with a *strategos* at its head, it is obvious that some

---

[1] *Constantini Porphyrogeniti De administrando imperio*, 42 (Bonn ed., pp. 177–179); *Theoph. Contin.*, III, 28 (pp. 122–124).   For the chronology of the erection of Sarkel see A. Vasiliev, *Political Relations*, pp. 137–138; Kunik, 'On the Report of a Gothic Toparch,' p. 145.   Both in Russian.   Also Bury, *op. cit.*, p. 416.

[2] Th. Uspenski, 'A Byzantine Table of Ranks,' *Izvestiya* of the Russian Archaeological Institute in Constantinople, III (1898), 115.

[3] Philotheos' table of ranks in *Constantini Porphyrogeniti De cerimoniis aulae byzantinae*, Bonn ed., pp. 713, 728; also in J. B. Bury, *The Imperial Administrative System in the Ninth Century, with a revised text of the Kletorologion of Philotheos* (London, 1911), pp. 137, 147; V. Beneshevick, 'Die byzantinischen Ranglisten,' *Byzantinisch-Neugriechische Jahrbücher*, v (1926), 122; G. Schlumberger, *Sigillographie de l'empire Byzantin* (Paris, 1884), pp. 236–237, 734.

danger common both to the Khazar state and to the region of Cherson was at that time threatening, so that speedy measures of the two friendly empires were required to avert the peril.   As the danger was felt in the region of Cherson, it evidently had already penetrated into the Crimean Peninsula; in other words, the Crimean Goths also were under a menace from the north.

The question arises first as to what danger at that time could threaten the Khazars and the Crimean Peninsula, and consequently the Crimean Goths; and secondly as to the extent of the new theme.

I do not believe that the formation of the new theme can be explained by domestic causes in Chersonesian life.   One of these, for instance, was the opposition to iconoclasm which was prevalent in Cherson, especially after the severe measures undertaken by Emperor Theophilus against venerators of icons.   One of the prominent representatives of veneration of icons Joseph the Hymnographos, was exiled to Cherson.[1]   But no doubt an external danger threatened both the Khazars and Cherson. Scholars, however, fail to agree what people in the twenties and thirties of the ninth century could have caused such alarm.   Some believe that Sarkel and other Khazar forts were erected first of all against the attacks of the Magyars;[2] some assert that Sarkel was built about 835 in order to protect Khazaria from the Patzinaks (Pechenegs);[3] others maintain that Sarkel was constructed against 'the savage hordes of the Turkish (Patzinaks, Magyars) and Alan peoples.'[4]   Bury writes that the fortification can not have been designed simply for defence against the Magyars and the Patzinaks, who had been neighbors of the Khazars for a long time. The danger which was impending over the Euxine lands, over both the Empire and Khazaria, must have been of more recent date, and Bury believes it was in the north, at Novgorod.   He concludes, in connection with the evidence given by the *Lives* of George of Amastris and of Stephen of Surozh, that the 'hostilities of Russian marauders, a stalwart and savage race, provide a complete explanation of the mission of Petronas to Cherson, of the institution of a *strategos* there, and of the co-operation of the Greeks with the Khazars in building Sarkel.'[5]   Finally, V. Lamanski explains the erection of Sarkel by the desire to protect Khazaria as well as

---

[1] Shestakov, *Outlines*, p. 44 (in Russian).   Cf. Bury, *A History of the Eastern Roman Empire*, p. 417, n. 1.

[2] J. Marquart, *Osteuropäische und ostasiatische Streifzüge* (Leipzig, 1903), p. 28; C. Macartney, *The Magyars in the Ninth Century* (Cambridge, 1930), pp. 74–77.

[3] F. Westberg, 'On the Analysis of Oriental Sources for Eastern Europe,' *Journal of the Ministry of Public Instruction*, March, 1908, p. 51 (in Russian).

[4] Vasilievski, *Works*, III, cxviii (in Russian).

[5] Bury, *op. cit.*, pp. 417–418.   Cf. Vasilievski, *Works*, III, cxiv; D. Ilovaiski, *Studies on the Origin of Russia* (Moscow, 1876), p. 248.   Both in Russian.

the northern possessions of the Empire against their 'new possible enemy' who had just begun to move from the north: the Varangians and 'their companions and new friends,' the Slavonic tribes of the Severians and Vyatichians (Viatichi).[1]

I do not believe that the Magyars were the enemy who induced the Empire and Khazaria to fortify their borders. In the first half of the ninth century the Magyars acknowledged the suzerainty of Khazaria; they were on very friendly terms with the Khazars and took part in their wars. The Khazar Khagan, as a reward for their bravery and military support, even gave a noble Khazar woman as wife to one of the Magyar chiefs. This was a sort of 'Magyar-Khazar alliance.'[2] Somewhat in contradiction to these friendly and allied relations between the Khazars and the Magyars is the evidence of an Arabic geographer, Ibn-Rostah (Rosteh), who wrote in the Persian city of Ispahan in the opening years of the tenth century; he says that 'for some time past the Khazars have entrenched themselves with a moat for fear of the Magyars and other neighboring peoples.'[3] On the basis of this statement, Marquart, as has been noted above, explained the construction of Sarkel as occasioned by the Magyar danger. But Ibn-Rostah is speaking generally and does not confine himself to the Magyars alone. Moreover, it is very probable that at the first appearance of the Magyars from the east in the steppes of present-day South Russia, the Khazars took measures to protect themselves against the newcomers, because at that time it was still uncertain what relations would be established between the two peoples. By the middle of the ninth century, the Magyars had left the South Russian steppes and moved westwards.[4] Thus the Magyar relations at that time explain neither the erection of Sarkel nor the organization of the theme of Cherson; the Patzinaks (Pechenegs) became dangerous at a later date,

[1] V. Lamanski, *The Slavonic Life of St Cyril* (Petrograd, 1915), p. 71 (in Russian). For a controversy between Vasilievski and Uspenski as to the date of the building of Sarkel see A. Vasiliev, *Political Relations between Byzantium and the Arabs during the Amorian Dynasty* (St Petersburg, 1900), Supplements, p. 138, n. 1 (in Russian). Without solid grounds Uspenski ascribed the erection of Sarkel to the opening of the tenth century. In the French edition of A. Vasiliev's book *Byzance et les Arabes*, Vol. I (Brussels, 1935), the note on Sarkel is omitted.

[2] *Constantini Porphyrogeniti De administrando imperio*, 38 (Bonn ed., p. 168). See C. Grot, *Moravia and the Magyars from the Ninth to the Beginning of the Tenth Century* (St Petersburg, 1881), pp. 189, 192, 204, 211–212, 217–219, 280 (in Russian); Bury, *op. cit.*, pp. 423, 490, 491; Marquart, *op. cit.*, pp. 33–35; C. Macartney, *op. cit.*, p. 108.

[3] Ibn Rosteh, *Kitâb al-alâk an-nafîsa*, De Goeje, *Bibliotheca geographorum arabicorum*, VII (Leyden, 1892), 143, ll. 1–3; D. Khvolson, *Accounts of Ibn-Dastah on Khazars, Slavs, and Russians* (St Petersburg, 1869), p. 27 (in Russian); Grot, *op. cit.*, p. 197 (in Russian); Marquart, *op. cit.*, p. 28.

[4] See J. Moravcsik, 'Zur Geschichte der Onoguren,' *Ungarische Jahrbücher*, x (1930), 89. Cf. C. Macartney, *The Magyars in the Ninth Century* (Cambridge, 1930), p. 76–77. See also F. Westberg, 'On the Analysis of Oriental Sources for Eastern Europe,' *Journal of the Ministry of Public Instruction*, March, 1908, pp. 49–51 (in Russian).

in the second half of the ninth century. Therefore we must turn to the attacks of the Russians in the first half of the ninth century.

According to the *Life* of Stephen of Surozh, which so far is known only in an old Russian version, in the first quarter of the ninth century a Russian prince Bravlin invaded the Crimea. 'A few years after the death of the Saint a huge Russian army under the very powerful prince Bravlin came from Novgorod. He took possession of the land, from Cherson [Korsunj] to Kerch [Korch]; then with a great force he came to Surozh. After ten days of violent fighting Bravlin forced the iron gate and entered the city . . . . Then he entered the Church of Saint Sophia and breaking down the door entered [the place] where stood the coffin of the Saint. On the coffin there were a royal shroud, pearls, gold, precious stones, golden candles, and many golden vessels. And he stole everything.'[1] Then follows the story of the miraculous baptism of Bravlin and his nobles (bolars). From this account we learn that Bravlin returned the sacred vessels he had taken in Surozh, Cherson, Kerch, and other places, as well as the captives, men, women, and children, taken 'from Cherson to Kerch.'[2]

Here we have the very interesting fact of an attack on the Crimea by the Russians, who devastated the coastland between Cherson and Kerch, took possession of Surozh (Sugdaia), and seized many captives and much rich booty. On good grounds, this is ascribed to the first twenty-five years of the ninth century.[3] From the evidence of the *Life* it is not to be concluded that such important fortified centers as Cherson and Kerch were also captured by the Russians.[4] But, however that may have been, the major part of the Peninsula suffered severely from this predatory campaign.

In addition, the *Life* of George of Amastris mentions an attack of the Russes (Russians — οἱ 'Ρῶς) earlier than 842, upon the city Amastris, which lay on the northern shore of Asia Minor, in Paphlagonia. We read in the *Life*: '[The Russians] spreading devastation from the Propontis[5] and overrunning the whole coastland reached the native city of the Saint

[1] Vasilievski, 'The Life of Stephen of Surozh,' *Works*, III, 95.

[2] Vasilievski, III, 95–96 (in Old Russian).

[3] Vasilievski, *ibid.*, p. cclxxvi; Westberg, *Viz. Vremennik*, XIV (1907), 234; Kartashev, 'Christianity in Russia before the Formation of the State,' *Khristianskoe Chtenie*, Mai, 1908, pp. 771–776; Golubinski, *A History of the Russian Church*, I, i, 2nd ed. (Moscow, 1901), 53 ff. All in Russian. Among Russian scholars there also exists an opinion, not very widely accepted, that Bravlin was the Russian Prince Saint Vladimir, so that the episode of Surozh related in the *Life* is to be referred to the tenth century, to Vladimir's campaign against Cherson (Korsunj). See Westberg, in the *Viz. Vremennik*, XV (1908), 235; Shakhmatov, *The Chersonesian Legend of Vladimir's Baptism* (St Petersburg, 1906), p. 121 ff. Both in Russian.

[4] Cf. Shestakov, *Outlines on the History of Chersonesus*, p. 48 (in Russian).

[5] The Propontis here means the Bosporan Straits, not the Sea of Marmora.

[i.e., Amastris]; they pitilessly killed those of both sexes and all ages, giving no mercy to old men nor sparing children; but raising their blood-stained arms against all, they hastened to make ruin as far as they could.'[1] The attack of this story is one of a series of Russian attacks; one of these, that upon the Crimea, has just been noted according to the *Life* of Stephen of Surozh. Now the Russians did not content themselves with ravaging the northern shores of the Black Sea; they extended their incursions to its southern coast.[2] The Byzantine chroniclers of the eleventh and twelfth centuries, who when they wrote of the events of the ninth century copied earlier sources, said that this 'rude and savage Scythian people of *Rus* (*Ros*) dwelt near the northern Taurus,' i.e., near the Crimean mountains.[3]

Here, then, is the new and unexpected danger which menaced Khazaria and the Crimea. The two friendly governments, Khazaria and Byzantium, were compelled to take energetic measures against Russian attacks which, beginning with the first twenty-five years of the ninth century, from that time on made themselves felt along the coasts of the Black Sea. By the thirties of this century the Russian danger was already a real fact to be reckoned with.

I have apparently somewhat deviated from the Gothic problem in the Crimea; but I believe that the facts just discussed refer directly to the Crimean Goths. The Russian raids into the Crimea, which devastated the territory between Cherson and Kerch and resulted in the capture of Surozh (Sugdaia), could hardly have failed to affect the Gothic regions. In spite of the lack of exact evidence on this subject, we may suppose that the Gothic territory in the Crimea was also devastated and pillaged. This was the first contact between the Crimean Goths and Russians; in the tenth century, as we shall see later, they came to a friendly understanding in order to get rid of the Khazar danger. It is quite possible that the first 'strategos of the Climata,' i.e., of the Chersonesian theme, Petronas Kamateros (Camaterus), with the acquiescence of the Khazar authorities in the Crimea, was entrusted, among other tasks, with protecting the Crimean Goths against Russian inroads.

In the so-called Pannonian *Life* of Constantine the Philosopher, who later took the name of Cyril, one of the two 'Apostles to the Slavs,' there is an account which is referred by Bury to the Crimean Goths. Constan-

---

[1] Vasilievski, 'The Life of St George of Amastris,' *Works*, III, 64 (Greek text and a Russian translation); also p. cix.

[2] Vasilievski, *ibid.*, pp. cxxvii–cxxxii (in Russian). Recently Miss Louillet tried to suggest that this attack on Amastris had taken place in 860; see A. Vasiliev, *Byzance et les Arabes*, I, ed. by H. Grégoire, M. Canard . . . (Brussels, 1935), 242, n. 1. The question deserves further investigation.

[3] Scylitzes = Cedrenus, II, 173; see also Zonaras, XVI, 5.

tine, on his mission to the Khazars, halted at Cherson. His journey took place, it is believed, before the middle of the ninth century. At Cherson he was notified that a Khazar governor had laid siege to one of the small cities in the neighborhood. Constantine went to the governor and by his preaching and instruction persuaded him to raise the siege and refrain from harming the Christian population of the city. On his way back to Cherson Constantine was attacked by the Magyars who 'howling like wolves' threatened to kill him; but when they saw him continue to pray, they were calmed 'by the will of God,' did reverence to him, and let him go unharmed with all his companions.[1] Probably this attack of the Magyar horde took place somewhere in the steppe regions of the Crimea, areas easily accessible to the predatory raids of the Magyar horsemen.[2] I have given this account because Bury, though without any good reason, supposed that the incident occurred on Gothic territory.[3]

In the Pannonian *Life* of Constantine there are two other passages which are often referred to the Crimean Goths. In one place the *Life* relates that on his coming to Cherson Constantine found there a Gospel and a Psalter which were 'written in Russian characters,' and met a man who 'spoke that language.' Constantine talked with the man, learned the new language, and was soon able to read and interpret the text.[4] After Constantine's *Life* was published, heated disputes arose among scholars on the subject of the writing of the Gospel and Psalter referred to. While some scholars have considered this passage a later interpolation, others have entertained no doubt that it was genuine. As to the language, scholars were at variance: most of them believed that the 'Russian characters' meant the Gothic language; some were inclined to see the Russian language, either that of the Azovo-Tmutarakan *Rus* or that of Kiev; finally, some were of opinion that the passage dealt with the Alan language, and that the Russian mentioned in the *Life* was an Alan.[5] More recently scholars have returned to the Gothic theory and asserted that the Gospel found by Constantine at Cherson was written in Gothic, in the alphabet established by Ulfila.[6]

[1] O. Bodianski, *Cyril and Methodius* (Moscow, 1862), p. 12 (in Russian); F. Pastrnek, *Dějiny Slovanských apoštolů Cyrilla a Methoda* (Prague, 1902), p. 175. Fr. Dvornik, *Les légendes de Constantin et de Méthode vues de Byzance* (Prague, 1933), p. 187–188.

[2] Grot, *Moravia and the Magyars*, p. 235 (in Russian).

[3] Bury, *A History of the Eastern Roman Empire*, p. 423, n. 4.

[4] O. Bodianski, *op. cit.*, p. 12; Pastrnek, *op. cit.*, p. 174.

[5] Kunik, 'On the Report of a Gothic Toparch,' pp. 139–140. Vasilievski, III, p. cclxxxii (Gothic writing); V. Parkhomenko, *The Origin of Christianity in Russia* (Poltava, 1913), pp. 52–56 (some bibliography is given); V. Lamanski, *A Slavonic Life of St Cyril* (Petrograd, 1915), pp. 180–193. All in Russian.

[6] G. Ilyinski, 'An Episode from the Chersonesian Period of the Life of Constantine the Philosopher,' *Slavia*, III (Prague, 1924–1925), 45–64 (in Russian); F. Dvornik, *Les Slaves, Byzance et Rome au IXe*

It is not irrelevant to recall that in another place in the Pannonian *Life* the Goths are mentioned as a nation.   During his stay at Venice Cyril had a discussion with some bishops, priests, and monks who attacked him for compiling books for the Slavs in the Slavonic language, on the ground that to praise God was allowed in only three tongues: Hebrew, Greek, and Latin.   Cyril explained that there were many peoples who had books and praised God, each of them in his own language.   The peoples were as follows: Armenians, Persians, Abasgians (Abkhaz), Iberians, Sogdians, Goths, Avars, Turks, Khazars, Arabs, Egyptians, Syrians, and 'many others.'[1]   Whatever view we take of the historical significance of the account in the *Life* of the discussion at Venice, the Goths here can mean only the Crimean Goths whom Constantine had known in the Crimea.[2]

In the same *Life* another account occurs which, without good reason, is sometimes connected with the Crimean Goths.   During his stay in the Crimea Constantine learned that the people of Phullae had an enormous oak near which they made pagan sacrifices; Constantine went to them and persuaded them to cut down the oak, root up the stump, and burn it.[3]   Of course we deal here with the city of Phullae which has already been mentioned in the *Life* of John of Gothia and the *notitia* published by C. de Boor.   Setting aside the question of the reliability of this account of Constantine,[4] I will note that Vasilievski wrote on this point: 'The fact that in spite of the Christian faith in the second half of the ninth century pagan rites continued to be performed here and that these superstitious customs were manifested in the worship of an oak, will in no wise contradict the hypothesis that the people of Phullae belonged to the Goths.'[5]   Hence it is obvious that aside from a mere mention of the Goths among other peoples given in the description of the discussion at Venice, the Pannonian *Life* of Constantine gives no evidence on the Crimean Goths.

---

siècle (Paris, 1926), p. 139, n. 3.   But cf. N. Nikolski, 'On the Question of the Russian Characters Mentioned in the Life of Constantine the Philosopher,' *Izvestiya po russkomu yazyku i slovesnosti*, I, (Leningrad, 1928), 1–37 (in Russian).   According to Nikolski, the Gospel and Psalter were written in a Slavonic script, called the Glagolitic alphabet or *Glagolitza*.   Nikolski's theory is not taken seriously by any reputable Slavist.

[1] Bodianski, *op. cit.*, p. 25; Pastrnek, *op. cit.*, p. 205.

[2] Lamanski, *op. cit.*, pp. 180–181.   Lamanski is perfectly right in rejecting the old opinion of Šafařik that the Byzantines of the middle of the ninth century identified the Varangian Russians with the Crimean Goths.   [3] Bodianski, *op. cit.*, p. 21; Pastrnek, *op. cit.*, p. 196.

[4] See Lamanski, *op. cit.*, pp. 213–214.

[5] Vasilievski, II, ii, 425.   Kulakovski saw here 'a Christian population which differed in their nationality both from the Greeks and from the Goths'; he believed them to be the Alans.   See Kulakovski, 'On the History of the Gothic Eparchy in the Crimea in the Eighth Century,' *Journal of the Ministry of Public Instruction*, Feb. 1898, p. 201 (in Russian).

Some hypotheses concerning the Crimean Goths have also been made in connection with the obscure question of the conversion of the Russians under the Patriarch Photius, in the sixties of the ninth century, i.e., a few years after the first attack on Constantinople by the Russians, 18 June 860.   In his circular letter of 867 Photius wrote that the cruel and murderous Russians had turned to Christianity and 'accepted a bishop and shepherd.'[1]   At a loss, like many other scholars, as to who those Russians were, Vasilievski was inclined to identify them previous to the middle of the ninth century with the Tauroscythians, whom he identified with the Goths, Valangoths, or Gothalans; knowing of course that the Crimean Goths had been Christians for a long time, he supposed that somewhere, north of Cherson, there might have been also some pagan Goths.[2]   But it goes without saying that Vasilievski's hypothesis has no serious basis whatever.

Finally another and more recent hypothesis has been advanced.   As it is extremely difficult to locate the bishopric which accepted a bishop and shepherd from Photius, a Russian scholar, Rosseykin, supposes that the Russians who were baptized under Photius and who lived near the Black Sea came under the jurisdiction of one of the existing Gothic bishops in the Crimea.[3]   But this attempt to clarify the obscure question of the conversion of the Russians under Photius is merely an hypothesis which has no support from our scanty evidence.

Thus both the Pannonian *Life* of Constantine and the fact of the conversion of some Russians under Photius have induced some scholars, in order to settle these questions, to refer to the Crimean Goths.   But these attempts, lacking any solid basis, not only have not clarified the problems but rather have obscured them further.

Late in the ninth century, as has been noted above, the Patzinaks (Pechenegs) who had come from the east settled in the steppes of South Russia; gradually spreading, they penetrated into the Crimea, so that some decades later, about 950, Constantine Porphyrogenitus wrote the following interesting lines: 'The Patzinaks occupy the whole country of Russia and Bosporus as far as Cherson, Sereth ($\tau\grave{o}$ $\Sigma\alpha\rho\acute{a}\tau$), Pruth ($Bov\rho\acute{a}\tau$) and thirty regions ($\tau\,\hat{\omega}\nu$ λ' $\mu\epsilon\rho\,\hat{\omega}\nu$).'[4]   Hence it is obvious that in the first half of the tenth century the Patzinaks were already occupying a considerable portion of the Crimean plain, and were to a certain extent

---

[1] *Photii Epistolae*, ed. Montakutius (London, 1651), p. 58; *Patr. Gr.*, cii, coll. 736–737.   The text under consideration is also given in Kunik, *Die Berufung der schwedischen Rodsen* (St Petersburg, 1845), pp. 335–336.   [2] Vasilievski, iii, pp. cclxxxi–cclxxxiii.

[3] T. Rosseykin, *The First Rule of Photius, the Patriarch of Constantinople* (Sergiev Posad, 1915), p. 482 (in Russian).

[4] *Constantini Porphyrogeniti De administrando imperio*, Ch. xlii, p. 179; cf. also Ch. xxxvii, p. 166.

menacing the Crimean Goths. This supposition is fully confirmed by another passage of the same work, where Constantine remarks: 'This people of the Patzinaks borders upon the region of Cherson, and if we are not on a friendly footing with them, they can march on Cherson, and raid and devastate both Cherson itself and the so-called *Climata* [i.e., the Gothic regions in the Crimea.]'[1] According to a letter of Patriarch Nicholas Mysticus to the Archbishop of Bulgaria, at the beginning of the tenth century, during the war between Byzantium and Bulgaria, the *strategos* of Cherson, John Bogas, many times called the attention of the Imperial government to the fact that the Bulgars, Patzinaks, and 'some other peoples who dwelt in those regions' were actively preparing to make war on the Empire and invade its territory.[2] This shows once more the growing might and importance of the Patzinaks in the north. I hesitate to admit that the Crimean Goths are included among 'some other peoples who dwelt in those regions.' The growing power of the Patzinaks in the Crimea meant a corresponding decline, and finally the collapse, of the Khazar predominance in the Peninsula; receding eastwards, the Khazars were forced gradually to evacuate the territory which they had been occupying for a long time. At the opening of the tenth century the period of Khazar predominance in the Crimea came to an end. We must not lose sight of the fact that the decline of the Khazar influence in the Crimea was also due partially to the clever diplomacy of the Byzantine government. As long as it was profitable, Byzantium had maintained friendly relations with the Khazars; but she rapidly realized the change which was occurring in the Crimea and adequately estimated the growing importance of the Patzinaks there. A friendly understanding with them became the corner-stone of Byzantine diplomacy, and the first chapters of Constantine Porphyrogenitus' work *On the Administration of the Empire* strikingly reflect this new attitude in the north. In addition, an-

---

[1] *Ibid.*, Ch. I, p. 68.

[2] *Nicolai Constantinopolitani Patriarchae Epistola IX:* '[Bogas] ὁ τῆς Χερσῶνος στρατηγὸς οὐ διαλιμπά-νει διηνεκῶς ἀναφέρων ὡς πᾶσαν σπουδὴν τίθενται Βούλγαροι, καὶ Πατζηνακῖται, καὶ εἴ τινα, ἕτερα ἐν ἐκείνοις ἔστι τοῖς τόποις ἔθνη, προσλήψεσθαι εἰς τὴν κατὰ Ρωμαίων ἔφοδόν τε καὶ τὸν πόλεμον,' *Patr. Gr.*, CXI, coli. 72–73. A Bulgarian translation of this letter by V. Zlatarski, 'The Letters of the Constantinopolitan Patriarch Nicholas Mysticus to the King of Bulgaria, Simeon,' *Sbornik za narodni umotvoreniya i knizhnina*, XI (1894), pp. 3–11. See V. Zlatarski, *A History of the Bulgarian State in the Middle Ages*, I, ii (Sofia, 1927), 383–391, 825 (in Bulgarian); on pp. 822–830 we have this letter reprinted in a Bulgarian translation. See Franz Dölger, *Corpus der Greichischen Urkunden*, A: Regesten, I: Regesten von 565–1025 (Munich and Berlin, 1924), p. 69, No. 575 (under the year 914); S. Runciman, *A History of the First Bulgarian Empire* (London, 1930), pp. 159–160. See also a very interesting Hungarian review of the Russian edition of my book on the Goths in the Crimea by Gyula Moravcsik, in the *Történeti Szemle*, 1929, pp. 240–249. I am greatly indebted to Professor Moravcsik for sending me a German translation of his Hungarian review; for the time being I am unfortunately unacquainted with the Hungarian language, which has become very important for Byzantine studies.

other passage of the same work notes that in order to keep an enduring and stable peace at Cherson and in the *Climata*, the Emperor from time to time instigated against the Khazars the Alans who dwelt in their rear.[1]

This change in the political conditions of the Crimea affected also the Crimean Goths.   While Khazar predominance in the Crimea was diminishing, the Crimean Goths were gradually freeing themselves from Khazar power and were again coming under the power of Byzantium.   Towards the middle of the tenth century the restoration of the power of the Empire over Gothia was an accomplished and very well-known fact.   Constantine Porphyrogenitus, who did not use the name 'Gothia' but called this region the *Climata* (τὰ Κλίματα), several times speaks of Cherson and the *Climata* (always in this combination, sometimes adding Bosporus) as of regions which must be protected by the Empire against the attacks of various enemies.[2]   Since Constantine Porphyrogenitus speaks of the *Climata*, i.e., of Crimean Gothia, as a region which was already under the power of the Empire, and considers this fact very well known, we may conclude that the restoration of Byzantine power in Gothia took place a number of years before his treatise *On the Administration of the Empire* was compiled,[3] i.e., supposedly at the close of the ninth century.[4]

4. The Period of the Russian Protectorate over Gothia in the Tenth Century and the Restoration of Byzantine Power in the Crimea

For the history of Crimean Gothia in the eighth century we possess the interesting source, the *Life* of John of Gothia; similarly for the tenth century we have tantalizing and interesting evidence, the puzzling *Report of a Gothic Toparch*.   Unfortunately this source deals with the history of only two or three years in the sixties of the tenth century; for the rest of this period we must content ourselves either with casual and fragmentary facts which are given disconnectedly among our scanty evidence or with hints which sometimes allow us to form more or less justified

---

[1] *De administrando imperio*, Ch. XI, p. 80.   The Patzinaks (Pechenegs) did not cross the Don until late in the ninth century; C. Macartney, *The Magyars in the Ninth Century* (Cambridge, 1930), p. 75.

[2] *De administrando imperio*, Ch. I, p. 68; Ch. XI, p. 80; Ch. XLII, p. 180.   See Kunik, 'On the Report of a Gothic Toparch,' pp. 76–79 (in Russian).

[3] The treatise was compiled about the middle of the tenth century.   See J. B. Bury, 'The treatise De administrando imperio,' *Byz. Zeitschrift*, xv (1906), 522–537.   Then see C. Macartney, *op. cit.*, p. 134–151.

[4] Here I give, without comment, a statement from Steven Runciman's *Byzantine Civilization* (New-York-London, 1933), p. 156: 'Possibly the Toparch of Gothia, an official who apparently existed in the early tenth century, was the head of the diplomatic bureau of Cherson.'   Runciman refers to Uspenski's Russian study, *Russia and Byzantium in the Tenth Century* (Odessa, 1888).

hypotheses.   The most interesting fact in the history of the tenth century in the Crimea is the establishment of the short-lived Russian protectorate over Gothia.

For the very beginning of the tenth century we have some brief information regarding the monastery of the Holy Apostles at Parthenit which, as has been noted above, was built in the eighth century by John of Gothia.

In 1884 at Parthenit a funeral inscription was discovered, as has been mentioned above, with the name of Nicetas, Abbot (Igumen) of the monastery.   According to this inscription,[1] Nicetas died on Sunday, 14 December 906.[2]   His funeral monument with its inscription was probably erected by a monk and presbyter of Bosporus, Nicholas, for the rather lengthy inscription ends with the following words: 'Pray, Father, for thy son Nicholas, a monk and presbyter of Bosporus.   May God have mercy upon me.'   The inscription gives no interesting information about Nicetas; compiled in the style of a synaxarium it runs as follows: 'Our Father Abba Nicetas, of blessed memory, inspired by God, Abbot (Igumen) of the monastery of the Holy Apostles, consecrated to God from his youth, brought up in monastic life, who worked, studied, and highly distinguished himself, recognized by all as hospitable and charitable, and who showed himself still more clearly to be a lover of Christ, breathed his last into the hands of the Living God, at fifty-three years of age.'   This inscription is important evidence that at the outset of the tenth century, at Parthenit, one of the trading centers in the Crimean region subject to the Goths, such an important religious center as the monastery of the Apostles Peter and Paul continued to exist.

In the first half of the tenth century the Russian danger began to make itself very strongly felt.   The text of the treaty concluded in 945 between the Russian Prince Igor and the Byzantine Emperor, which has survived in the Russian annals, gives us very interesting confirmation of this statement.   After the failure of Igor's campaign against Constantinople, among other conditions of the treaty of peace, we read the following: 'In the matter of the country of Cherson and all the cities in that region the Prince of Rus shall not have the right to make war in these localities, nor shall that district be subject to him.'[3]   It is obvious that this point

---

[1] Latyshev, *A Collection of Christian Inscriptions*, No. 69, p. 74.

[2] The tombstone discovered at Parthenit was later transported to St Petersburg, where it was studied by Latyshev.   After its return to its owner, Mr Rayevski, at Parthenit, it disappeared.   But later it was discovered again by Latyshev at Tsarskoye (now Detskoye) Selo, near Leningrad.

[3] The Laurentian text of the Russian Primary Chronicle, under 945 (*P.S.R.L.*, 2nd ed., 1926, coll. 50–51).   Shakhmatov, *The Tale of Bygone Years* (*Povest Vremennykh Let*), I (Petrograd, 1916), 57; *The First Sofian Chronicle*, in the *Complete Collection of Russian Chronicles*, v, 100–101; The

was included in the text of the treaty because Cherson (Korsun) and the cities 'in that region' had before undergone Russian attacks. Unfortunately the Greek originals of the treaties between the first Russian Princes and Byzantium are unknown; therefore it is impossible to be certain of the original version. But we may say with certainty that the Russian word *chastj* — 'portion' or 'section' ('the cities in *that region*' in an English translation) which occurs in the Russian annals is a rendering of the Greek word μέρος which is used by Constantine Porphyrogenitus in his work *On the Administration of the Empire* in the sense of 'region.' Therefore the words of the Russian annals 'the country of Cherson and all the cities in that region' probably form a direct analogy with 'Cherson and the *Climata*' mentioned several times in Constantine Porphyrogenitus' work. If this is so, we are justified on the basis of Igor's treaty of 945 in drawing the conclusion that in the first half of the tenth century the Gothic regions in the Crimea, the so-called *Climata*, suffered Russian raids, and that the treaty of 945 which was dictated by the victorious side, i.e., by Byzantium, obliged Igor henceforth to put an end to such aggressions. According to the treaty, 'So be it good that the Great Prince Igor shall rightly maintain these friendly relations that they may never be interrupted, as long as the sun shines and the world endures henceforth and forevermore.'

Now let us turn to the puzzling source which was called by A. Kunik first *Anonymus Tauricus*, and later *The Report of a Gothic Toparch* (*Zapiska Gotskago Toparkha*). By the latter name this text is known at the present time.

The three fragments of this *Report* which have come down to us were published in 1819 in the Parisian edition of Leo the Deacon. Their editor, the distinguished French philologist Charles-Benoit Hase (1780–1864), published the fragments among his valuable notes to the *History* of Leo the Deacon, which he edited on the basis of a Greek manuscript in the Bibliothèque Nationale (then Royale) of Paris. This manuscript contained various letters of Saint Basil, Phalaris, and Gregory of Nazianzus, and was ascribed by Hase to the end of the tenth century. On two folios of the manuscript Hase discovered these fragments, written in a very bad hand, with many blots and corrections.[1] In Hase's preface to his edition of Leo the Deacon, dated 1 January 1818, he tells us that at that time he was working on the description of the Greek manuscripts which had been recently brought to Paris from Italy.[2] But when Hase

---

Voskresenskaya Chronicle, ibid., VII, 281. See S. H. Cross, *The Russian Primary Chronicle* (Cambridge, 1930), pp. 159–163.   [1] See *Leo Diaconus,* Bonn ed., p. 496.

[2] See Hase's *Praefatio,* reprinted in the Bonn edition, pp. xvi, xxxi.

published the fragments he wrote in the notes, 'Thus, in this codex which had *previously* belonged to the Royal Library,' etc. From the collation of these two statements it appears that the manuscript which contained the fragments was brought from Italy to Paris shortly before 1818, but in 1818 was no longer in Paris. Therefore we are right of course in conjecturing that the manuscript was brought by Napoleon from Italy as booty among other works of art and learning, and that after the Congress of Vienna and the Peace of Paris, in 1814–1815, it was returned to Italy. It is worth noting that after Hase no one has seen this manuscript and all trace of it has been lost. It is obvious that unless this manuscript perished on its way back to Italy it ought to have been discovered later in one of the Italian libraries. However, so far all attempts to trace it in Italy have failed.[1] But we must remember that systematic and complete catalogues of the Greek manuscripts preserved in the richest libraries of Italy have begun to appear only recently; so that we may still reasonably hope, it seems to me, that this manuscript may yet be discovered somewhere in Italy. In my own view, there is absolutely no reason to imagine that Hase himself compiled these fragments, or that we are dealing here with a forgery.

I have allowed myself to dwell at some length on the original history of the fragments because I take them to be one of the most important sources for the Gothic problem in the Crimea, which is so poorly provided with systematic information. I do not intend to examine the vast number of studies on this obscure source, which have been almost exclusively published in Russian. I have no doubt whatever that the events treated in the *Fragments* refer to the Crimea. Therefore I will not take into consideration the attempts of some scholars to transfer the scene of events to other regions, as, for example, V. Vasilievski, P. Milyukov, and Bănescu, who lay the scene on the Lower Danube, or Th. Uspenski, who is inclined to refer the account to the Lower Don. The doubts of previous scholars as to time are now of no importance whatever, because the chronology of the events reported in the *Fragments* has been since firmly established.[2]

The three fragments, which represent portions of one historical account, were printed by Hase as they occurred in the manuscript, that is

---

[1] On the correspondence between Hase and E. Miller concerning the Vatican Library see Vasilievski, *Works*, II, 144. See also Kunik, 'On the Report of a Gothic Toparch,' p. 66. Both in Russian.

[2] For a critical review of the literature on the *Fragments* see F. Westberg, 'Die Fragmente des Toparcha Goticus (Anonymus Tauricus) aus dem 10. Jahrhundert,' *Mémoirs of the Academy of Sciences*, v, 2 (St Petersburg, 1901), 3–13; *idem*, 'The Report (Zapiska) of a Gothic Toparch,' *Viz. Vremennik*, xv (1908) 73–84 (in Russian); N. Bănescu, 'Les premiers témoignages byzantins sur les Roumains du Bas Danube,' *Byzantinisch-Neugriechische Jahrbücher*, III (1922), 306–310.

to say, not in chronological order.   Chronologically, the second fragment must be read first, then the third, and lastly the first.[1]   Hase was of opinion that the chief of the embassy with which the *Fragments* deal had with him during the expedition the manuscript which contains the *Fragments* and wrote an account of his journey on its blank pages.[2]   If this were so, which I doubt, we should possess the original text of the Toparch's records.

It is very important to note that the date of one of the facts referred to in the Fragments can be exactly established.   The *First Fragment* describes a snowstorm which burst after the Toparch crossed the Dnieper; during this storm 'Saturn (Κρόνος) was at the beginning of its passage across Aquarius, while the sun was passing through the winter [signs].'[3] In order to clarify this question Westberg applied to Russian and foreign astronomers, who after examination of the text came to the following conclusion: 'During the period between the middle of January 904 (or it is better to say, the second half of December 874, for the passage of Saturn in 903–904 in all probability should not be taken into account) and the middle of December 1021 Saturn only once had the position among the stars indicated in the *First Fragment*, namely at the outset of January 963.'[4]   In our further discussion we must always keep in mind this chronological definition.

First of all, general conditions of the political life of Byzantium at that time did not allow the government to devote much attention to the far-off Crimean borderland.   Towards the beginning of the sixties of the tenth century the Empire was thoroughly absorbed in its struggle with the Arabs, especially in Syria, where Saif-ad-Daulah, the energetic emir of Aleppo, was fighting against Byzantium.   Byzantine troops were waging an almost continuous war in Syria and Mesopotamia which at the end of 962 resulted in the temporary occupation by the Greeks of one of the most important centers of Syria, Aleppo.   At the same time the Byzantine navy was occupied in hostilities against the island of Crete, which belonged to the Arabs.   The Cretan expedition of 949, which was undertaken with an enormous force and complete equipment, ended in complete failure; a second Cretan expedition in 960–961 was more successful and resulted in the annexation of the island to the Empire.   Of course these undertakings diverted all the naval forces of the Empire from any

[1] I do not know why Shestakov believes that Hase printed the *Fragments* in chronological order.

[2] *Leo Diaconus*, Bonn ed., p. 496.   I shall refer to the text of the *Fragments* printed in the Bonn edition of *Leo the Deacon*, pp. 496–504.

[3] *Leo Diaconus*, Bonn ed., p. 497; Westberg, *op. cit.* (1901), p. 16 (in German); *idem., op. cit.* (1908), p. 282 (in Russian).

[4] Westberg, in German, pp. 109–126; in Russian, pp. 263–271.

interests and expeditions elsewhere. It is not surprising that during this period Byzantine influence in the Crimea was in a state of decline, and the peoples who at that time were playing an important rôle in South Russia took advantage of these difficulties. It should be remembered, however, that the importance of the Empire's relations with the northern peoples was theoretically fully recognized by the Imperial government; we know that in the middle of the tenth century Constantine Porphyrogenitus, who was unable to take the measures he wished in the north, in his work *On the Administration of the Empire* gave to his son and heir several thoughtful and wise pieces of advice as to which policy should be followed towards the barbarians who dwelt on the northern shore of the Black Sea.

The decline of Byzantine power in the Crimea affected the position of the Crimean Goths. The treaty with Igor in 945 seemed to have reëstablished the imperial power, obliging the Russian Prince to cease further attacks on the Gothic *Climata*. This paragraph of the treaty was imposed on Igor by the victory of Byzantium over him. But owing to the general conditions noted above the Empire, after 945, was unable to enforce this clause of the treaty; in other words, it could not succor efficiently in case of need Cherson and the Gothic *Climata*. Crimean Gothia, left to its fate, was forced to defend its own interests. Such was the situation in the Crimea towards the opening of the sixties of the tenth century. For this time the *Report (Zapiska) of a Gothic Toparch* must be considered a very important source for the history of Crimean Gothia.

The *Fragments* give the record of an unknown man who played the chief rôle in a war of which I shall speak later, and who headed an embassy to the ruler 'who reigned north of the Ister';[1] the aim of the embassy was to make a treaty. From a literary point of view the *Fragments* are no mere collection of notes; they are, without doubt, a piece of serious literary work. Krumbacher characterized the style of the anonymous author as remarkably skillful and even humorous.[2] It was later pointed out that the author was very familiar with Thucydides; he does not repeat phrases of the great Greek historian, but he adopted his general style and, what is more important, he was undoubtedly affected by the most tragic passages of his history.[3]

The account is written in the first person. No one of the peoples who are mentioned in the *Fragments* is called by name. There are also very few topographical names: the *Second Fragment* mentions 'the north of

---

[1] *Leo Diaconus*, Bonn ed., p. 503: 'πρὸς τὸν κατὰ τὰ βόρεια τοῦ Ἴστρου βασιλεύοντα.'

[2] Krumbacher, *Geschichte der byzantinischen Litteratur*, p. 269.

[3] See a very interesting article by S. V. Melikova, 'The Toparch of Gothia and Thucydides,' in *Izvestiya* of the Russian Academy of Sciences, 1919, pp. 1063–1070 (in Russian).

the Ister' (τὰ βόρεια τοῦ "Ιστρου) and the *Climata* (τὰ Κλήματα); in the *Third Fragment* occur a ruler 'who reigned north of the Ister' as noted above, and the *Climata* once more; in the *First Fragment* the river Dnieper (ὁ Δάναπρις), a settlement or village, Borion (ἡ κώμη ἡ Βορίων), and Mauro-castron (Μαυρόκαστρον).

The most definite point is the *Climata*, by which we mean the Gothic territory in the Crimea.   The spelling τὰ Κλήματα for τὰ Κλίματα need not puzzle us, because this is the common manuscript confusion between the Greek letters η and ι.[1]   In the *Fragments* the *Climata* mean rather a city than a country.[2]   But we have already met something similar in the name of the Gothic region Dori with its various forms, when in some sources Dori signified a region and in others a city or fort.

The origin of the author of the *Report* is not certain.   He may have been, as A. Kunik asserts, a Greek 'who was very familiar with the Gothic language'; but in my opinion he may have been a Crimean Goth who was well acquainted with the Greek language.   This question is of secondary importance.   It goes without saying that after a long period of cultural and political Byzantine influence on the Crimean Goths, a considerable part, if not all, of them must have mastered the Greek language.   They were doubtless an example of those bilingual peoples who, preserving their own language in common use, employ the state and more refined language in their official relations and literary works.   The Crimean Goths may be termed the Gotho-Greeks (Γοτθογραῖκοι) — the name given in Byzantine sources sometimes to designate the hellenized Goths of Asia Minor or some other places.[3]   From the Crimea, of course, came the merchant, a 'hellenized Goth' (*Grechanin Gotfin*) whom in the twelfth century St Antonius the Roman met in Novgorod, and who spoke Latin, Greek, and Russian.[4]

In my opinion, the best designation for the unknown ruler of the *Climata* who is mentioned in the *Fragments* would be the Toparch of

---

[1] See *De administrando imperio*, p. 68, l. 24, and a note to the latter.

[2] See the end of the *Second Fragment*, p. 502; Westberg, § 7 (in German, p. 23; in Russian, p. 285).

[3] See *Theophanis Chronographia*, ed. de Boor, p. 385; 'Acta Graeca SS. Davidis, Symenois et Georgii Mitylenae in Insula Lesbo,' 34, *Analecta Bollandiana*, XVIII (1899), 256: 'φίλου γάρ τινος ἐν τοῖς Γοτθογροικίας λεγομένης ὑπάρχοντος μέρεσι.' On the name 'Γοτθογροικία' the editor of the *Life* offers the following note: 'Hoc nomine rarius usurpato Gotthiam seu Chersonesum Tauricam designari putaverim.' More correctly Kulakovski refers this passage to Asia Minor, to the theme *Optimaton*, Kulakovski, *History of Byzantium*, III (Kiev, 1915), 415–416 (in Russian).   E. Stein supports the hypothesis of the *Life's* editor, E. Stein, *Studien zur Geschichte des byzantinischen Reiches* (Stuttgart, 1919), pp. 126–127.

[4] 'The Tale of the Life . . . of Antonius the Roman,' in the *Pravoslavni Sobesednik*, II (Kazan, 1858), 165–166; also in the *Monuments (Pamyatniki) of Old Russian Literature*, ed. by Kushelev-Bezborodko, I (St Petersburg, 1860), 265.   Both in Old Russian.

Gothia.   A. Kunik holds this view and it can be justified by the sources
given above, for example, the letters of Theodore of Studion.

Following chronological order, we shall begin with the *Second Frag-
ment*.[1]   The story is told in the first person, sometimes plural, sometimes
singular, i.e., from our point of view either in the name of the Crimean
Goths or better of the population of Crimean Gothia, or directly in the
name of the Toparch himself.   The story begins with the decision of the
Crimean Goths to anticipate a barbarian attack by attacking first.   The
Fragment gives the following description of these unnamed barbarians.
They most cruelly ruined and destroyed all, like wild beasts, raging in
every way; ferociously and causelessly they decided to make the country[2]
a prey to the Mysians[3] [i.e., to raze everything to the ground].   The
former mildness and justice of these barbarians had allowed them to attain the greatest triumphs; cities and peoples had willingly joined them.
But then they revealed injustice and despotism towards their subjects;
they determined to enslave and destroy their subject cities instead of supporting and aiding them; innocent chiefs could not escape death.   In the
regions bordering on Gothia more than ten cities and no less than five,
hundred villages had been totally deserted; innocent people protected by
oaths had fallen a prey to hands and swords.   Finally fate brought these
barbarians to the region of the Toparch, who took energetic steps to avert
the serious danger.   The war between the Toparch and the barbarians
broke out without formal declaration when winter was near at hand, because the sun was already not far from the winter [signs], that is, late in
the autumn.   The barbarians with a large number of horse and foot
plundered and devastated the Toparch's regions, and razed to the ground
the walls of his chief city, so that his subjects were forced to dwell in, and
make sallies from, the destroyed city, which was little better than a village.   But in spite of this the Toparch, opposing archers to the barbarian
foot and cavalry to their horse, forced them towards night to retreat;
afterwards he determined to repeople the *Climata*.   For this purpose he
built a fort ($\phi\rho o\acute{v}\rho\iota o\nu$), planning from this starting point to rebuild the
whole city.   Here the *Second Fragment* ends.

The *Third Fragment*[4] (chronologically the second) opens with the account of the rapid construction of the fort and a surrounding moat.   The
most important possessions were stored in the fort, and everything else

---

[1] Hase, in the Bonn edition of *Leo the Deacon*, pp. 500–502; Westberg, in German pp. 19–23, in
Russian pp. 283–285.

[2] In the manuscript there occurred originally ‘$\tau\grave{\eta}\nu$ $\dot{\eta}\mu\hat{\omega}\nu$ $\gamma\hat{\eta}\nu$’; later this was corrected to ‘$\tau\grave{\eta}\nu$ $a\dot{v}\tau\hat{\omega}\nu$
$\gamma\hat{\eta}\nu$.’   [3] This is a Greek proverb denoting anything that can be plundered with impunity.

[4] Hase, in the Bonn edition of *Leo the Deacon*, pp. 503–504; Westberg, in German pp. 23–26, in
Russian pp. 285–286.

somewhere outside, in another enclosure of the city. The barbarians apparently withdrew and at least temporarily gave up the war, for more than a hundred riders and three hundred slingers and archers whom the Toparch led out to battle were unable to discover their enemy. Taking advantage of this interval in hostilities, the Toparch set to work to restore the old wall and to prepare his troops for future warfare. At the same time he sent messengers to his 'adherents' (πρὸς τοὺς ἡμῖν προσέχοντας); coming from all quarters they held a meeting of nobles, called in the text 'best' men. The Toparch, forseeing future complications with the barbarians, proposed that they should consider which ruler they should first approach in order to profit as much as possible. 'Either because they had never enjoyed the Imperial favor and were not influenced by Greek customs and first of all sought autonomy, or because they were neighbors of the ruler north of the Danube (πρὸς τὸν κατὰ τὰ βόρεια τοῦ "Ιστρου βασιλεύοντα), who possessed a strong army and was proud of his military forces and from whose people they did not differ in customs and manners, they determined to make a treaty with him and surrender to him; and they unanimously decided that I should do the same.' The Toparch went to the northern ruler and briefly explained the cause of his coming. Much struck with the importance of the matter, the ruler willingly reinstated the Toparch in his authority over the *Climata*, added one satrapy more, and granted him annual revenues from the ruler's own country. Here the *Third Fragment* ends.

The *First Fragment*[1] (the longest, and chronologically the third) describes the Toparch's return home. His way crossed the Dnieper; but on account of the breaking up of the ice the Toparch and his companions could not cross the river. A few days later, however, the Dnieper froze over, so that the embassy crossed safely and arrived in the village Borion (τὴν Βοριῶν), where they intended to rest a few days and then proceed to Maurocastron (τὸ Μαυρόκαστρον).[2] But a violent blizzard which raged for many days prevented them for a considerable time from returning to their own country. In the description of this storm we find the astronomical information mentioned above of the passage of Saturn across Aquarius which occurred at the opening of January, 963. Finally, the embassy set out; according to the *Fragment*, 'the local population cordially welcomed us, all clapping their hands in my honor (εἰς ἐμέ) and everyone regarding me as his kinsman and giving me his best wishes.' The

---

[1] Hase, in the Bonn edition of *Leo the Deacon*, pp. 496–498; Westberg, in German pp. 14–19, in Russian pp. 281–283.

[2] *Maurocastron* means *black fort:* on Italian maps *Nigropolis*. For Borion and Maurocastron see A. Bertier Delagarde, 'On the location of Maurocastron in the Report of the Gothic Toparch,' *Zapiski* of the Odessa Society of History and Antiquities, XXXIII (1919), 1–20 (especially 18–20).

return journey was extremely difficult, owing to deep snow and heavy winds. At night they slept on their shields. They were all filled with despair. Because of the storm the guides lost their direction and led the embassy astray. In addition, from a friendly country the Toparch and his companions entered a hostile territory. 'On account of this our situation was dangerous; calamity threatened us from both winter and enemies.'

Here end the *Fragments* published by Hase. Let us consider them in more detail.

The date of the embassy has been exactly fixed: the Toparch's return journey from the northern ruler occurred at the beginning of January, 963; on the other hand, hostilities between the Toparch and the barbarians, which resulted in the embassy, began according to the *First Fragment* late in the autumn, that is, late in the autumn of the previous year, 962. Without doubt, 'the ruler north of the Ister (Danube) possessing a strong army and proud of his military forces,' as he is characterized in the *Third Fragment*, can be none other than the Russian Prince Svyatoslav. In the Russian Primary Chronicle under the year 6472 (964), we read a characterization of Svyatoslav which is analogous to that of the *Third Fragment*: 'When Prince Svyatoslav had grown up and matured, he began to collect a numerous and valiant army. Being valiant himself and stepping light as a leopard, he undertook many campaigns.'[1] Leo the Deacon calls Svyatoslav 'a man rash, valiant, strong, and active.'[2] Most probably the Toparch met Svyatoslav in Kiev,[3] and there came to the agreement mentioned at the end of the *Third Fragment*; Svyatoslav reinstated the Toparch as ruler of the *Climata*, added to his jurisdiction one more region (satrapy), in all likelihood also in the Crimea, and promised to grant him an annual remuneration from Svyatoslav's own revenues. Thus, beginning with the winter of 962, when this agreement was made, we must admit a Russian protectorate over Crimean Gothia. In my opinion, we have no ground for believing that this protectorate was established earlier. Therefore A. Kunik's view that 'from a purely historical standpoint it is most probable that this protectorate originated before 940'[4] cannot be accepted. On the other hand, according to the treaty with Igor Byzantine authority over Gothia was reëstablished in 945. The Russian protectorate over Gothia was of very short duration; it lasted only ten years, from 962 to 972. I shall speak of this subject below.

[1] Ed. Shakhmatov, p. 75; *The Russian Primary Chronicle*, ed. S. H. Cross (Cambridge, 1930), p 170. [2] *Leonis Diaconi Historiae*, v, 2 (Bonn ed., p. 77).

[3] Bruun considered it possible that this meeting might not have been in Kiev but 'in some other place north of the Danube, especially if the ruler were Prince Svyatoslav'; Kunik, 'On the Report of a Gothic Toparch,' p. 126 (in Russian). [4] Kunik, *op. cit.*, p. 91; see also p. 89.

Who were the barbarians who raided the Toparch's territory? As we know, their name is not given in the *Fragments*; but general considerations and the information which we can draw from the *Fragments* give us solid ground for recognizing the Khazars. We have already spoken sufficiently of the Khazar predominance in the Crimea and of the system of government in the Khazar Empire. In the eighth and ninth centuries, friendly relations between Byzantium and Khazaria had existed, and the policy of these empires in the Crimea was regulated by this friendship. But in the tenth century circumstances changed. At that time Byzantine influence in the Crimea was in a state of decline At the same time, because of the raids and attacks of the Magyars and Russians throughout the ninth century, and of the Patzinaks (Pechenegs) at the close of this century, the Khazar empire was also declining and was no longer able to play the leading part in the south-east of present-day Russia. Such a weakening of Khazaria, of course, was felt in the Crimea, where Gothia was eager to throw off the last traces of her Khazar dependence. It seems to me that the account in the *Fragments* most clearly refers to the Khazars. According to the *Fragments*, the barbarians had formerly distinguished themselves by mildness and justice; thanks to this cities and peoples had voluntarily joined them. Of all the peoples of that period who dwelt in the south of Russia, such a characterization could apply only to the Khazars and their Khagans who by their political wisdom and religious tolerance succeeded in keeping under their power a number of peoples and in creating a vast and economically prosperous state, which was bound by ties of friendship with the great Eastern Empire. It goes without saying that neither the Magyars nor the Russians nor the Patzinaks could boast of such qualities. Only later, in the tenth century, during their final decline and the dismemberment of their empire did the Khazars who remained in the Crimea become such cruel barbarians as those depicted in the *Fragments*. But at that time they evidently still preserved some remnants of their former military organization, and they attacked the Gothic region with a considerable number of horse and foot.

The aim of the Toparch's embassy to Svyatoslav at Keiv was to secure the latter's protection against the Khazars. Svyatoslav, who was greatly interested in Khazaria, heartily welcomed the Toparch's proposition; according to the *Fragments*, 'he considered this matter very important.' Pledging himself to defend the Gothic *Climata*, Svyatoslav did not confine himself to promises only; he at once rendered Gothia real aid. This action, of course, entirely suited his own political plans and interests. In this connection the Russian Primary Chronicle is of great help to us; it gives very interesting information on Svyatoslav's relations with the Khazars, which we must correlate with the accountof the *Fragments*. Under the year 6472 (964) the Russian Chronicle notes that Svyatoslav inquired of the Vyatichians to whom they paid tribute; and they made answer that they 'paid a silver piece per ploughshare to the Khazars';[1] in other words, at that time the Khazars still had authority among Svyatoslav's neighbors. Then, because of his own political interests and his treaty with the Toparch, Svyatoslav in 6473 (965) 'sallied forth against the Khazars. When they heard of his approach, they went out to meet him with their Prince, the Khagan, and the armies came to blows. When the battle thus took place, Svyatoslav defeated the Khazars and took their city of Byelavyezha,' i.e. Sarkel.[2] Afterwards proceeding south he conquered also the Yasians and Kassogians. In the following year, 6474 (966), he conquered the Vyatichians, who paid tribute to the Khazars, and made them his tributaries.[3]

It is well known that the chronology of the Russian Chronicles for the early period of the history of Russia is not exact. But since we know the exact date of the Toparch's return from Kiev to the Crimea, January, 963, we may with full confidence ascribe Svyatoslav's campaign against the Khazars to the same year, 963, instead of to the year given by the Russian Chronicle, 6473 (965), or, more precisely, the period from 1 September 964 to 1 September 965.

The question now arises as to who were the Toparch's 'adherents,' the 'best' men who met together to decide to whom they should appeal for help. According to the *Fragments*, the Toparch's 'adherents' were not under the power of Crimean Gothia, but belonged to some neighboring people. From the *Third Fragment* we learn that they 'never enjoyed Imperial favor nor were influenced by Greek customs but first of all sought autonomy.' It is obvious that the text can not refer to the Crimean Goths, who for a considerable time were under an Imperial, i.e. Byzantine, protectorate and were very much influenced by Greek customs; the question of autonomy or independence never arose among the Crimean Goths, who lived first under Byzantium and then under the Khazars. Furthermore the same *Fragment* notes that the Toparch's 'adherents' were neighbors of a ruler who reigned north of the Ister (Danube) . . . and that in their own customs and manners they did not differ from his people, i.e., they did not differ from Svyatoslav's Russians.

In my opinion, the Toparch's 'adherents' were the Russes (*Rusj*, 'Ρῶs) who, according to the evidence of the *Lives of the Saints* discussed above, in the first half of the ninth century raided the Crimea and, of course, re-

---

[1] Ed. Shakhmatov, p. 76; S. H. Cross, *op. cit.*, p. 171.
[2] *Ibid.* On Byelavyezha or Sarkel see above.   [3] *Ibid.*

mained there in the tenth century.   Where these Russes came from originally I am as yet unable to say.   The statement of the *Fragments* that 'they never enjoyed Imperial favor nor were affected by Greek customs but first of all sought autonomy' applies very well to the Russians in the Crimea.   They probably obtained autonomy soon after by founding the Princedom of Tmutarakan.   These Russes suggested to the Toparch that he call for aid on the powerful northern Prince, Svyatoslav.

Finally, the last question connected with the *Fragments* is, who were the enemies whose territory the Toparch's embassy entered on its return? I believe that this question may be easily answered: these enemies were the Patzinaks, who in the first half of the tenth century occupied the south of Russia and a portion of the Crimea, where, as has been pointed out above, their growing power balanced the Khazar decline.

We may sum up as follows our consideration of the *Report of a Gothic Toparch*.   Wishing to restore their tottering predominance in the Crimea, the Khazars in 962 resorted to violence and pillaging; more than ten cities and no less than five hundred villages in the Crimea were devastated, according to the statement of the *Fragments*, which is obviously exaggerated.   Late in the autumn of the same year (962), the Khazars burst upon Gothia with a large number of horse and foot, devastated the country, and leveled the walls of the chief city to the ground.   It would be most natural to consider this chief city the well-known center of Gothia Dory — Doros; but in the *Third Fragment* this city is called the *Climata*. It might be possible for the author to give to the city the name of the whole region; but even if we admit this, we must confess that the account in the *Fragment* of the construction of a fort with a moat near the *Climata*, and some additional defense, does not agree with the position of Dory, of which we have spoken above.[1]

The Toparch with his troops repulsed the Khazars and forced them to discontinue hostilities for a time at least.   The Toparch rapidly restored the fort, and realized that without foreign support he would be unable to withstand the Khazars.   Without hope of aid from Byzantium, he called on the Russians who were at that time in the Crimea, and who as well as, perhaps even more than, the Goths were suffering from the Khazars. These Russians persuaded the Toparch to appeal to the Russian Prince, Svyatoslav.   Early in the winter of 962, apparently, since his conflict

---

[1] Cf. L. Schmidt, *Geschichte der deutschen Stämme bis zum Ausgang der Völkerwanderung*, 2nd ed. (Munich, 1934), p. 400: 'After a fight with the Khazars in 962, when Doros was destroyed, the Toparch decided to transfer the chief city to Mankup, which had been recently built in the neighbourhood.   Doros continued to be a settlement, but not a fortress, and in the sixteenth century it was completedly abandoned.'   Cf. the results of recent Russian archaeological expeditions in the Crimea mentioned in the preface of this book.

with the Khazars took place as we know late in the autumn of that year, the Toparch set out north to Kiev.

It is a great pity that the report of the Toparch's interview with Svyatoslav has not come down to us in the three published *Fragments*. We know, however, that Svyatoslav willingly agreed to keep control over the Gothic *Climata*, confirmed the Toparch in his authority as his vassal, added to his territory another region (satrapy), and granted him annual revenues from his own country. After the agreement was concluded, late in 962 the Toparch left Kiev for the Crimea. For some days the breaking up of the ice on the Dnieper prevented the embassy from crossing. But soon the Dnieper froze over, so that the Toparch and his companions safely crossed the river and arrived in the village of Borion. There early in January 963, as we know exactly from astronomical data, a violent blizzard broke out. Only after the storm had ceased could the embassy continue its journey. The account in the *Fragments* of the hearty welcome of the embassy by the local population, who 'clapped their hands and regarded the Toparch as their kinsman, giving him their best wishes,' shows that at that time, before the beginning or the first half of January, the embassy was still in allied and friendly territory. When they left the Russian possessions, they were badly harassed by the Patzinaks (Pechenegs). The *Fragments* give no information as to how the Toparch reached his Crimean residence.

Thus, beginning with the winter of 962, when the treaty between the Toparch and Svyatoslav was concluded in Kiev, the Gothic *Climata* or Crimean Gothia fell under a Russian protectorate. This did not affect Chersonesus, which continued under the power of the Empire. But as we learn from the treaty between Svyatoslav and the Empire in 971. Chersonesus or Korsun was several times raided by the Russians. These new conditions in the Crimea must have directed the attention of the Byzantine government to Svyatoslav, the more so as the Khazars were no longer dangerous.

Because of Bulgaria Byzantium became involved in a war with Svyatoslav and after a long and stubborn struggle defeated him. In July, 971,[1] John Tzimisces made a treaty of peace with the Russian Prince. A portion of this treaty has survived in the Russian Primary Chronicle, where among other provisions Svyatoslav takes the following oath: 'I will therefore contemplate no attack upon your territory, nor will I collect an army or foreign mercenaries for this purpose, nor will I incite any other foe

---

[1] The chronology of the war between John Tzimisces and Svyatoslav has been recently reconsidered and challenged by D. Anastasievié in five articles. I shall not deal with this problem here. See F. Dölger, 'Die Chronologie des grossen Feldzuges des Kaisers Johannes Tzimiskes gegen die Russen,' Byzantinische Zeitschrift, xxxii (1932), 275–292 (especially 292).

against your realm or against any territory pertaining thereto, and particularly against the district of Cherson, or the cities thereto adjacent,
or against Bulgaria.   But if any other foe plans to attack your realm, I
will resist him and wage war upon him.'[1]

From this statement it is obvious that after the establishment of his
protectorate over Gothia Svyatoslav attacked Chersonesus.   The passage concerning Cherson in Svyatoslav's treaty should be compared
with the corresponding clause in Igor's treaty, of which we have spoken
above.   Igor's treaty speaks of 'the country of Cherson and all the cities
in that region,' which, as I have proved above, refers to 'Chersonesus and
the *Climata.*'   I believe, therefore, that Svyatoslav's treaty contains an
identical statement, in which for the words in Igor's treaty 'the cities
in that region' occurs simply 'the cities thereto adjacent.'   Hence it is
clear that according to the treaty of 971 the defeated Svyatoslav pledged
himself not only not to attack Chersonesus but also to give up his recent
protectorate over the Gothic *Climata.*   Therefore, I believe, the Russian
protectorate over Gothia which was established late in 962 came to an
end in 971, when the Gothic *Climata* or Crimean Gothia was restored to
the power of Byzantium.   As a result of the final decline of the Khazar
rule, the Empire regained, for some period of time, its dominating influence
in the Crimea.

To the period of Svyatoslav should also be referred the mention of the
main Gothic center in the Crimea in its later form 'Mankup,' in an answer
of the Khazar King Joseph to Khazdai-ibn-Shaprut, a very prominent
Hebrew under the califs of Spain.   Khazdai's letter is usually regarded
by scholars as genuine; but the authenticity of King Joseph's letter is
often doubted.   Before 1875 Joseph's letter had not been discovered in
any manuscript, but was known only in a brief version printed in 1577 in
Constantinople by Isaak Akrish under the title 'Qol Mebasser' (Announc-
ing Voice).   But among the manuscripts brought from Egypt in the nineteenth century by a Russian Hebrew scholar, Firkovich, and later discovered in St Petersburg (Leningrad) there has been found a complete
text of Joseph's letter, which was published, translated into German and
later into Russian, by A. Harkavy.[2]   Firkovich's name, however, has
several times been connected with falsified documents, so that his discovery of the text of Joseph's letter has not been entirely accepted.

---

[1] Ed. Shakhmatov, p. 86; Cross, *op. cit.*, p. 176.

[2] A. Harkavy, 'Ein Briefwechsel zwischen Cordova und Astrachan zur Zeit Swjatoslaw's (um 960),
als Beitrag zur alten Geschichte Süd-Russlands,' *Russiche Revue*, VI (1875), 70, 79–80; *idem*, 'Accounts of the Khazars, Khazar Letters,' *Evreiskaya Biblioteca*, VII (1879), 153–162 (in Russian).
Both versions have been translated also by P. Cassel, *Der Chazarische Königsbrief aus dem 10. Jahrhundert* (Berlin, 1877), pp. 25 ff.

Scholars dealing with the letter have fallen into two groups: supporters of its authenticity (Harkavy, Cassel, Westberg), and opponents (Marquart). Some students, as for instance Cassel, consider the brief version published in the sixteenth century as genuine, disparage Firkovich's manuscript, and believe its additions are only later interpolations.[1]

This discrepancy is of importance for our purpose, because the passage in which we are interested is lacking in the printed version of 1577, and is found only in Firkovich's manuscript. In this passage, speaking of the limits of the Khazar state, Joseph wrote: 'West [lay] Sharkel, Samkrz, Kerz, Sugdai, Alus, Lambat, Bartnit, Alubika, Kut, Mankup, Budak (Burak?), Almam, and Gruzin.'[2] Instead of this enumeration the printed version has only: 'West dwell thirteen powerful nations.'[3] Of the thirteen places given above, the majority of which can be easily recognized by their modern names in the Crimea, two are particularly interesting, Kut and Mankup. Mankup, which has survived down to the present, is as we know the Tartar name of Theodoro. Some scholars recognize in the name 'Kut' Iskut or Uskut, or Kutlak near Sudak;[4] others consider it the region or the fortress of the Crimean Goths (κάστρον Γοτθίας).[5] In my opinion, Mankup and Kut are different names of the same place. Perhaps we may suppose in the manuscript a hyphen between Kut and Mankup (Kut-Mankup), indicating that we are dealing with two names for one place.

If this passage in Firkovich's manuscript had been beyond doubt, it would have proved the interesting and, I may say incomprehensible existence of the name Mankup for the Gothic center in the Crimea as early as the tenth century. But since Turko-Tartar names in the Crimea appear later than the tenth century and in my opinion can in no wise be explained so early, I believe that the list of thirteen geographic points in Firkovich's manuscript is really a later interpolation.

We might have supposed that the capture of Cherson (Korsun) — Chersonesus by the Russian Prince Vladimir in 988 or 989 also affected to a certain extent Crimean Gothia, and that Vladimir thus regained his power over the Gothic *Climata*. But this was not the case.

Our sources for Vladimir's campaign against Cherson (Korsun) afford

---

[1] Harkavy, "Accounts of the Khazars: B, History of Khazar Letters in the European Scholarly World in the Course of Three Centuries,' *Evreiskaya Biblioteca*, VIII (1880), 140; Westberg, 'On the Analysis of Oriental Sources for Eastern Europe,' *Journal of the Ministry of Public Instruction*, March, 1908, p. 35; J. Marquart, *Osteuropäische und ostasiatische Streifzüge* (Leipzig, 1903), pp. 9, 11. P. Kokovtzov, *A Hebrew-Khazar Correspondence in the Tenth Century* (Leningrad, 1932), xv–xx (in Russian).   [2] Harkavy, *op. cit.*, *Russische Revue*, VI, 87, and *Evreiskaya Biblioteca*, VII, 160.

[3] Harkavy, *Evreiskaya Biblioteca*, VII, 165.

[4] Harkavy, *Russische Revue*, VI, 87, 94 ff., and *Evreiskaya Biblioteca*, VII, 165.

[5] Westberg, *Izvestiya* of the Academy of Sciences of St Petersburg, II (1899), 309.

no clear indication as to whether he came by land or by sea from Kiev
into the Crimea. There are supporters of both views. Generally speaking, with the exception of the Toparch's embassy, there is no evidence in
our sources of any land campaign from Kiev to the Crimea; it is hard to
believe that considerable forces could make their way by land through
hostile nomadic peoples. The Russian Primary Chronicle gives the following statement: 'Vladimir marched with an armed force against Cherson, a Greek city, and the people of Cherson barricaded themselves therein. Vladimir halted in the harbor on the further side of the city.'[1] On
the basis of this rather vague passage and some other considerations, most
scholars have recently come to the conclusion, which in my opinion is
correct, that Vladimir undertook this campaign by water: he went down
the Dnieper by the usual 'Greek' way, and then sailed along the shores of
the Crimea.[2] Vladimir possessed Chersonesus for a short while.[3] According to the Russian Chronicle, when he married the Byzantine princess 'as a wedding present for the Princess he gave Cherson over to the
Greeks again, and then departed for Kiev.'[4]

Like former Russian naval enterprises, Vladimir's naval campaign
against Cherson aimed at no vast offensive results. I agree with those
scholars who assert that Vladimir soon surrendered Cherson because he
'had no need whatever of this city and was absolutely unable to keep it.'[5]
Vladimir did not even reach the territory of the Gothic *Climata*. I have
lingered over this episode because some scholars declare that during this
campaign Vladimir revived again old claims to the Tauric ports and
Chersonesian *Climata*. They adduce as further proof the last miracle in
the *Life* of Stephen of Surozh, although the beginning of the text is very
obscure and therefore debatable. However, scholars claim to discover
in the text the name of the Byzantine Princess Anna, Vladimir's wife, and
accordingly they refer the miracle to his time; they state that besides
Chersonesus Vladimir conquered Surozh (Sugdaia, Sudak) and Korchev

[1] In the Russian text 'v limeni,' i.e., 'in the gulf or port.' The word *limen* (*v limeni*) in the Russian
Chronicle is the Greek word λιμήν, ed. Shakhmatov, p. 137; Cross, p. 199. Cross translates 'v
limeni' as 'beside the bay.' In a letter to me Professor Cross suggests that this passage be translated: 'Vladimir disembarked,' etc., instead of 'V. halted'; and he adds: 'This is obviously stretching
[the Slavonic verb in the Annals] *sta* a little, but that is obviously what the passage means.' I agree
with him.

[2] Bertier Delagarde, 'How Did Vladimir Besiege Cherson?,' *Izvestiya Otdeleniya Russkago Yazyka
i Slovesnosti*, XIV (1909), 6, 38 (reprint). This study gives a complete bibliography of the question.

[3] In the Russian Chronicle the beginning of the siege, the capture and transfer of Cherson to Byzantium, with all other relevant facts, are related under one year, 6496. But apparently all this
took a longer time; see Bertier Delagarde, 'On Chersonesus,' *Izvestiya* of the Archaeological Commission, XXI (1907), 167–168 (in Russian).

[4] Shakhmatov, p. 148; Cross, p. 204.

[5] Bertier Delagarde, 'How Did Vladimir Besiege Cherson?,' p. 59.

(Kerch), so that there is a probability 'of the restoration of the Russian protectorate over Gothia.'[1]

This miracle of the healing of the Queen of Cherson is told in the Old Russian text of the *Life* of Stephen of Surozh; its opening lines, according to a manuscript of the Spiritual Academy of Moscow, are as follows: 'When the Empress Anna proceeded from Cherson to Kerch'; but in other manuscripts this passage reads: 'A inaya tsaritsa' (another empress) or 'a i tsaritsa' (and the empress).[2] In other words, in all other manuscripts the name Anna is not given.   Therefore it is extremely conjectural on these grounds alone, to refer the episode to the Byzantine Princess Anna, Vladimir's wife.   In the brief Greek text of the *Life* which has survived, tales of miracles are lacking.   I believe that in Vladimir's campaign one fact only is firmly established: the siege and capture of Chersonesus — Korsun (Cherson).   Crimean Gothia was not touched by Vladimir's military operations and continued under the power of the Byzantine Empire.

The friendly relations established between the Empire and the Russian principality after Vladimir's marriage to the Byzantine Princess and his conversion to Christianity led to the fact that in 1016 the two states were acting in the Crimea in common in order definitely to reëstablish Byzantine authority there.[3]   Although the Khazar state had been crushed by the Russians in the sixties of the tenth century, some groups of Khazars evidently still remained in the Crimea and at times raided the Byzantine regions there.   According to a Byzantine chronicler of the eleventh and twelfth centuries, in 1016 Emperor Basil II sent to Khazaria a fleet under the command of Mongus, son of Andronicus, and with the aid of Sfengus, Vladimir's brother, conquered the country; its ruler George Tsulus was taken prisoner in the first battle.[4]   This expedition sailed no doubt to the Crimea, since Khazaria or Gazaria was the name given to the Crimea in the Middle Ages because of the former Khazar predominance there. This was an attempt of the Byzantine government to do away with the remnants of the Khazars who were hostile to the Imperial interests in the Crimea.   It was brilliantly successful, and from 1016 on the Byzantine power in the Peninsula was completely restored as far east as Bosporus and Kerch, where in the eleventh century, according to a seal, the *pro-*

---

[1] See Tomaschek, *Die Goten in Taurien*, p. 38.   Braun (*Die letzten Schicksale der Krimgoten*, p. 20) and Loewe (*Die Reste der Germanen*, p. 218) follow Tomaschek.

[2] Vasilievski, *Works*, III, 96 (in Russian).

[3] Perhaps this Russo-Byzantine expedition may help to clarify the unsolved problem whether or not from Vladimir's period on Russia was a vassal state of Byzantium.   See A. Vasiliev, 'Was Old Russia a Vassal State of Byzantium?,' *Speculum*, VII (1932), 350–360.

[4] Cedrenus, II, 464.   Russian Chronicles do not mention this expedition.   Sfengus, Vladimir's brother, is unknown otherwise.

tospatharius and *strategos* of Bosporus, Arcadius, was a governor appointed by the Emperor.[1]

As for church organization, the Gothic eparchy as an archbishopric was under the jurisdiction of the Patriarch of Constantinople. In a *notitia* which probably belongs to the opening of the ninth century, the period of Patriarch Nicephorus (806-815),[2] we find the following statement: the Constantinopolitan Patriarchate comprises the regions 'as far west as Sicily, the Cyclades as far as the Pontus, Cherson, Abasgia, Khaldea, Khazaria as far as Cappadocia, and all northern *Climata*.'[3] 'All northern *Climata*' here means of course also the Gothic archbishopric, which in the tenth century is mentioned in several *notitiae*, along with other Crimean archbishoprics. The so-called *notitia* of Leo the Wise, which depicts the conditions of 901–907, in listing the archbishoprics under the jurisdiction of Constantinople puts Cherson in the nineteenth place, Bosporus in the thirty-seventh, Gothia (ἡ Γοτθία) in the forty-fourth, Sugdaia in the forty-fifth, and Phullae in the forty-sixth.[4] The *notitia* called *Nova Tactica*, of the epoch of Constantine Porphyrogenitus (913–959), gives the same five centers in the Crimea, but numbers Cherson 21, Bosporus 39, Gothia 46, Sugdaia 47, and Phullae 48.[5] Finally, the *notitia* of the time of John Tzimisces (969–976) puts the Archbishop of Cherson in the twenty-second place and the Archbishop of Bosporus in the thirty-ninth, and ascribes them both to the eparchy of Zikhia; it also places the Archbishop of Sugdaia forty-third, the Archbishop of Gothia (ὁ Γοτθίας) forty-fifth, and the Archbishop of Phullae forty-sixth.[6] In this *notitia* the Archbishop of Gothia is ranked lower than the Archbishop of Sugdaia. I believe this is to be explained merely by an error in the manuscript, because in the later *notitiae* of the eleventh and twelfth centuries the Gothic Archbishopric always occurs before that of Sugdaia.

---

[1] G. Schlumberger, *Mélanges d'archéologie byzantine* (Paris, 1895), pp. 206–207. Schlumberger incorrectly refers this seal to the Thracian Bosporus, which has never been a separate province. He ascribes the seal to the tenth or eleventh century.

[2] H. Gelzer, *Jahrbücher für protestantische Theologie*, XII (1886), 556.

[3] *Hieroclis Synecdemus et notitiae graecae episcopatuum*, ed. Parthey (Berlin, 1866), p. 140 (Not. 5).

[4] Gelzer, 'Ungedruckte und ungenügend veröffentlichte Texte der Notitiae episcopatuum,' *Abh. Philos.-philol. Cl. der Bayer Akad.*, XXI (1901), 551.

[5] H. Gelzer, *Georgii Cyprii Descriptio orbis Romani* (Leipzig, 1890), pp. 60–61.

[6] *Idem*, 'Ungedruckte . . . Texte,' pp. 571–572.

CHAPTER III

THE PERIOD OF POLOVTZIAN (CUMAN) DEPEND-ENCE AND SECESSION FROM BYZANTIUM

(FROM THE MIDDLE OF THE ELEVENTH CENTURY TO THE YEAR 1204)

1. POLOVTZIAN PREDOMINANCE

IN the history of the Crimean Goths the period from the middle of the eleventh century to the opening of the thirteenth is, as F. Braun remarks,[1] perhaps even more obscure than the previous epoch. During this period the Polovtzi-Cumans, a Turkish nomadic tribe, were predominant in the steppes of the Black Sea, and they apparently exercised some power also over the plains of the Crimea. Their influence spread also over the mountainous regions of the Peninsula. The Arab geographer of the twelfth century, al-Idrisi (Edrisi), who compiled his important work at the court of the Sicilian King Roger II, notes that the way from Cherson to Yalta (Djalita) lay in the region of the Cumans.[2] At any rate, it may be stated with great probability that some regions of mountain Crimea inhabited by the Goths had to pay tribute to the Polovtzi for a considerable time. William de Rubruquis, a Minorite who in 1253 was sent by Louis IX, King of France, on a mission to the Tartars, and who gives us very reliable information, went from Constantinople to the shores of the Crimea, and sailing by Cherson landed on May 21 at Soldaia (Sugdaia — Surozh), whence about the first of June he proceeded by land to the Tartars. Rubruquis writes that beyond the Crimean mountains and a beautiful wood 'there is a mighty plain which stretches out for five days' journey to the very border of the province northward, and there is a narrow isthmus or neck of land, having sea on the east and west sides, so that there is a ditch (fossatum) made from one sea to the other. In this plain before the Tartars came were the Cumans, who compelled the above-mentioned cities and castles to pay tribute to them.'[3]

---

[1] Braun, *Die letzten Schicksale der Krimgoten*, p. 20.

[2] *Géographie d'Edrisi, traduite de l'arabe en français par A. Jaubert*, II (Paris, 1840), 395. See Harkavy, 'The Crimean Peninsula before the Mongol Invasion in Arabic Literature,' *Trudy* (Works) of the Fourth Archaeological Congress, II (Kazan, 1891), 244 (in Russian).

[3] *Recueil de voyages et de mémoires*, IV (Paris, 1839), 219; *The Texts and Versions of Plano Carpini and William de Rubruquis*, ed. Beazley (London, 1903), pp. 146–147; *Contemporaries of Marco Polo*, ed. M. Komroff (New York, 1928), pp. 57–58; a Russian translation by A. Malein (St Petersburg, 1910), p. 68. In the last sentence Braun (*op. cit.*, p. 21) incorrectly reads the Tartars for the Cumans. Following Braun, Loewe (*op. cit.*, p. 219) plainly states: 'Rubruquis' remark indicates that the Goths paid tribute to the Tartars.'

This account is of great importance for our subject. At first sight it might seem that Rubruquis' account referred to a rather later epoch, i.e., the middle of the thirteenth century, but we must not forget that the Tartars made their appearance in the South-Russian steppes and in the Crimea, putting an end to the Polovtzian preponderance there, early in the second decade of the thirteenth century, in other words, only thirty years before Rubruquis collected his information. According to the notes in a Greek synaxarium discovered by Archimandrite Antoninus in one of the manuscripts of the library in the island Khalki, near Constantinople, the Tartars made their first raid in the Crimea on Sugdaia on 27 January 1223.[1] Therefore Rubruquis' statement deserves serious attention. Apparently for a number of years some at least of the Gothic possessions in the Crimea were dependent upon the Polovtzi, who exacted tribute.[2] In a monograph on the Goths in the Crimea Tomaschek has advanced an hypothesis, supported by no evidence whatever, that the famous Gothic stronghold Doros was probably founded by the Cumans (Polovtzi).[3]

It goes without saying that the predominance of the barbarians in the South-Russian steppes considerably hampered trade relations between the coast of the Black Sea in general and the Crimea in particular, and the north. However, according to the *Life* of St Antonius the Roman, for the opening of the twelfth century we have very interesting evidence of the coming to Novgorod of a Hellenized Goth from the Crimea. A Russian chronicle relates that in 1106 Antonius 'came by water to Novgorod the Great from Rome'; in 1116 he laid the foundation of 'the stone church of the nativity of our Holy Lady,' which as a cathedral of the monastery has survived almost intact down to our day; and he died in 1147.[4] The *Life* of Antonius the Roman, which has come down to us only in later

---

[1] Archimandrite Antoninus, 'Notes of the Twelfth–Fifteenth Centuries concerning the Crimean City Sugdaia (Sudak) Written Down in a Greek Synaxarium,' *Zapiski* of the Odessa Society of History and Antiquities, v (1863), 601, No. 33. For other information on this question see Vasilievski, *Works*, iii, 172–173. By this time the famous battle on the river Kalka near the Azov Sea had taken place, in which the Tartars crushed the Russians.

[2] In the eighteenth century the Danish historian P. F. Suhm wrote: 'I doubt very much that the Uzes (i.e. Polovtzi) ever possessed the Crimea,' P. Suhm, 'An Historical Study on the Uzes or Polovtzi,' transl. from Danish into Russian by S. Sabinin, *Chteniya* of the Society of Russian History and Antiquities, xiii (Moscow, 1848), No. 8, p. 23 ff.

[3] Tomaschek, *Die Goten in Taurien*, p. 51.

[4] *Novgorod Annals*, published by the Archaeographic Commission (St Petersburg, 1879), pp. 187–188. See also the *Novgorod Annal* according to the Synodal transcript, published by the Archaeographic Commission (St Petersburg, 1888), pp. 121–122 and 137. Both in Old Russian. An English translation by R. Michell and N. Forbes, *The Chronicle of Novgorod 1016–1471* (London, 1914), p. 9 (under the year 1117): 'The same year the *Igumen* Anton laid the foundation of the stone church of the monastery of the Holy Mother of God'; also p. 19 (Camden Society, 3rd Series, vol. xxv).

versions of the sixteenth to the eighteenth centuries, is attributed to
Andrew, Antonius' disciple and his successor as Abbot (Igumen) of the
Monastery.   After relating Antonius' miraculous arrival at Novgorod
upon a stone which floated on the water, the *Life* continues as follows:
'The holy man landed from the stone and went to the city; there he met a
Greek merchant who spoke Roman, Greek, and Russian.'   Antonius
asked him about his city, and 'the Goth (*Gotfin*) told everything in detail
to the holy man. . . .   Hearing these stories from this Greek (Grechanin)
the holy man rejoiced in his soul . . . then the holy man asked the Greco-
Goth (*Grechanin-Gotfin*) and said . . . '[1]   This merchant is of very great
importance for our subject: he spoke Latin, Greek, and Russian; he is
called in the tale a Greek, and, what is particularly interesting, a Goth
(Gotfin) or a Greco-Goth (Grechanin-Gotfin).   The merchant was of
course a Hellenized Goth, who owing to his commerical relations with
Novgorod had become acquainted with the Russian tongue.   In the
twelfth century this Goth could have come to Novgorod only from the
Crimea, where at that time the Goths dwelt; of course, after a long period
of Byzantine influence they were very familiar with the Greek language.[2]
Thus, early in the twelfth century the Crimean Goths who spoke Greek,
safely passing among the South-Russian nomads, were travelling for
commercial purposes to the far-off north, i.e., they took part in Russo-
Byzantine trade.   It is most probable that Cherson, which was in direct
communication with Constantinople and Asia Minor, was the trade
center in the Crimea whence commercial operations spread to the north.

   But generally speaking the Cuman predominance must, as has been
pointed out, have hampered and interrupted trade relations between
south and north.   Under the year 1167 (6675) a Russian chronicle states
that the Polovtzi 'going to the cataracts began to do mischief to the
Greeks.'[3]   This passage refers, of course, to Greek merchants who journeyed on the Dnieper from Constantinople or Cherson (Korsun) and who
were attacked by the Polovtzi in the Dnieper cataracts.

   There is a well-known passage in the Old Russian epic *The Tale of the
Host of Igor* about Gothic girls singing on the shore of the Blue Sea; this
also is to be referred to the period of Cuman predominance in the south,
i.e., to the end of the twelfth century.   The passage is as follows: 'Thus

   [1] 'The Tale of the Life of Antonius the Roman,' *Pravoslavny Sobesednik*, II (Kazan, 1858), 165–166;
also *Monuments (Pamyatniki) of Old Russian Literature*, published by Kushelev-Bezborodko, I (St
Petersburg, 1860), 265.   In Old Russian.
   [2] Kunik ('On the Report of a Gothic Toparch,' p. 142) calls this merchant 'Gotho-Greek' and remarks: 'This also explains how the Goths became hellenized, and afterwards "tartarized".'
   [3] *The Hypatian Chronicle*, under the year 6675, *Voskresenskaya letopis* (chronicle) under the year
6674, in the *Complete Collection of Russian Chronicles*, VII, 78.   In Old Russian.   See Karamzin,
History of the Russian State, II, 410 (in Russian).

the fair maidens of the Goths sang on the shore of the blue sea, tinkling in Russian gold.   They sing the time of Bus; they cherish the revenge for Sharokan.'[1]   By comparing this passage with other references in this epic we may conclude that the 'blue sea' means the Sea of Azov.[2]   The Gothic maidens, i.e., girls of the Crimean Goths, were perhaps carried off by the Polovtzi in one of their incursions to the shores of the Sea of Azov, which at that time belonged to the Polovtzi.   Some scholars believe these girls were forced to attend Cuman festivals and celebrate in song the deeds of Cuman chiefs.[3]   Another passage in the same epic shows that girls were carried off in Russo-Cuman conflicts of the time; in this passage we find that this time it was the Russians who after their first victory over the nomads 'carried off the fair maidens of the Polovtzi.'[4]

Setting aside various opinions as to what was the Russian gold in which the Gothic girls were tinkling, I shall say a few words on their song of 'the time of Bus.'   At present the opinion has been almost abandoned that this name means a Polovtzian prince, Bolush (Blush, Bulush, Blyush) mentioned in Russian chronicles under the year 1054 or 1055.[5]   In the song of 'the time of Bus' some scholars are now inclined to see a recollection of early Gothic struggles with the Antes when the Goths were still dwelling in the South-Russian steppes, i.e., late in the fourth century, and particularly an episode related by Jordanes in his *Gothic History.*[6] Jordanes says that the Ostrogothic Prince Vinitharius, after his victory over the Antes, as a terrible example crucified their king, named Boz (Box, Booz), together with his sons and seventy nobles.   Following other commentators on Jordanes' narrative, A. Shakhmatov thought it very probable that the song of the Gothic girls referred to Vinitharius' struggle with the Antes; he adds: 'Perhaps Boz is not a Russian name; cf. Boso, the count of Provence, who in 879 became the King of Burgundy.'[7]   For my own part I may add that in its Greek form this name is given by Constantine Porphyrogenitus as 'βόζων.'[8]   Tomaschek compares the name in *The Tale of the Host of Igor*, *Bus*, with that of a Bulgarian

---

[1] *The Tale of the Armament of Igor A.D. 1185*, edited and translated by Leonard A. Magnus (London-Oxford, 1915), p. 13, ll. 407–411; 'The Lay of the War-Ride of Igor,' translated from the Old Russian by A. Petrunkevitch in collaboration with Wanda Petrunkevitch, *Poet-Lore*, xxx (Boston, 1919), 296.   [2] See Kunik, 'On the Report of a Gothic Toparch,' p. 141 (in Russian).

[3] See Bruun, 'Notices historiques et topographiques concernant les colonies italiennes en Gazarie,' p. 13.   By the Blue Sea of *The Tale of the Host of Igor* Bruun seemingly means the Black Sea, which is incorrect.   [4] *The Tale*, by L. Magnus, p. 4, l. 139; by A. Petrunkevitch, p. 293.

[5] See L. Magnus' speculations as to the name *Bus* in his edition of the *Tale*, p. 50.

[6] *Jordanis Getica*, Ch. xlviii (ed. Mommsen, p. 121).

[7] Shakhmatov, *The Earliest Fortunes of the Russian People*, pp. 9–10 (in Russian).   For Bozo see R. Poupardin, *Le royaume de Provence sous les Carolingiens* (Paris, 1901), pp. 41–141.

[8] *De administrando imperio*, Ch. xxvi (Bonn., p. 116).

chief Busa, who in 488 resisted Theoderic during his march on Italy.[1]
The words of *The Tale of the Host of Igor* that the Gothic maidens 'cherish
the revenge for Sharokan' refer to the Polovtzian (Cuman) Prince Sharu-
kan mentioned under the year 1107 in the Russian Primary Chronicle,
who after a Russian victory over the Polovtzi barely escaped death.

I must admit that it is much more natural to refer the passage of *The
Tale of the Host of Igor*, 'they sing the time of Bus,' to some Polovtzian
prince than to recognize in the name *Bus* an allusion to the conflicts of the
fourth century.[2] We must not forget that the text of the *Tale* leaves
much to be desired, especially as to proper names. At any rate, the
passage about the Gothic girls must be included among our scanty and
fragmentary evidence on the Goths during the Polovtzian (Cuman)
predominance.

2. The Title 'Gothicus' used by the Byzantine Emperors of the Twelfth Century

According to Rubruquis' account quoted above, we learn that in the
twelfth century most of the Crimea, including the Gothic *Climata*, paid
tribute to the Polovtzi; in other words, during this period Byzantine
authority in the Peninsula was in a state of decline. The Byzantine
government could not submit easily to such a situation and must have
taken some measures to restore its prestige. Unfortunately our sources
are silent on this subject. But perhaps it may be possible to discover in
the sources some hints of a temporary restoration of Byzantine authority
in the Crimea in the second half of the Twelfth century.

Manuel Comnenus (1143–1180) in 1166 issued a novella on the interrelation between God the Father and Jesus Christ[3] which was engraved on
a stone slab and placed in Saint Sophia.[4] This novella gives the solemn
title of the Emperor in a form that we have not met since the period of
Heraclius, i.e., since the seventh century. The preamble of the novella
reads as follows: 'Manuel, Emperor faithful in Christ God, Porphyrogenitus, Autocrat of the Romans, most pious, ever reverend Augustus, Isauricus, Cilicius, Armenicus, Dalmaticus, Ugricus, Bosniacus, Chrobaticus,
Lazicus, Ibericus, Bulgaricus, Serbicus, Zikhicus, Azaricus, Gothicus,

---

[1] Tomaschek, *Die Goten in Taurien*, p. 40.

[2] There are some geographic names in the south of Russia, for instance in the Kharkov province,
which apparently refer to the name Bus: Bus' Ravine (*Busov yar*), Bus' river, Bus' farmhouse
(*Buzov khutor*), etc. See N. Aristov, 'On the Polovtzian Land (O zemle Polovetzkoi),' *Izvestiya* of
the Historico-Philogical Institute at Nezhin (Nezhin, 1877), p. 219 (in Russian); V. N. Peretts,
Slovo o Polku Igorevim (Kiev, 1926), p. 264.

[3] Zachariae von Lingenthal, *Jus Graeco-Romanum*, III (Leipzig, 1857), p. 485.

[4] See S. G. Mercati, 'Epigraphica, III: Sull' editto di Manuele I Comneno del 1166 inciso nel tempio
di Santa Sofia,' *Rendiconti della Pontificia Accademia Romana de Archeologia*, III (1925), 206.

guided by God, heir to the crown of the Great Constantine,' etc. In this title, the Goths ('Gothicus') are mentioned among many other peoples. Is this pompous title a purely formal list of names for the Emperor's greater exaltation, and perhaps unconnected with the real situation of his epoch? Or does it reflect the real state of things in the Empire in the twelfth century (of course before 1166, when the novella was issued)?

In his review of the Russian text of my study on *The Goths in the Crimea* Franz Dölger[1] points out that solemn titles such as this often have no real importance and are often omitted in Imperial edicts; it is misleading ('abwegig') to use such titles to prove the dependence upon Byzantium of the peoples mentioned. They are 'victory titles' ('Siegestitel') which may only mean that the emperor (or one of his commanders) 'victoriously' fought these peoples. I agree perfectly that solemn Imperial titles are not such reliable evidence as to justify definite conclusions. Often such a title has nothing to do with the epoch of the ruler who bears it, reflecting only events of the past. None the less, if after careful consideration of the title it becomes clear that all the names may be satisfactorily explained by events of the period of the emperor concerned, I believe we may use the document as a source and with due reservation advance some hypotheses.

We first notice that up to this time few titles of this sort are known. The earliest analogous title, as far as I recall, belongs to Justinian the Great; others are used by his immediate successors, Justin II and Tiberius, and finally by Heraclius in his novella of 612. From the last novella down to the novella of Manuel Comnenus in 1166, this ethnic element in imperial titles occurs neither in novellae nor in inscriptions.[2] Apparently, then, these titles from Justinian to Heraclius correctly reflect the real attitude of the Empire towards neighboring peoples, and therefore have real historical significance.

It is not surprising that Manuel restored the old form of the title which reminded him of the brilliant epoch of Justinian. The political ideology of Manuel was identical with the political ideology of Justinian. He dreamed of the restoration of the Roman Empire to its former bounds by means of the annexation of west-European regions which had once been under the power of the Empire. The pompous title admirably fitted the tastes and ideas of such a political dreamer as Manuel.

Let us now examine the ethnic elements in Manuel's title and try to

---

[1] In the *Byz. Zeitschrift*, XXVIII (1928), 200.

[2] Dölger (p. 200) mentions an analogous edict of 681, but, as he says himself, 'of course without solemn title' ('freilich ohne Triumphal titel'); this edict in Mansi, *Conciliorum Amplissima Collectio*, XI, 700. See also F. Dölger, *Regesten der Kaiserurkunden des oströmischen Reiches*, I (Munich und Berlin, 1924), 29, No. 245.

explain them by the political relations in the eleventh and twelfth centuries which brought the Empire into contact with the Slavonic peoples in
the Balkan Peninsula, Ugria (Hungary), Isauria, Cilicia, as well as with
various peoples of the Caucasus.   The title contains fourteen ethmic
names.   Manuel was called 'Isauricus' because the region in the south of
Asia Minor, Isauria, the Byzantine theme Seleucia, which in the second
half of the eleventh century had been occupied by the Seljuq Turks, was
restored to the Empire during the First Crusade and remained under its
power in Manuel's reign.[1] 'Cilicius' and 'Armenicus' may be explained
by the annexation by Manuel's predecessor, John Comnenus, of the
Princedom of Lesser Armenia, which was situated in Cilicia.   The result
of John's campaign was the expansion of the Empire down to the bound-
ary of the Princedom of Antioch.   An uprising which broke out in Lesser
Armenia under Manuel was put down after some difficulty so that shortly
before 1166 the Byzantine Emperor's authority was restored there.[2]
The surnames 'Dalmatius,' 'Ugricus,' 'Bosniacus,' 'Chorvaticus,' and
'Serbicus' are to be considered in connection with the Hungarian policy
towards Byzantium in the twelfth century.   The alliance of the two
Empires, Eastern and Western, Byzantine and German rulers, which had
been made under John Comnenus and remained for some time the foundation of the external policy of Byzantium under Manuel, brought Hungary
(Ugria) between two fires.   Therefore it is not surprising that the King
of Hungary, Geza (Geisa), as a counterstroke determined to make an
alliance with the King of the Two Sicilies, Roger, the enemy and rival of
Byzantium.   Then Hungary began to develop in the Balkan Peninsula
a policy which was hostile to the interests of the Eastern Empire.   During the time of Manuel, Hungary supported Serbia, which rose up against
Byzantine domination.   The Serbian uprising of 1150 was quelled by
Manuel.   Then .Hungary tried to establish itself in Dalmatia, on the
Adriatic Sea, a policy which also strikingly encroached upon the interests
of Byzantium and Venice, the latter being at that time on a friendly footing with the Empire.   Finally, Manuel could not forgive Hungary its
hostilities against his friends and allies, the Russian princes, Vladimirko
of Galich[3] and Yuri Dolgoruki.   For these combined reasons Manuel
opened a vast offensive in the Balkan Peninsula.   In 1165 the Byzantine
troops entered Dalmatia and quickly subdued it; in this case Dalmatia
is to be understood not in its narrow sense of the coastland with the cities

---

[1] F. Chalandon, *Les Comnène: études sur l'Empire byzantin aux XI° et XII° siècles*, II (Paris, 1912),
112.

[2] Chalandon, *op. cit.*, II, 112–118, 417–418; N. Jorga, *Geschichte des osmanischen Reiches*, I (Gotha,
1908), 101 ff.; H. Tournebize, *Histoire politique et religieuse de l'Arménie* (Paris, 1910), pp. 174–181.

[3] Galich was a city on the Dniester.

which once formed Byzantine Dalmatia, but in the wider sense which was more often used among the Byzantines: this included the *former* Croatia (south of the Save river), the so-called Rama, perhaps the whole of Bosnia, and lastly Dalmatia proper.[1]   A Byzantine historian notes that after this campaign Byzantium subjugated thirty-seven cities of Dalmatia and a Serbo-Croatian tribe of the Kachichi.[2]   A Byzantine governor appointed to Spalato was called *dux Dalmatiae et Croatiae*.[3] Bosnia, conquered by Manuel, had only shortly before his campaign acknowledged the suzerainty of Hungary.   Perhaps it is relevant to point out that even in the twentieth century the Magyars liked to refer to the short-lived dependence of Bosnia upon Hungary in the twelfth century, considering this as giving them a right to Bosnia when the question arose of the annexation of this province to Austria-Hungary.[4]   On the basis of these facts the titles 'Dalmaticus,' 'Croaticus (Khorvaticus),' and 'Bosnia-cus' are easily explained.   The title 'Bulgaricus' needs no comment, for after Basil II's conquest of the first Bulgarian kingdom in 1018, Bulgaria was a mere province of the Empire down to the eighties of the twelfth century.   The title 'Ugricus,' of course, does not mean the occupation of Hungary by Manuel.   But hostilities between Manuel and Hungary occurred several times and sometimes ended in a complete defeat of the Hungarian troops; for instance, in 1165 the Magyars lost Zemlin, and Byzantine authority was restored in the whole region of Sresh; Magyar *župans* (nobles), at the command of the victorious Emperor, were forced to present themselves before him barefooted and bareheaded, with ropes around their necks.   Immediately after this victory Hungary lost Croatia Bosnia, and Dalmatia proper, as we have said above.[5]   All this fully empowered Manuel to assume the title 'Ugricus.'

Let us turn now to Manuel's Caucasian titles.   'Lazicus' must be explained by the relations between Byzantium and Trebizond in the twelfth century.   Trebizond, which lay in the region of the Lazi, seceded in the twelfth century from the Empire, and organised an independent princedom of its own with the family of the Gabrades at its head, of which we shall speak later.   But in the sixties of the twelfth century Trebizond was restored to the Empire, and Nicephorus Palaeologus was appointed there as Manuel's governor.[6]   'Ibericus' is a little less obvious.   This title goes back to the period of Basil II Bulgaroctonus.   At the very end

---

[1] C. Grot, *From the History of Ugria (Hungary) and the Slavs in the Twelfth Century* (Warsaw, 1889), pp. 345–346 (in Russian).   For the geographic term 'Rama' see *ibid.*, pp. 32–33.

[2] Cinnamus, *Historiae*, p. 249.   [3] C. Jiriček, *Geschichte der Serben*, I (Gotha, 1911), 253.

[4] See A. Pogodin, *History of Serbia* (St Petersburg, 1909), p. 30 (in Russian).

[5] C. Grot, *op. cit.*, pp. 344–346 (in Russian).

[6] *Nicetas Choniata*, p. 295.   Cf. W. Miller, *Trebizond, the Last Greek Empire* (London, 1926), p. 13.

of the tenth century the ruler of a portion of Iberia (Gruzia), *Curopalates*
David, died childless, bequeathing his possessions to Basil II.   The latter
immediately came from Tarsus to his new lands, where he was met by
the King of Abkhazia, Bagrat, who had come especially for this purpose,
and by his father, the King of 'Inner' Iberia, Gurguen.   Basil bestowed
the title of *curopalates* on the former and that of *magister* upon the latter.
In the twelfth century Iberia seems to have depended upon Byzantium.[1]
'Zikhicus' signifies the vassal dependence of the Caucasian tribe Zikhi
(probably later Djigeti), who dwelt on the north-eastern coast of the
Black Sea.   Let us recall that several episcopal *notitiae* mention the
Archbishopric Zikhia (Ζηχία, Ζικχία, Ζηκχία) under the jurisdiction of
Constantinople.   Lastly, 'Azaricus' (ἀζαρικός) indicates the suzerainty
of the Empire over the Caucasian region Atzara (Azara, Adjara) which
according to Constantine Porphyrogenitus[2] was a region bordering on
Romania, i.e., the Byzantine Empire.   Thus almost all geographical
elements in Manuel's title have a real significance entirely corresponding
to the international position of the Empire in his period.

If we turn now to the title 'Gothicus' and ask who were the Goths in
the twelfth century, only one answer may be given: they were the Crimean Goths, for in the twelfth century we know no other Goths.[3]   We
know that in the twelfth century the Goths paid tribute to the Polovtzi.
No doubt the Byzantine government could not submit easily to this dependence of Crimean Gothia upon the Polovtzi.   Therefore I am inclined
to interpret the title 'Gothicus' in the novella of 1166 as a proof of the
fact that for a certain time in the twelfth century, at any rate before 1166,
Byzantium succeeded in restoring its power over the Crimean Goths
after freeing them from dependence on the Polovtzi.   It is well known
that in some other places, for instance, in the Danubian region, Manuel
was successfully fighting against the Polovtzi before 1166.[4]

There is another indirect indication of the increase of Byzantine power
under Manuel on the northern shore of the Black Sea, namely, in the
treaty concluded in 1169 between Byzantium and Genoa, in which the
Emperor grants exceptionally favorable trade privileges to Genoa within
the Empire; among other clauses we read the following: 'Genoese ships

[1] Brosset, *Histoire de la Géorgie*, I (St Petersburg, 1849), 297; *Idem, Additions et éclaircissements à l'histoire de la Géorgie* (St Petersburg, 1851), pp. 105, 185–186; G. Schlumberger, *L'épopée byzantine*, II (Paris, 1900), 163–164, 179 ff.   Fr. Dölger (*Byz. Zeitsch.*, XXVIII [1928], 200) doubts very much whether the Iberians really depended upon the Byzantine Empire in 1166.

[2] *Constantini Porphyrogeniti, de administrando imperio*, p. 206.   See also Brosset, *Additions et éclaircissements*, p. 105.

[3] I am in doubt as to whether the Goths of Asia Minor may be included in this novella, as Fr. Dölger believes in the *Byz. Zeitsch.*, XXVIII (1928), 200.   [4] Chalandon, II, 323–325, 474.

may traffic in all regions of my Empire, except Rosia (Rusia, Rossia, Russia) and Matrakha (Matraka), unless special permission to this effect is granted by our Majesty.'[1]   Since the trade settlement Rosia lay, in my opinion, on the lower Don, and Matrakha, i.e. Tamatarkha-Tmutarakan, in the Kerch Peninsula, it is obvious that Manuel felt himself the master not only of the northern coast of the Black Sea but also of the Azov Sea.[2] It is very probable that his strong power in the far-off north was connected with his success over the Polovtzi in the Crimea.   Perhaps this signified that under Manuel and before 1166 Crimean Gothia was again under the power of Byzantium.

3. Church Life in Gothia in the Eleventh and Twelfth Centuries

In the political history of Gothia we deal almost entirely with more or less probable hypotheses; but for church relations we possess some exact though scanty evidence.

The *notitiae* of the eleventh and twelfth centuries always list the Archbishopric of Gothia under the jurisdiction of Constantinople, along with other archbishoprics in the Crimea: Cherson, Bosporus, Sugdaia, and Phullae; sometimes the two latter are combined into one, Sugdaphullae. In the eleventh century the Archbishopric of Gothia is mentioned in two *notitiae*: the first, which formerly was incorrectly ascribed to the period of Leo the Wise, belongs to the epoch of Alexius Comnenus and was compiled after 1084 (Gothia is found here in the thirty-fourth place);[3] the second is to be referred to the period immediately preceding the First Crusade (Gothia also in the thirty-fourth place).[4]   The Archbishopric of Gothia is three times mentioned in the *notitiae* of the twelfth century.

---

[1] F. Miklosich and J. Müller, *Acta et diplomata graeca medii aevi*, III (Vienna, 1865), 35; Zachariae von Lingenthal, *Jus Graeco-Romanum*, III, 496; A. Sanguineti and G. Bertolotto, 'Nuova serie di documenti sulle relazioni di Genova coll'impero bizantino,' *Atti della Società Ligure di storia patria*, XXVIII (1896–1898), 351, 355, 360. See Fr. Dölger, *Regesten der Kaiserurkunden*, II (1925), 82 (No. 1488) and 99 (No. 1610).

[2] I do not agree with C. Manfroni in considering the names of Rosia and Matrakha not definite geographic points but merely a general indication of the extreme limits of the eastern and northern regions of the Black Sea, in order thereby absolutely to interdict the Genoese from sailing in Crimean and Azov waters. Cf. C. Manfroni, 'Le relazioni fra Genova, l'Impero bizantino e i Turchi,' *Atti della Società Ligure*, XXVIII (1896–1898), 593, 611, n. 1.   M. Canale, reading in this treaty Matica (see Zach. von Lingenthal, *op. cit.*, III, 496) or Moetica for Matrica incorrectly recognizes here Maeotis or Lake Maeotis, i.e., the Azov Sea, M. G. Canale, *Nuova istoria della repubblica di Genova*, I (Firenze, 1858), 311, 317.

[3] *Hieroclis Synecdemus*, ed. Parthey, p. 100.   For the time of the compilation of the *notitia* see Gelzer, in the *Jahrbücher für protestantische Theologie*, XII (1886), 529 ff., 541, 556; *idem*, in the *Abhandlungen der philos.-philol. Cl. der Ak. der Wissenschaften zu München*, XXI (1901), 549.

[4] H. Gelzer, 'Ungedruckte und wenig bekannte Bistümerverzeichnisse der orientalischen Kirche,' *Byz. Zeitsch.*, I (1892), 255; 281–282.

In the *notitia* of Nilus Doxopater compiled under Roger II the Sicilian (1101–1154) Gothia is in the twenty-eighth place; in this *notitia* all the Crimean archbishoprics are named as subject to Constantinople and 'as not subject to any metropolite nor having any bishoprics under their jurisdiction.'[1]   The second *notitia*, compiled in 1189 under Isaac Angelus (1185–1195), remained in force during the Empire of Nicaea, until 1256 at least (Gothia in the twenty-ninth place).[2]   The third *notitia*, drawn up under the Angeli late in the twelfth century or perhaps in the opening years of the thirteenth, notes not only the Archbishopric of Gothia but also its chief center Kodros (ἡ Κόδρος) in which the distorted name of Doros is recognizable.[3]   This note is of great interest, for it shows that the residence of the Gothic archbishops in the Crimea, Doros, existed in any case up to the beginning of the thirteenth century.   In this *notitia* Gothia is in the thirtieth place.

Archbishops of Gothia rather often took part in the councils convened in Constantinople.   Under Patriarch John Xyphilinus an Archbishop of Gothia whose name is not given attended two local councils in Constantinople: 26 April 1066, and 19 March 1067.[4]   The epoch of the Comneni was crowded with church troubles caused by manifold doctrines which differed from that held by the government.   These problems were discussed at various councils in the presence of the most prominent representatives of the Byzantine Church.   Among them an Archbishop of Gothia was often found; sometimes in the documents referring to the councils there is mentioned only the fact of the participation of a Gothic Archbishop without a name; sometimes a list of the members of the council is given, and the name of the Archbishop of Gothia is specified.

In 1140 under John Comnenus and Patriarch Leo Styppes, among others an Archbishop of Gothia was present[5] at the Council of Constantinople which dealt with the heresy of Constantine Chrysomalus, closely related to the Paulician or Bogomile heresy.   In the opening years of Manuel's reign an Archbishop of Gothia attended the following councils convoked in Constantinople to handle the development of Bogomile

---

[1] *Hieroclis Synecdemus*, ed. Parthey, pp. 303–304.

[2] Gelzer, *Analecta byzantina*, Index scholarum of the University of Jena 1891–1892 (Jena, 1891–1892), pp. 6, 10; *idem*, in the *Abhandl. der Ak. zu München*, XXI (1901), 590; 593.

[3] *Hieroclis Synecdemus*, ed. Parthey, p. 201; Gelzer, in the *Jahrbücher für protestantische Theologie*, XII (1886), 544, 550, 556; *idem*, in the *Abh . . . zu München*, XXI (1901), 591.

[4] *Jus Canonicum Graeco-Romanum*, *Patr. Gr.*, CXIX, coll. 756 and 757.

[5] Leo Allatius, *De ecclesiae occidentalis atque orientalis perpetua consensione* (Cologne, 1648), col. 644; Mansi, *Conciliorum Collectio*, XXI, 552.   For the council itself see Chalandon, *op. cit.*, II, 23; N. Grossu, 'The Attitude of the Byzantine Emperors John II and Manuel I Comneni towards Union with the West,' *Trudy* (Transactions) of the Spiritual Academy of Kiev, December, 1912, p. 623 (in Russian).

heresy: in August and October, 1143, and in February, 1144, all three under Patriarch Michael Kurkuas Oxites (Oxeites).[1] In February, 1147, a council presided over by the Emperor himself convened in Constantinople; the question to be dealt with was the case of Patriarch Cosmas Atticus, accused of relations with the monk Niphon, who had been charged with Bogomile heresy. The council condemned the Patriarch as a follower of Bogomile heresy and deprived him of Patriarchal rank. The act of Cosmas' deposition was signed by numerous members of the council; among other signatures there are those of the two representatives of the Crimean Church, the 'humble' Archbishops Constantine of Gothia and Theophanes of Cherson.[2]

A Gothic Archbishop also attended the Council of Constantinople in 1166 which dealt with the correct interpretation of the words of Jesus Christ in Saint John's Gospel, 'My Father is greater than I' (14:28). In the second half of the twelfth century this question was of great importance in the internal life of Byzantium, and for many years it agitated the Byzantine church and state.[3] The documents pertaining to this council give the names of the two 'humble' Archbishops of Gothia: John was present at the third meeting, and Constantine at the eighth.[4] Since John attended the third meeting, March 6, and Constantine the eighth, May 6, we may conclude that in March or April 1166 a change of Archbishops occurred, Constantine being appointed to take the place of John, who had probably died in the meantime.[5]

But the disputes which seemed to be settled at the Council of 1166 in reality continued both in the provinces and in the capital. On 30 January 1170, Manuel convoked in Constantinople a new council for the examination of Constantine, Metropolitan of Corcyra, who had accused the late Patriarch Lucas Chrysobergus of heresy. Among many other representatives of the Byzantine clergy was present the Archbishop of Gothia, Constantine. The Council condemned the errors of the Metropolite of Corcyra; and the Archbishop of Gothia, as well as the Bishops of Cypsalla (Ipsala), Brysis, Lemnos, Heracleia, and Anchialus, made the following statement: 'On the basis of what we have heard today, we believe that

---

[1] Allatius, *op. cit.*, coll. 671, 674, 678; Mansi, xxi, 584, 600, 601. For the councils themselves see Chalandon, *op. cit.*, p. 635 ff.

[2] Allatius, *op. cit.*, coll. 685–686; Mansi, xxi, 705, 708. On the Council itself Chalandon, *op. cit.*, pp. 636–683; A. Lebedev, *Historical Sketches of the Conditions of the Byzantine Eastern Church from the End of the Eleventh to the Middle of the Fifteenth Century*, 2nd ed. (Moscow, 1902), pp. 174–177 (in Russian).

[3] Th. Uspenski, *Essays on the History of Byzantine Civilization* (St Petersburg, 1892), pp. 225–236 (in Russian); Chalandon, *op. cit.*, pp. 646–651; Lebedev, *op. cit.*, pp. 131–137 (in Russian).

[4] *Nicetae Choniatae ex libris Thesauri orthodoxae fidei*, *Patr. Gr.*, cxl, coll. 261, 281.

[5] On these councils see *ibid.*, coll. 252–261 and 276–281.

the Bishop of Corcyra deserves deposition and anathema.' The act of this Council was sealed, among others, by the signature of the Archbishop of Gothia, Constantine.[1] The Archbishop of Gothia was also present at the meeting of 20 February 1170, when anathema was actually pronounced against Constantine of Corcyra.[2]

The act concerning church properties of a council under Patriarch Lucas Chrysobergus (1156–1169) is very interesting for the Crimea because of its signatures; in this document are the signatures of the Archbishops of Gothia, Matrakha (Tamatarkha-Tmutarakan), and Sugdophullae. Their names are not given.[3] From the period of the same Patriarch Lucas Chrysobergus, on 19 November 1169, is another mention of a Metropolitan of Gothia, who together with other members of the synod took part in an examination about conveying a monastery to two persons.[4] As far as I know, from 1170 to the beginning of the thirteenth century, there is no mention of the participation of Gothic Archbishops in the councils of Constantinople.

Thus, beginning with the second half of the eleventh century the Archbishops of Gothia not infrequently took part in the Constantinopolitan councils, so that there was still a real connection between the Gothic eparchy in the Crimea and the capital of the Empire; their names, however, are not always given in the documents. For this period the names of the Archbishops of Gothia are as follows: at the council in February, 1147, Constantine; in March, 1166, John, but in May of the same year, Constantine, who evidently was not identical with Constantine of 1147. Constantine mentioned in May, 1166, was also a member of the council in January, 1170.[5]

The writer and encyclopedist of the twelfth century, John Tzetzes, in his work *Chiliades*, which was compiled probably between 1144 and 1170,[6] refers very harshly to a certain Archbishop of Gothia. This rather obscure passage is found in the chapter on Cato.[7] At its beginning he depicts Cato the Elder, laying special stress on Cato's education of his son; he states that in their outward and inward qualities, with a few excep-

---

[1] L. Petit, 'Documents inédits sur le concile de 1166 et ses derniers adversaires,' *Viz. Vremennik*, xi (1904), 480, 486, 489.   [2] *Ibid.*, p. 489.

[3] Leunclavius, *Jus graeco-romanum*, i (Frankfurt, 1596), 282; Mansi, xxi, 841–842; *Patr. Gr.*, cxix, col. 885.

[4] Papadopulos-Kerameus, 'Ἀνάλεκτα ἱεροσολυμιτικῆς σταχυολογίας, iv (St Petersburg, 1897), 107.

[5] See an incomplete list of the Archbishops of Gothia in the eleventh and twelfth centuries in Bishop Hermogenes, *The Tauric Eparchy* (Pskov, 1887), p. 149; Arsenius, 'The Gothic Eparchy in the Crimea,' *Journal of the Ministry of Public Instruction*, clxv (1873), 69.

[6] Krumbacher, *Geschichte der byzantinischen Litteratur*, 2nd ed., p. 528.

[7] *Joannis Tzetzae, Historiarum variarum Chiliades, instruxit Theophilus Kiesslingius* (Leipzig, 1826), *Chiliades*, iii, Hist. 70, vv. 102–231 (pp. 84–88).

tions, he himself and Cato are very much alike. Then Tzetzes relates how much Cato the Younger was disgusted with Sulla's cruelties; he asked why nobody killed Sulla and was answered that all feared him. Cato replied, 'Give me a sword, and I will free my country from cruel tyrants.'[1] Tzetzes continues that he himself is filled like Elijah with ire and zeal which burn his heart; if he could he would kill for their follies the worshippers of shame; the archbishops (ἀρχιερεῖς) at their own will serve the archonts; filled with greed they live like slaves, and perform lay functions; ignominious priests and deacons ruin themselves by lewd women as by gangrene; this Cretan filth,[2] and so on. Then there is a passage which runs as follows: 'Among them was a Goth from Gothia, filled with stench, I may say, *triacontaphyllos*,[3] a one-eyed cyclops, or to be more correct, an eyeless one, who being blind like Haman blinds everything;[4] for if justice is blinded, everything becomes blind. How is it possible to carry on state affairs properly where the blind lead those who see? And behold this *triacontaphyllos* prolongs the whole Council, directs it, and pulls it as he pleases, as of old the blind Orion carried Cedalion.[5] But thou, oh supreme and all-seeing power, send down brilliant lightnings and burn by fire all this filth. Let not the Divine Name be defamed; let not sacred ranks be sold to debauchees.'[6]

Tzetzes' *Chiliades* may be considered as a detailed commentary in

---

[1] Vv. 199–200 (p. 87).

[2] 'τὸ βδέλυγμα τὸ Κρητικόν' (v. 210, p. 88). Here I believe the author hints at the horrible vices for which the Cretans were notorious. Cf. a mediaeval saying: 'The three worst *kappas* are Cappadocia, Cilicia, and Crete,' *Anthologia Graeca*, XI, 237, *The Greek Anthology with an English translation* by W. R. Paton, IV (London-New York, 1926), 183. The same epigram is also found in *Constantini Porphyrogeniti De thematibus*, p. 21. Cf. the *Epistle of Paul to Titus* (I, 12): 'The Cretans are always liars, evil beasts, slow bellies.'

[3] 'Τριακοντάφυλλος'; cf. 'Τριαντάφυλλον' (a rose). The editor of the *Chiliades*, Kiessling, asks: 'an τριακοντάφυλλον intelligit quendam, qui non plus quam triginta folia vel legerit vel scripserit vel possideat' (Kiessling, p. 88, n. 218). Pressel believes with more probability that Tzetzes invented the word 'Τριακοντάφυλλος' i.e., 'qui rosam olet vel aquam vel oleum rosarum,' Th. Pressel, *Joannis Tzetzae epistolae* (Tübingen, 1851), p. 106. The passage quoted refers to the clergymen who like women anointed themselves with oil or water of roses, which according to Tzetzes resulted not in *fragrance* but in *stench*. It is to be noted that the family name *Triacontaphyllos* was known in Constantinople. For instance, Romanus III Argyrus bought a house from one Triacontaphyllos and rebuilt it as the monastery of the Holy Virgin Peribleptos; he was later buried there (Cedrenus, II, 497). A Russian pilgrim, Antonius of Novgorod, mentions 'a monastery *Troyandophilitza*,' Antonius' *Pilgrimage*, ed. Savvaitov (St Petersburg, 1872), p. 116; ed. Loparev, in the *Palestinsky Sbornik*, LI (St Petersburg, 1899), 25 (in Old Russian).

[4] Here Tzetzes probably refers to the Biblical story of Haman, *Esther*, Chapters 3–7.

[5] According to a legend of Chios, Orion, Poseidon's son, was blinded for violating the daughter of King Oenopion, son of Dionysos. He groped his way, however, to Lemnos, and met there one of Hephaestus' workmen, the lame Cedalion. Orion set him on his shoulders and with his help reached the extreme east where the sun rose; and in its radiance he regained his sight.

[6] *Chiliades*, III, Hist. 70, vv. 217–230 (p. 88).

verse (12674 political verses) upon his collected letters, and the letters as
a detailed index to the *Chiliades*; in other words, the connection between
these two works is very close, each completing and explaining the other;
some hints which are incomprehensible in one work are often satisfactorily clarified in the other. Unfortunately, the passage from the
Chiliades quoted above has not survived in the letters. According
to the author himself, the first collection of his letters was partly destroyed, partly distorted, partly disarranged by someone.[1] Tzetzes restored from memory what he could; but he was unable to replace the
destroyed letters, to one of which the passage quoted above refers.[2] It
is obvious that Tzetzes has in view some Archbishop of Gothia who took
part in one of the councils noted above. But I can not identify the 'one-
eyed' Archbishop, 'filled with stench,' who 'prolonged' the meetings of
the council.[3]

4. The Rupture between Gothia and Byzantium

At the end of the twelfth century a change of great importance occurred
in the political life of Crimean Gothia. It broke from its political dependence upon Byzantium and in the thirteenth century came under the
control of the new Empire of Trebizond, which was established in 1204.
We know this from the fact that in the detailed treaty of the partition
of the Empire in 1204 (*Partitio Romaniae*) the northern coast of the Black
Sea, politically and economically important as it was, was passed over in
silence; Byzantine possessions in the Crimea are mentioned neither among
the regions which after 1204 remained under Byzantium nor among the
centers which were ceded to triumphant Venice or other Latin peoples.
Meanwhile, as we shall see a little later, in the twenties of the thirteenth
century Crimean Gothia was dependent upon Trebizond. The puzzling
question now arises as to when and how the secession of Gothia from
Byzantium took place: whether in 1204 in connection with the fatal results of the Fourth Crusade, or earlier. It is very probable that the suzerainty of the Emperors of Trebizond over Cherson, Gothia, and Sugdaia
might from time to time have existed in name only, especially in the first
half of the thirteenth century, when the Polovtzi and later the Tartars
had the upper hand in the Peninsula. We know that beginning with 1170
the evidence which is available at present no longer speaks of the presence
of the Gothic clergy at the Constantinopolitan councils; this silence is un-

---

[1] *Tzetzae Epistolae*, ed. Pressel, p. 61.

[2] G. Hart, 'De Tzetzarum nomine, vita, scriptis,' *Jahrbücher für classische Philologie*, XII, Supple-
mentband (Leipzig, 1881), 41, 47.

[3] Loewe, who knew this passage from the *Chiliades*, following his preconceived theory, considers
it possible that Tzetzes meant here the Caucasian Goths, Loewe, *Die Reste der Germanen*, pp. 218–219.

doubtedly more than a mere accident; it probably indicates that late in the twelfth century the political break between the Empire and Gothia was an accomplished fact, and so prevented the Gothic Archbishops from going to Constantinople.   The fact that in the *notitiae* of the end of the twelfth century and the beginning of the thirteenth the Gothic Archbishopric is noted under the jurisdiction of Constantinople need not trouble us.   Of course from the point of view of ecclesiastical subordination the Gothic Archbishop was still under the jurisdiction of Constantinople; in reality, however, because of new political conditions in the Peninsula, he was sometimes prevented from visiting Constantinople.

We have examined the title 'Gothicus' in Manuel's novella of 1166 in connection with the Byzantine-Genoese treaty of 1169, and have come to the probable conclusion that Gothia, which in the twelfth century was in a state of dependence upon the Polovtzi, at any rate before 1166 came again under the power of Byzantium.

In 1192 Emperor Isaac Angelus confirmed the Genoese privileges of 1169, and in this document the statement about Rosia and Matrakha, which is of great importance for our subject, remained intact.   In the original Greek text of the treaty of 1192 we read the following: 'Genoese vessels shall have full right ($\check{\epsilon}\chi\omega\sigma\iota\nu$ $\dot{\epsilon}\pi'\dot{a}\delta\epsilon\dot{\iota}as$) to traffic in all the regions of my Empire with the exception of Rosia ('Pωσία) and Matrakha unless special permit has been granted by my Imperial Majesty.'[1]   That in 1192 the Emperor was able to confirm in full this passage of the treaty of 1169 indicates that in 1192 Isaac Angelus was still master in the Crimean and Azov waters, and that in this year there were no political complications or new international relations in the Peninsula.

In November, 1198, under Isaac Angelus' successor, Alexius Angelus, and after long negotiations, a treaty was concluded between Byzantium and Venice.[2]   In addition to the renewal of the offensive and defensive alliance between these two states, the *chrysobull* of 1198 contains a special and very elaborate declaration which establishes for Venice freedom of trade within the Empire, and then gives a detailed list of all the provinces and separate points in the Empire open to Venetian traders.   This is an almost complete picture of the geographic composition of the Empire at the end of the twelfth century, which makes this document exceptionally important.[3]   This list mentions no Crimean point whatever un-

---

[1] Miklosich and Müller, *Acta et diplomata*, iii, 35; A. Sanguineti and G. Bertolotto, *Atti della Società Ligure*, xxviii (1896–1898), 422, with a Latin translation, p. 432 (in Latin, 'Russiam et Matracham').

[2] Tafel und Thomas, *Urkunden zur älteren Handels-und Staatsgeschichte der Republik Venedig*, i (Vienna, 1856), 248–278; Zachariae von Lingenthal, *Jus Graeco-Romanum*, iii, 553–565 (he gives the incorrect year for this treaty, 1199 for 1198).

[3] On this treaty see W. Heyd, *Histoire du commerce du Levant au moyen-âge*, i (Leipzig, 1885), 226–228, F. Dölger, *Regesten*, ii (1925), 104–105 (No. 1647); a bibliography is given.

less there is a possible reference in the conclusion, 'And generally speaking
in any possession (*in omni tenumento*) which is under my power, either
on the coast or within the country.'[1]   But it is very difficult to admit
that a treaty including even secondary points could have omitted such
an important center as Cherson in the Crimea.   Apparently in 1198 the
Crimean regions previously held by Byzantium were not under the authority of the Constantinopolitan government.   If in 1198 the Crimea
was already out of reach of Byzantium, it is not at all surprising that the
Crimean possessions are not mentioned in the so-called *Partitio Romaniae*
in 1204.   Some scholars, however, believe that the Crimea shook off the
power of Constantinople in 1204; they attempt accordingly to discover
in the treaty of this year some places in the Crimea.   Bruun, interpreting
the geographic names of the treaty, which are not always clear, somewhat
arbitrarily recognizes in the name Sagudai the Crimean city Sugdaia —
Surozh.[2]   But according to the context of the treaty Sagudai is located
among other places situated near Chersonesus of Thrace, i.e., near the
Strait of Hellespont (Dardanelles) and along the coast of the Sea of
Marmora.[3]   It is relevent to recall that one of the editors of the text of
the *Partitio Romaniae*, Tafel, in spite of his vast knowledge of mediaeval
geography, could not identify Sagudai and in a note to this passage remarked that the name was unknown to him.[4]   But Anna Comnena says
that near Nicaea there was a large settlement, Sagadaus; some scholars
are inclined to identify this with Saccudion, where Theodore of Studium
(Studion) lived.[5]   Of course this place is Sagudai of the treaty of 1204,
for its geographic location is in complete accordance with the context of
the treaty.

Thus the secession of the Byzantine possessions in the Crimea occurred
before 1204, that is, at the end of the twelfth century, perhaps between
1192 and 1198.   The opinion that the Crimea seceded before 1204 was
casually expressed long ago.   In 1854 A. Kunik wrote: 'Under the
Comneni Cherson seems not to have been entirely freed from the Byzantine government; but in 1204 or even under the Angeli it had already
been left to its own fate.   . . . But soon afterwards the republic of Cherson

---

[1] Tafel und Thomas, *Urkunden*, I, 272, Zachariae von Lingenthal, *op. cit.*, III, 561.

[2] Bruun, *Notices historiques*, pp. 8, 14.

[3] Bruun's opinion was refuted by Heyd, *op. cit.*, I, 217.   Cf. Bruun, *Chernomorye*, I, 197; Vasilievski, *Journal of the Ministry of Public Instruction*, CCVI (1879), 110–111.   Both in Russian.

[4] Tafel und Thomas, *Urkunden*, I, 467.

[5] *Annae Comnenae Alexias*, XV, 2 (ed. Reifferscheid, II, 269), *The Alexiad of the Princess Anna
Comnena*, translated into English by Elizabeth Dawes (London, 1928), p. 393.   See W. Tomaschek,
'Zur historischen Topographie von Kleinasien im Mittelalter,' *Sitzungsberichte der Ak. der Wiss. in
Wien., Philos.-philol. Cl.*, CXXIV (1891), 10 (pagination of a reprint), A. Dobroklonski, *The Blessed
Theodore, Confessor and Abbot of Studion*, I (Odessa, 1913), 320 (in Russian).

received new masters in the persons of the Comneni of Asia.'[1]   Later Heyd remarked, 'Probably in the epoch of the treaty (1204) these over-seas territories had already seceded from the Empire.'[2]

On the other hand, we know that at the beginning of the thirteenth century the Byzantine possessions in the Crimea depended upon the Emperors of Trebizond.   How and when was Byzantine authority in the Crimea replaced by that of Trebizond?   Let us turn to the first part of this question.   But we must promise that we shall deal mostly with hypotheses, more or less probable, since the poverty of our evidence gives no solid ground for definite conclusions.

Pursuing his belief, of which we shall speak below, that the rulers of Mankup in the thirteenth century did not belong to the family of the Comneni, F. Braun writes[3] that the rulers of Mankup must have belonged to a Greek line of dynasts which, originating either from the Toparchs of Trebizond or perhaps from Byzantine governors, became in the course of time independent.   'As to this line, on the basis of Russian sources *Khovra* was the most probable form from which for the first time on Russian soil the family name *Chovrin* was formed . . . Under the Comneni in Byzantium we find the noble Greek line of Gabras or Gavras (Γαβρᾶς), the latter name almost identical in sound with the Russian *Chovrin.* Michael Gabras (Gavras) was an eminent commander under Manuel Comnenus.   Therefore it is not impossible that one of the members of this family was appointed by the Emperor Toparch of Gothia and that this line finally rose to the condition of an almost independent dynasty . . . Perhaps the future will bring some new material which may help to solve this question.'

It is time, in my opinion, to reconsider Braun's hypothesis and take into account some new evidence.   The Gabrades family is of great interest for our subject.   This was a well-known Trebizond family, probably of Armenian origin, which produced a number of outstanding members who fought against the Empire for the independence of Trebizond at the end of the eleventh and during the twelfth century.   F. Braun mentions only one representative of the family, Michael Gabras, who for our question is the least characteristic and important.   Before making some conjectural conclusions concerning the secession of the Crimea in general and Gothia in particular from the Byzantine Empire, I wish to turn to the history of the most prominent members of the Gabrades family.   Three are of particular interest: Theodore, Gregory, and Constantine.

[1] A. Kunik, 'The Foundation of the Empire of Trebizond,' *Uchenyya Zapiski* of the Imperial Academy of Sciences in St Petersburg, 1st and 3rd Sections, II (1854), 732.

[2] W. Heyd, *op. cit.,* I, 297.

[3] F. Braun, *Die letzten Schicksale der Krimgoten,* pp. 44–45.

Theodore Gabras (Gavras), born in Chaldaea, an excellent warrior and able commander, was appointed under Alexius Comnenus duke (*dux*) of Trebizond. Freeing Trebizond from the temporary domination of the Turks, he became, about 1091, almost independent ruler of the city, or, as Anna Comnena says, 'allotted it to himself as if it were his special portion.'[1] In order to prevent the danger of the open secession of Trebizond, Alexius Comnenus kept in Constantinople Theodore's son, the young Gregory Gabras. Some time later Theodore took the field against the Turks, who were besieging Paipert (now Baiburt). After mentioning this, Anna Comnena interrupts her narrative to say, 'But the result of Gabras' enterprise and his origin and character shall be reserved for a fitting place.'[2] But there is no further mention of him in the *Alexiad*. A synaxarium compiled in his honor gives information of his later life. Defeated and captured by the Agarenes (i.e., Turks) he was brought to Theodosiopolis (Erzerum) and suffered there a martyr's death.[3] The warrior Theodore Gabras became the saint and holy martyr Theodore Gabras of Trebizond.[4] Later his body was transported to Trebizond, where at that time his nephew Constantine Gabras was ruling, and solemnly buried there. In after days a monastery and a church of Theodore Gabras were built.[5] The memorial of the holy martyr Theodore Gabras occurs under October 2 in the Orthodox calendar, where his death is erroneously dated 1080.[6] In a fragment of a Sinai manuscript of the year 1067, which is now preserved in the Public Library of Leningrad there is a picture of Theodore Gabras, i.e., a miniature in which Jesus Christ puts his hand upon the head of a man, and there is an inscription 'Θεόδωρος πατρίκιος καὶ τοποτηρητὴς ὁ Γαβρᾶς δοῦλος Χριστοῦ.'[7]

---

[1] Anna Comnena, VIII, 9 (ed. Reiffersheid, II, 23); translation by Dawes, p. 211. See Chalandon, *Essai sur le règne d'Alexis I Comnène* (Paris, 1900), p. 146. A lead seal was issued with Theodore Gabras' name, Schlumberger, *Sigillographie de l'Empire Byzantin* (Paris, 1884), p. 665. See also Uspenski, 'The Secession of Trebizond from the Byzantine Empire,' *Seminarium Kondakovianum*, I (Prague, 1927), 27–30 (in Russian).

[2] Anna Comnena, XI, 6 (II, 121), translation by Dawes, p. 284. See Chalandon, *op. cit.*, p. 241, and a correction to this page in his *Jean II Comnène et Manuel I*er *Comnène* (Paris, 1912), p. 37.

[3] Papadopulos-Kerameus, 'On the history of Trebizond,' *Viz. Vremennik*, XII (1905), 135–136; *Idem, Collection of the Sources on the History of the Empire of Trebizond*, I (St Petersburg, 1897), 59.

[4] Zonaras, XVIII, 22: 'Τοῦ Γαβρᾶ ἐκείνου Θεοδώρου τοῦ σεβαστοῦ καὶ μάρτυρος' (ed. Dindorf, IV, 240). DuCange could not understand this phrase. S. Lambros, ''Ο Μαρκιανὸς κῶδιξ 524,' *Νέος Ἑλληνομνήμων*, VIII (1911), 17: See also W. Fischer, 'Trapezus im 11. und 12. Jahrhunderten,' *Mitteilungen des Instituts der oesterreichischen Geschichtsforschung*, X (1889), 193–194.

[5] Miklosich and Müller, *Acta et diplomata*, III, 133; Papadopulos-Kerameus, 'On the History of Trebizond,' *Viz. Vremennik*, XII (1905), 137.

[6] Archimandrite Sergius, *The Complete Liturgical Calendar (Menologion) of the Orient*, 2nd ed. (Vladimir, 1901), II, 306 (in Russian).

[7] This miniature was for the first time published by N. Malitzki, 'Notes on the Epigraphy of Mangup,' *Izvestiya* of the State Academy for the History of Material Culture, LXXI (Leningrad, 1933),

In Theodore's lifetime, his son Gregory Gabras, as has been noted above, lived in Byzantium as a hostage; his attempts to escape and reach his father failed; he was caught, brought back, and closely guarded.[1] There is some discrepancy concerning Gregory's later life.   Some believe that on becoming the *dux* of Trebizond he, like his father, sought for independence from the Empire, but was not so successful as his father. Alexius Comnenus sent against him an expedition which ended in Gregory's defeat; he was captured and brought to Constantinople; but later, owing to the intercession of influential persons, he was released and obtained his freedom.   Scholars holding this opinion identify Gregory Gabras with Gregory Taronites whom Anna Comnena mentions in this connection,[2] that is, the family of the Gabrades is presented by Anna as related to the well-known Armenian family of the princes of Taron.[3] But other scholars, on the basis of Anna Comnena's statement that the duchy of Trebizond had been transferred to the Taronites,[4] distinguish two Gregories.[5]   In my opinion, Gregory Gabras is identical with Gregory Taronites.   Anna Comnena begins the narrative of Gregory's secession thus: 'The Gregory already mentioned who had long been hatching rebellion on being appointed Duke (δούξ) of Trapezus disclosed his secret.'[6] A few lines below she calls him simply 'the Taronites.'   The only Gregory mentioned earlier in her history is Gregory Gabras; therefore Gregory Gabras and Gregory Taronit are one and the same person.   Thus like his father but less successfully Gregory Gabras worked for the complete secession of Trebizond from the Empire.[7]

Constantine Gabras is also mentioned.   According to some scholars, he was Gregory Gabras' son,[8] according to others, Theodore Gabras' son,[9] and according to the synaxarium Theodore's nephew.[10]   Setting aside a

---

24, Plate 5.   On the other leaf of the same Manuscript there is a miniature representing Gabras' wife, Irene.   See V. Beneshevich, *Monumenta Sinaitica archaeologica et palaeographica*, i (Leningrad, 1925), col. 52, Plate 37; Malitzki, *op. cit.*, p. 24, pl. 6.

[1] Anna Comnena, VIII, 9 (II, 23–27); translation by Dawes, pp. 210–213.   See Chalandon, *Essai sur le règne d'Alexis Ier Comnène*, p. 146.

[2] Anna Comnena, XII, 7 (II, 163–164); transl. Dawes, p. 315.

[3] Fallmerayer, *Geschichte des Kaiserthums von Trapezunt* (Munich, 1827), pp. 19–20; K. Hopf, *Griechische Geschichte*, I, 178; Gelzer, *Abriss der byzantinischen Kaisergeschichte*, p. 1036.   A historian of the fourteenth century, Pachymeres, traces the Gabrades family from the Caucasian Lazi (I, 282).

[4] Anna Comnena, XII, 7 (II, 163); transl. Dawes, p. 315.

[5] Vasilievski, *Journal of the Ministry of Public Instruction*, CCIV (1879), 331 (in Russian); W. Fischer, *op. cit.*, pp. 200–201; Chalandon, *Essai*, p. 241, n. 7.

[6] Anna Comnena, XII, 5 (II, 163); transl. Dawes, p. 315.   Cf. G. Buckler, *Anna Comnena* (London, 1929), p. 374.

[7] For the later life of Gregory and his struggle against the Turks see Fallmerayer, *op. cit.*, p. 20; Hopf, *op. cit.*, I, 178.   [8] Fallmerayer and Hopf, *ibid.*

[9] Chalandon, *Jean II Comnène et Manuel 1er Comnène*, p. 37.

[10] *Viz. Vremennik*, XII (1905), 136.

discrepancy among scholars as to time and details of Constantine's uprising, which is not important for our subject,[1] we may point out that in the twenties of the twelfth century, i.e., under John Comnenus, Constantine stood at the head of Trebizond and governed there for a long time as an absolutely independent ruler.[2] But in the sixties of the twelfth century, as has been noted above, Trebizond was again dependent upon the Empire, the imperial governor Nicephorus Palaeologus being appointed there.[3] After Constantine Gabras there is no mention in our evidence of the family of the Gabrades as ruling in Trebizond. In the first half of the twelfth century, the Byzantine government had finally the upper hand over the separatist tendencies of Trebizond. Since the separatist movement had been headed by the Gabrades, and since Theodore, Gregory, and Constantine had energetically worked for independence, we may be almost certain that the triumphant Emperor not only deprived the rebellious family of its rule over Trebizond but also exiled thence its most dangerous members.[4] I find some confirmation for this hypothesis in a passage of the Syriac chronicle of the twelfth century compiled by Michael the Syrian. Under the year 1130 (in the *Chronicle* under the year 1442 of the Seleucid era) he mentions a plot formed in the East against Emperor John Comnenus. 'When the Emperor was preparing to meet the Turks, his brother and some nobles formed a plot against him. As the Emperor wished to catch them, his brother fled to the Emir Gazi. The latter welcomed him, treated him with great honor and sent him to Trebizond to Gabras. The Emperor returned to Constantinople and sent into exile those who had plotted against him.'[5] On the basis of this text we see that the conspirators were exiled. Gabras, who received the Emperor's brother and was on a friendly footing with the Turkish Emir, Gazi, a political enemy of the Empire, also took part in the plot, and evidently was also exiled when the Emperor succeeded in recapturing Trebizond. The fact of Gabras' exile is very important for the point I am about to discuss. Gabras in Michael the Syrian's chronicle is identical with Constantine Gabras who, as we have noted above, became an independent ruler of Trebizond in the twenties of the twelfth century, i.e., shortly before the plot was formed.

Others of the Gabrades are known in the twelfth century both in the Turkish service and in the Imperial service under Manuel. One of the

---

[1] L. Petit, 'Monodie de Théodore Prodrome,' *Izvestiya* of the Russian Archaeological Institute in Constantinople, VIII (1902), 3–4. His conclusions were refuted by S. Papadimitriu, *Theodore Prodromus* (Odessa, 1905), pp. 98–104 (in Russian). See E. Kurtz, in the *Byz. Zeitschr.*, XIII (1904), 536.   [2] *Nicetas Choniatus*, p. 45.

[3] *Idem*, p. 295.   [4] Fallmerayer, *op. cit.*, pp. 20–21.

[5] *Chronique de Michel le Grand*, ed. Chabot, III (Paris, 1903), 230.

Gabrades who possessed a satrapy, according to Cinnamus, 'originated from the Romans but was brought up and educated in Persia';[1] he was captured by the Byzantines and executed.   Among the Imperial troops under Manuel there were some commanders from this family, for instance Michael Gabras,[2] and Constantine Gabras, who in the sixties was sent as ambassador from the Emperor to the Sultan Kilydj-Arslan and betrayed his master.   This Constantine may have been a son of the Constantine mentioned above.[3]   At the end of the thirteenth, and during the four-teenth century, Michael Gabras and John Gabras, probably Michael's brother, are mentioned in Byzantine literature.[4]   In the fourteenth cen-tury there existed in Constantinople the monastery of Gabras.[5]

Thus Constantine Gabras was exiled and we know nothing about the end of his life.   Let us not forget that the sources, for some reason, say nothing as to how Trebizond passed into the power of Byzantium proba-bly under Manuel and what was the end of Constantine Gabras' inde-pendent rule there.   The sources state only the accomplished fact of the subjugation of Trebizond to the Empire, of which we have spoken above. Fallmerayer is inclined to explain the silence of the sources on this point by the fact that Trebizond was reunited with the Empire, not after a successful military campaign which the sources would not have failed to recapitulate, but because of an internal revolution in Trebizond, which transferred the power to the Empire without any parade.[6]

Setting aside the question of how Trebizond became subject to Byzan-tium, I believe that the disappearance of Constantine from our sources may be explained by the fact that he was sent into exile after the occupa-tion of Trebizond by Byzantium; since the Crimea was the usual place of exile for dangerous political criminals, he was exiled there.   This hypothe-sis may explain the further course of events.   Gabras undoubtedly brought to the Crimea the innate tendency of all his family to struggle against Byzantium.   He perhaps obtained in Gothia considerable influ-ence.   When at the end of the rule of the weak and untalented Angeli an opportunity presented itself, he probably sided with Trebizond, his na-tive city, to attain that freedom for which three members of his family

---

[1] Cinnamus, ii, 8 (p. 56).

[2] Cinnamus, v, 8 (p. 226); 13 (pp. 238–239); vi, 3 (p. 258); vii, 1 (p. 293); 2 (p. 296), 3 (p. 299). The same Gabras is apparently mentioned among the members of the Council of 1170, L. Petit, in the *Viz. Vremennik*, xi (1904), 490.

[3] *Nicetas Choniatus*, p. 159.   See Chalandon, *John ii Comnène*, pp. 467, 678.   Hopf erroneously believes (i, 178) that it was the same Constantine.

[4] See Krumbacher, *Geschichte der byzantinischen Litteratur*, 2nd ed., pp. 482, 483, 558–559; S. Lambros, "Ἀρχοτέλειαι ἐπιστολῶν," Νέος Ἑλληνομνήμων, xii (1915), 424.

[5] *Joannis Cantacuzeni Historiae*, iii, 23 (ii, 104).   See DuCange, *Constantinopolis Christiana*, iv, 44 (p. 157).   [6] Fallmerayer, *op. cit.*, p. 21.

had fought.   The family name of Gabrades still exists in Trebizond up
to the present day.[1]   As a survival of the influence of the Gabrades
(Gavrades) in Crimean Gothia may serve the name of the village Gavri,
Gavry, or Gavra, east of Mankup, near Belbek.[2]   The family name Gav-
rasov-Gavradov still exists among the Greeks of the district (*uyezd*) of
Mariupol, on the northern coast of the Sea of Azov, in Urzuf or Kizil-Tash.
At the end of the eighteenth century, with the permission of the Russian
government under Catherine II, more than 31,000 Christians emigrated
from the Crimea; among them were already tartarized descendants of the
Crimean Goths; they were Christians but spoke only Tartar.[3]   This emigration explains the appearance of the family name Gavradov at Urzuf.
Thus our hypothesis helps to explain the fact, obscure at first glance, of
the dependence of Crimean Gothia upon the Empire of Trebizond.

   Moreover, the same hypothesis confirms the possible origin of the Russian family name *Khovrini* from a certain Khovra, i.e. Gabras, who late
in the fourteenth century came from the Crimea to Moscow.   In the
sixteenth century Prince Kurbski, who under Ivan IV the Terrible fled
from Russia to Lithuania, testifies to the fact that the name of the
Khovrini was of Greek origin; he writes, 'The same day his brother-in-
law, Peter Khovrin, a man of a very noble and rich Greek family, was
killed with him.'[4]   In any case, the Russian family name *Khovrini* has
nothing to do with the Comneni, as is usually stated, especially in the
books on the origin of the family name *Golovini*, which derive this name
from *Khovrini*; the authors try to recognize in the latter name a distorted
name of the Comneni through the form *Comrin*.[5]

   Perhaps a passage in the historical work of an Arabic writer of the
thirteenth century, Ibn-al-Athir, may give us a hint as to the growing
power of Trebizond at the very beginning of the thirteenth century in the
basin of the Black Sea, and probably in the Crimea.   Under the year
1205–1206 (602 of the Hegira) Ibn-al-Athir relates that the sultan of
Iconium, Guiyath-ad-din-Kay-Khusru I, 'prepared war against the city
of Trebizond and besieged its lord, because the latter had disobeyed and
harassed him.' Ibn-al-Athir continues: 'On account of this the routes by

---

[1] Ἰωαννίδου Ἱστορία καὶ στατιστικὴ Τραπεζοῦντος (Constantinople, 1870), p. 42.

[2] Köppen, *Krymsky Sbornik*, p. 77 (in Russian); Braun, *Die Schicksale der Krimgoten*, p. 45.

[3] Kunik, 'On the Report of a Gothic Toparch,' p. 142 (in Russian).   Braun, *op. cit.*, pp. 70–75.
For a very brief summary of the Gabrades see also Malitzki, *op. cit.*, pp. 22–23 (in Russian).

[4] Prince Kurbski, *Works*, I (St Petersburg, 1914), 281, *Russian Historical Library*, XXXI (in Russian).

[5] P. Kazanski, *The Village Novospasskoe, or Dedenevo and the Genealogy of the Golovini* (Moscow,
1847), p. 113; N. Golovin, *Some Words on the Family of the Greek Princes Comneni* (Moscow, 1854),
pp. 11–12; P. Petrov. *A History of the Families of Russian Nobility (dvoryanstva)*, I (St Petersburg,
1886), 268.   All three in Russian.

land and sea from Asia Minor, Russia, and Kipchak [i.e., from the land of the Polovtzi] were blocked, so that no one came thence into the land of Guiyath-ad-din; and great harm befell the men, because they carried on trade with them [the Russians] and the Kipchaks [Polovtzi] and visited their cities; and traders were proceeding to them from Syria, Irak, Mosul, Djezireh, and so on; and many of them gathered in the city of Sivas. But since the road was not open, they suffered great damage, and he was lucky who saved his principal.'[1]

This text shows that the Emperor of Trebizond, whose Empire had just been formed in 1204, attained such power and authority on the Black Sea that he was able to interrupt commercial relations between the Turks and the people of the northern coast of the Black Sea in general and the Crimea in particular; this is indicated by Ibn-al-Athir's mention of the Kipchaks, as the Arabs called the Polovtzi, who in the opening years of the thirteenth century still played the chief rôle in the Crimea. If the breaking off of commercial relations between the south and north harmed the Turks, as Ibn-al-Athir relates, the Polovtzi in the north for their part were also discontented. Since the Emperor of Trebizond none the less was able to stop trade, this circumstance can indicate only that he could lay an embargo in the Crimea on Polovtzian trade with the Turks; and he was able to do so most successfully because he himself held power and strength in the Crimea. Therefore I consider it possible to use this passage of Ibn-al-Athir for a proof, though indirect, that in 1205–1206 a portion of the Crimea, namely Crimean Gothia, was already dependent upon Trebizond.

On the basis of these sources, we reach a conclusion which is not entirely proved, but is possible and indeed probable. We conclude that Crimean Gothia became independent of Byzantium before 1204, that is, at the very end of the twelfth century, perhaps between 1192 and 1198.[2]

---

[1] *Ibn-el-Athiri Chronicon*, ed. Tornberg, xii (Leyden, 1853), 160; also in the *Recueil des historiens des croisades, Historiens orientaux*, ii, i (Paris, 1887), 101–102. A Russian translation of this fragment in Kunik, *The Foundation of the Empire of Trebizond*, p. 730, and in A. Yakubovski, 'An account of Ibn-al-Bibi on the Campaign of the Turks of Asia Minor against Sudak, Polovtzi and Russians at the Outset of the Thirteenth Century,' *Viz. Vremennik*, xxv (1927–1928), 65–66. See Vasilievski, *Works*, iii, p. 169 (in Russian). Th. Houtsma, *Ueber eine türkische Chronik zur Geschichte der Selguqen Klein-Asiens*, in the *Actes du VIe Congrès International des orientalistes tenu en 1883 à Leide*, ii (Leiden, 1885), p. 377.

[2] My conclusions concerning the importance of the Gabrades in the process of the secession of Gothia from Byzantium have been accepted by N. Bănescu, 'Contribution à l'histoire de la seigneurie de Théodoro-Mangoup en Crimée,' *Byz. Zeitschrift*, xxxv (1935), 37.

CHAPTER IV

THE EPOCH OF THE LATIN EMPIRE (1204-1261) AND THE DEPENDENCE OF GOTHIA UPON THE EMPIRE OF TREBIZOND

IN the preceding chapter we reached the conclusion that in the year 1204, when the Fourth Crusade resulted in the capture of Constantinople, the founding of the Latin Empire, and the partition of the Byzantine Empire among the Crusaders, Crimean Gothia was not under the power of Byzantium, but depended upon Trebizond. The Empire of Trebizond proclaimed under the dynasty of the Great Comneni in the very year of the founding of the Latin Empire became for the thirteenth century one of the three Greek centers which for a long time were to uphold the traditions of Hellenism. These three were the Empire of Trebizond, the Empire of Nicaea, and the 'Despotate' or Principality of Epirus, whose despot, Theodore Angelus, in 1222 conquered Thessalonica (Salonica) and proclaimed the short-lived Empire of Thessalonica (1222–1230).

In the first half of the thirteenth century the dependence of Crimean Gothia or the Gothic *Climata* upon Trebizond was manifested by the payment of an annual tribute. Valuable evidence on this subject is preserved in a compilation (synopsis) of the miracles attributed to St Eugenius, the famous patron of Trebizond. The author of this compilation, John Lazaropoulos, lived in the second half of the fourteenth century in Trebizond; he was a high official of the clergy, and in 1364, under the name of Joseph, was elected Metropolitan of Trebizond; in 1367 he retired and in 1368, because of the attack of the Turks upon Trebizond, left for Constantinople, where he probably ended his days.[1] According to the Greek text of the miracles of St Eugenius,[2] the Emperor of Trebizond, Andronicus I Gidon or Gidos (1222–1235) and the Seljuq

---

[1] See A. Papadopulos-Kerameus, *Fontes historiae Imperii Trapezuntini*, I (St Petersburg, 1897), viii–xi (in Russian). On the error of Fallmerayer, who attributed the compilation to a certain Lazarus who never existed, see *ibid.*, p. ix. From Fallmerayer this error passed into the first edition of the *Bibliotheca hagiographica graeca* (Brussels, 1895), p. 41; see also the second edition (1909), pp. 84–85; also Archbishop Sergius, *The Complete Liturgical Calendar (Menologion) of the Orient*, 2nd ed. (Vladimir, 1901), II, i, 20, and II, ii, 34 (in Russian).

[2] The Greek text in Papadopulos-Kerameus, *op. cit.*, pp. 117–118. The first edition of this text by Fallmerayer, 'Original-Fragmente, Chroniken, Inschriften und anderes Materiale zur Geschichte des Kaiserthums Trapezunt,' Erste Abtheilung, *Abhandlungen der hist. Classe der K. Bayerischen Akademie der Wissenschaften*, III, Dritte Abtheilung (Munich, 1843), pp. 71–72. A Russian translation of the Greek text in Th. Uspenski, *Outlines of the History of the Empire of Trebizond* (Leningrad, 1929), pp. 51–58.

Sultan, Melik, made a treaty of peace, so that 'the population dwelling round the forts could live quietly.' But this agreement was violated by Melik's subordinate official, Hetum, the governor of Sinope ('Ραΐση τοῦ 'Ετούμη). In 1223 a vessel named the *Serion* (τὸ Σέριον) carrying the money collected from Cherson and the Gothic *Climata* to be paid to Andronicus Gidon as annual tribute, sailed to Trebizond. The vessel had on board the *archon*, Alexis Paktiares, who evidently collected the annual taxes, and some other notables (ἄρχοντες) of Cherson. But by a violent storm the vessel was driven to Sinope where the governor, Hetum, seized vessel, money, passengers, and sailors; in addition he sent ships to plunder the territory of Cherson. When the news reached Trebizond, Andronicus, angry at the violation of the treaty with the Sultan and the damage caused by Hetum, despatched a fleet and troops against Sinope. They landed at Karusa (εἰς Κάρουσαν), not far from Sinope, and plundered the whole district right up to the harbor.[1] They slew or captured the crews of the ships lying in the harbor. The relatives of these crews and of the commanders of the ships revolted against the governor and heaped him with injuries. Instead of retaliating, Hetum sent envoys to Trebizond to make peace. After long negotiations the Emperor finally exchanged his captives for Alexis Paktiares, the *Serion*, and the sums which had been taken from him, as well as all the plunder carried off from the *Climata* of Cherson. After this the Trebizond fleet 'returned home cheerful.' This episode provoked a war between Andronicus Gidon and the Sultan Melik, which ended in the latter's defeat.[2]

For our subject it is extremely important to emphasize the fact that in the first half of the thirteenth century the Emperor of Trebizond was the suzerain of Cherson and Crimean Gothia, or, in other words, of a considerable section of western and mountain Crimea. These dependencies of the crown of Trebizond, as we shall see later, were given in the title

---

[1] 'ἄχρι καὶ αὐτοῦ ἐμπορίου Σινώπης' (p. 117). The Greek word 'ἐμπόριον' means a 'trading place,' 'market place,' 'mart.' Uspenski, (*op. cit.*, p. 51) translates it 'the harbor'; W. Miller, 'the mart.' W. Miller, *Trebizond, The Last Greek Empire* (London, 1926), p. 20.

[2] See A. Kunik, 'The Foundation of the Empire of Trebizond in 1204,' *Bulletin* (*Uchenyya Zapiski*) *of the Imperial Academy of Sciences*, ii (St Petersburg, 1854), 734; Vasilievski, *Works*, iii, clxxiv–clxxv; J. Kulakovski, *The Past of the Tauris*, 2nd ed. (Kiev, 1914), p. 96; Uspenski, *op. cit.*, pp. 48–58; G. Finlay, *A History of Greece*, ed. by Tozer, iv (Oxford, 1877), 328–336; W. Miller, *Trebizond* (London, 1926), pp. 20–23; G. Bratianu, *Recherches sur le commerce génois dans la Mer Noire au XIIIe siècle* (Paris, 1929), pp. 169–170. See a rather misleading passage in Alb. M. Condioti, *Historia de la institución consular en la antigüedad y en la edad media*, i (Madrid, Berlin, Buenos-Aires, Mexico, 1925), 544: 'The Crimean Goths, famous for their humanity towards foreigners, were allies of the Greeks and were incorporated in the Empire, until the establishment of the Latin Empire made them, along with the whole southern coast of the Crimea, dependent on the Empire of Trebizond'; also p. 600, n. 2.

of the Emperors of Trebizond as 'the overseas land' ($\dot{\eta}$ $\pi\epsilon\rho\alpha\tau\epsilon\acute{\iota}\alpha$); their dependence was outwardly manifested by the payment of an annual tribute,
which was conveyed yearly from the Crimea to Trebizond.   Andronicus
Gidon took very seriously his obligations to his vassal possessions in the
Crimea, so that after the incident at Sinope he did not stop at sending a
punitive expedition against the governor Hetum, but even became involved in a war with the Seljuq Sultan himself.   It is not clear what ad-
vantages Cherson and Crimean Gothia enjoyed in return for recognizing
the suzerainty of the weak Empire of Trebizond, whose independence in
the thirteenth century was of brief duration.   A few years after Andronicus' success over the Seljuq Sultan Melik, Trebizond became the vassal
of the Sultan of Iconium.   Communication between Trebizond and the
Crimea became very insecure, the more so as the Turks themselves also
set up a fleet in the Black Sea.   In addition, at that time new events in
the Crimea itself changed the situation.   A new foe appeared in the
Crimea: the Mongols or Tartars.

The Mongolian hordes crossed the Caucasus Mountains, and passing
through the steppes of the Don, penetrated into the Crimea.   In January,
1223, the Tartars for the first time attacked Sudak (Sugdaia, Surozh) on
the shores of the Black Sea, as is noted in a synaxarium of Sugdaia.[1]   An
Arab historian of the thirteenth century Ibn-al-Athir, gives more information on this point.   According to him, the Tartars took possession of
Sudak, and its inhabitants abandoned their city.   Some of them with
their families and possessions ascended the mountains; others took ship
and sailed to the Seljuq states in Asia Minor.[2]   Setting aside Ibn-al-
Athir's rather obscure statement about the departure of the Christian
population of Sudak to the Muhammedan states in Asia Minor,[3] we may
conclude that a portion of the threatened population of Sudak took refuge
in the mountains; it is very probable that many of the fugitives found
shelter in the territory of Crimean Gothia, which was partly mountainous
(its capital, Theodoro-Mankup, was on the top of a mountain).   During

[1] Archbishop Antoninus, 'Notes of the Twelfth–Fifteenth Centuries Referring to Sugdaia and
Written in a Greek Synaxarium,' *Zapiski* of the Odessa Society of History and Antiquities, v (1863),
601, No. 33 (in Greek and Russian).   This is a collection of brief Lives of the Saints (synaxarium) of
the twelfth century with some interesting notes on its margins made by the possessors of the code in
the thirteenth to the fifteenth centuries.

[2] Ibn-al-Athir, *Chronicon*, ed. Tornberg, xii (Leyden, 1853), 248, *Recueil des historiens des Croisades, Historiens orientaux*, ii, i, 160; V. Tisenhausen, *A Collection (Sbornik) of the Materials Referring to the History of the Golden Horde*, i (St Petersburg, 1884), 26 (in Russian); Abulfeda, *Annals*, in
the *Recueil des Croisades, Hist. Or.*, i, 96.   See A. Yakubovski, 'The Account of Ibn-al-Bibi on the
campaign of the Turks of Asia Minor against Sudak, Polovtzi, and Russians at the Outset of the
Thirteenth Century,' *Viz. Vremennik*, xxv (1927–1928), 58 ff. (in Russian).

[3] See Vasilievski, iii, clxxiii; Uspenski, *Outlines of the History of the Empire of Trebizond*, pp. 47–48.
Both in Russian.

this campaign the Tartars defeated the Polovtzi or Cumans, who before this, as we have seen, had been very powerful in the Crimea. This Mongolian invasion of the Crimea was of brief duration; in the same year, 1223, the Mongols left the Peninsula and crushed the Russian and Cuman forces on the river Kalka near the Sea of Azov. After this the Tartars turned eastward and disappeared as suddenly as they had come. A Russian chronicler wrote: 'We know not whence they came, nor where they hid themselves again; God knows whence he fetched them against us for our sins.'[1] It is very interesting to note that after the departure of the Tartars trade and commerce were reëstablished in the Crimea.[2] Probably during this first very short visit of the Tartars to the Crimea the territory of Gothia was not invaded.

Fifteen years later in 1238 the Tartars once more visited the Crimea. This was the epoch of the famous campaign of the Mongolian Khan Baty against Russia. An enormous territory was conquered by the Tartars, who in 1240 sacked Kiev and in their irrepressible rush westwards crossed the Carpathians into Hungary and Poland. But in Bohemia Baty was checked; he retreated and retraced his march to the lower Volga. This was the beginning of the Tartar yoke in Russia. Parallel to this main stream of the invasion, the Tartars once more appeared in the Crimea.

According to the Synaxarium of Sudak already mentioned, in 1239 the Tartars once more visited Sudak and plundered the city; but ten years later, in 1249, they left Sudak, and the city solemnly celebrated its liberation.[3] Gothia also was invaded and devastated by the Tartars. Sanudo Marino Senior, who died about 1337, summarizing under the year 1242 all devastations inflicted by the Tartars, mentions Gothia among other countries.[4] One of the greatest Byzantine scholars and writers of the fourteenth century, Nicephorus Gregoras, also relates that among the peoples neighboring on Lake Maeotis and dwelling on the shores of the Black Sea, who in the thirteenth century were invaded by the Tartars,

[1] *The Chronicle of Novgorod 1016–1471*, transl. R. Michell and N. Forbes, Camden Society, 3rd Series, xxv (London, 1914), 66.

[2] See Vasilievski, *ibid.*; Uspenski, *op. cit.*, p. 47.

[3] Arch. Antoninus, *op. cit.*, *Zapiski* of the Odessa Society, v (1863), 597, No. 10, and 611, No. 104. See Vasilievski, iii, pp. clxxvi–clxxvii; G. Bratianu, *Recherches sur le commerce génois dans la Mer Noire au XIIIe siècle* (Paris, 1929), p. 203; Virginie Vasiliu, 'Sur la seigneurie de "Tedoro" en Crimée au XVe siècle, à l'occasion d'un nouveau document,' *Mélanges de l'école roumaine en France* (Paris, 1929), i part, 317–318.

[4] Marinus Sanutus dictus Torsellus, *Liber Secretorum Fidelium Crucis super Terrae Sanctae recuperatione et conservatione*, iii, 11, 16: 'Sequenti vero anno (1242) in partibus Aquilonis, Tartari vastant Rusiam, Gasariam, Sugdaniam, Gotiam, Ziquiam, Alaniam, Poloniam, caeteraque regna usque triginta; et usque ad Theotoniae fines prosiliunt'; Bongars, *Gesta Dei per Francos*, ii (Hanover, 1611), 217. Tomaschek (*Die Goten in Taurien*, p. 42) gives an incorrect reference, 'iii, 12, 16' for 'iii, 11, 16.' From Tomaschek this inexact reference passed to Vasilievski, *Works*, iii, clxxvi, n. 2 (iii, 12).

were the Goths.[1]   None the less, the whole Crimea was not really conquered.   However, the Tartars firmly established themselves in the eastern part of the Crimea, along the shores of the Black Sea, from Caffa
to Sugdaia, with a Tartar governor resident at Solkhat (Eski-Krim, Old-
Krim), in the interior of the country, one day's journey on post-horses
from the shore.[2]   Sugdaia was at that time a very important economic
center for trade with the south, Constantinople, Trebizond, and the coast
of Asia Minor, as well as a very active intermediary port for trade with
Central Asia.   Other regions of the Crimea were obliged to pay tribute
to the Tartars, Gothia among them.   F. Braun wonders 'whether the
Goths had only to pay tribute to the Tartars or whether their dependence
was greater.'[3]   Our evidence is scanty and fragmentary, but, in my opinion, in the thirteenth century the dependence of Crimean Gothia upon
the Tartars consisted only in tribute; there is no indication whatever that
a Tartar governor resided in Theodoro-Mankup.

In connection with the creation in the thirteenth century of the huge
Mongolian Empire stretching from the Pacific in the east to the Adriatic
Sea in the west and the establishment for a considerable time of order and
safety all over the colossal territory of the new state, the mysterious depths
of Central Asia and the Far East were opened to Europe.   Many missionaries and traders streamed into Asia, and by reason of the manifold
results of their remarkable discoveries and achievements they may be
regarded as the real predecessors of Christopher Columbus and Vasco da
Gama.   The best known travellers of the thirteenth century were John
de Plano Carpini, William de Rubruquis, and Marco Polo.   Plano Carpini, a Franciscan monk who passed through Russia in 1246 on a mission
from the Pope to the Mongol Khan at Karakorum, in Central Asia, did
not touch the Crimea and made no mention of the Goths.   But he has
preserved an oral statement of his companion and interpreter, Friar
Benedict the Pole (Benedictus Polonus), in which the name of the Goths
is given.   The statement, in Plano Carpini's version, runs as follows:
'The Friars journeying through Comania had to their right the land of
the Saxons whom we believe to be Goths, and they are Christians; then
the Alani who are Christians; then the Gazari who are Christians; then
the Circassians, and they also are Christians.'[4]   Thus, according to Plano

---

[1] *Nicephori Gregorae Historiae*, II, 5 (Bonn ed., I, 36): 'τὰ δὲ ὁμοροῦντα τῇ Μαιώτιδι καὶ τὴν τοῦ
Πόντου πληροῦντα παράλιον, Ζικχοί τ' 'Αβασγοί τε ἦσαν, Γοτθοί τε καὶ 'Αμαξόβιοι, Ταυροσκύθαι τε καὶ
Βορυσθενεῖται.'   Nicephorus Gregoras relates this under the reign of John III Ducas Vatatzes (1222–
1254).   [2] See Vasilievski, III, clxxxi, n. 2.

[3] F. Braun, *Die letzten Schicksale der Krimgoten*, p. 21.

[4] 'Fratres euntes per Comaniam a dextris habuerunt terram Saxonum, quos nos credimus esse
Gotos, et hii sunt christiani; postea Alanos, qui sunt christiani; postea Gazaros, qui sunt christiani;
deinde Circassos, et hii sunt christiani,' *Recueil de voyages et de mémoires publié par la Société de*

Carpini, Benedictus Polonus identified the *Saxones* with the Goths. Plano Carpini himself mentions the *Sassi* among many other peoples conquered by the Mongols.[1] But Benedict the Pole was wrong in identifying the Saxones with the Goths; his *Saxones* and Plano Carpini's *Sassi* must have been a north-Caucasian people dwelling on the river Terek, Chechentsy, Sasones-Sarmatiae in the *Tabula Peutingeriana*, Σάσονες in Ptolemy, still later Σάσοι in Laonikos Chalcocondyles, Sassoni or Sasoni in some other sources, who together with the Circassians became later fanatical Muhammedans.[2] Apparently the name of a German people, the Saxons, caused Benedict to make the mistake; only one German people lay on his way eastwards, the Goths in the Crimea. However, he knew that somewhere in the south of the east European steppes the Goths existed; otherwise he could not have identified them with the Saxons.

On 21 May 1253 William de Rubruquis with his companions and interpreter landed in Soldaia (Surozh) from Constantinople, as we have said above. He not only gives us an extremely interesting description of the Crimea, including a mention of the Goths, but he also makes for the first time a statement, valuable at first glance, that the Goths used the Germanic tongue. Rubruquis' description runs as follows:

There are high promontories on the seashore, from Kersona unto the mouth of Tanais. There are forty castles between Kersona and Soldaia, every one of which almost has its proper language; among whom there were many Goths, who spoke the Teutonic tongue ('quorum idioma est Teutonicum'). Beyond the said mountains towards the north there is a most beautiful wood growing on a plain full of fountains and freshets. And beyond the wood there is a mighty plain, continuing five days' journey unto the very extremity and borders of the said province northward, and there is a narrow Isthmus having sea on the east and west sides thereof, insomuch that there is a ditch made from one sea unto the other. In the same plain, before the Tartars came were the Comanians [Comani] wont to inhabit, who compelled the foresaid cities and castles to pay tribute to them. But when the Tartars came, the great multitude of the Comanians entered into that province, and fled all of them unto the sea shore . . . .[3]

Géographie, éd. M.d'Avezac, IV (Paris, 1839), 776; *The Journey of William de Rubruck to the Eastern Parts of the World (1253–55) with two Accounts of the Earlier Journey of John of Pian de Carpine*, translated by W. W. Rockhill (London, 1900), p. 36.

[1] *The Texts and Versions of John de Plano Carpini and William de Rubruquis*, ed. C. R. Beazley (London, 1903), p. 68. Some manuscripts give *Cassi* for *Sassi* (see *ibid.*, notes, p. 261).

[2] See Tomaschek, *op. cit.*, p. 44.

[3] *Itinerarium fratris Willielmi de Rubruquis de ordine Fratrum Minorum, Galli, anno gratiae 1253 ad partes Orientales, Recueil de voyages et de mémoires publié par la Société de Géographie*, éd. M. d'Avezac, IV (Paris, 1839), 219; *The Texts and Versions of John de Plano Carpini and William de Rubruquis*, ed. C. R. Beazley (London, 1903), pp. 146–147 (English version, p. 187); *The Journey of William of Rubruck to the Eastern Parts of the World*, transl. by W. W. Rockhill, pp. 50–51; *Contemporaries of*

Of course Rubruquis' most important statement is that in the thirteenth century the Crimean Goths still spoke German.   His information about the forty castles ('quadraginta castella') seems confirmed by an Arabic geographer of the fourteenth century, Abulfeda, who died in 1331. In his geographic work completed in 1321 Abulfeda describes certain places in the Crimea, Sary-Kerman (i.e. Cherson), Kerker or Kerkri, Sudak, Solgat (Solkhat), Kafa (Alkaffa), Kerch (Alkerch).   For our subject Kerker or Kerkri (Qyrq-ier, now Chufut-Kalé) is of great interest. Abulfeda writes:

Kerker or Kerkri, the 55th degree and a half of longitude and the 50th degree of latitude.   Kerker is situated at the extremity of the seventh climate, in the country of the Asses.[1]   Its name signifies in Turkish 'forty places.'[2]   This is a fortified castle, hard of access: indeed it leans against a mountain which cannot be scaled.   On the mountain is a plateau where the inhabitants of the country (in time of danger) take refuge.   This castle is some distance from the sea; the inhabitants belong to the race called Ass.   In the neighborhood there is a mountain which rises high in the air and is called Djathir (Chatyr)-dagh [in Turkish, Tent Mountain].   This mountain is visible to vessels sailing on the Crimean Sea.   Kerker is located north of Sary-Kerman; between these two places is about a day's distance.[3]

In his description Abulfeda considers Kerker a single settlement, which is perfectly correct; we know that Kerker or Qyrq-ier is now Chufut-Kalé.[4]   Rubruquis on his journey through the Crimea from Sudak did not visit personally the western part of the Peninsula, and therefore took Qyrq-ier, which is a name meaning 'forty places,' for forty different castles.   Perhaps we deal here with an earlier use of the name Qyrq-ier (forty places), when it signified not one single place, but the southern part of the Crimea between Cherson and Soldaia (Sudak); the name was later limited to one place, namely the present Chufut-Kalé.[5]   Whether or not this was really the case we do not know.   In this connection

---

Marco Polo, ed. M. Komroff (New York, 1928), pp. 57–58; a Russian translation by A. Malein (St Petersburg, 1910), p. 68.   A portion of Rubruquis' description has already been given above, in connection with the Polovtzian (Cuman) predominance in the Crimea.

[1] The Asses-Ass are the Alans.   In his English translation of the Russian Primary Chronicle S. H. Cross calls them the Yasians (p. 171), a name closer to the old Russian form *Yasi*.

[2] Reinaud's translation, (see the following note) gives 'quarante hommes,' which is incorrect.   The second part of the name *Qyrq-ier* is a Turkish word *ier*, 'a place,' not *ĕr*, 'a man.'   See Tomaschek, *Die Goten in Taurien*, p. 43.

[3] *The Arabic Text of Abulfeda*, ed. M. Reinaud and M. de Slane (Paris, 1840), p. 214; *Géographie d'Aboulféda, traduite de l'arabe en français par M. Reinaud*, II (Paris, 1848), 319.

[4] Defining the geographic term *Crimea* Abulfeda says, 'The Crimea (Alkirim) is the name of a country which contains about forty cities,' Arabic text by M. Reinaud and M. Slane, p. 200; French translation by M. Reinaud, II, i, 282.

[5] Tomaschek, *op. cit.*, p. 43; Braun, *Die letzten Schicksale*, p. 53.

Rubruquis' statement that the Crimean Goths used the Germanic (Teutonic) tongue perhaps loses some of its authenticity, which at first sight seemed indubitable.　Rubruquis himself failed to visit Gothia; he did not hear the Goths speak, and he received his information by hearsay, from some inhabitants of the Crimea, most probably at Soldaia (Sudak).[1]　But in any case Rubruquis' description rightly reflects the very heterogeneous population of the Peninsula where 'almost every one of forty castles spoke its own language' ('quorum quodlibet fere habet proprium idioma').　We are well assured that juxtaposition of various races has always been a characteristic feature of the ethnic composition of the Crimea.

It is relevant to emphasize here Abulfeda's very interesting statement about the Alans (Asses, Ass) dwelling in the neighborhood of Cherson and Qyrq-ier (Chufut-Kalé), or in other words including very probably some part of Crimean Gothia.　In this connection it is not amiss to say a few words about the 'Epistle of Theodore, Bishop of the Alans to Constantinople and the bishops living therein' (Θεοδώρου ἐπισκόπου ᾿Αλανίας λόγος ἐπιστολιμαῖος πρὸς τὴν Κωνσταντινούπολιν καὶ τοὺς ἐνδημοῦντας τῶν ἐπισκόπων').[2]　This document belongs to the year 1240 or thereabouts and gives very interesting data on the Alans dwelling near Cherson.　Theodore was ordained Bishop of Alania by the Patriarch of Nicaea, Germanus III (1222–1240); he sailed to the place of his bishoprics via the Chersonesian Bosporus, whence he sailed eastwards and landed some where on the Caucasian coast.　But this was not the end of his exhausting voyage; from the coast he proceeded by land and after a sixty days' journey finally reached the confines of his far-distant flock.　From there Theodore wrote the epistle.[3]　For our subject, Theodore's passage about the Alans is very interesting; they dwelt in the neighborhood of Cherson, but they were 'neither wanted nor voluntary [settlers]'; they served the city as 'a sort of wall and fortified enclosure.'[4]　They lived under very primitive conditions, 'scattered in the mountains, deserted places and caves, having neither cattle folds nor huts.'[5]　Thus by the middle of the thirteenth century the Alans lived in the neighborhood of Cherson and had to defend and protect the city against an enemy, probably the Tartars.　It

---

[1] Cf. Braun, *op. cit.*, p. 53: 'Die erste sichere Nachricht von der germanischen Sprache der Krimgoten erhalten wir durch den Bericht des Franziskanermönches W. Ruysbrock [Rubruquis].'　See also R. Loewe, *Die Reste der Germanen am Schwarzen Meere*, p. 114.

[2] Mai, *Patrum Nova Bibliotheca*, VI, 379 ff.; *Patr. Gr.*, CXL, coll. 387–414; a Russian translation by Kulakovski, *Zapiski* of the Odessa Society of History and Antiquities, XXI (1898), 15–27.

[3] Tomaschek (*op. cit.*, p. 42) seems to believe that Theodore's bishopric was among the Alans, near Cherson, which is incorrect.　See a misprint in C. Macartney, *The Magyars in the Ninth Century* (Cambridge, 1930), p. 49, n. 4 ('Theodosius, Bishop of Alania,' for 'Theodore').

[4] 'οὐχ ἧττον θελητθέντες ἢ θελήσαντες, ὡς οἷόν τι περιτείχισμα ταύτῃ καὶ περιφρούρημα,' Mai, VI, 383; *Patr. Gr.*, CXL, col. 393.　　　[5] *Ibid.*

is hardly to be supposed that in the thirteenth century the Chersonesian Alans had to protect the city against Gothia, because, as we know, the Gothic *Climata* and Cherson were both at that time vassal possessions of Trebizond; in addition, the common danger from the Tartars must have made them forget internal rivalry and friction.   One thing is certain, that the Alans also occupied some portion of the territory of Gothia.[1]

Towards the end of the thirteenth century the famous traveller Marco Polo (1254–1324), who spent many years in the Far East (1271–1295), mentions Gothia among other countries conquered by the Tartars under Baty.   He writes:[2] 'The first lord of the Tartars of the Ponent was Sain,[3] a very great and puissant king, who conquered Rosia and Comania, Alania, Lac,[4] Menjar,[5] Zic, Gothia, and Gazaria; all these provinces were conquered by King Sain.   Before his conquest these all belonged to the Comanians. . . .'

All the missionaries journeying to the Far East were provided with special papal instructions and privileges; the chief aim of the Popes at this time was to convert the pagan Eastern peoples to Christianity and to bring back the schismatics to the bosom of the Catholic Church.   Some papal instructions mention the Goths among other peoples.   In a letter of Pope Gregory IX, 11 June 1239, to the 'Fratribus ordinis Minorum in terras Sarracenorum, paganorum, Graecorum, Bulgarorum, Cumanorum aliorumque infidelium proficiscentibus'[6] the name of the Goths is not mentioned.   But they are included among the 'alii infideles,' because a letter of Pope Innocent IV, 22 March 1245, which practically confirmed the instructions of the previous letter, reads as follows: 'Dilectis filiis fratribus de ordine fratrum Minorum in terras Sarracenorum, paganorum, Grecorum, Bulgarorum, Cumanorum, Ethiopum, Syrorum, Iberorum, Alanorum, Gazarorum, *Gothorum*, Zicorum, Ruthenorum, Jacobinorum, Nubianorum, Nestorinorum, Georgianorum, Armenorum, Indorum, Mesolitorum aliarumque infidelium nationum Orientus seu quarumcunque aliarum partium proficiscentibus.   Cum hora undecima — nulli ergo,'

---

[1] On Theodore, Bishop of Alania, see *Patr. Gr.*, CXL, coll. 385–388, and especially Vasilievski, *Works*, III, clvii–clviii, and J. Kulakovski, *The Past of the Tauris*, 2nd ed. (Kiev, 1914), pp. 98–100.

[2] *The Book of Ser Marco Polo*, translated and edited with notes by Sir Henry Yule, 3rd ed., revised by Henri Cordier (of Paris), II (New York, 1903), 490 (Book IV, Chapter XXIV).

[3] This is Baty himself.   He bore the surname of *Sain Khan*, or 'the Good Prince.'

[4] The Yule-Cordier edition states that *Lac* means here the Wallachs.   Bratianu sees in *Lac* a Caucasian tribe *Lesgi*, now the Lezguins, G. Bratianu, *Recherches sur le commerce génois dans la Mer Noire au XIIIe siècle* (Paris, 1929), pp. 295–300 (especially p. 299).

[5] The interpretation of this name is uncertain.   Perhaps 'Mingrelians'?

[6] A. Potthast, *Regesta Pontificum Romanorum*, I (Berlin, 1874), 911, No. 10763.   See P. G. Golubovich, *Biblioteca bio-bibliografica della Terra Santa e dell' Oriente Franciscano*, II (Quaracchi, 1913), 316.

etc.[1]   No doubt the Goths were also meant in another letter by the same Pope, 25 March 1245, in which he 'universos patriarchas, archiepiscopos, episcopos in terris Bulgarorum, Blacorum, Gazarorum . . . ceterorumque christianorum Orientis rogat et obsecrat, ut ad unitatem sacrosanctae Romanae ecclesiae redeant, eisque fratres ordinis fratrum Minorum latores praesentium commendat.'[2]   From these letters it is obvious how far-reaching were the papal plans and interests in the thirteenth century, especially in connection with new perspectives opened to the Popes by the creation and internal organization of the immense Mongol Empire. Is extremely interesting that the Crimean Goths were well known to the papal curia and considered on a level with many other peoples in the East in whom the Roman Catholic Church, particularly in the thirteenth century, became intensely interested.

In the thirteenth century also, Bartholomaeus Anglicus, an English Franciscan, wrote a sort of encyclopaedia which gives a good idea of the general culture of his day.   This compilation was the most popular encyclopaedia of that century, which has been called the age of encyclopaedias.   Enumerating the countries in Eastern Europe, the author mentions Alania, Maeotides Paludes, Gothia, Dacia, Rhaetia, Germania, etc.; but his authority is 'As Isidore says.'[3]   Bartholomaeus of course refers to Isidore of Seville, who lived in the seventh century and was the author of the *Etymologies*, another encyclopaedia.   If we compare the text of Bartholomaeus with that of Isidore, we see at once that the former merely reproduced Isidore's text with minor modifications; accordingly Bartholomaeus' mention of Gothia in the thirteenth century is of no importance whatever.[4]

Between 1204 and 1261 a new factor of great importance appeared in the Crimea: the Italian colonies, which after 1261 began to play a preponderant part in the political and economic life of the Peninsula.   In 1204, after the capture of Constantinople by the crusaders, Venice secured the lion's share of the partition of Romania, so that a considerable number of extremely important centers on the soil of the former Empire passed into the hands of the Republic of St Mark, and the Venetian merchants

---

[1] *Les registres d'Innocent* iv, ed. Élie Berger, i (Paris, 1884), 208, No. 1362.   A few words in A. Potthast, *Regesta*, ii (Berlin, 1875), p. 985, No. 11607; Golubovich, *op. cit.*, ii, 316.   A fragment of this letter without the address in Baronius-Raynaldus, *Annales Ecclesiastici*, xxi (Bar-le-Duc, 1870), p. 295, § 19.   [2] A. Potthast, *Regesta*, ii, 985, No. 11613; Golubovich, *op. cit.*, ii, 316.

[3] *Bartholomaei Anglici De genuinis rerum coelestium, terrestrium, et infernarum proprietatibus Libri XVIII* (Frankfurt, 1609), xv, cxlviii, p. 701: 'ut dicit Isidorus lib. 14.'

[4] *Isidori Hispalensis Etymologiae*, xiv, iv, 3; *Patr. Lat.*, lxxxii, col. 504.   See G. E. Se Boyar, 'Bartholomaeus Anglicus and His Encyclopaedia,' *Journal of English and Germanic Philology*, xix (1920), 177, 182; L. Thorndike, *History of Magic and Experimental Science*, ii (New York, 1923), 425, n. 2.   He gives Bartholomaeus' list of provinces.

enjoyed exceptional commercial privileges all over the new Latin possessions in the East.   In the middle of the thirteenth century the Venetians
penetrated into the Crimea.   Of course this was only the bare beginning
of Italian penetration in the Peninsula, because at that time more powerful nations were in control there.   After 1204 the Empire of Trebizond
exercised its suzerainty over Gothia, Cherson, and perhaps Soldaia
(Sudak), and the Tartars replaced there the Polovtzian (Cuman) predominance, so that the Latin Empire, so closely united with Venice,
politically and economically, was unable to support effectively Venetian
interests in the Crimea, where the Latin Emperors had no power or influence.   In March, 1261, a few months before the capture of Constantinople by Michael Palaeologus and the restoration of the Byzantine Empire, at Nymphaeum, close to Nicaea, in Asia Minor, a very important
treaty was concluded between Michael Palaeologus and the Genoese, who
received exceptionally favorable privileges.   Free trade with no time
limit was granted the Genoese throughout all present and future provinces of the Empire.   Among many other clauses of the treaty the most
essential for our subject provided that the Black Sea ('Majus mare') was
to be closed to all foreign merchants except Genoese and Pisans, the faithful subjects of Michael.   This was a real offensive and defensive alliance
against Venice which put an end to the commercial supremacy of the
Venetians in the Levant.   With the year 1261 begins a new era in the
history of the Crimean Peninsula: the activities and rivalry of the two
Italian republics and especially the powerful growth, prosperity, and political and economic significance of Genoa, whose Crimean colonies often
were to collide with Gothia in the fourteenth and fifteenth centuries.

CHAPTER V

THE PRINCIPALITY OF GOTHIA IN THE FOUR-
TEENTH AND FIFTEENTH CENTURIES
AND ITS FALL IN 1475

1. The Founding of Caffa. Papal Missions. The Plague of 1346

THE most important fact in the history of the Genoese colonies in
the Crimea was the founding by the Genoese of their colony Caffa
(Kaffa) about 1266. The colony was founded and masterfully organized
on territory bought from some Tartar landlord.[1] This did not mean that
the *city* of Caffa was founded at that time. In the tenth century Constantine Porphyrogenitus had twice mentioned a settlement in the Crimea,
Kafa (Καφᾶς).[2] But about 1266 a real Genoese center was established
there, and it prospered so rapidly that in later times Caffa was called
Lesser Constantinople by the Tartars and Turks.[3] Caffa, which was the
center of the Genoese colonies in the Crimea, was to play, as has been
noted above, a very important part in the history of Gothia. The Pisans
were not powerful enough in the Black Sea to be dangerous rivals to the
Genoese. The only people who were able to compete with Genoa were
the Venetians, who were temporarily excluded from commerce on the
Black Sea. But fortunately for Venice the friendship between Michael
Palaeologus and Genoa was of short duration. Hardly four years had
elapsed after the conclusion of the treaty at Nymphaeum which granted
Genoa exceptional privileges, when Michael Palaeologus broke the treaty
and allowed the Venetians to settle on the shores of the Black Sea. Venetian merchants made their appearance in the Crimea. The influence of
the Republic of St Mark increased, so that in 1287 a Venetian consul appointed to Soldaia (Sudak) was entrusted with the management of the
whole of Gazaria (Khazaria), as in the Italian documents of that time the
Crimea was often called. The Genoese exerted all their energy to maintain their influence and keep the commercial privileges for Caffa.[4] Thus

---

[1] For the founding of Caffa see W. Heyd, *Histoire du commerce du Levant au moyen-âge*, II (Leipzig.
1885; or reimpression of 1923), 163–165 ('very little after 1266'); F. Braun, *Die letzten Schicksale*,
p. 22 (in 1266); E. Skrzinska, 'Inscriptions latines des colonies génoises en Crimée,' *Atti della Società
Ligure di Storia Patria*, LVI (1928), 7–8; G. Bratianu, *Recherches sur le commerce génois dans la Mer
Noire* (Paris, 1929), p. 219.

[2] *Constantini Porphyrogeniti De administrando imperio*, pp. 252, 255.

[3] V. E. D. Clarke, *Travels in Various Countries of Europe, Asia, and Africa*, 2nd Amer. ed. (New
York, 1813), 294, 356, note; E. Skrzinska, 'Le colonie genovesi in Crimea, Theodosia (Caffa),'
L'Europa Orientale, XIV (Rome, 1934), 145.

[4] V. M. G. Canale, *Della Crimea del suo commercio e dei suoi dominatori*, II (Genoa, 1856), 441;
Bruun, *Chernomorye*, II, 142 ff.; Vasilievski, *Works*, III, clxxxv–clxxxvi (these two works in Russian);
Heyd, *op. cit.*, II, 168–170.

Gothia entered a very complicated political period: the Tartars, the Genoese, and the Venetians were competing and sometimes colliding with each other in the Crimea, and in some places the vacillating influence of the Empire of Constantinople was felt, as was perhaps also the lessening suzerainty of the Empire of Trebizond. The most powerful people in the Crimea were the Tartars, with whom all other nations represented there at that time had to reckon.

In connection with the overwhelming Tartar influence in the Crimea we may observe the very interesting process of the assimilation of the local population with the Tartars in language, customs, and manners. A statement given by George Pachymeres (1242–1310) in his *History* is of great interest and importance. Dealing with the period of Michael Palaeologus (1261–1282), Pachymeres writes: 'In the course of time the peoples dwelling in the inland parts [of the Peninsula and neighboring countries], I mean the Alans, Zikhi, Goths, Russians and other different neighboring peoples, mixed with them (the Noghai-Tartars); they adopted their customs, assumed their tongue and clothes, and became their allies.'[1] In 1263 the envoys of the Egyptian Sultan Baibars (Beibars), the most famous of the Mamelukes, arrived in the Crimea. The contemporary Arab writers who deal with this embassy give the name of the Crimea and say that this country was inhabited by the Kipchaks (Kifchaks; Tartars), Russians, and Alans.[2] They give no mention of the Goths, and fail to distinguish them from other peoples dwelling in the Crimea.

[1] *Pachymeris Historiae de Michaele Palaeologo*, v, 4 (Bonn., I, 345): ὡς δὲ χρόνου τριβομένου ἐπιμιγνύντες σφίσιν οἱ περὶ τὴν μεσόγαιον κατῳκημένοι, Ἀλανοὶ λέγω Ζίκχοι τε καὶ Γότθοι, Ῥῶσοι καὶ τὰ προσοικοῦντα τούτοις διάφορα γένη, ἔθη τε τὰ ἐκείνων μανθάνουσι, καὶ γλῶσσαν τῷ ἔθει μεταλαμβάνουσι καὶ στολὴν καὶ εἰς συμμάχους αὑτοῖς γίνονται'; Tomaschek, *op. cit.*, p. 45; Loewe, *op. cit.*, p. 114; G. Bratianu, 'Vicina, I, Contributions à l'histoire de la domination byzantine et du commerce génois en Dobrogea,' *Bulletin de la section historique de l'Académie Roumaine*, x (Bucarest, 1923), 143 (31).

[2] Ibn Abd al-Zahir (died in 1292–1293), in V. Tisenhausen, *Collection of Materials Referring to the History of the Golden Horde*, I (St Petersburg, 1884), 54 (Arabic text) and 63 (Russian translation). The complete historical work of Ibn Abd al-Zahir is not yet published. See *Encyclopédie de l'Islam*, II (1927), 376; C. Brockelmann, *Geschichte der arabischen Litteratur*, I (Weimar, 1898), 318–319 (a very brief note); Mufazzal ibn-Abil-Fazaïl, *Histoire des Sultans Mamlouks*, Texte arabe publié et traduit en français par E. Blochet, in the *Patrologie Orientale*, xii (1919), 457 (115); the Arabic text and a Russian translation in Tisenhausen, *op. cit.*, 180–181, and 192. Mufazzal completed his work in 1358; he was a Christian Copt in Egypt. On Mufazzal see Blochet, *op. cit.*, Introduction, pp. 345–361 (3–19). The Arab historian and jurist Nowairi, who died in 1332 and whose chronicle served as the basis for that of Mufazzal, gives the same information. The complete text of his *Chronicle* is not yet published, but the relevant passages are given in Blochet, *op. cit.*, pp. 456–457 (114–115). See also M. Quatremère, *Histoire des Sultans Mamlouks de l'Egypte, écrite en arabe par Taki-Eddin-Ahmed-Makrizi, traduite en français*, I (Paris, 1837), 213–218. V. Smirnov, *The Crimean Khanate under the Domination of the Ottoman Porte to the Beginning of the Eighteenth Century* (St Petersburg, 1887), p. 38–39 (in Russian). A Russian version of Quatremère's translation by Ph. Bruun, in the *Zapiski* of the Odessa Society of History and Antiquities, vi (1867), 612–622 (with notes).

A document exists which states that on 23 September 1277, Guglielmo de Monte di Asti sold to Giovanni da Vado in Genoa for eight *libre* a swarthy she-slave by name Gota who came from Zikhia.[1] Perhaps we have here an indication that among the slaves sold in the Crimea there were sometimes Goths.   It is very possible.

Let us now turn to a statement which has been connected by scholars with the Crimean Goths, but which in my opinion must be eliminated from our evidence as based on an incorrect manuscript reading.   In the beginning of the fourteenth century a Minor Friar, John of Monte Corvino, 'one of the most intrepid and attractive Friars,'[2] went as a missionary to China; he was the founder of the Latin Church in China, became Archbishop of Cambalec (Pekin) and died there about 1328.   In the first letter, dated 8 January 1305, and narrating his missionary successes in China, he refers to the roads leading to the Far East.   This letter has been several times published and translated, but scholars have always reproduced and translated the text as it was published in the seventeenth century by Wadding in the sixth volume of his *Annales Minorum seu historia trium ordinum a S. Francisco institutorum* (Lyons, 1625–1648).   The passage in which we are interested runs as follows: 'As for the road hither (i.e., to China) I may tell you that the way through the land of the Goths, subject to the Emperor of the Northern Tartars, is the shortest and safest; and by it the friars might come, along with the letter-carriers, in five or six months.'[3]   This very interesting though not very clear mention of the Goths has been referred to by scholars, and Tomaschek wrote that the way to the interior of Asia through the Crimea was not only shorter but also safer than through Armenia.[4]   But in 1914 A. C. Moule republished Monte Corvino's letter; for this purpose he studied its original manuscript, which is now preserved in the Bibliothèque Nationale of Paris (*MS. Latin 5006;* our passage on fol. 171ʳ, col. 2) and discovered that Wadding, whom all later scholars followed, erroneously transcribed the manuscript word *Cothay* as *Gothorum*; the passage under consideration therefore really reads as follows: 'De via notifico quod per terram Cothay

---

[1] Arturo Ferretto, 'Codice diplomatico delle relazioni fra la Liguria la Toscana e la Lunigiana ai tempi di Dante,' *Atti della Società Ligure di Storia Patria*, xxxi, ii (Rome, 1903), 167, n. 1: 'ii 23 sett. (1277) Guglielmo de Monte di Asti vende a Giovanni da Vado una schiava olivastra per nome Gota que est ranga de partibus Zechie per L. 8.'

[2] *Travel and Travellers of the Middle Ages*, ed. A. P. Newton (London, 1926), p. 146.

[3] 'De via notifico, quod per terram Gothorum Imperatoris Aquilonarium Tartarorum est via brevior et securior; ita quod cum nunciis intra quinque vel sex menses poterunt pervenire,' I. L. Moshemii (Mosheim), *Historia Tartarorum ecclesiastica* (Helmstadi, 1741), Appendix, No. 44, p. 116; Baronius-Raynaldus, *Annales Ecclesiastici*, xxiii (Bar-le-Duc, 1871), 372, §20; H. Yule, *Cathay and the Way Thither*, i (London, 1866), 200; new edition by H. Cordier, iii (London, 1914), 48.

[4] Tomaschek, *op. cit.*, p. 46.

Imperatoris Aquilonarium Tartarorum est via brevior,'[1] etc.   As P.
Pelliot suggests, the name *Cothay* stands for Marco Polo's Toctai, in
Chinese T'o-t'o, a descendant of Chingis' eldest son Chu-ch'ih, Khan of
Kipchak, whose capital was at Sarai on the Volga.[2]   Thus Monte Cor-
vino's first letter must be now eliminated from our evidence concerning
the Goths in the Crimea.

In his letter to the King of France Philip VI, written in 1334, Marino
Sanudo mentions the Goths among other peoples who were under the
power of the Tartars.[3]

In connection with the papal missionary activities in the East and the
establishment of the Italian colonies in the Crimea the Roman Catholic
Church made its appearance in the Peninsula.   The Italian colonies became the chief centers for the Roman Catholic propaganda, which dealt
not only with the non-Christian nomads but also with the 'Greek schismatics.'   About 1318 the Archbishop of Bosporus (Vospro), Franciscus de
Camarino, had under his jurisdiction five suffragans, among whom was
the Bishop of Cherson, Richard, an Englishman (Ricardus Anglicus
Episcopus Cersonensis).   A letter of Pope John XXII, dated 5 July 1333,
is of great interest.[4]   The Pope writes that he is reliably informed that
in ancient times the Christian faith was strong in the wide and populous
country of Gothia ('in terra Gothie diffusa et populosa') which lies in the
East ('in partibus orientis'); but alas! through the increasing wickedness
of time the observance of this faith has ceased so that the inhabitants of
that country, blindly deviating to the darkness of faithlessness, have been
involved in the nets of error and become open schismatics; but owing to
the indefatigable labors in those regions of Friars Predicatores and Minors
to convert both schismatics and other infidels, a considerable number will
be converted to the true light which is Christ.   According to information
received by the Pope, in the country of Gothia ('in prelibata terra Got-
thie') there is a place called *Cersona* which is said to have been a city of

---

[1] A. C. Moule, 'Documents Relating to the Mission of the Minor Friars to China in the Thirteenth
and Fourteenth Centuries,' *Journal of the Royal Asiatic Society*, 1914, pp. 533–599; M. Corvino's first
letter, pp. 545–551; our passage, p. 550.   See anonymous review of Vol. III of *Cathay and the Way
Thither*, ed. by H. Cordier, in the *Athenaeum*, 25 Dec. 1915, pp. 478–479.   Also H. Cordier's note in
his edition *Cathay and the Way Thither*, IV (London, 1916), 269–270; he refers to the anonymous article mentioned above.   [2] Moule, *op. cit.*, p. 550; H. Cordier, *op. cit.*, IV, 270.

[3] *Epistola Marini Sanudi ad Philippum Francorum regem*; datum Venetiis die XIII, Octobris anno
1334: 'Sunt etiam in Galgaria (*sc.* Gazaria) et in aliis locis subjectis Tartaris de septentrione aliqui
populi, scilicet Gothi et aliqui Alani et aliquae aliae plures nationes, quae sequntur Graecorum
vestigia.'   Friedrich Kunstmann, 'Studien über Marino Sanudo den Aelteren mit einem Anhange
seiner ungedruckten Briefe,' *Abhandlungen der historischen Classe der K. Bayerischen Akademie
der Wissenschaften*, VII (1855), 801.   See also Bruun, *Chernomorye*, II, 137.

[4] A. Theiner, *Vetera Monumenta Poloniae et Lithuaniae gentiumque finitimarum historiam illustrantia*, I (Rome, 1860), 347–348 (No. CDLVII).

old; it is reported a populous, convenient, well-ordered, and prosperous place.   Then the Pope writes: 'Following the advice of the Friars and by virtue of the plenitude of the Apostolic power we raise again this place of Cersona into a city, and confer on it the name of city; by Our Apostolic authority we order that in this city a cathedral dedicated to the Blessed Clement shall be founded and built.   We order and decree that the above-mentioned Church of Cherson (ecclesia Cersonensis') shall be subject for ever ('perpetuis futuris temporibus') to the Church of Bosporus ('ecclesie Vosprensi') as its Metropoly.'

In another letter of 16 July 1333 to Richard (Ricardo Anglico), Bishop of Cherson, Pope John XXII confirms his decision expressed in the preceding letter to build a cathedral at Cherson, and mentions 'the place of Cherson in the country of Gothia.'[1]   Thus in the fourteenth century Gothia became a center of Roman Catholic propaganda.

In 1334, on his way from Sinope to the East, an Arab traveller, Ibn-Batuta, landed at Soldaia (Sugdaia), where he stayed a few days before continuing his journey by land to Caffa.   He wrote of the preparations for this journey, 'One of the merchants in our company hired some waggons from the Qipchaqs who inhabit this desert, and who are Christians.' Caffa (Kafa) was 'a large town extending along the sea-coast, inhabited by Christians, mostly Genoese.'[2]   This testimony that there were Christians at that time among the Qipchaqs, i.e., the Tartars, is very interesting.   Of course these were not the Tartars proper but some Christian peoples dwelling in the Peninsula who had adopted Tartar customs and manners, and possibly the Tartar language, so that in the eyes of the Arab traveller they appeared Qipchaqs.   This account must be correlated with the statement of George Pachymeres quoted above that towards the end of the thirteenth century many peoples in the Crimea, including the Goths, had become tartarized.   We must also note that the Genoese settlement Caffa impressed Ibn-Batuta as a large town.

In 1346 a terrible plague befell the Crimea.   This was the so-called Black Death, which had been carried from the interior of Asia to the

---

[1] A. Theiner, *op. cit.*, pp. 349–350 (No. CDLXI).   For some papal letters of 1333 which mention several times the names 'Franciscus, archiepiscopus Vosprensis,' and 'Richardus, episcopus Cersonensis,' see Baronius-Raynaldus, *Annales Ecclesiastici*, XXIV (Bar-le-Duc, 1872), 514–515.   See also C. Eubel, *Hierarchia Catholica medii aevi*, I (Münster, 1898), 190; P. G. Golubovich, *Biblioteca bio-bibliografica della Terra Santa e dell'Oriente Franciscano*, III (Quaracchi, 1919), 205; Tomaschek, *op. cit.*, p. 47; Loewe, *op. cit.*, p. 219.

[2] *Voyages d'Ibn Batoutah, texte arabe accompagné d'une traduction*, ed. C. Defrémery and B. B. Sanguinetti, II (Paris, 1877), 357; Tisenhausen, *Collection of Materials Referring to the History of the Golden Horde*, p. 280 (in Russian); *Ibn Batuta, Travels in Asia and Africa, 1325–1354*, translated and selected by H. A. R. Gibb (London, 1929), p. 142.   Gibb is preparing a complete English translation of Ibn Batuta's travels for the Hakluyt Society.

coast of the Maeotis (the Sea of Azov) and to the Crimea. The infected Genoese trade-galleys sailing from Tana and Caffa carried the plague to Constantinople in 1347; then from Byzantium it spread in 1348 over West Europe, through Italy, Spain, France, England, Germany, and Norway, and in the following years penetrated through the Baltic Sea and Poland into Russia.

We have a very interesting contemporary document on the outbreak of the plague in the Crimea written by a notary of Piacenza, in Italy, Gabriel de Mussis (Gabriele de' Mussi). It was formerly believed that he spent the years 1344–1346 in the East and was an eyewitness of the outbreak of the Black Death in the Crimea.[1] But this is erroneous, because later study of the archives of Piacenza has shown that Mussi stayed in Piacenza through the forties of the fourteenth century and therefore could not have been in the Crimea. Probably he obtained his information concerning the East from some of his compatriots who together with the Genoese were trading in the Crimea.[2] Gabriel de Mussi relates that in 1346 in the East an enormous number of Tartars perished from an inexplicable disease; at that time some Italian merchants expelled from Tana by the Tartars had taken refuge within the walls of Caffa, which was immediately besieged by the Tartars. A violent disease broke out among the besiegers, which carried off thousands of men. Driven to despair, the Tartars ordered the corpses to be thrown by machines over the walls into the city in order to spread the disease there and thus force the Genoese to surrender. Mussi lists the names of many Eastern peoples affected by the plague, Armenians, Tarsians, Georgians, Mesopotamians, Turks (*Turchumani*), Greeks, and others; but he fails to mention the Goths.[3] This need not surprise us because at that time the Goths, as we have already seen, were so tartarized that they could not be readily distinguished from the Tartars by the travellers and merchants who landed at Soldaia or Caffa and then, without any particular attention to the Crimea, continued their journey through Solkhat to the East. But despite the silence of our evidence we may be certain that the plague af-

---

[1] See A. Henschel, 'Documente zur Geschichte des schwarzen Todes,' *Archiv für die gesamte Medicin*, published by H. Haeser, II (1842), 28–29; H. Haeser, *Lehrbuch der Geschichte der Medicin und der epidemischen Krankheiten*, 3rd ed., III (Jena, 1882), 99 and n. 1.

[2] See A. G. Tononi, 'La peste dell'anno 1348,' *Giornale Ligustico*, XI (Genoa, 1884), 141–144. Heyd was acquainted with the results of Tononi's article, W. Heyd, *Histoire du commerce du Levant*, II, 196 and n. 1; Ch. Creighton, *A History of Epidemics in Britain from A.D. 664 to the Extinction of Plague* (Cambridge, 1891), pp. 144–148.

[3] Gabriel de'Mussi's text was first published by A. Henschel, *op. cit.*, in *Archiv für die gesamte Medicin*, II (1842), 45–57; reprinted by H. Haeser, in his *Lehrbuch*, III (Jena, 1882), 157–161; a new edition by A. Tononi, in the *Giornale Ligustico*, XI (1884), 144–152. In his account of the Black Death M. Kovalevski incorrectly calls de'Mussi 'De Muissi,' M. Kovalevski, *Die ökonomische Entwicklung Europas*, transl. by M. Kupperberg, V (Berlin, 1911), 231, 234.

fected not only Caffa and some other places in the Crimea but the whole Peninsula as well, so that Gothia also undoubtedly lived through the horrors of the Black Death.[1]

2. The Treaties between Genoa and the Tartars in 1380, 1381, and 1387

Soon after the plague a war broke out in the Crimea between Genoa and Venice; this war ended in 1355. Although successful in the field and in her diplomacy, Genoa was forced to give up her original plan of making Caffa the sole center of commerce in the Crimea and on the shores of the Sea of Azov; thus after the peace of 1355 the Venetians regained full liberty to renew commercial relations with the Crimean regions occupied by the Tartars. Extending their influence in the Crimea, the Genoese profited by the period of anarchy which occurred among the Crimean Tartars after the death of their Khan Berdibeg and took possession of Soldaia and eighteen other localities in that district. Under their new leader Mamai, the Tartars tried to reconquer the lost territory and gained a brief temporary advantage. But the Genoese won the day and in 1365 recaptured Soldaia and some territory along the sea. Finally, after more conflict a treaty was made between the Genoese and Tartars; this treaty is of great importance for our subject.[2]

The first treaty was concluded on 28 November 1380; as a second treaty almost identical in content is dated 23 February 1381, we may be almost certain that the version of 1380 was only a preliminary text of the treaty confirmed in February, 1381.[3] The text published by Silvestre de Sacy is a translation from the original Mongol text ('lingua Ugaresca'), which, as the introductory note asserts, was translated into Latin in 1383 at the order of the consul of Caffa, Meliaduce Cataneo.[4] It is not very obvious whether by 'Latin translation' the author of the note meant the Genoese dialect, as Silvestre de Sacy is inclined to believe, or, as Oderico supposes, a real Latin translation from which a Genoese rendering was made.[5] The

---

[1] For the most recent bibliography, not absolutely complete, see Anna Montgomery Campbell, *The Black Death and Men of Learning* (New York, 1931), pp. 181–195.

[2] On these events see Braun, *Die letzten Schicksale der Krimgoten*, p. 23; Vasilievski, *Works*, III, cxcvii–cxcix (in Russian); Heyd, *op. cit.*, II, 196–205.

[3] The text of the preliminary treaty was published in Genoese dialect with a French translation by a French scholar, M. Silvestre de Sacy, 'Pièces diplomatiques tirées des archives de la République de Gènes,' *Notices et extraits des manuscrits de la Bibliothèque du Roi*, XI (Paris, 1827), 53–55 (Genoese text) and 55–58 (French translation). The Genoese text of this treaty is also reprinted by C. Desimoni, 'Trattato dei Genovesi col Chan dei Tartari nel 1380–1381 scritto in lingua volgare,' *Archivio Storico Italiano*, 4th Series, XX (1887), 162–165 (second column). Before Silvestre de Sacy an Italian scholar, Gaspar Ludovico Oderico, had been acquainted with the text and made use of it in his book *Lettere Ligustiche* (Bassano, 1792), Letter XVII, pp. 137–138.

[4] See Silvestre de Sacy, *op. cit.*, p. 53; Desimoni, *op. cit.*, p. 161.   [5] *Ibid.*

preliminary treaty of 1380 was drawn up on one side by Jarkass (Jhar-
cas), governor of Solkhat, acting in the name of the Khan and in his own
name, and on the other side by the consul of Caffa and 'of all the Genoese
in the Empire of Gazaria,' Giannone del Bosco, assisted by some other
colonial officials, in the name of the 'Great Commune' of Genoa.   The
most important part of the treaty is the cession by the Tartars of two
territories in the Crimea to the 'Great Commune' of Genoa.   The first
territory comprised Soldaia (Sudak) with eighteen neighboring settlements or villages; according to the treaty these places 'shall be at the disposal and under the power of the Commune and the Consul, and be freed
from the (Tartar) Empire.'[1]   The second territory ceded by Jarkass to
the Commune of Genoa was Gothia: 'Gothia with its settlements and
people who are Christians, from Cembaro to Soldaia, shall belong to the
Great Commune, and the settlements mentioned above, people as well
as territory and waters, shall be freed [from the Tartar Empire].'[2]   Among
other provisions is a very important one about commercial relations, according to which 'all the merchants who go and come shall enjoy complete security in the territory of the (Tartar) Empire.'   A representative
of the Tartar authority was to reside in Caffa to arrange business between
subjects of the Khan.   This preliminary treaty was drawn up between
Caffa and the mountain Sachim, before the 'Three Fountains' ('davanti
li trey pozi'), in the year 782 of the Hegira, the last day of the month
Shaban (28 November 1380).

Three months later this preliminary treaty was confirmed at a second
conference, which took place on 23 February 1381 ('Zulqa'da 28,' 782 of
the Hegira).   The representative of the Tartars was not Jarkass, but
Elias, son of Cotolbega, who at that time was governor of Solkhat; he was
probably Jarkass' successor.   The Genoese delegates were the same as
in 1380.   The final text of the treaty of 23 February 1381 is identical with
the preliminary text,[3] so that in 1381 Gothia 'with its settlements and
people, from Cembaro to Soldaia,' was definitely annexed to the Great
Commune, and 'the settlements mentioned above as well as Gothia and
their people with territory and waters' were free from the [Tartar] Empire.[4]   The final text of the treaty omits the words 'who are Christians'

---

[1] 'Queli dixoto casay li quai eran sotemixi e rendenti a Sodaja . . . queli dixoto casay sean in la
voluntay e bayria de lo comune e de lo consoro, e sean franchi da lo imperio,' Silvestre de Sacy, pp.
54, 57; Desimoni, p. 163.

[2] 'Someieyoenti la Gotia, con li soy casay e cum lo so povo, li quay sum cristiani, da lo Cembaro fim
in Sodaya, sea de lo grande comun, et sean franchi li sovrascriti casay, lo povo cum li soy terren cum
le sue aygae,' Silvestre de Sacy, p. 54, 57; Desimoni, pp. 163–164.

[3] The text of the treaty of 23 February 1381 is published by C. Desimoni, 'Trattato dei Genovesi
col Chan dei Tartari nel 1380–1381 scritto in lingua volgare,' *Archivio Storico Italiano*, 4th Series, xx
(1887), 161–165.   [4] Desimoni, *op. cit.*, pp. 163–164.

which were inserted in the preliminary text.   The population of the ceded territory included Muhammedans as well as Christians, so apparently the final decision was that the population as a whole should be ceded to the Genoese.   The name of Gothia is mentioned only once in the preliminary text and twice in the final version.   At Christmas, 1380, during the negotiations preceding the conclusion of the treaty of 23 February 1381, Eliasbey, governor of Solkhat and chief delegate of the Tartars, was entertained in Caffa by a banquet given in his honor by the Genoese consul. The sum of 478 aspers (aspri; a piece of silver money) was spent for the maintenance of the *vicarius Gotiae* and ambassadors of the Khan.[1]   Anthonius Mazurro, a *notarius*, as well as his staff, was rewarded by a considerable amount of money for many journeys to Solkhat and 'all over Gothia as far as Cembalo' in connection with the preliminary negotiations which led to the conclusion of the treaty.[2]

For the Genoese Republic the year 1381 was of great importance.   In this year the war between Genoa and Venice ended with the peace of Turin.   Genoa's attempt to eliminate Venice from the Black Sea seemed successful.   According to the treaty Venice was forbidden for two years to sail to Tana, at the mouth of the River Don, the most important Venetian station in the basin of the Black Sea.   In addition she was forbidden to sail to the district 'de Zagora,' ('ad partes de Zagora subditas Dobrodice'), i.e., the present-day Dobrudja, on the western shore of the Black Sea.[3]   But in spite of these restrictions, a few years later, in 1386, normal commercial relations were reëstablished with the ports of the Black Sea, so that the Venetians regained their access to Tana and other places.

The treaties of 1380–1381 failed to end hostilities between Genoa and the Tartars.   Shortly after, a new war broke out which resulted in a new treaty dated 12 August 1387.[4]   For the Tartars the treaty was concluded by the governor of Solkhat and some other Tartar representatives in the name of the 'most dignified Emperor of the Tartars,' Tokhtamysh, a vassal of the famous Turko-Mongol conqueror, Timur (Tamerlane); Gentile

---

[1] N. Iorga, *Notes et extraits pour servir à l'histoire des Croisades au XVe siècle*, I (Paris, 1899), 16 (document of 8 February 1382).

[2] *Ibid.*, p. 17 (document of 11 May 1381): 'pro Anthonio Mazurro, notario, et sunt quos habuit pro ipsius faticha et mercede de componendo instrumenta . . . de dacitis factis de Gotia et aliis locis datis Communi per dominum Sorchati . . . de casilibus [*sic*] Gotie Communi, et ipsius faticha de eundo in Sorchati per plures vices ac per totam Gotiam usque ad Cimballum . . . .'

[3] See M. Silberschmidt, *Das orientalische Problem zur Zeit der Entstehung des türkischen Reiches nach venezianischen Quellen* (Leipzig and Berlin, 1923), p. 6; N. Iorga, *Notes et extraits pour servir à l'histoire des Crusades au XVe siècle*, I (Paris, 1899), 11, n. 3; *idem*, 'La politique vénitienne dans les eaux de la Mer Noire,' *Bulletin de la Section Historique de l'Académie Roumaine*, II (Bucarest, 1914), 305–306. Cf. G. Bratianu, *Recherches sur Vicina et Cetatea Albă* (Bucarest, 1935), pp. 138–139.

[4] The Latin text of this treaty is published by Silvestre de Sacy, *op. cit.*, in the *Notices et extraits*, XI (1827), 62–64.

dei Grimaldi and Giannone del Bosco represented Genoa.   The original Mongol text of the treaty ('lingua Ugarica') was translated into Latin by a citizen of Caffa, Francesco de Gibeleto.   This treaty 'ratified, approved, and confirmed' all the 'peace provisions, precepts, agreements, and engagements the complete mention of which is found in documents mentioned above'; all the clauses of the treaty were to be 'observed inviolably,' and 'a true and good peace between the two parties was to be perpetually kept and observed.'   Thus the hostile relations between the Tartars and Genoa which existed in the eighties of the fourteenth century ended in 1387 with the conclusion of the final treaty which confirmed the stipulations of the previous treaties of 1380 and 1381.   Genoa had long been interested in this region, and her consuls in Alushta (Lusca), Parthenit (Partinita), Gurzuf (Gorzoni), and Yalta (Jallita), in other words, along the coast ceded by the treaties of 1380–1381, had been working there and preparing for the annexation of this territory many years before the war broke out.   In 1374 Anthonius de Acursu and Johannes de Burgaro had been sent to Gothia apparently on some special mission.[1]

Now let us see what importance the treaties of 1380–1381 and 1387 have for our subject.   From this standpoint, the most essential clause in the treaties is the cession by the Tartars of Gothia with its villages ('con li soy casay') and Christian people from Cembalo to Soldaia to the Commune of Genoa.   According to the Genoese documents of Caffa, dated 1381–1382, Gothia extended from Cembalo to Soldaia inclusive; the names of the villages ceded are given; each place was headed by a *Propto* (*Proto*, 'first') and all together were under the jurisdiction of a *Vicarius ripariae marinae Gotiae*.[2]   The names of the places ceded follow: Cembalo (now Balaklava), Fori (now Foros, southeast of Balaklava), Chichineo (now Kikineis, near Foros),[3] Lupico (now Alupka), Muzacori (now Myskhor, between Alupka and Ai-Todor), Orianda (now the same name), Jallita (now Yalta), Sikita (now Nikita, between Yalta and Gurzuf), Gorzovium (now Gurzuf), Pertenite (now Parthenit, near Ayudagh), Lambadie (now the villages of Biyuk (Great)-Lambat and Kutchuk (Little)-Lambat), Lusta (now Alushta), and Soldaia (Sudak).[4]   The authors of these treaties meant by Gothia the narrow coast strip from Balaklava to Sudak bounded on the north by the mountains of Yaila,

[1] See N. Iorga, *Notes et extraits pour servir à l'histoire des Croisades au XVe siècle*, i (Paris, 1899), 7–8 (document of 4 November 1374).

[2] This information from 'Cartolari della Masseria di Caffa del 1381–1382' was published by C. Desimoni and L. T. Belgrano in their edition of 'Atlante idrografico del medio evo posseduto dal prof. Tammar Luxoro,' *Atti della Società Ligure di Storia Patria*, v (Genova, 1867), 253–254.

[3] In the published text there is a misprint, 'Chinicheo' for 'Chichineo' (p. 254).

[4] See F. Braun, *Die letzten Schicksale*, pp. 24–25.

the so-called *riparia marina Gotia*.   According to the treaties mentioned above the Genoese took real possession only of a smaller part of Gothia; but the major part of Gothia, i.e., the mountain section north of the Yaila, 'the heart of old Gothia,'[1] was not ceded and probably, beginning with the middle of the fourteenth century, as we shall see later, was governed by its own princes.

According to the same treaties the Commune of Genoa received Soldaia with eighteen villages ('dixoto casay'); their names are known and can for the most part be identified:[2] (1) Casale Coxii (Kos, Koz, about seven miles east of Soldaia-Sudak); (2) Casale Sancti Johannis (about seven miles east of Alushta, in the valley Kuru-Uzen, the ruins of a rather large church of St John, with a cemetery); (3) Casale Tarataxii (Taraktash, about two miles north of Sudak); (4) Casale Louolli (Voron, northwest of Sudak?); (5) Casale de lo Sille (Shelen, close to Voron); (6) Casale de lo Sdaffo (Osdaffum; the ruins of a village in the valley Edy-Evler, about four miles east of Alushta?); (7) Casale de la Canecha (now Kanaka, a stream close to the ruins of a settlement between Tuak and Uskjut); (8) Casale de Carpati (now Arpat, on the river of the same name, west of Shelen); (9) Casale de lo Scuto (Uskjut, southwest of Arpat); (10) Casale de Bezalega (uncertain); (11) Casale de Buzult (doubtful; perhaps Elbuzly, north of Sudak, but Elbuzly lies about ten miles from the sea); (12) Casale de Cara-ihoclac or Carachoclac (either Tokluk, east of Sudak, or Kutlak, west of Sudak); (13) Casale de lo Diavollo (perhaps Tuak, near Kuru-Uzen; not absolutely certain); (14) Casale de lo Carlo (at the foot of Kearly-burnu, the ruins of a village with a church and cemetery, near Kutlak); (15) Casale Sancti Erigni (uncertain); (16) Casale Saragaihi (rather doubtful; either the mountain Sara-kaya, not far from Alushta, or the village Ai-Seres, northwest of Sudak); (17) Casale Paradixii (perhaps some ruins of settlements in a bay near Sudak); (18) Casale de lo Cheder (uncertain).

This period marked the greatest territorial expansion of the Genoese power in the Crimea.   Neither Cherson in the west nor Kerch in the east ever belonged to Genoa.   All these new acquisitions became exceedingly important to Caffa from the point of view of her political power in the Peninsula, and, especially, from the point of view of her economic significance and prosperity.[3]   As the title *Vicarius ripariae marinae Gotiae*

---

[1] F. Braun, *Die letzten Schicksale*, p. 26.

[2] The list of these villages is published by C. Desimoni and L. Belgrano in the *Atti de la Società Ligure*, v, 254–255.   The list with some notes is also given by F. Braun, *op. cit.*, pp. 25–26; Bruun, in his review of the publication by Desimoni and Belgrano just mentioned, in the *Zapiski* of the Odessa Society of History and Antiquities, VIII (1872), 293–294 (in Russian).

[3] For these events see P. Köppen, *Krymsky Sbornik* (St Petersburg, 1837), pp. 81–86; Vasilievski, *Works*, III, cxcvii–cxcix; Heyd, *op. cit.*, II, 207–211; F. Braun, *Die letzten Schicksale*, pp. 23–27; E.

mentioned above does not occur in Genoese documents after 1381–1382 but is later replaced by that of *capitaneus (capitanus) Gotie*, we may conclude that *Vicarius ripariae marinae Gotiae* was a temporary title established by the Genoese after the peace of 1380 and of 1381; but after the final peace of 1387 the new territory was turned over to the *Capitaneatus Gotie*, and its governor-general was entitled *capitaneus (capitanus) Gotie*.[1] Apparently his residence was in Caffa.

Evidently Genoa's political longings in the Crimea went much farther. From official documents we learn that the Genoese authorities apparently regarded the principality of Gothia as their vassal state, and its princes as rebels when they acted for the benefit of their own country without regard to Caffa. But Genoa's claim was only theoretical; it was beyond the power of Caffa to exert real suzerainty. Therefore Bruun, I believe, was wrong in stating that simultaneously with the cession to Genoa by the Tartars of maritime Gothia in 1380 the prince of Theodoro passed from the suzerainty of the Tartars to that of the Genoese Commune, at least as regards part of his domains.[2] This new situation signified considerable weakening of the Tartar influence both in the Genoese colonies in the Crimea and in Gothia.

3. THE PRINCIPALITY OF THEODORO IN THE FOURTEENTH CENTURY

Beginning with the middle of the fourteenth century there are some indications of the existence of the independent principality of Theodoro. The circumstances under which the rulers of Theodoro or of Gothia proclaimed themselves independent are veiled in obscurity. In the thirteenth century Gothia or the Gothic *Climata* depended on the Empire of Trebizond, and the dependence manifested itself in annual tribute to the oversea Empire. This dependence, never very strong because of the weakness of the distant Empire, became still weaker when the Tartar-Mongolian preponderance made itself felt in the Peninsula. Doubtless Gothia's political dependence on Trebizond was then replaced by subjugation to the Tartars. Usually the Tartars were satified with imposing

---

Marengo, C. Manfroni, G. Pessagno, *Il Banco di San Giorgio* (Genoa, 1911), p. 486; a few words in Federico Donaver, *La storia della Repubblica di Genova*, ɪ (Genoa, 1913), 361; Kulakovski, *The Past of the Taurus*, 2nd ed. (Kiev, 1914), pp. 109–110 (in Russian). Kulakovski is wrong in stating (p. 110) that Cherson was definitely delivered to the Genoese by Emperor Andronicus in 1350. This never occurred, and in 1350 not Andronicus but John v was Emperor of Byzantium. A. M. Condioti, *Historia de la institucion consular en la antigüedad y en la edad media*, ɪ (Madrid, Berlin, Buenos-Aires, Mexico, 1925), 545–546 (on the treaty of 1381).

[1] See the Statute of Caffa of 1449, published by Yurguevich in the *Zapiski* of the Odessa Society of History and Antiquities, v (1865), 726, ed. by P. Vigna in the *Atti de la Società Ligure di Storia Patria*, vɪɪ, ii (Genova, 1879), 628. Several later documents on the *Capitaneatus Gothiae* will be referred to below. [2] Bruun, *Notices historiques*, p. 63.

annual tribute and leaving internal administration practically independent, and probably they were satisfied with this in the case of Gothia.

Our earliest evidence concerning independent Gothia is found in a book
on the origin of the Ottoman Emperors written by Theodore Spandugino,
'Constantinopolitan patrician.' Spandugino was born about 1453 but
the year of his death is unknown; after 1538 we lose track of him.[1] He
remarks that Emperor Andronicus III Palaeologus (1328–1341) came into
conflict with the Prince of Gothia, the Bulgarians, and Stephen, King of
Serbia.[2] In another place he writes that also in the fourteenth century
the Turkish Sultan, Amurath, made a league with the Bulgarians, Wallachs, Goths, and the Emperor of Constantinople against the Kingdom
of Hungary.[3] At the end of the fourteenth century, Spandugino states,
the Sultan Yildirim Bayazid (1387–1402) observed strong disagreements
existing among the Christian princes, especially the King of Serbia, the
Goths, and the Wallachs, who were all contending with the Emperor of
Constantinople Manuel Paleologus (1391–1425).[4] In his account Spandugino deals with the Prince of Gothia or of the Goths as equally important
with the King of Serbia, the Bulgarians, and the Wallachs.

Our second piece of evidence is given by Martin Bronevski (Martinus
Broniovius), ambassador of the Polish King Stephen Batory to the Khan
of the Crimea in 1578. In his description of the Crimea in the chapter on
Yamboli or Balaklava, he writes that this city was built and fortified on
a high mountain of stone by the Genoese, who had taken it without meeting any resistance from the proud, careless, and quarrelling Greek princes
who then possessed that portion of the Tauris.[5] The Genoese must have
taken Symbolon or Balaklava before 1340; at that time the Khan of the
Crimea, Djanibek, was fighting in the south of the Crimea against the
Genoese,[6] and the Tartars captured Balaklava from the Genoese proba-

[1] Theodoro Spandugino, patritio Constantinopolitano, *De la origine deli imperatori Ottomani, ordini
de la corte, forma del guerreggiare loro, religione, rito, et costumi de la natione,* in Sathas, *Documents
inédits relatifs à l'histoire de la Grèce au moyen-âge,* IX (Paris, 1890). Spandugino's biography in the
preface, pp. iii–xxxi.

[2] Sathas, IX, 143: 'et havendo controversie il detto Andronico Paleologo con il principe di Gothia et
con li Bulgari, con il re Stephano di Servia . . . .'

[3] *Ibid.,* p. 146: '[Amurath] fece poi una legha con li Bulgari, Valacchi et con li Gotti, et lo imperator
di Constantinopoli, contra il regno di Ungaria . . . .'

[4] *Ibid.,* pp. 146–147: 'Ildrim Baiasit-vedendo le altercatione grande che erano tra principi Christiani
et massimamente il re di Servia, li Gotti et li Valachi che contendeano tutti con lo imperator di
Constantinopoli Emanuel Paleologo.'

[5] *Martini Broniovii Tartariae Descriptio* (Cologne, 1595), p. 7: 'superbis et pessime inter se conveni-
entibus ac ignavis Graecorum qui tunc eam partem Tauricae tenebant, ducibus ignominiose sine
aliquo eorum praesidio ab eis erepta fuit.' For a Russian translation see *Zapiski* of the Odessa Society of History and Antiquities, VI (1867), 343.

[6] See V. Smirnov, *The Crimean Khanate under the Power of the Ottoman Porte up to the Beginning of
the Eighteenth Century* (St Petersburg, 1887), p. 126 (in Russian).

bly shortly before 1345.[1]   This was not a final annexation of Balaklava
to the possessions of the Crimean Khan.   The struggle continued, and
as we know by the treaties of 1380, 1381, and 1387 the southern coast of
Gothia from Sugdaia to Balaklava was ceded by the Tartars to Genoa.
Even before that a Genoese consul, Simone dell'Orto, is mentioned in
Balaklava in 1357.[2]

In connection with the supposed independence of the principality of
Theodoro in the fourteenth century another account must be taken into
consideration.   The fourteenth century was marked by the growth of the
political power of the Grand Principality of Lithuania under the princes
Gedimin (1317–1341), Olgerd (1341–1377), and Vithold (Vitovt, 1392–
1430).   On the south-eastern border of the Principality the Lithuanians
were neighbors of the Tartars, with whom they fought at length.   According to our sources Olgerd won a brilliant victory over the three Khans
at the Blue Water, at the mouth of the Dnieper.   But scholars disagree
as to whether this Olgerd was the Grand Prince of Lithuania who ruled
from 1341 to 1377 or a general under Vithold (1392–1430); according to
one view or the other, this victory has been attributed by scholars approximately either to 1362–1363 or to 1396.   This question has recently
been carefully reconsidered by a Russian scholar, N. V. Malitzki.   In his
excellent study on the inscriptions connected with Theodoro-Mankup, he
concludes decisively that the defeat of the three Khans at the Blue Water
is to be referred to the period of the Grand Prince Olgerd, i.e., to the
sixties of the fourteenth century.[3]   Most of our sources say that Olgerd
took the field southward and defeated three Tartar princes, Kadlubak
(Kutlubak), Kachibei (Khochebi), and Demetrius.[4]   On the other hand,

[1] See Braun, *Die letzten Schicksale der Krimgoten*, pp. 26–27, 29; Bruun, *Notices historiques*, p. 59.
Both refer to the old book by V. A. Formaleoni, *Storia filosofica e politica della navigazione, del commercio e delle colonie degli antichi nel Mar Nero*, II (Venice, 1789), Ch. XXII, pp. 88–90.   This book
gives neither date nor references.   Both Bruun and Braun incorrectly refer to Chapter XXI for Chapter XXII.

[2] V. Yurgevich, 'Genoese Inscriptions in the Crimea,' *Zapiski* of the Odessa Society of History and
Antiquities, V (1863), 175: 'in 1357 . . . tempore regiminis discreti viri Simonis de Orto, consulis et
castelani.'   See E. Skrzinska, 'Inscriptions latines des colonies génoises en Crimée,' *Atti della Società
Ligure di Storia Patria*, LVI (1928), 129–130, where other editions of the inscription are given, and
Bruun, *Notices*, p. 59, Heyd, *op. cit.*, II, 210.

[3] N. V. Malitzki, 'Notes on the Epigraphy of Mangup,' in the *Izvestiya* of the Academy of the
History of Material Culture, LXXI (Leningrad, 1933), 11–14 (in Russian).

[4] *Western Russian Chronicles, Suprasl Version (Codex Suprasliensis), A Chronicle of the Grand
Princes of Lithuania*, in the *Complete Collection of Russian Chronicles*, XVII (1907), 81 ('Khochebi,
Kutlubugh, and Dmitrey'), *Chronicles of the Grand Princes of Lithuania, ibid.*, p. 170 ('Khachebei,
Sakutlubugh and Dmitrey'), both in Old Russian; *Wielkiego Xiestwa Litweskiego i Žmodskiego
Kronika, ibid.*, pp. 453–454 ('Chaczabeia, Kukubuha, Dmitreia'); *Bykhovetz Codex, ibid.*, p. 496
('Chaczybeja, a Kutlubuhu, a Dmitreja'), both in Polish; *Stanislai Sarnicii Annales sive De origine
et rebus gestis Polonorum et Lituanorum Libri VIII*, 1st ed. (Cracow, 1587).   I use here the edition of

there is information that Olgerd, 'a noble Lithuanian,' under Vithold routed near the Don three Khans, of the Crimean, Kirkelian, and Monlopian Tartars.[1]   In all likelihood Kirkel is the very well-known city in the Crimea, Qyrq-ier.   But what is Monlop?   No such place is known. I think this name must be a distorted form of Mankup (Mangup).   Thus one of the princes subject to the Tartars who was defeated by Olgerd was a prince of Mankup, i.e., a prince of Gothia.   If we now take into consideration the fact that a Christian name, Demetrius, is given by several sources for one of the defeated princes, we may conclude with reason that Demetrius was a Christian prince and a prince of Monlop, i.e., Mankup, or in other words a prince of Gothia.[2]

We turn now to a very interesting result of the study by Malitzki quoted above.   In 1913 R. Loeper discovered a dated inscription on Mankup, and without publishing its Greek text gave a Russian translation, neither complete nor exact.   The original text of the inscription was printed by Malitzki only in 1933.[3]   The inscription invokes the blessing

---

Sarnicki published in *Joannis Dlugossi seu Longini Historiae Poloniae liber XIII et ultimus*, II (Leipzig, 1712), col. 1134 (*s.a.* 1333): 'Progressus [Olgerdus] enim cum suis copiis usque ad Boristhenem et ostia ejus, totum robur Tartarorum, et tres duces eorum Kadlubachum, Demetrium, et Kaczibeium . . . armis suis attrivit, profligavit, et disiecit.' The author of this Chronicle, Sarnicki, died in 1592; see *Praefatio ad lectorem*, pp. xxxii–xlv; also Ludwik Finkel, *Bibliografia Historyi Polskiej*, I (Lwów, 1891), 425 (in Polish). See Karamzin, *History of the Russian State*, 2nd ed., v (St Petersburg, 1819), 17 (in 1363) and n. 12 (p. 7), in Russian; Bruun, *Notices*, pp. 50–51 (in 1392 or 1396), cf. p. 89: 'Olgerd défait trois chefs mongols' (under 1331); Tomaschek, *Die Goten in Taurien*, p. 51 (in 1396); Braun, *Die letzten Schicksale*, p. 79 (addition to p. 27); he incorrectly refers to Dlugosz for Sarnicki; D. Ilovaiski, *A History of Russia*, II (Moscow, 1884), 74–75 (about 1362); M. Lyubavski, *A Sketch of the History of the Lithuanian-Russian State up to and including the Union of Lyublin* (Moscow, 1911), p. 24 (under the Grand Prince Olgerd).   Both in Russian.   On other Russian historians see Malitzki, *op. cit.*, pp. 12–13; Hrushevski, *Istoriia Ukraini-Rusi*, IV (Lwów, 1903), 70 ff. (in Ukrainian).

[1] See A. L. Schlözer, *Geschichte von Littauen als einem eigenen Grossfürstenthume bis zum J. 1569* (Halle, 1785), p. 109 (under 1396), in the *Fortsetzung der Allgemeinen Welt-historie durch eine Gesellschaft von Gelehrten in Deutschland und England ausgefertiget*, L: 'drey Chane der Krimschen, Kirkelschen und Monlopischen Tartaren.' It is interesting to notice that this important passage has been overlooked by some Russian historians who have dealt with this particular question, such as Dashkevich and Molchanovski.   See Malitzki, *op. cit.*, p. 13.   In his recent study Bănescu states that the exact date of Olgerd's victory, 1396, has been established by Thunmann and Schlözer; Bănescu, 'Contribution à l'histoire de la seigneurie de Théodoro-Mangoup en Crimée,' *Byz. Zeitschrift*, XXXV (1935), 36.

[2] See P. Köppen, *Krymsky Sbornik* (St Petersburg, 1837), p. 310 (in Russian); W. Tomaschek, *Die Goten in Taurien*, p. 51; also a short popular history of Lithuania by I. A. Katzel, *A History of Lithuania*, I (Kovno, 1921), 30, (in Russian).   A Spanish traveller of the fifteenth century, Pero Tafur, speaks of Vithold's wars with the Tartars, 'Andanças é viajes de Pero Tafur,' ed. D. M. Jiménez de la Espada, *Coleccion de libros españoles raros ó curiosos*, VIII (Madrid, 1874), 164; *Pero Tafur, Travels and Adventures*, translated by Malcolm Letts (New York and London, 1926), p. 134. See also V. Smirnov, *The Crimean Khanate under the Domination of the Ottoman Porte up to the Beginning of the Eighteenth Century* (St Petersburg, 1887), pp. 159–166 (in Russian).

[3] R. Loeper, in the *Izvestiya* of the Tauric Archive Commission, LI (Simferopol, 1914) 298; Bertier

of Jesus Christ upon the builders of the wall, and proceeds, 'This tower of the upper city of ancient Poiki [?] was constructed with the help of God and St Demetrius, and by the care of our most honorable ἑκατοντάρχης Khuïtani; and the restoration of Theodoro [was completed], and Poiki was built in 6870.'[1]

Loeper dated the inscription 1362–1363; but Malitzki has shown that its real dating is 1361–1362.[2] Apparently we have here the first mention of the name Theodoro, which is so well known in documents of the fifteenth century. According to the inscription, Poïki or Poïka was the name of the upper city, where a tower was constructed, marked by this memorial inscription. The topographical name Poïka remains obscure. Loeper believed that it was a barbarian name for the citadel or a tower of the city of Theodoro. Bertier Delagarde hazarded the guess that Poïka was the whole or part of the front wall of Tabana-Dere; but this wall, as Repnikov properly observes, was built in later times. Finally, in 1928 A. Markevich called attention to the name of a mountain range near Mankup, Boïka, on which are found some ruins of old buildings: a church, walls, and the remains of a settlement. In his opinion the similarity of the names Poïka and Boïka cannot be mere coincidence; Poïka perhaps signified a region in Gothia.[3] In spite of efforts of various scholars to identify Poïka, the question remains open. The builder of the tower, the ἑκατοντάρχης Khuïtani, although perhaps not a local prince of Mankup-Theodoro, certainly belonged to those who possessed and commanded the city. Doubtless also despite his Tartar name Khuïtani was a Christian, for the inscription begins with an address to God. At first sight the mention of the martyr St Demetrius is rather incomprehensible. Malitski is right in saying that if a church were in question here the reference might be explained by the fact that the church was consecrated to this saint; but in our inscription this is not the case. Malitski concludes: 'It is evident that the name of St Demetrius is connected with the name of the builder Khuïtani, i.e., we must admit that Khuïtani's Christian name was Demetrius.' He then makes the extremely interesting and novel observation that Khuïtani-Demetrius of the inscription is none other than Demetrius, prince of Monlop (Mankup), one of the three Tartar princes defeated by Olgerd; thus in the sixties of the fourteenth cen-

---

Delagarde, 'Kalamita and Theodoro,' *ibid.*, LV (1918), 6, n. 1, and p. 32. The Greek text in Malitzki, *op. cit.*, p. 9. See A. Vasiliev, 'The Goths in the Crimea,' in the *Izvestiya* of the Russian Academy for the History of Material Culture, I (1921), 51 (pagination of a reprint; in Russian). See this book, p. 49.

[1] The last words in the inscription run as follows: 'και ο ανακαινισμος της Θεωδωραω μετα τον Ποϊκαν εκτισθαν ομου επι ετει ͵ϛωδ.'

[2] Malitzki, *op. cit.*, p. 10, n. 1.   [3] All references in Malitzki, *op. cit.*, p. 10.

tury a prince named Demetrius possessed Mankup, which may serve to confirm the fact that the defeat of the three Tartar princes at the Blue Water belongs to the period of the Grand Prince of Lithuania, Olgerd, not to that of Vitovt.   Otherwise we must admit that two princes named Demetrius ruled over Mankup at the very end of the fourteenth century, which is improbable.[1]   As we shall see later, our tables of the rulers of Mankup would allow no space for the second Demetrius.

Under 20 December 1374 an unpublished Genoese document mentions 'Theodoro Mangop.'[2]

In 1890 Braun discovered an inscription on Mankup which informs us that (a tower) was built by the $\dot{\epsilon}\kappa\alpha\tau o\nu\tau\acute{\alpha}\rho\chi\eta s$ $T\zeta\iota\zeta$ ($\iota\kappa\iota os$?)[3] under the rule of the Tartar Khan of the Golden Horde, Tokhtamysh, in whose name, as we have noted above, the treaty of 1387 with Genoa was concluded. During the eighties of this century Tokhtamysh's influence was preponderant in the Crimea, so that the inscription in question is to be attributed to that time.   As we shall see later, in the tenth decade of the fourteenth century Theodoro was devastated by Tamerlane, Tokhtamysh's rival, and remained in a state of decay for several years.   Thus we may conclude that about 1380 a building connected with the fortification of the place, perhaps a tower, was constructed by a man with a Turkish name ($\tau\zeta\iota\tau$ . . . ?).[4]   At that time Tartar influence was very strong in Gothia, so that its rulers were no doubt tributary to the Tartar Khan; Tokhtamysh was suzerain of Gothia and apparently did not oppose the fortification of Theodoro.   It is interesting to note that in both inscriptions we have been considering, that of 1361–1362 and that of about 1380, the person in charge of the fortification or restoration of Theodoro bore the Greek title $\dot{\epsilon}\kappa\alpha\tau o\nu\tau\acute{\alpha}\rho\chi\eta s$.

Although Gothia was a dependency of the Tartars, and therefore forced to take part in their expeditions, the Emperors of Trebizond continued to mention Gothia in their title under the name of *Perateia*, or 'the land

[1] Malitzki, *op. cit.*, pp. 9–14.

[2] 'Theodoro Mangop contrata bazariorum,' Bănescu, *op. cit.*, 21; he refers to *Archivio di Stato* of Genoa, Massaria Caffe 1374–1375, fol. 37ᵛ.

[3] F. Braun, 'Excavations on Mankup,' in the *Otchety* (Accounts) of the Imperial Archaeological Commission for the Year 1890 (St Petersburg, 1893), p. 19.   The Greek text in Latyshev, *Collection of Greek Inscriptions of Christian Times from South Russia*, p. 55 (No. 46); Malitzki, *op. cit.*, p. 5.

[4] On this inscription see Malitzki, *op. cit.*, pp. 5–9.   The name of Tokhtamysh in the inscription is beyond question, so that Latyshev and Kulakovski have no grounds for wondering whether the name of Tokhtamysh occurs here or that of another Tartar Khan, Tokhta, who died about 1313. Latyshev, *op. cit.*, pp. 54–55; J. Kulakovski, *The Past of the Tauris*, 2nd ed. (Kiev, 1914), p. 117 (in Russian).   On Tokhtamysh and his activities see W. Barthold's accurate article under this name in the *Encyclopédie de l'Islam*, livraison M-bis (1930), pp. 850–852.   The tomb of Tokhtamysh's daughter, Nenkedjan-Khanym, is found at Chufut-Kalé, 'Arabic and Turkish Inscriptions of Baghchesaray,' *Zapiski* of the Odessa Society of History and Antiquities, ii (1855), 527.

beyond the sea,' as if Gothia still belonged to Trebizond.   Thus in a *chrysobull* granted to the Venetians in 1364 by the Emperor of Trebizond, Alexius III (1349–1390), the Emperor's signature is as follows: 'Alexius the faithful in God Emperor and Autocrat of all the East, the Iberians, and the Transmarine Provinces (*Perateia*).'[1]   No doubt in this title *Perateia* is merely a memory of the past, that is, of the situation which existed in the thirteenth century, when, as we have seen above, Gothia or the *Climata* was tributary to Trebizond.[2]

4. TAMERLANE AND GOTHIA

At the end of the fourteenth century the south of present-day Russia suffered severely from the invasion of Tamerlane.   On 14 September 1395 he destroyed Tana, a flourishing Italian colony at the mouth of the Don.[3] He also devastated the Crimea.   A very interesting document which evidently refers to Tamerlane's invasion of the Crimea has been recently published.   This is a rhetorical poem in verse containing 153 lines and devoted to a description of Theodoro.[4]   Its author, named in the title, was a monk (*hieromonachus*) Matthew.   The editor and translator of the text, an Italian scholar, S. G. Mercati, identified the author with the *hieromonachus* Matthew who in the summer of 1395 went to Khazaria (Gazaria) as a representative (vicar) of the Patriarch of Constantinople to administer Yalta and some other places in the Crimea.[5]   In spite of the rhetorical style the description is not a poetical invention but depicts a real journey.   The city itself is called in the poem 'θεοῦ δῶρον'; Mercati could not identify this place and apparently thought of Theodosia-Caffa.[6] But during the Byzantine Congress at Belgrade in 1927 N. Iorga called Mercati's attention to the Crimean castle of *lo Theodoro*.[7]

[1] D. A. Zakythinos, *Le Chrysobulle d'Alexis III Comnène empereur de Trébizonde en faveur des Vénitiens* (Paris, 1932), p. 37.   In this book the four earlier editions of the *Chrysobull* are indicated (pp. 15–17).   Some scholars give the year 1374: Bruun, *Chernomorye*, II, 134; Braun, *Die letzten Schicksale*, p. 21.   The correct year is 1364.

[2] See Braun, *Die letzten Schicksale*, p. 22; Th. Uspenski, *Sketches of the History of the Empire of Trebizond* (Leningrad, 1929), p. 2 (in Russian); Zakythinos, *op. cit.*, p. 92.

[3] See Max Silberschmidt, *Das orientalische Problem zur Zeit des Entstehung des türkischen Reiches nach venezianischen Quellen* (Leipzig and Berlin, 1923), pp. 127–140; on the destruction of Tana, pp. 128–129.

[4] S. G. Mercati, 'Versi di Matteo Ieromonaco, Διήγησις τῆς πόλεως Θεοδώρου,' *Studi Bizantini*, II (Rome, 1927), 19–30; Greek text, 26–30; Italian translation, with some omissions, 21–22.

[5] See Miklosich and Müller, *Acta et diplomata graeca*, II (Vienna, 1862), No. 492 (p. 249), August, 1395, and No. 497 (p. 258), September, 1395.   [6] Mercati, *op. cit.*, pp. 25–26.

[7] S. Mercati, 'Note critiche,' *Studi Bizantini*, II, 294–296; N. Iorga, 'Chronique,' *Revue Historique du sud-est européen*, VI (April–June, 1929), 185.   Cf. N. Iorga, 'Une source négligée de la prise de Constantinople,' *Bulletin de la section historique de l'Académie Roumaine* (Bucarest, 1927), p. 68: 'Parmi ces Grecs qui purent quitter Constantinople faut-il compter ce moine Mathieu qui décrivit en vers son voyage en Gazarie (Crimée) et l'aspect du château de Théodore, ou plutôt des Théodores, de Mangoup, en tatar . . . .'

The poem is entitled *The Story of the City of Theodoros by a Simple and Most Humble Monk, Matthew*.   At the beginning of the poem the author says that he wished to go abroad and traverse Khazaria; he gives an enthusiastic description of the fertility of the country, of the harbors rich in fish, of the delicious drinking water, of the mountains, hills, and plains. One day in his wanderings he saw the ruins of a delightful and beautiful city surrounded by hills, plains, and mountain passes.   The wonderful city, 'an awe-inspiring and extraordinary marvel , unheard of and almost unbelievable,' stood in the midst of the plain 'like a six-cornered table, and its walls seemed made by heaven but not by the hands of men.' Filled with admiration, Matthew found an old road which winding like a spiral stair brought him to a beautiful gate.   'Who, my friend,' writes the author, 'will tell without tears and sorrow of the beauty of the porticoes,' of the huge and well-adjusted stones, colonnades, pylons, and other marvelous buildings?   He saw a magnificent temple, wells of sweet water, irrigated gardens, fountains playing, and he noted that the place was fresh and airy.   The floors of the temple were covered with mosaics; the cupolas were long and spherical.   From a tower he admired a vast and beautiful panorama, magnificent temples and palaces, sculptured sepulchres, porticoes, and columns.[1]   With deep sorrow he saw also heaps of corpses and skulls.   Later he descended and observed many other objects of interest.   Then he re-ascended and looked at the view.   He remarks: 'One can see from here a distance of three days' journey over land; but who can measure the view by sea?'

The author, who is henceforth referred to as a stranger, now meets a man who is really the personification of the city of Theodoro, and they have an imaginary conversation.

Stranger: O most marvelous city called gift of God [θεοῦ δῶρον], who was thy supreme and wonderful builder, who erected moats, mountain passes, heights, most marvelous natural walls without lime, bricks, or hewn marble, without architects, workers, or masons, without large quadrangular stones, without instruments, saws and tools, without shouts and sighing, without guards, without crowds of people, carts, and wood, without imperial command and without cost? The high walls which surround thee rise high above the ground and are well seen by land and by sea.   How hast thou sweet crystal wells, meadows, plains, hills, and ravines?   Thou art not a small city, but a 'megalopolis,' far from Constantinople.   Marvel of marvels, thy creation amazes me!

---

[1] Cf. the description of Theodoro-Mankup by Martin Broniovius, who visited the place in 1578: 'Mancopia civitas ad montes et sylvas magis porrecta, et mari non jam propinqua est, arces duas in altissimo saxoso et peramplo conditas, templa Graeca sumptuosa et aedes, plurimos rivos, qui ex saxo decurrunt, limpidissimos et admirandos habuit,' *Martini Broniovii Tartariae Descriptio* (Cologne, 1595), p. 7; a Russian translation in the *Zapiski* of the Odessa Society of History and Antiquities, vi (1867), 343.   See N. Bănescu, *op. cit.*, 31–32.

City: Thou admirest my simple construction? But it is very easy for the artificer (God). He who established the heaven and founded the earth, the glorious architect, the all-wise artificer who first completed the roof and then established the ground, who lighted the heaven with the beauty of the stars and filled the sun and the moon with light, who adorned the earth with most various flowers, mountains, and plants, who brought forth wells, seas, and rivers from the depth of the abyss, who created everything by (His) word, without material, or instruments, without cost, He who is omnipresent and fills everything — He erected my structure, o stranger!

Stranger: Thou hast well answered me, and I thank thee. I see magnificent temples, beautiful palaces, marvelous many-colored sculptures on the ground, and above columns and painted sepulchres. But why art thou deserted and empty? Even if the land of Khazaria [ἡ γῆ τῆς Χαζαρίας] had no houses, it would be fitting, O all-delightful one, that thou shouldst be inhabited!

City: Weeping from the depth of my soul, I speak from (my) mournful heart. I see thou art a wise, intelligent, and sagacious stranger, but clothed in tatters, wandering alone. I see thou wearest a poor and sad garment [χιτῶνα]. I can tell thee of my many losses, wars, horrors, battles; of peoples who surrounded me for seven years, the numberless armies of the Agarenes ['Αγαρηνῶν φοσσάτα], massacres and fears of besieged and besiegers, raids and ambushes, neighing of horses; inside the people lamenting and weeping, enduring the ninth year (of siege), destitute of food, children, women, and men lamenting; they suffered so from the violence of famine that they ate asses, dogs, weasels. [I can tell thee] how driven to despair they surrendered me; o stranger, I should be overcome with lamentations and wailings and I should make thee also sob and weep. But before thou succumbest, o stranger, and art overwhelmed, direct thy mind in the right way, glorifying [our] Lord. I am filled with sorrow, but coming to my right mind I laud the Creator who is the just judge and whose judgments are right. This happened to me through the ire of God on account of many iniquities committed by the men of that time.

Stranger: Thou saidest well, o most marvellous creature of God. When God is wrathful, disasters occur. This world is like a harvest [ὡς πανηγύριν]: whatsoever a man sows, that shall he also reap.[1] There is nothing stable or firm in the world. Everything passes, everything is vanity; this life is shadow, dream, and smoke. Only one good thing exists: to save your soul, to believe in the Maker and Creator, to love Him with all your heart, and to love your neighbor as God. The whole law rests upon these commandments, as our Lord says in the gospels, to whom be glory and honor, power and might, now and forever, world without end.

This poem has considerable historical interest. As the author went to the Crimea about 1395, a fact confirmed by the sources mentioned above, we may be certain that the text deals with the invasion of Tamerlane,

---

[1] In Greek: 'ὡς πραγματεύετ' ἕκαστος, οὕτως ἀπολαμβάνει.' I think the text refers to the Epistle to the Galatians, VI, 7.

who after having destroyed Tana in September 1395 invaded the Crimea. We learn for the first time from this poem that the Tartars surrounded Theodoro for almost nine years. Of course this was not a regular siege directed by Tamerlane himself; he promptly left the Crimea for other distant military campaigns. But the Tartars who were under his power continued hostile to Theodoro for nine years after his departure, cutting it off from food supplies so that the population lived through the horrors of famine. The buildings of the city, palaces, churches, and private houses, were evidently mostly destroyed by Tamerlane himself when he first attacked Theodoro. If we admit that Tamerlane's invasion in the Crimea took place in the same year that he destroyed Tana, 1395, which is almost certain, and add the nine years of the Tartar occupation of Theodoro, we shall get 1404, the year of Tamerlane's death (in January). After his death his huge empire entered a period of disturbance and disruption, so probably it was easy for Theodoro to shake off the Tartar domination and under the energetic rule of its prince Alexis set about restoration of the city buildings. In my opinion, the nine years given in the poem signify the period of the preponderance of Tamerlane's empire in the Crimea.

Giving the variants of the name of the city — Theodoro, Tedori, Tedoro, οἱ Θεόδωροι — Mercati explains the latter plural form by the fact that the city was dedicated to the two saints, its protectors, Theodore Tyron and Theodore Stratelates. The plural accusative form 'Θεοδώρους,' which is found in the title of the Codex Vaticanus which contains the text of the poem, may perhaps be explained by the common usage 'στοὺς Θεοδώρους,' like 'Setines' and 'Stivas' in the documents on Athens and Thebes.[1] I am very doubtful as to the plausibility of Mercati's interpretation, supported by N. Iorga, of the form 'οἱ Θεόδωροι,' because there is no proof whatever as to the existence of the two saints as protectors of Theodoro. The most plausible solution of this question is to be found in Bănescu's recent study. In Genoese documents the name of the place is given as Tedoro, Todoro, Theodori, Teodori, Thodori, Tedori, Todori; these forms are to be explained as deriving from the Greek names of this place used with definite article τὸ λεγόμενον Δορός, τὸ λεγόμενον Δόρος, and especially ἡ χώρα τὸ Δόρυ (Procopius). From the point of view of Bănescu the combination 'a governor τῆς χώρας τὸ Δόρος would not be inadmissible.' Thus τὸ Δόρος or τὸ Δόρυ have given Genoese names Theodoros, Todoros, Todori, etc.[2]

---

[1] Mercati, 'Note critiche,' *Studi Bizantini*, II (Roma, 1927), 295, note. For the form 'Θεοδώρους' see Mercati, *ibid.*, p. 26, in the critical apparatus. Iorga also calls Theodoro 'le château des SS. Théodores,' in the *Revue Historique du sud-est européen*, VI (1929), 185; also VII (1930), p. 254: Théodori ('Théodore Tiron et Théodore Stratélate'). [2] N. Bănescu, *op. cit.*, 35–36.

To the period of Tamerlane's invasion of the Crimea I am inclined to refer a very obscure inscription discovered in one of the towers of Tabana-Dere on Mankup, and preserved in a very fragmentary form.[1]   Although modern methods of photography have given us a much better copy of this inscription than Latyshev had, none the less its general content is uncertain.[2]   The first line gives the end of the title, indicating that the inscription was set up by the *Theodoritai*, i.e., by the inhabitants of Theo-doro, in eternal commemoration of a certain event which cannot be pre-cisely determined.   Then after mentioning cavalry the inscription says that they (?) killed ten pairs of oxen and their driver and . . . herd; he raised young and old (μικρου εος μεγαλους) against the barbarians and pursued them up to . . . (μεδήους ?) . . . of the fortress Theodoro pro-tected by God, drove and assailed them up to Zazale (Ζαζαλε ?).   Lines 7–9 are as yet undecipherable.   No doubt line 8 gives the date of the in-scription, because the word 'ετους' can be read; then follow the two letters 'sω'; after 'ω' the letters are completely erased.   Here, then, is the begin-ning of the date 6800 (s̄ = 6000 and ω = 800); in other words, our inscrip-tion belongs to the fourteenth century.[3]   Of course it is quite impossible to be sure of the meaning of this inscription; but since it deals with a barbarian attack on and devastation of Theodoro in the fourteenth cen-tury, I am inclined to attribute it to the very close of that century and connect it with Tamerlane's invasion of Theodoro, which took place, as we have noted above, in 1395.   For this invasion the poem on Theodoro written by the monk Matthew, which I have discussed above, serves as an interesting and fresh source.[4]

5. Gothia in the Fifteenth Century.   Alexis, Prince of Gothia

At the beginning of the fifteenth century we have very interesting in-formation concerning the existence of the Gothic tongue in the Crimea. The evidence is given by a Bavarian soldier, Hans Schiltberger,who took part in the battle of Nicopolis in 1396 and was taken prisoner by the Turks.   During many years' wandering in the East (1394–1427) he visited various countries and described their customs and manners.[5] Among other things, in Chapter xx of his travels he relates the story of

---

[1] On the discovery and study of this inscription see Malitzki, *op. cit.*, pp. 15–17.

[2] Latyshev, *Collection of Greek Inscriptions of Christian Times*, p. 57 (No. 47).   A new and more complete edition in Malitzki, *op. cit.*, p. 18.   [3] See Malitzki, *op. cit.*, pp. 18–19.

[4] Malitzki is evidently not acquainted with this poem.

[5] *Hans Schiltbergers Reisebuch*, ed. V. Langmantel (Tübingen, 1885), in the *Bibliothek des Littera-rischen Vereins in Stuttgart*, clxxii).   An English translation: *Johann Schiltberger, The Bondage and Travels*, translated by J. B. Telfer, with notes by Ph. Bruun (London, 1879), in the series of the Hakluyt Society.   A Russian translation with very valuable notes by Ph. Bruun (see the English translation just quoted) in the *Zapiski* of the University of Novorossiya, i (Odessa, 1867), 1–157.

Tamerlane's death and says that he was in Tamerlane's service for six years.[1] In the section on the Crimea he mentions the country called Kipchaq with its capital Solkhat and gives a detailed and valuable description of Caffa. Then he writes: 'There is a city called Karkery (Karckery, Kercueri) in a good country called Sudi (Sutti, Suti); but the Infidels call it That (Thatt, Than); there are Christians of the Greek faith in it, and there are good vineyards. It lies near the Black Sea, and in this country S. Clement was thrown into the Sea. Close by is a city called in the Infidel tongue Serucherman.'[2] In Chapter LVI (LX) Schiltberger notes that 'the seventh (tongue) is the *Kuthia* tongue [Sprauch] which the Infidels call That.'[3] The city Karkery with some manuscript variants is of course Chufut-kalé, which has been discussed above. In the distorted form *Sudi (Sutti, Suti)* we may no doubt recognize *Guti*, i.e. Gothia, where Karkery is found; this is the mountain section of the Crimea or Gothia, called by the Tartars *That*, the name given by Turkish tribes to 'a subject people.'[4] For the 'Kuthia Sprauch' (tongue) we have also another variant, 'Ruthia.'[5]

Schiltberger's account consists of two parts: in the first in a distorted form he gives the geographic term 'Gothia,' which is well known and is confirmed by many other sources; secondly, listing the tongues in which divine service is performed according to the Greek faith, he in the seventh place gives the 'Kuthia sprauch,' i.e. the Gothic language. But like Rubruquis, of whom we have spoken above, Schiltberger gives this information by hearsay, so that I should not venture to say that the Gothic language survived in the territory of Gothia at the outset of the fifteenth century. Schiltberger's statement is interesting as showing that in the recollection of some people in the Crimea the tradition of older times, when the population of Gothia was neither hellenized nor tartarized, was still fresh.

The anonymous account of a voyage from Venice to Tana has been preserved. The voyage was made from 1404 to 1407.[6] The traveller, evidently a merchant, sailed through the Hellespont to Constantinople, which he admired greatly; he then entered the Black Sea. He writes:

---

[1] Ph. Bruun says that Schiltberger doubled the years of his service with Tamerlane, so that in reality he served only three years (*Zapiski*, p. 27, n. 1).

[2] Ed. Langmantel, p. 68; Telfer, pp. 49–50; Bruun, pp. 57–58 (in Russian).

[3] Langmantel, p. 140 (Ch. LX); Telfer, p. 78 (Ch. LVI); Bruun, p. 102 (Ch. LVI).

[4] See Bruun, *op. cit.*, p. 58, n. 4 (in Russian).

[5] See variants in Langmantel, *op. cit.*, p. 140.

[6] N. Iorga, 'Un viaggio da Venezia alla Tana,' *Nuovo Archivio Veneto*, XI, i (1896), 5–13. The text is published from a manuscript of the *Biblioteca Ambrosiana* in Milan. For dating see p. 6. See M. Kovalevski, 'On the Early History of Azov,' *Trudy* of the Twelfth Archaeological Congress in Kharkov, II (Moscow, 1905), 152 (in Russian).

'We cross the sea, and finally the lands of the Goths appear to us . . . . Then the huge city of Caffa presents itself . . . . The Genoese dominate there.   Leaving the lands of the Goths to the left, we see the lands of the Tartars on the same side.'[1]   Then the travellers left the Black Sea, entered Maeotis (the Sea of Azov), and reached Tana, 'where merchants of various countries bring their wares.'[2]   This account of the Venetian merchant certifies once more that the region Gothia was well known at that time.

After the death of Tamerlane in 1404 and the disruption of his empire, and before the Ottoman Turks made their appearance in the Crimea after the capture of Constantinople in 1453, three powers existed in the Peninsula: the Tartars, Genoa, and Gothia.   At the beginning of the fifteenth century, from Tamerlane's dismembered empire a new Tartar khanate came into being in the Crimea, under the dynasty of the Gireis.   Hadji-Girei (*circa* 1420–1466) is considered the first khan of the Crimean Tartars.   His residence was in Solkhat, north of Caffa.   Genoa and Gothia were usually rivals with strained or openly hostile relations; but sometimes both of them, Genoa in particular, realized that their own welfare and security, especially in view of the ever-increasing power of the Ottoman Turks and the uncertain attitude of the Tartars, required a policy of mutual confidence and peaceable understanding.   Let us not lose sight of the fact that after the treaties of 1381–1387 Genoa regarded Gothia as a vassal state, though the rulers of Gothia opposed this view.   These affairs serve as background for a very interesting figure, a prince of Gothia, Alexis of Theodoro.

Various scholars have believed that Alexis was related to an Imperial family, either that of the Palaeologi or that of the Comneni of Trebizond.   Bruun writes that Alexis was a member of the family reigning in Constantinople.[3]   Heyd remarks that the name Alexis which was borne by most of the rulers of Gothia indicates kinship with the Imperial house of Trebizond.[4]   But for such a statement there is no proof whatever.   As we have seen above, Alexis' family was of Greek origin and was very probably connected with a noble family of Trebizond, the Gabrades, who had been exiled to the Crimea.[5]   The fact that Alexis' family had no Imperial blood may now be considered definitely established.

---

[1] 'Transfretamur pelagus et tandem nobis Gothorum apparent terre . . . se nobis pendebit ingens urbs Caffa . . . huic dominantur Ianuenses.   Relictis his a leva Gothorum terris, ab eadem parte se nobis Tartarorum pendent terre' (p. 12).

[2] 'Ibi pagum reperimus que Tana nuncupatur, ad quam mercatores diversarum regionum merces deferunt' (p. 13).   It is interesting to note that Tana rapidly recovered from its destruction by Tamerlane in 1395.   [3] Bruun, *Chernomorye*, II (Odessa, 1880), 230 (in Russian).

[4] Heyd, *Histoire du commerce du Levant*, II, 212.   I do not know why Heyd states that most of the rulers of Theodoro bore the name of Alexis.   I know only two princes of this name (see below).

[5] See Braun, *op. cit.*, pp. 26, 44–45; Vasiliev, *The Goths in the Crimea*, II, 275–280 (in Russian). See this book, pp. 153–157.

In 1883, from a Paris manuscript of the seventeenth century written by a Greek monk, Cosmas, a French scholar, Emile Legrand, published a Greek epitaph to a prince's son ('τῷ Αἰθεντοπούλῳ') of ninety-five lines in verse, composed by John Eugenikos.[1] To this text a Greek scholar, N. G. Polites, wrote a note without arriving at any positive conclusion.[2] From 1883 to 1928 this text was ignored. In the latter year a Russian scholar, D. S. Spiridonov, reprinted the Greek text of the epitaph, gave its Russian translation, and wrote a very interesting commentary on it.[3] The author of the epitaph, John Eugenikos, a native of Trebizond, lived in the first half of the fifteenth century and was the author of many rhetorical descriptions of different cities, beginning with his own native city, Trebizond, as well as of some theological treatises.[4] Unfortunately we do not know the date of his death; but he died in all likelihood about 1450, because the *Codex Parisinus graecus* 2075, containing most of his works, was written by himself in 1439.[5]

In spite of the rhetorical character of the epitaph, a style perfectly suitable for such literary work, the poem gives us new information on the genealogy of the ruling line of Theodoro. The epitaph is dedicated to Alexis, who died in childhood, a grandson of the famous Alexis of Theodoro. According to the epitaph, the father of the dead child was a prince of Khazaria ('αἰθέντης Χαζαρίας'), John, son of 'a wonderful and most powerful father' (ll. 20–21). Then the epitaph continues: 'Who does not know of the great Alexis, a man terrible and vigorous in war, quick in thought and still quicker in action, a firm pillar of Khazaria, a bright luminary to his subjects, a warrior undaunted in wars, who by his mere appearance puts his enemies to flight? During his life he is the sun circling the sky and illuminating the whole land of Gothia with his beams.'[6] As we see, there is no mention here of Alexis' Imperial origin; had this existed, the author would no doubt have included it.

[1] "Ἰωάννου τοῦ Εὐγενικοῦ Ἐπιτάφιον τῷ Αἰθεντοπούλῳ,' edited by Em. Legrand, in the Δελτίον τῆς ἱστορικῆς καὶ ἐθνολογικῆς Ἑταιρίας τῆς Ἑλλάδος, ι (Athens, 1883), 455–458 (text, 456–458).

[2] N. G. Polites, *ibid.*, pp. 459–461.

[3] D. S. Spiridonov, 'Notes on the History of Hellenism in the Crimea, ι: On the Family History of the House of Mangup,' *Izvestiya* of the Tauric Society of History, Archaeology, and Ethnography, ιι (Simferopol, 1928), 1–7 (in Russian). I use a reprint of the article. One line, between lines 30 and 35, is probably omitted (Spiridonov, p. 4).

[4] See Krumbacher, *Geschichte der byzantinischen Litteratur*, 2nd ed., pp. 495–497, 117.

[5] See Krumbacher, *op. cit.*, pp. 117, 496. Spiridonov believes that John Eugenikos died after 1453 (p. 6).

[6] Spiridonov, ll. 22–30. Referring to these lines, Spiridonov (p. 4) remarks: 'As to Alexis the epitaph uses the present tense (lines 22, 28 and 30); evidently he is still alive (line 29: "τὸν κὲν βίῳ ἥλιον οὐρανοδρόμον").' But in my opinion, this is a rhetorical description of the personality of Alexis; and the Greek present ('τίς οὐκ ἀκούει') and the two Greek present participles ('τρέχοντα' and 'καταυγάζοντα') may be attributed to Alexis deceased as well as alive. Therefore I am inclined to believe that the epitaph deals with Alexis after his death.

Then there follows an extremely interesting passage of the epitaph: 'His first son is the father of the deceased, the great John, of blessed name, who has quickly reached the highest glory, a perfect model of piety, just, ingenious, active, magnanimous, modest, straightforward, considerate, humble, brilliant, liberal, pleasant, gentle, mild, approachable, a friend to all, a harmonious personification of all virtues.'[1]   I may point out that we have here for the first time the real name of Alexis' possible successor, John, of whom I shall speak a little later.   The statement of the epitaph that John was the first son of Alexis implies that he was not Alexis' only son, but that he had brothers, which, as we shall see later, is positively confirmed by other sources.   Referring to John, Spiridonov writes: 'The epitaph calls him a prince of Khazaria.   Does it follow henceforth that John was co-ruler with his father?   The qualities which our author points out in his characterization indicate that he was in private life and did not at that time perform state duties; at least the author does not estimate him from this point of view.'[2]   In this respect I disagree with Spiridonov.   John was actually Prince of Khazaria after the death of his father, so that there can be no question of his being co-ruler.   That John was actually Prince of Gothia the following references in the epitaph show: 'αἰθέντης Χαζαρίας' (l. 20), 'the great John' (l. 32), 'who reached the highest glory' (l. 33).   Now we pass to the information given by the epitaph concerning the dead child's mother, that is, John's wife.   Her name was Maria.   On her father's side she was related to the 'illustrious family of the Asans and to the purple-flowering [πορφυρανθής] tree of the Palaeologi emperors; on her mother's side to the wonderful Tzamblakon [Τζαμπλακόμων τῶν θαυμαστῶν μητρόθεν].[3]   On her arrival the marriage celebrations were brilliant.   She was young, illustrious, most distinguished, noble, God-loving, most pious, grave, loving goodness, very discreet, mild, kind to the poor, affable, pleasant, charitable, compassionate, sweet, liberal, very clement, the serene Maria, having thousands of epithets and wonderfully distinguished for all gifts, by mercy of God the august princess [σεπτὴ κυρία] related to our holy empress' (ll. 41–55).   Thus, according to the reliable information of the epitaph, the male line of the princes of Gothia or Theodoro belonged to a noble Greek family, in all likelihood, to the Trebizond family of the Gabrades; while, by the marriage of Alexis' son John to Maria, they became connected with the Imperial dynasty of the Palaeologi.

---

[1] Spiridonov, ll. 31–40.   [2] *Idem*, p. 4 (in Russian).

[3] The family of the Tzamblakon was related to the family of the Palaeologi.   See Miklosich and Müller, *Acta et Diplomata*, ii (1862), 324: "Ο οἰκεῖος τῷ κρατίστῳ καὶ ἁγίῳ μου αὐτοκράτορι, ἐν ἁγίῳ πνεύματι ἀγαπητὸς υἱὸς τῆς ἡμῶν μετριότητος, κῦρις Ἀλέξιος Τζαμπλάκου ὁ Καβαλλάριος' (Doc. December 1399). See also N. Bănescu, 'Peut-on identifier le Zamblacus des documents ragusains?,' *Mélanges Charles Diehl*, i (Paris, 1930), 32; N. Iorga, *Revue hist. du sud-est européen*, viii (1931), No. 4–6, p. 154.

But the author's attention is concentrated mainly on the child Alexis. The epitaph opens with the following words:

O child, flower of the family, offspring of the Graces, combination of all good, of marvelous nature, wonderful stature, exquisite beauty, what painter could picture thy form and the brilliancy which rested on thee? Who [could describe] the innate charm of thy soul which thou hast manifested all thy childhood, or the fame of thy noble family? But why if he reproduces thy appearance and the charm emanating from it, and thy inimitable beauty, does the painter not express the virtues of thy soul, nor point out thy ancient nobility nor thy imperial relationship and power? Or, acting well and reasoning wisely, does he leave all this to be described in words? Then we shall tell that which the painter passes over in silence. The [deceased] springs from a noble root and from a branch of imperial blood (ll. 1–19).

After the rhetorical description which we have translated above of the virtues and noble lineage of the grandfather, father, and mother, the author turns again to the infant Alexis. The epitaph continues:

Such were the parents of this golden offspring, the delightful Alexis, a golden star, the golden Alexis. Oh, terrible sorrow! Alas, who envied our happiness? How the heavy and deadly sickle mercilessly deprived thee of life, before like an ear of corn thou mightest have matured and ripened with time, and put thee in the heavenly granaries gloriously to inhabit paradise, in the longed-for bosom of Abraham! Thy eyes, pleasant welcome, sweet words have vanished. Where is thy golden countenance like a rose? Where are the streams of words, marvelous for thy age, where is thy captivating and sweet voice, like a harmonious and melodious song? Where is thy considerateness, wise courage, and natural tendency to all good? What a loss we have seen! The all-destroying scythe of untimely death has cut off this plant, high, noble, and beautifully flowering! Indeed, that choicest couple, the parents, in their ardent feeling of love for their child, were destined to suffer this terrific blow and live through this bitter sorrow! Thus to console themselves in their pain and alleviate this greatest calamity, the parents ordered the picture of the child to be made, and now they look at him as if he lived and breathed, and they add the following verse: 'O visitor [ὦ θεατά], do not look carelessly at this tomb or this picture, but coming here bend thy head gently, shed a compassionate tear, and in this contemplation know thyself, condemn this bitter life, and give all thy goods to the poor. Although the mouth of the golden child is silent, it yet has the power to speak without words, and becomes a teacher of life for thee' (ll. 56–96).

By means of a rather debatable interpretation of the text of the epitaph supported by data from other sources, Spiridonov has come to the following conclusions. John's marriage to Maria Palaeologina took place in Trebizond, where, as we shall see later, his sister, also Maria, in 1426 married David, destined to be the last Emperor of Trebizond. There John's and Maria's first child, Alexis, was born and died. In Trebizond also John Eugenikos composed his epitaph to Alexis. John and Maria left the Crimea for Trebizond between 1440 and 1446; the death of the child and the composition of the epitaph fall in 1446–1447.

In his recent study Malitzki disagrees with Spiridonov and finds the latter's chronological speculations doubtful; he rejects as ungrounded Spiridonov's dating of the child's death, 1446, and points out that advancing the composition of the epitaph to 1446–1447 and John's marriage with Maria to approximately 1440 does not take into account John's age. John was the eldest son of Alexis of Mankup, who, Malitzki believes, began to rule at the outset of the fifteenth century and even at that time was not a young man. John's sister, Maria, married David of Trebizond in 1426 (see below). Malitzki asks: 'How could John's marriage have taken place fourteen years after that of his sister?' He ventures the hypothesis that the child's death must have happened not later than 1426, and that possibly John's marriage was performed about 1420. However, he says, 'Matters may have fallen out in an entirely different way.'[1] Thus, although he refutes Spiridonov's opinion, Malitzki himself does not come to any positive conclusion.

Before discussing what is known regarding the beginning of Alexis' rule in Gothia, his activities, and his death, I will go back to the fourteenth century and endeavor to trace the list of the Princes of Gothia at that period.

We have seen that in the middle of the fourteenth century Demetrius ruled in Theodoro, the prince who was defeated by Olgerd (1341–1377). Whether or not this Demetrius is to be identified with Khuïtani, as Malitzki believes on the basis of the inscription of 1361–1362, is a secondary question.

According to the old genealogical lists of the Russian nobility, at the close of the fourteenth century under the Russian Grand Prince Vasili I Dmitrievich (1389–1425), a Greek prince, Stepan Vasilyevich, i.e. Stepan, son of Vasili, surnamed Khovra (Khomra or Komra), former master of the cities Sudak, Mankup, and Balaklava, emigrated from the Crimea to Moscow, and established the famous Russian family name Golovin; in Russia, however, he did not bear the title of prince.[2] Another old genealogical work, the *Barkhatnaya Kniga* (the Velvet Book), tells us that 'Prince Stepan Vasilyevich and his son Grigory (Gregory) came from their estate of Sudak and Cafa to Grand Prince Vasili Dmitreevich.'[3] But ac-

---

[1] Malitzki, *op. cit.*, pp. 30–32.

[2] *A Russian Genealogical Book Published by Prince Peter Dolgoruky*, III (St Petersburg, 1856), 105. See also Bruun, *Chernomorye*, II (Odessa, 1880), 231. Both in Russian.

[3] *A Genealogical Book of Russian as Well as Immigrant Princes and Nobles, Containing a Genealogical Book Collected and Compiled in the Razryad under Tsar Theodore Alexeyevich and at Times Augmented,*

cording to Köppen, the manuscript of the *Barkhatnaya Kniga* has a different version: he quotes it as follows. 'Under the Grand Prince Dmitri Ivanovich (Donskoi, 1363–1389) Prince Stepan Vasilyevich came to Russia from his estate of Sudak, Mankup, and Kafa. The families of the Khovrins and the Golovins sprang from his son, Grigory Khovra.'[1] This version states that Stepan Vasilyevich came to Russia not under Vasili I Dmitreevich but under his father, Dmitri Donskoi.

A prayer inserted in old lists of the members of the Golovin family, the *synodica*, contains the following words: 'Remember . . . Prince Stephan who when he became a monk was called Simon, and his children: Gregorius, and Alexis who was killed at Balaklava.[2] From the old genealogical lists of the Russian nobility we learn that Prince Stephan (Stephen) with his son Gregorius emigrated to Russia at the close of the fourteenth century (in 1391 or 1399)[3] or at the outset of the fifteenth (in 1403).[4] His son Gregorius founded a monastery in Moscow called Simonov after his father's monastic name Simon.[5] I am inclined to accept the year 1391 and connect the emigration of Stephan, Prince of Sudak, Mankup, and Balaklava, with the results of the war between Genoa and the Tartars in the eighties of the fourteenth century, when after the final peace of 1387 Stephan lost Sudak and Balaklava to Caffa. No doubt serious friction must have arisen with the Khan of Solkhat, who was the suzerain of Gothia. Stripped of Maritime Gothia with her important ports, such as Sugdaia (Sudak) and Cembalo (Balaklava), and facing difficulties with the Khan, Stephan was forced to emigrate; he left Gothia reluctantly, yielding to force of circumstances, perhaps even secretly. Braun writes that Stephan died in 1400,[6] of course in Russia, but cites no authority.

Thus from the sources cited above we learn that in the second half of the fourteenth century there were three Princes of Gothia or Mankup: (1) Demetrius; (2) Vasili, Stephan's father; and (3) Stephan (Stepan Vasilyevich) who ended his days in Russia. It is possible that Vasili was Deme-

Known as *Barkhatnaya Kniga*, ed. N. Novikov, II (Moscow, 1787), 270; see also pp. 304, 396, 423. See also Vasilievski, *Works*, III (Petrograd, 1915), ccii. Both in Russian. Vasilievski writes that Stepan Vasilyevich Surozhski (i.e. of Surozh=Sudak) came to Grand Prince Vasily in 6911=1403. Malitzki (*op. cit.*, p. 22) gives the year 1399. A *razryad* was one of the departments in pre-Petrian Russian administration, and *razryadnaya kniga* (book) was an official record of Russian genealogies.

[1] Köppen, *Krymsky Sbornik*, p. 291, n. 432. Cf. P. Petrov, *A History of the Families of the Russian Nobility*, I (St Petersburg, 1886), 268; N. Golovin, *Some Words on the Family of the Greek Princes Comneni* (Moscow, 1854), pp. 11–12. All in Russian.

[2] N. Golovin, *op. cit.*, pp. 11–12. See also Malitzki, *op. cit.*, p. 25, n. 1, 38–39.

[3] P. Kazanski, *The Village Novospasskoe, or Dedenevo and the Genealogy of the Golovini* (Moscow, 1847), p. 113 ('in 1391'). N. Golovin, *op. cit.*, pp. 11–12 ('in 1399').

[4] Vasilievski, *op. cit.*, p. ccii.   [5] Malitzki, *op. cit.*, p. 39.

[6] F. Braun, *Die letzten Schicksale*, p. 41 (genealogical table).

trius' son.   Stephan's surname was Khovra (Khomra or Komra) or in the
Russian form Khovrin, i.e., a slightly distorted form of Gabras, as we
have pointed out above.   According to a very plausible hypothesis of
my own, originally but briefly advanced in 1890 by F. Braun, the family
of Gabrades appeared in the Crimea in the twelfth century and some time
later controlled Gothia, originally in all likelihood with the title of
Toparchs.   As Toparchs in the thirteenth century they lived through a
period of loose dependence upon Trebizond.   Is it possible that the governor (*sebastos*) who resided at Sugdaia (Sudak) and in 1249 freed the city
from the Tartars, so that the city solemnly celebrated its liberation (see
above), was the ancestor of the rulers of Mankup?[1]   But soon afterwards
the Tartars regained their power and the Toparchs of Gothia fell under
the political influence of the Crimean Tartars.   Gothia became a sort of
vassal state with its own ruling family of Gabrades, who by that time had
obtained the title of princes, and in the fourteenth century fought with
the Tartar Khans against Olgerd of Lithuania.   We do not know how
Gothia became a principality; it is obvious that this change happened in
the first half of the fourteenth century, with the consent and approbation
of the Tartar authorities.

Malitzki has some doubts as to my hypothesis that in the twelfth century the family of Gabrades grew powerful in the Crimea in general and
in Gothia in particular.   'As far as Mankup is concerned,' he adds, 'we
have seen that in the fourteenth century men of Turkish or Tartar origin
stood at its head, although perhaps they maintained relations with the
Greek world, especially with Trebizond.   The establishment of the power
of the family of Gabrades (i.e. Alexis' family) ought to be attributed to
the very beginning of the fifteenth century.'[2]   But as far as I understand
the general situation in the Crimea in the fourteenth century, Gothia's
vassalage to the Tartars would explain the presence in Mankup of Tartar
officials rather than Tartar rulers, especially after the Tartar-Genoese war
of 1380–1387, when the Prince of Gothia himself emigrated to Russia,
or earlier, when Demetrius of Gothia fought against Lithuania in alliance
with the Tartar Khans.   Some of these representatives with Tartar
names may have been Christians.

In connection with the emigration of Stepan Vasilyevich Khovra to
Moscow Bănescu says: 'Baron Igor von der Launitz, the last descendant
of the *seigneurs* of Theodoro, writes to us that this refugee belonged to the

---

[1] G. Bratianu, *Recherches sur le commerce génois dans la Mer Noire au XIIIe siècle* (Paris, 1929),
p. 204; Virginie Vasiliu, 'Sur la seigneurie de "Tedoro" en Crimée,' *Mélanges de l'école roumaine en
France* (Paris, 1929), Part I, p. 318.

[2] Malitzki, *op. cit.*, p. 23; cf. p. 20: 'At the outset of the fifteenth century the possession of Mankup
passes to a Greek family in the person of Alexis, who calls himself lord and master of Theodoro.'

very well known family of the Gabrades, who had, for a certain time, an independent situation in Trebizond. He is mentioned in Russian sources as Stepan Vasilyevich Khovra and was entitled the sovereign of the cities of Mangup, Balaklava, and Sudak. Expelled by the Emperor of Trebizond, Manuel III (in 1393), he took refuge in Moscow, where he was received with honour and became the head of the important families of Khovrin and Golovin.'[1] As far as I am concerned, I do not know why Baron Igor von der Launitz is the last descendant of the *seigneurs* of Theodoro, and what is the source of his statement that Stepan Vasilyevich was expelled by the Emperor of Trebizond, Manuel III, in 1393. In other respects, the information given by Baron von der Launitz to Bănescu can be compared with my presentation of this question.

According to the old genealogical lists of the Golovin family, Stephan Vasilyevich, who emigrated to Russia about 1391, had two sons: Gregorius, who left with his father for Moscow, and Alexis. The latter is the most prominent, energetic, and famous personage among the Princes of Gothia or Theodoro-Mankup,[2] and his name occurs frequently in our sources. We do not know exactly when he began to rule. After the emigration, or perhaps it is better to say the flight, of Stephan and Gregorius to Russia in 1391, the Tartars must have been much occupied with affairs in Gothia. At that time Alexis was evidently very young,[3] because he died between 1444 and 1447 (see below) as a Prince of Gothia after a very long reign. It may be supposed that after 1391 either an interregnum lasted for several years or a sort of regency over the child Alexis was established by the Tartars. The first information about Alexis given by our printed sources belongs to the year 1411, when he was regarded by Caffa as a very important element in the political life of the Crimea.[4] In this year in the records of the Genoese colony of Caffa we read that on 8 July a present offered to Alexis, Prince of Theodoro, cost 1121 aspers.[5] On 26 August 1411 a sum of money was paid to Alexis' ambassador.[6] On 24 October, 260 aspers were paid to Alexis' ambassador to

---

[1] Bănescu, *op. cit.*, p. 37.

[2] Braun's casual remark that Demetrius might have been Alexis' father is to be ignored; Braun, *op. cit.*, p. 79 (Nachträge).

[3] Cf. Malitzki, *op. cit.*, p. 25: 'If Alexis remained in the Crimea after his father had gone to Moscow, he was then at any rate an adult.'

[4] We shall speak later of the inscription of 1403, which probably, though not certainly, belongs to Alexis' reign.

[5] N. Iorga, *Notes et extraits pour servir à l'histoire des Croisades au XVe siècle*, I (Paris, 1899), 21: 'pro exenio facto Alecxi, domino de lo Tedoro . . . asp. ımcxxı.' See a very conscientious recent article by Virginie Vasiliu, 'Sur la seigneurie de "Tedoro" en Crimée au XVe siècle, à l'occasion d'un nouveau document,' *Mélanges de l'école roumaine en France* (Paris, 1929), Part I, pp. 303–306.

[6] N. Iorga, *Notes et extraits*, I, 22: 'pro quodam nuncio Alichssi . . . .'

Caffa for a robe,[1] evidently intended as a gift to Alexis. The ambassador's name was Cheaassus, because on the same October 24 we have an assignment of 50 aspers to Cheaassus, ambassador of the Prince of Theodoro.[2] In the same year the ambassador from Caffa to Alexis was George Torsello, to whom was allotted a sum of 100 aspers.[3] The active relations between Alexis of Gothia and Caffa in 1411, marked by the present to him and the exchange of ambassadors, may indicate that Alexis began to rule in or shortly before this year; realizing the importance of maintaining friendly relations with the new prince, Caffa behaved most cordially to him. Later, on 25 September 1420, a certain sum was spent by Caffa for the reception of an ambassador from Alexis,[4] and on 7 January 1421, 200 aspers were allotted to George Vacha, who was sent to Gothia on a mission with five Genoese officials.[5] Evidently the negotiations ended in failure; political relations between Gothia and the Commune of Caffa became strained, and in 1422 both sides were at war. Considerable amounts of money were allotted by the Genoese for the protection of Genoese maritime Gothia, especially Cembalo (Symbolon-Balaklava), which was 'the head of all Gothia.'[6] The relations of the Tartar Khan, Hadji-Girei, with Caffa were very strained, so that in engaging in war with Genoa Alexis was sure of friendly neutrality if not of actual support from the Khan; this was of great assistance to him. The cause of the conflict was Alexis' anxiety to obtain access to the sea. He considered Cembalo-Balaklava not only an outlet to the sea, but also a strategic fortress, and also an extremely important economic port on the south coast of the Crimea, from which commercial relations could be easily developed and maintained. The Genoese well understood Alexis' plan, and therefore during the war their chief attention was concentrated on the defense of Cembalo-Balaklava and the organization of its food supplies in case of siege. A sum of 16,460 aspers was assigned, 9 October 1422, for the provisioning and defense of Cembalo and all of Gothia.[7] On 31 October and 9 November more money was allotted for the defense of Lusce (Alushta).[8] On 29 November, 12 aspers were assigned to a

---

[1] *Ibid.*, 22: 'pro una rauba data nuncio misso a domino de lo Tedoro in Caffam . . . , asp. CCLX.'

[2] *Ibid.*, 22: 'pro Cheaassi, nuncio misso a domino de lo Tedoro . . . asp. L.'

[3] *Ibid.*, p. 22: 'pro Georgio Terselle, misso ad dominum Thedori . . . asp. C.' This was George Torsello who in May of 1411 was sent to Comania (*ibid.*, p. 24: 'pro Georgio Torsello, transmisso in Comania').   [4] *Ibid.*, p. 25: 'pro convivio facto ambassiatori domino [*sic*] de lo Tedoro.'

[5] *Ibid.*, p. 26: 'pro . . . Georgio Vacha, misso in Gotia cum orguxiis quinque pro suprascriptis agendis publicis . . . , asp. CC.'

[6] *Ibid.*, p. 385: 'insolentis Alexii, ex cujus insidiis timere cogimur loco Cimbali, qui est caput totius Gothie' (doc. 25 January 1425).

[7] *Ibid.*, p. 28: 'expense facte et fiende in provisione et custodia loci nostri Cimbali et tocius Gottie, occaxione guerre Alexii, domini de lo Tedoro . . . , asp. XVIMCCCCLX'; Bănescu, *op. cit.*, 35, n. 1.

[8] *Ibid.*, p. 28: 'expense facte et fiende in guerra (cum) domino de lo Tedoro, occaxione loci Lusce . . . *Item,* die VIIII Nov., pro . . . qui portavit certos homines promissos in Lusce loco . . . , asp. XLV.'

Greek who brought a letter from Alexis.[1] We do not know the subject of this letter. In the following year, 1423, a brigantine was fitted out for the war with Alexis at a cost of 881 aspers.[2] On 4 March and 9 October new sums of money were assigned for the same purpose.[3] The garrison of Cembalo was strengthened.[4] A Genoese citizen, Pietro Giovanni Maynerio, took active part not only in the defense of Cembalo but also in its liberation, for which service he received in 1424 from the Republic of Genoa an important post in Caffa.[5] From the text just cited we learn that during the war Cembalo was seized by Alexis but immediately after relieved by Pietro Maynerio. In March of 1423, 246 aspers were spent to repair a galley.[6] In May, 9,313 aspers were allotted for a vessel whose captain was Marco Spinula de Luculo, a Genoese citizen; the vessel was intended to protect Cembalo and Soldaia.[7] In October, 16,460 aspers were again spent for the provisioning and defense of Cembalo and all of Gothia.[8] In the record of 9 October 1423 Alexis is called a rebel from the Commune of Caffa.[9] During the war, by the order of the consul of Caffa and *Officium Guerre Caffensis*, a Genoese noble, Negrono de Nigro, arrived with his vessel at Calamita, no doubt to raid this very important part of Gothia; for this service he was promised a sum of money and a reward, which still remained unpaid by the authorities of Caffa at the outset of the year 1426.[10] Apparently the war ended at the beginning of 1424, because in February of this year a certain Simon the Armenian,

[1] *Ibid.:* 'pro quodam Grecho, qui portavit litteras ab Alexio . . . asp. xii.'

[2] *Ibid.*, p. 27: 'die 11 Martii. Brigantinum nuper armatum . . . , occaxione guerre domini de lo Tedoro, debet nobis . . . asp. dccclxxxi.'

[3] *Ibid.*, p. 28: 'expense facte et fiende, occaxione guerre domini de lo Tedoro'; p. 29: 'expense facte occaxione guerre domini de lo Tedoro debent nobis . . . asp. 27,850.'   [4] *Ibid.*, p. 29.

[5] *Ibid.*, p. 361: 'Cum attentis virtute et meritis viri probi Petri Johannis Maynerii, quondam Andree, precarissimi civis nostri, necnon laboribus magnis per eum passis in guerra contra Alexium de Theodoro, pro defensione et liberatione loci Cimbali, eum elegerimus et deputaverimus . . . .'

[6] *Ibid.*, p. 29: 'Die vi Marcii . . . Galeota que nuper reparatur . . . , occaxione guerre domini de lo Tedoro . . . , asp. ccxlvi.'

[7] *Ibid.*, p. 29: 'die viii Maii. Galeota patronizata per Marchum Spinulam, civem Januensem, armata . . . occaxione guerre domini de lo Tedoro et securitate Cimbali et Soldaie . . . , asp. viiiimcccxiii'; see p. 34, 'die xxxi Jan. (1434): Galleota Cafe, olim patronizata per Marchum Spinulam de Luculo, armata tunc occasione guerre vigentis inter Commune nostrum et dominum de lo Tedoro . . . .'

[8] *Ibid.*, p. 31: 'expense facte et fiende in provisione et custodia loci nostri Cimbali et tocius Gotie, occaxione guerre Alexii, domini de lo Tedoro . . . , asp. xvimcccclx.'

[9] *Ibid.*, p. 31: 'Alexii, rebelis Communis.'

[10] *Ibid.*, p. 414: 23 January 1426, a letter from the government of Genoa to the consul, *massarii*, councillors, and *Officium Provisionis* of Caffa: 'Recepta supplicatione viri nobilis Negroni de Nigro, dilecti nostri, petentis sibi satisfieri de debito stipendio et mercede sibi perveniente pro tempore quo alias servivit Communi Caffe, ad locum Calamite, quo, jussu et requisicione tunc consulis et Officii Guerre Caffensis, accessit cum quadam sua navi, sub certis pactis et promissionibus, temporibus vigentis guerre inter Commune Caffe et dominium de lo Theodoro.' Following this letter payment was ordered of the money claimed.

an *orguxius*[1] of Caffa, was sent to Alexis of Gothia for negotiations; his mission cost the Commune 60 aspers.[2] It is interesting to note that in March, 1423, i.e., during the war, Bexada, an ambassador of the Sultan of Solkhat, on his way to Alexis passed through the Genoese territory and for two days was entertained by the Genoese authorities, at a cost of 100 aspers.[3] Possibly the peace between Caffa and Gothia was concluded through the mediation of the Sultan of Solkhat. The war apparently did not end successfully for Alexis, because Cembalo-Balaklava remained in the hands of Caffa.

During the war Alexis had seized Cembalo, though the Genoese soon after recaptured it; and, taught by this experience, immediately after the conclusion of peace Caffa set to work on the fortification of Cembalo. An interesting document, probably of January 1425, pictures the feverish activities of the Genoese authorities.[4]

Taking into account the very great pertinacity and ingratitude of the insolent Alexis, whose treachery we have to fear in Cembalo, which is the head of all Gothia, and in order to avert the dangers which this place may easily incur, we, being informed that this may easily and successfully happen, have quickly decided, and we direct you, since you are unable to free our republic from this danger, to arrange and take speedy pains that the castle [castrum] of Cembalo may have on the side of the town [burgus] bank bulwarks (?),[5] ditches, and other things which may separate the castle itself from the town and fortify it, so that if — God forbid! — something sinister happens in the town, the castle shall be able to maintain itself and render assistance to the town both in victuals and in men, by the road made in the rocks down to the sea. For permanent guard of the castle we wish sent at least four to six 'socios' from Caffa who have no families or wives in Cembalo. The consul shall stay in the castle and have necessary ammunition [*munitionem habere necessariam*] for four months at least.

---

[1] *Orguxius* or *argusius* was a judge, judicial officer, see V. Smirnov, *The Crimean Khanate under the Domination of the Ottoman Porte up to the Beginning of the Eighteenth Century*, pp. 43–44 (in Russian).

[2] N. Iorga, *Notes et extraits*, I, 33: 'die XXVI Febr. (1424), pro Simone Armeno, orguxio et sunt pro ejus mercede, eundo ad dominum Teodori et ibi stando et redeundo pro negociis Communis . . . , asp. LX.' Miss V. Vasiliu fails to make use of this document in this place and believes that the war was still going on in 1425. At that time, she thinks, the situation of Cembalo was critical; and she conjectures that peace was made in 1426, Vasiliu, *op. cit.*, pp. 305–306. But on p. 312, n. 3, she refers to this document, without however coming to my conclusion that the war between Alexis and Caffa ended in 1424.

[3] N. Iorga, *Notes et extraits*, I, 30: 'die XXVII Marcii (1423), pro una alafa data Bexada Saraceno, ambassiatori dominorum Surchatensium, qui ivit ad Alexium, dominum Thedori, pro duabus diebus . . . , asp. c.'

[4] *Ibid.*, p. 385. This document contains instructions given by J. de Isolanis, 'Sancti Eustachii cardinalis, ducalis gubernator Januensis, et Consilium Antianorum ac Officium provisionis Romanie, consuli, massariis et provisoribus civitatis Caffe . . . ' (p. 384).

[5] In the text 'ripagula.' Iorga remarks: 'Ce doit être un diminutif rare de *ripa*' (p. 385, n. 4). I do not know the real meaning of this word.

Miss V. Vasiliu, who supposes, as we have noted above, that the war ended in 1426, believes that this document refers to the critical year of the war, when Genoa feared to lose Cembalo. But we know that the war ended in 1424. This document, accordingly, which probably should be dated 1425,[1] shows that the Genoese authorities took measures after the temporary loss of Cembalo in 1423 to avoid a repetition of this disaster, and therefore ordered new works of fortification executed. The severe characterization of Alexis as an insolent man of the greatest pertinacity and ingratitude, despite the fact that peace had been concluded, may be surprising at first sight; but it is quite natural in a document not intended to be made public. The Genoese never trusted Alexis, did not consider the peace durable, and often used harsh terms in reference to him. After the conclusion of the peace in 1424 there was no open war between Caffa and Gothia till 1433; and just for this period of outwardly peaceful relations the records of Caffa, under the years 1424 and 1428–1429, mention a bishop of Theodoro (Episcopus de Tedoro).[2]

Alexis did not abandon his cherished dream of taking possession of this important fortress and port; and his plans and activities in this respect unexpectedly became involved in the war declared in 1431 between Genoa and Venice.

In this year the Duke of Milan, Filippo Maria Visconti, drew Genoa into the war which he had been waging against Florence and Venice for many years. A most essential problem for both Genoa and Venice in this war was the protection of their numerous colonies in the East in general, and in the Black Sea in particular, where the Genoese were obviously superior to the Venetians. The Venetian colony Tana at the mouth of the Don river, could be easily cut off by the Genoese, and the Venetians taxed all their energy to maintain relations with this far-off factory.[3] It was thus exceedingly important to them to find an ally in the north, and of course no better ally could be found there than Alexis of Theodoro in the Crimea, sworn enemy of the Genoese, who had not given up his plans of taking possession of Maritime Gothia, to which the first step was the capture of Cembalo. The stage was set for a friendly understanding between Alexis and Venice. We do not know who took the initiative; but it is clear that in 1432 Alexis made certain promises to the Republic of St Mark in return for support in his plans concerning Caffa. On the motion of the Doge, on 1 June 1432, the senate of Venice decided that the

---

[1] *Ibid.*, p. 384.

[2] Bănescu, 'Contribution à l'histoire de la seigneurie de Théodoro-Mangoup en Crimée,' *Byz. Zeitschrift*, XXXV (1935), 35. He refers to unpublished documents, Mass. Caffe 1424, fol. 122ʳ, 1428–29, fol. 67ᵛ. Unfortunately Bănescu gives no text of the records, so that it is impossible to draw any conclusion from this interesting indication.

[3] Among other writings on this war, see V. Vasiliu, *op. cit.*, pp. 306–310.

vessels maintaining communication with Tana and Romania should sail
25 June in order to make their voyage during the good season, to succor
Tana, and 'to carry out that which Alexis, Prince of Gothia, intends to do
for our country.'[1]   The Doge's motion was passed by a decided majority:
110 for, 14 against, 15 not voting.[2]   Genoa, aware of these negotiations,
feared that the Venetians might accept Alexis as their ally.[3]

Alexis' attention was concentrated on Balaklava-Cembalo; as we know,
his dream was to take possession of this important castle and port. It is
hardly to be doubted that in this plan Alexis was supported, perhaps en-
couraged, by Hadji-Girei, the founder of the independent Tartar dynasty in the Crimea, Alexis' suzerain and friend, and the sworn enemy
of Genoese Caffa.[4]   Hadji-Girei's rule in the Crimea lasted nearly forty
years, from about 1420 or 1428 to 1466 (1467),[5] so that he had time
enough to establish a definite policy in the Peninsula, especially towards
Gothia and Caffa, and he survived the fall of Constantinople, when the
rise of the Ottoman power forced him to change his political orientation
and to incline to the side of the victorious Muhammed II.   Of course in
regard to Cembalo, Alexis was no mere blind tool in Hadji-Girei's
hands; but his interests coincided with those of the Crimean Khan.   As
we shall see later, in the inscription of 1425 Alexis entitled himself 'Prince
of Theodoro and the Maritime Region.'

In 1433 Alexis succeeded in gaining over a party among the Greek
population of Cembalo-Balaklava.   At the end of February of this year
a revolt broke out in the city.   The rebels took arms, drove out the
Genoese, overcame the garrison, seized the citadel, and delivered the city
to Alexis.   On 16 June 1433, the government of Genoa notified the Duke
of Milan that 'at night, about the end of February, Alexis of Theodoro
took a precious city of this state, located in the eastern regions, which is

---

[1] Iorga, *Notes et extraits*, I, 554: 'tam pro faciendo viagium suum bono tempore, quam pro succur-
rendo loco Tane et pro executione rerum quas dominus Alexius, dominus Gothie, intendit facere
nostro dominio.'

[2] *Ibid.*   [3] See *ibid.*, p. 559.

[4] See an interesting Russian study by L. Kolli, 'Hadji-Girei and his Policy,' *Izvestiya* of the
Tauric Learned Archive Commission, L (1913), 99–139; Elena Sczrzinska, 'Inscriptions latines des
colonies génoises en Crimée,' *Atti della Società Ligure*, LVI (1928), 10; Malitzki, *op. cit.*, pp. 37–38.
Cf. Vasiliu, *op. cit.*, pp. 311–312.

[5] See W. Barthold, *Hadji-Girai*, in the *Encyclopédie de l'Islam*, II (1927), p. 217.   Barthold does not
mention Kolli's study which I have quoted in the preceding note.   Hadji-Girei's dates are not definitely established: A. M. Stokvis, *Manuel d'histoire, de généalogie et de chronologie de tous les états
du globe depuis les temps les plus reculés jusqu'à nos jours*, II (Leyden, 1889), 360: '1420–1466';
S. Lane-Poole, *The Mohammadan Dynasties*, p. 236: '*circa* 1420–1466'; a Russian translation by W.
Barthold (St Petersburg, 1899), p. 196: '1420–1466'; E. de Zambaur, *Manuel de généalogie et de chronologie pour l'histoire de l'Islam* (Hanover, 1927), p. 247, No. 234: 'from about 823–871 after the Hegira'=about 1420–1466; Hrushevski, *Istoriia Ukraini-Ruzi*, IV (Lwów, 1903), 258 ff. (in Ukrainian).

called Cimbalum.'[1]   The Italian chroniclers who mention under 1433 the fact of Alexis' taking Cembalo speak of him as 'a certain noble of Greek descent who is commonly called Dominus de Lotedoro and whose own name is Alexis,' or 'a noble Greek called Alexis, prince of Theodoro,' or simply 'Alexis, a certain Greek, prince of Theodoro.'[2]   It seemed that Alexis' desire was fulfilled.

Naturally Genoa could not submit easily to the loss of so important a city, which played no small rôle in trade activities on the shores of the Black Sea and the loss of which considerably affected the security of the other Genoese possessions in the Crimea.   The Genoese authorities in Pera (Constantinople) were very pessimistic as to the general position of the Genoese in the Crimea.   In a document from the Genoese colony in Pera written at the end of July 1433 we read that the Genoese merchants of Pera were seriously affected by events in the Crimea.   They believed that Caffa in its miserable condition could not long survive the fall of Cembalo; the loss of Cembalo was very harmful to commerce, and their own attempts to recover Cembalo had failed.   Messages were sent to Genoa 'by land and sea' urging the Republic to do all in her power to re-cover Cembalo; if she failed, other places might be exposed to similar danger; peace was urgently desired.   At the close of this document it is repeated that the situation had a very bad effect on mercantile activities.[3]

---

[1] Iorga, I, 558–559: 'Alexio de lo Tedoro [occupied] tempore noctis, circa finem mensis februarii proxime exacti . . . opidum preciosum hujus civitatis in orientalibus partibus situm, Cimbalum vocatum.'   Cf. Malitzki, *op. cit.*, p. 38: 'Cembalo was taken late in the autumn.'

[2] *Johannis Stellae Annales Genuenses*, Muratori, *Scr. Ital.*, xvii, col. 1311: 'Castrum Cimbaldi, quod in partibus orientalibus situm est intra Mare Majus, quod erat de potentatu Communis Januae, opera quorumdam Graecorum Burgensium Castri illius conjuratione facta datum est in potestatem cujusdam nobilis de Graecorum progenie, qui vulgo Dominus de Lotedoro dictus est, et proprio nomine Alexius vocatus est'; A. Giustiniani, *Annali della Repubblica di Genova*, 3rd ed., ii (Genova, 1854), 325–326: 'misero quella in mano di un nobile Greco nominato Alessio signor del Tedoro, che è luogo vicino al Cembalo' (Bk. v, *s.a.* 1433); Folieta (Foglieta), *Historiae genuensium libri* xii, J. G. Graevius, *Thesaurus antiquitatum et historiarum Italiae, Tomi primi pars prior* (Leyden, 1704), col. 567 (Bk. x, *s.a.* 1433): 'Eo anno Graeci incolae Cembali, Tauricae Chersonesi urbis, conjuratione in Genuenses urbis dominos facta, armis improvisa arreptis, Genuensibus ejectis, urbem Alexio cuidam Graeco Theodori Domino, quod oppidum parvo intervallo abest a Cembalo, tradiderunt.' See *Petri Bizari Senatus populique Genuensis rerum domi forisque gestarum historiae atque annales* (Antwerp, 1579), p. 243; Braun, *Die letzten Schicksale*, p. 29; Heyd, *Histoire du Commerce du Levant*, ii, 381; E. Marengo, C. Manfroni, G. Pessagno, *Il Banco di San Giorgio* (Genoa, 1911), p. 486; J. Kulakovsky, *The Past of the Tauris*, 2nd ed. (Kiev, 1914), p. 118 (in Russian).

[3] L. T. Belgrano, 'Prima Serie di documenti riguardanti la colonia di Pera,' *Atti della Società Ligure*, xiii (1877–1884), 200–202: 'nam quasi totam racionem meam in Caffa habeo et in parte pannis, de quibus propter miseram condicionem loci dubito de lunga fine . . . fuit occupata dicta navis cum illa Cepriani de Mari et aliis . . . pro negociis Cimbali amissi; et secundum sentivimus nostri nichil facere potuerunt in recuperacione dicti loci, de quo vehementer dolemus, et scripsimus tam per terram quam per mare Dominacioni circa provixionem fiendam in recuperatione loci quoniam necessitat valde; aliter periclitarent cetera loca nostra granditer.   . . . Hic parum fit ex mercantia et omnia cum pauca consumacione.'

The first attempt to recover Cembalo was apparently made in June 1433, when Bartholemy de Levanto sailed with a fleet from Pera to Cembalo.[1] This expedition accomplished nothing whatever. But Alexis' possession of Cembalo was of short duration. The Genoese authorities acted energetically. In October 1433, to the sound of the bells and the applause of all the citizens, Carolo Lomellino was elected captain of a fleet to be prepared for the recapture of Cembalo; the unanimous desire of the citizens was to wrest the city from the hands of the Greek enemy, 'the prince of Theodoro (Lotedoro).'[2] In March 1434 the fleet left Genoa under Lomellino's command. It consisted of twenty vessels and carried more than six thousand men. On March 31, after staying several days at Porto Venere, the fleet sailed from there for the Orient.[3] Lomellino's expedition, as far as Cembalo was concerned, was completely successful.

On June 4 the Genoese fleet reached Cembalo.[4] A galley under the command of a high officer had been sent from the entrance into the Black Sea along the shores of Asia Minor to Sinope. There the officer landed, pretending to sail for Trebizond; but he immediately reëmbarked and joined his fleet, which had already arrived in Cembalo. This ruse was evidently to divert the attention of Sinope from the real aim of the expedition. On Saturday, June 5, early in the morning, boats were lowered into the water and towed to the port. After a violent fight the chain which barred access to the port was broken, and the same day the vessels, one

[1] *Ibid.*, pp. 200–201: 'Recepta de Peira die xxx julii 1433: Adavisunt Johannes de Levanto nuper hic venit, et ut dicitur restare debet in loco fratris sui Bartholomei qui ivit pridie in Ci . . . (probably *Cimbalo*) cum armata nostra.'

[2] *Johannis Stellae Annales Genuenses*, in Muratori, xvii, col. 1312: 'Anno ipso (1433) de mense Octobris per Dominium Januense spectabilis Dominus Carolus Lomellinus militiae baltheo decoratus in Capitaneum classis parandae pro recuperatione Castri Cimbaldi . . . eligitur sub sono campanae majoris et applausu omnium civium, qui uno animo unoque voto satagebant Castrum praedictum evellere de manu hostis illius Graeci Domini de Lotedoro.'   [3] *Ibid.*

[4] For the expedition of Lomellino to Cembalo we have an excellent contemporary source unexpectedly discovered in Italy, in the archives of the Council of Basel: the diary of a chronicler of Padua, Andrea Gatari, who, though it had no connection with the events of the Council, inserted into his diary a detailed account of the expedition of Lomellino to the Crimea. Gatari's Diary was published by C. Coggiola, *Concilium Basiliense, Studien und Quellen zur Geschichte des Concils von Basel*, v: *Tagebücher und Acten* (Basel, 1904), 'Diario del Concilio di Basilea di Andrea Gatari 1433–1435' (Lomellino's expedition on pp. 406–408); we know little concerning Gatari's life (see pp. xxxvii–xlv). This text was reprinted by C. Manfroni, 'Due nuovi documenti per la storia della Marineria Genovese,' *Giornale Storico e Letterario della Liguria*, v (La Spezia, 1904), 36–38. This source was used by L. Kolli in his interesting study, 'Hadji-Girei Khan and his Policy,' *Izvestiya* of the Tauric Learned Archive Commission, L (Simferopol, 1913), 113–121 (in Russian); on pp. 116–120 a Russian translation of the text is given. On the basis of Kolli's account Malitzki (*op. cit.*, p. 38), gives some passages from the *Diary*. According to Bertier Delagarde, Gatari's *Diary* is a very interesting document, unfortunately incomplete, confused both in dates and in topography, but correct in substance, Bertier Delagarde, 'Calamita and Theodoro,' *Izvestiya* of the Tauric Learned Archive Commission, LV (1918), 7 and note 1 (in Russian). I cannot agree with Bertier Delagarde's statement concerning Garati's confusion in dates; as far as I understand, his chronology, day after day, is very exact.

after another, with many large bombards and machines, reached the port, each taking up its place. On Sunday, June 6, troops landed and laid siege to the fortress. A severe battle followed in which many people fell on both sides. On June 7 the Genoese unloaded some small bombards ashore and began to cannonade a tower; shortly after a considerable part of the tower and a large piece of wall fell. In terror some of the inhabitants of Cembalo begged the commander of the Genoese fleet to open negotiations with them for the surrender of the city, on condition that he should spare their lives and property; but he demanded that the terms should be left to his discretion. Thereupon fighting was resumed.

Among the Greeks fighting in Cembalo was Alexis' son. When on June 8 one of the Cembalo gates was taken by the Genoese, Alexis' son and seventy other men retreated into the interior of the fortress. The Genoese in pursuit entered the fortress, occupied the hills above the city and massacred many people; they spared the lives of Alexis' son, his companions, and a certain Candiote, i.e., a Cretan. All of these were brought on board the vessel in chains. Afterwards the city was given to the soldiers for pillage; a great number of people were murdered.

On June 9, the ships left the port and debarked infantry at Calamita. This city was ordered to surrender. The people answered that they would surrender the next day in the evening, on condition that their lives and property be spared. The following day, June 10, many Genoese soliders who were at Cembalo proceeded to Calamita by land. Since none of the besieged population was seen, the soldiers, with ladders and other equipment, drew nearer, and without meeting resistance entered the city, and then realized that all the inhabitants had fled with their belongings. The soldiers burnt the whole city, so that of Calamita only the walls remained. Thereupon the soldiers returned to Cembalo. After the departure of the Genoese, the city was no doubt re-occupied by Alexis.

The land troops were ordered to devastate the territory of Gothia, while the fleet busied itself with pillaging the coastland, demanding obedience to the Genoese from the inhabitants.

On Saturday, June 12, a military council was held concerning subsequent plans.

Knowing that Alexis had been supported by Hadji-Girei, Lomellino marched towards Solkhat, the Khan's residence. But Lomellino was thoroughly defeated by Hadji-Girei, so that he could take no further advantage of his brilliant victory over Alexis. On June 27 about two hundred Tartar horsemen, elated by the recent victory over Lomellino, galloped up to the gates of Cembalo and ordered the Genoese garrison to surrender their arms. After negotiations which came to nothing, peace was made and the Tartars rode away.[1] After this set-back for the Genoese, it might have been expected that Alexis would be able to retake Cembalo. But this time Alexis lost Cembalo forever.[2]

However, this was not the end of the war, and in spite of the loss of Cembalo Alexis continued to fight. In 1438 a galley of Caffa pillaged 'the territory of Alexis.'[3] The war ended in 1441, and in the records of Caffa we find that on November 22 of this year a certain amount of money was allotted to provide for the captives of Gothia who 'were liberated on the occasion of the peace made with Alexis.'[4] Perhaps Alexis' son, who had been captured at the taking of Cembalo, returned to Theodoro in accordance to this agreement. The war thus lasted from 1433 to 1441.[5]

In connection with this war I shall devote some space to the discussion of a newly published document from the *Atti Secreti* of the Genoese Archives. This is an undated letter addressed by a Venetian *baile* in Constantinople to Alexis of Theodoro (*Copia lettere Baili Venetorum Constantinopolis scripte Alexio de Lo Tedoro*).[6] The text is in several places insufficiently clear; but we learn from it that the Venetian *baile* was corresponding with Alexis via Moncastro (Mocastro, Cetatea-Albă in Roumanian), the chief city of the Moldavian principality at the mouth of the Dniester river, and that one of Alexis' vessels ('lo monero vostro'),[7] which

---

[1] Gatari, ed. Coggiola, p. 408; Manfroni, p. 38; Kolli, p. 119–120.

[2] Gatari, p. 407–408; Giustiniani, *Annali*, II, 326; Folieta, Bk. x, *s.a.* 1433, in Graevius, col. 567; Marino Sanudo, *Vite de Duchi de Venezia*, in Muratori, XXII, col. 1036: 'in questo tempo (1434) i Genovesi con armata presero Ciambano, ch'è appresso Caffa, il qual luogo era . . . ' (lacuna); Kolli, *op. cit.*, p. 119. See also *Petri Bizari Senatus populique Genuensis rerum domi forisque gestarum historiae atque annales* (Antwerp, 1579), pp. 243–244; Heyd, *Histoire du commerce du Levant*, II, 381–382; Vasiliu, *op. cit.*, pp. 313–314; Malitzki, *op. cit.*, p. 38; Alb. M. Condioti, *Historia de la institución consular en la antigüedad y en la edad media*, I (Madrid, Berlin, Buenos-Aires, Mexico, 1925), 534–535.

[3] Iorga, *Notes et extraits*, III (Paris, 1902), 145: Doc. 13 January 1444, mention of a pillage committed in 1438 by a galley of Caffa 'in territorio Alexii.'

[4] *Idem*, I, 37: 'MCCCCXXXXI, die XXII Novembris. Racio captivorum Gotie captorum per Johannem Montanum et socium et qui liberati fuerunt occaxione pacis facte cum Alexio.'

[5] I believe Miss Vasiliu is inexact in saying that this peace ended hostilities which began in 1422 and lasted for twenty years (Vasiliu, *op. cit.*, p. 314). As we have seen above, there was no open war from 1424 to 1433.

[6] Virginie Vasiliu, 'Sur la seigneurie de "Tedoro" en Crimée au XVe siècle, à l'occasion d'un nouveau document,' *Mélanges de l'école roumaine en France* (Paris, 1929), Part I, pp. 299–336; the text of the letter, pp. 335–336. See N. Iorga, in the *Revue Historique du sud-est européen*, VII (1930), pp. 253–254 (a few lines on Miss Vasiliu's study). The text has not been satisfactorily published by Miss Vasiliu, so that her translation and interpretation are in several places incorrect. Miss Vasiliu herself and N. Bănescu have later improved both the text and the translation. See Vasiliu, in the *Revue Historique du sud-est européen*, VIII (1931), p. 160; Bănescu, 'Le bulletin roumain,' in *Byzantion*, V (1930), 540–541; *idem, Byzantinische Zeitschrift*, XXXI (1931), 166–167. In spite of the corrections, some passages in this letter are still rather obscure.

[7] *Monero* — in Greek μονήρης and in Latin *moneris* — a ship with one bank of oars.

he had sent to Constantinople, returned to Calamita, a port of Gothia, after leaving some merchandise with the *baile*, who promised to take care of it as of his own belongings. Then the letter mentions an epidemic among the cattle of Gothia which had killed many of them, no doubt a very severe economic blow to mountain Gothia. Informed of Alexis' illness, the *baile* seems anxious about his health and advises him how to improve it. A very interesting but obscure passage follows. From corrections made in the published text it is obvious that Alexis asked the *baile* — we do not know for what purpose — to send him some poisoned pastry or cakes ('de confeti atosigati'). The *baile*, a little hesitant, answered, 'I believe that you want them for the infidels, so I will get them from Venice.'[1] In the second part of his letter the *baile* gives information on the situation in Genoa, class hostility there between nobles and commons, and the possibility of Venice's interference in the internal affairs of Genoa; but the *baile* is waiting for more precise news from Italy that may be brought by galleys from Italy to Constantinople; it will then be possible to discuss the question in all desirable detail. Referring further to the war in Italy the *baile* mentions the names of Francesco Sforza ('le conte Francesco'), Niccolò Piccinini ('Nicolo Picenino'), and King Alfonso of Aragon ('lo Re de Aragone').[2] The *baile* ends the letter with a statement that his 'words' are not intended to be told to all; but 'seeing your good will, I manifest to you everything; as to other matters to come, you will be notified.'

Miss Vasiliu supposes that this letter is to be referred to the years 1442–1443; but her proofs are not convincing, and N. Bănescu remarks that the mention of Francesco Sforza, Niccolò Piccinini, and King Alfonso suits better an earlier period than the year 1441, when peace was concluded between the Venetians and Florentines acting together, and the Duke of Milan.[3] The first interesting indication in the letter is that correspondence between the *baile* and Alexis was maintained via the Moldavian city, Moncastro. This was possible after the years 1435 and 1436. On 19 April 1435 the Venetian Senate accepted the proposition of the ruler of Maurocastrum to open commercial relations with Venice; thereafter a vessel *de Romanie* stopped in Maurocastrum, and on April 27 in-

---

[1] 'E che in quelli spenda non volentera fasso queste cose, ma considero che le voleti per infideli, providero de venecia,' Vasiliu, *op. cit.*, p. 335. Some words following this passage are differently interpreted by Bănescu ('sinon, il s'agit de réputation'), *Byzantion*, v, 541, and by Miss Vasiliu ('puisque ce n'est pas chose ayant trait à la réputation'), *Revue Hist. du sud-est européen*, VIII, 160. Miss Vasiliu's original interpretation was erroneous: 'Il lui promet de faire apporter de Venise des gâteaux de noix' probably for the Turks and Tartars, 'grands amateurs de sucreries,' Vasiliu, 'Sur la seigneurie de "Tedoro",' p. 320.

[2] A misprint occurs in Vasiliu (p. 336): '*la* Re de Aragone.'

[3] Vasiliu, *op. cit.*, pp. 322–323; Bănescu, *Byz. Zeitschrift*, XXXI, 166.

structions on this subject were given the *baile* in Constantinople.[1] In
March 1436 Francesco Duodo was appointed first vice-consul of Venice
in Maurocastro.[2] Only after these arrangements had been effected were
regular relations between Moncastrum and Venice established, and only
then could the *baile* of Constantinople have carried on his correspondence
with Alexis of Theodoro by means of Moncastrum. Alexis' unexpected
demand for poisoned cakes shows that the war was not over. Of course
he had no intention of using poison against the Tartar Khan or any other
Tartar authority, with whom he was on friendly terms. This perfidious
plan, which was quite in accordance with the customs of that epoch,[3]
was in all likelihood framed against the Genoese; but we do not know precisely against whom. The peace which ended the war between Genoa
and Theodoro and in which Venice was involved was made in 1441. I am
almost certain that it is no mere coincidence that this peace was concluded
in the same year as the peace in Italy mentioned above, 1441, in which
Venice also participated. These two peaces of 1441 ended only one war,
which had been simultaneously carried on in Italy and the Crimea. The
baile's letter therefore was written before 1441. For our subject the letter
is interesting because it shows once again a friendly understanding between Venice and Theodoro based on their hostile attitude towards
Genoa whether in Italy or in the Crimea; it indicates the political and
economic importance of the main port of Gothia, Calamita; it mentions
a great economic calamity in Gothia, a serious epidemic among the cattle;
and finally it pictures Alexis as a ruler who did not disdain in case of need
to resort to methods of getting rid of his enemies which were of dubious
character though in harmony with his age.

After his failure to reach the south coast and organize a political and
economic base at Cembalo, Alexis began to construct a port at Kalamita
(Calamita, now Inkerman), close to Sevastopol. The names of Gothia
and Calamita are often given on mediaeval charts and Italian *portolani*,
which shows once more the economic significance of those places.[4] In

---

[1] Iorga, *Notes et extraits*, i (Paris, 1899), 573–574.

[2] *Ibid.*, p. 581. See also N. Iorga, *Studiĭ istorice asupra Chilieĭ şi Cetăţiĭ-Albe* (Bucarest, 1900), p. 93.

[3] On this subject see L. de Mas Latrie, 'Projets d'empoisonnement de Mahomet II et du Pacha de
Bosnie, accueillis par la république de Venise,' *Archives de l'Orient Latin*, i (Paris, 1881), 653–662. In
this study Mas Latrie published some extremely interesting documents of 1477–1478, from which we
learn that the Venetian Council of the Ten decided to consider the proposition of a Jew named
Salamoncinus and his brothers to bring about the death of Muhammed II through the Sultan's doc-
tor, and another proposition of a certain Amico 'dandi scilicet mortem Turco,' i.e. to Muhammed.
A similar plan to destroy the Pasha of Bosnia is mentioned and discussed in these documents. Much
material on the use of poison for getting rid of one's political enemies in the fifteenth and sixteenth
centuries may be found in V. Lamanski, *Secrets d'État de Venise* (St Petersburg, 1884).

[4] See K. Kretschmer, *Die italienischen Portolane des Mittelalters* (Berlin, 1909), p. 643: La Gotia
(a rather misleading commentary); Caramit-Calamit-Calomit-Callamita=Kalamita.

their general report on the economic and political situation in the Genoese colonies in the Crimea, the Genoese authorities pointed out that Alexis with his brothers 'was making a port at Kalamita,' and accordingly it was decided to arm a galley.   Many times by special messages Alexis was urged to live according to the agreements and treaties which he had made with Caffa; but to no avail.   The answers of the Gothic princes were often rude.   'However,' we read in the report, 'we expect a fitting moment and do not doubt that they shall endure due punishment; because they are very ungrateful and elated, which, in our judgment, the Lord should not suffer.   They boast openly that they fear nobody as long as their father and the emperor of the Tartars live.   From this you can understand their plans.   But matters will be taken care of according to circumstances, and we shall always notify you.'[1]   This report, in my opinion, contains a contradiction.   In the opening lines of the passage quoted Alexis and his brothers are spoken of, while at the end we read 'as long as their father and the emperor of the Tartars live.'   I think the opening line should read 'Alexis with his sons,' which is in complete accordance with our sources, which state that Alexis' son John had brothers.[2]   This report testifies once more that Alexis and his family were on a friendly footing with the sultan of Solkhat, who in our document is called the Emperor of the Tartars.

Evidently Alexis was at war with some one else besides the Genoese. There is a rather vague indication that the Goths were also in conflict with the Emperor of Byzantium, Manuel II Palaeologus (1391–1425).[3] In all probability the result of this conflict was not favorable to Alexis, because in his will Manuel left 'the Pontic regions bordering on Khazaria' as an appanage to his fourth son, Constantine, destined to be the last Emperor of Byzantium.[4]   I believe these Pontic regions bordering on

---

[1] 'Un quadro generale dello stato economico, politico ecc. di Caffa, 1455 . . . agosto,' *Atti della Società Ligure*, VI (1868), Doc. CL, p. 361: 'Alexius cum omnibus fratribus male se habet.   cum quibus simulamus donec tempus congluum nobis videbitur.   faciunt portum in Callamitta.   pro quo etiam laudatum fuit armare galeam quam obluamus pro . . . omnino.   Predictis non obstantibus simulationibus eis semper scripsimus eos ortando in bene vivendo secundum conventiones et pacta inter ipsum et nos vigentes, et paucum valuit et sepe rescripserunt et potissimum unus ex ipsis scripsit aliqua verecundamur scribere.   tamen expectamus tempus et nil dubitamus penas debitas patientur. Nam ingratissimi et ilati sunt.   quod dominus judicio nostro sufferre non debet.   jactant se multum non timere posse aliquem vivente eorum patre et domino imperatore tartarorum.   ex quo intelligere potestis eorum intentionem.   Verum negotia secundum tempus consulenda sunt, de quo avisabimus semper.'   [2] See Malitzki's doubts as to this document (pp. 39–40).

[3] *Theodoro Spandugino*, 'De la origine deli imperatori ottomani,' in Sathas, *Documents inédits*, IX (Paris, 1890), 146–147: 'et massimamente il re di Servia, li Gotti et li Valachi che contendeano tutti con lo imperator di Constantinopoli Emanuel Paleologo.'

[4] Ducas, Ch. XXIII (Bonn, p. 134): 'ὁ τέταρτος Κωνσταντῖνος ὃς καὶ τὰ Ποντικὰ μέρη τὰ πρὸς Χαζαρίαν ἐκληρώσατο.'

Khazaria are the territory of Gothia, or perhaps a portion of it, which theoretically became a vassal state of Byzantium after the unsuccessful conflict with Manuel II. It is hardly to be supposed that Constantine ever went to his appanage; we know that later he was the ruler of Mistra in the Peloponnesus.[1] On the other hand, we must not lose sight of the fact that under Manuel II and his son and successor John VIII the Empire was so shrunken in territory and crippled in power and resources that it could not retain the far-off land in the Crimea.

In 1426 Alexis became related to the Imperial family of Trebizond. In this year Alexis' daughter Maria left Theodoro for Trebizond, where she arrived in November and married David, the last Emperor of Trebizond.[2] She was his first wife.

Alexis was not only anxious to increase the political might and economic resources of his princedom; he was also an active builder. In this respect two inscriptions and a poor fragment of a third are extremely interesting. According to the first, discovered by R. Loeper in 1912 on Mankup, in October 1425 Alexis erected a palace and castle.[3] The inscription contains five lines, but the first half of each is lacking. Loeper restored the missing lines with the help of the inscription of 1427, of which we shall speak a little later, the text of which is very close to that of the inscription of 1425. Some of Loeper's restorations were rejected by Bertier Delagarde. I agree with the latter's suggestion that the first line reads not 'ὁ οἶκος' but 'ὁ πύργος,'[4] i.e., not 'a house' but 'a tower,'

---

[1] See Köppen, *Krymsky Sbornik* (St Petersburg, 1837), pp. 93–94 (in Russian); Bruun, *Notices historiques*, p. 63; Bruun, *Chernomorye*, II, 134 (in Russian); Tomaschek, *Die Goten in Taurien*, p. 52.

[2] M. Panaretus, 'Chronicle of Trebizond,' Ch. LVII, ed. S. Lambros, in the Νέος Ἑλληνομνήμων, IV (1907), p. 294: 'Τῷ δὲ αὐτῷ ἔτει (1426), μηνὶ Νοεμβρίου ἦλθε καὶ ἀπὸ Γοτθίας ἡ βασίλισσα κυρὰ Μαρία, ἡ τοῦ κῦρ Ἀλεξίου ἐκ τῆς Θεοδώρας θυγάτηρ, καὶ εὐλογήθη μετὰ εὐσεβοῦς δεσπότου, τοῦ ἀνδρὸς αὐτῆς κῦρ Δαβὶδ τοῦ μεγάλου Κομνηνοῦ.' J. Fallmerayer, 'Original-Fragmente, Chroniken, Inschriften und anderes Materiale zur Geschichte des Kaiserthums Trapezunt, Zweite Abteilung,' *Abhandlungen der III Classe der Ak. der Wissenschaften zu München*, IV (1846), 40 (in German, p. 69); in French in Lebeau, *Histoire du Bas-Empire*, ed. Saint Martin and Brosset, XX (Paris, 1836), 509; in Russian by Khakhanov, in the *Publications* (*Izdaniya*) of the Lazarev Institute of Oriental Languages in Moscow, XXIII (1905), 18. Heyd, (*Histoire du Commerce*, II, 381, n. 2), and Bertier Delagarde ('Kalamita and Theodoro,' p. 34, in Russian) erroneously state that Maria was Alexis' sister. See W. Miller, *Trebizond, the Last Greek Empire* (London, 1926), p. 97.

[3] R. Loeper, 'Archaeological Investigations in Mankup in 1912,' *Accounts* (*Soobscheniya*) of the Archaeological Commission, XLVII (St Petersburg, 1913), 78–79:

'[ἐκτίσθη ὁ οἶκος οὖ]τος μετὰ τοῦ παλατ =
[ιου καὶ σὺν τῷ εὐ] λογημένῳ κάστρ =
[ῳ, ὁ νῦν ὁρᾶται, ὑπὸ] ἡμερῶν κυροῦ Ἀλ =
[εξίου αἰθέντου πόλεω]ς Θεοδωροῦς, καὶ πα =
[ραθαλασσίας μηνὶ Ὀκτ]οβρίῳ ἔτους SϠΛΔ' (6934 = 1425 A.D.)

See also pp. 149–154. On p. 150 is given a plan of the building where the inscription was discovered. On this inscription see N. Malitzki, 'Notes on the Epigraphy of Mangup,' pp. 33–35 (in Russian).

[4] Bertier Delagarde, 'Kalamita and Theodoro,' p. 31 (in Russian).

which is more suitable in referring to a palace and a castle.   In the fourth and fifth lines we have Alexis' official title: 'Alexis prince of the city of Theodoro and the maritime region' ('Αλέξιος αὐθέντης πόλεως Θεοδωροῦς καὶ παραθαλασσίας).   On this inscription have been preserved the Genoese escutcheon, Alexis' monogram, and the escutcheon of the Palaeologi.

The second inscription, that of 1427, says that a church 'with a divinely protected castle was erected under Alexis, prince of the city of Theodoro and the maritime region, and builder of the church of the Holy Great Emperors and Equals to the Apostles, Constantine and Helen.'[1]   The origin of this inscription is rather uncertain.   Some scholars believe that its original place was in Inkerman (Calamita), which belonged to the principality of Theodoro and has been, as we know, erroneously identified with the city of Theodoro.   Others think that the inscription comes from Theodoro-Mankup.[2]   The most recent writer on this subject, the author of an excellent monograph on the inscriptions on Mankup, N. Malitzki, is inclined to support the first group of scholars.[3]   Our difficulty is that, though we know this inscription was found in a garden in the village of Sably, in the Crimea, about 1830, we do not know exactly from what place it came to Sably.   In the inscription Alexis is called not only prince of Theodoro and the maritime region but also the builder of the church of Constantine and Helen.   Now the question arises whether the church mentioned in the first line of the inscription as erected by Alexis is the church of Constantine and Helen mentioned at the end of the inscription, or whether we are dealing here with two different churches, one erected in 1427, and the other, that of Constantine and Helen, some time earlier. In my judgment the words 'builder of the church of Constantine and Helen' cannot be a part of Alexis' official title.   Malitzki points out that the style of the inscription is not good if it indicates the consecration of the church not at the beginning but at the close in Alexis' title, without making it clear that the church referred to is the one mentioned in the

---

[1] This inscription has been well known for a long time: "Ἐκτίσθη ὁ ναὸς οὗτος σὺν τῷ εὐλογημένῳ κάστρῳ ὃ νῦν ὁρᾶται, ὑπὸ ἡμετέρου κυροῦ Ἀλεξίου αὐθέντου πόλεως Θεοδωροῦς καὶ παραθαλασσίας καὶ κτήτορ(ος) τῶν ἁγίων ἐνδόξων θεοστέπτων μεγάλων βασιλέων καὶ ἰσαποστόλων Κωνσταντίνου καὶ Ἑλένης, μηνὶ ὀκτωβρίῳ ἰνδικτιῶνος ἕκτης ἔτους 6936,' *Corpus Inscriptionum Graecarum*, ed. E. Curtius and A. Kirchhoff, IV (1877), No. 8742 (p. 341); Latyshev, *Collection (Sbornik) of Greek Christian Inscriptions in the South of Russia*, No. 45 (pp. 50 f.); idem, 'Notes on the Christian Inscriptions of the Crimea,' IV, *Zapiski* of the Odessa Society, XXIII (1901), 76.   Both inscriptions are now in the Central Museum of the Tauris (in Simferopol, in the Crimea), Nos. 2747 and 2748.   See Spiridonov, *On the Family History of the House of Mangup*, p. 3, n. 1 (in Russian).   See also Köppen, *op. cit.*, pp. 95, 218–220; Tomascheck, *op. cit.*, p. 52; Braun, *Die letzten Schicksale*, pp. 27–28; Kulakovski, *The Past of the Tauris*, p. 117 (in Russian); Malitzki, *op. cit.*, pp. 26–32 (in Russian).

[2] For different opinions see Latyshev, *Collection of Greek Inscriptions of Christian Times*, pp. 50–53. Latyshev himself is of opinion that the inscription of 1427 was originally placed in Mankup-Theodoro.

[3] Malitzki, *op. cit.*, pp. 27–28.

first line.[1]   But the style of inscriptions in general is often far from perfect.   Martin Bronevski (Broniovius), who visted Mankup in 1578, saw
there the church of St Constantine in a state of decay.[2]   Bronevski also
saw several Greek inscriptions in Inkerman; but in Inkerman no church
of Constantine and Helen is known.   Accordingly I am inclined to admit
that the inscription of 1427 came from Theodoro-Mankup and that it
describes Alexis as the builder of the church of Constantine and Helen in
Theodoro.   This inscription also has Alexis' monogram, the Genoese
escutcheon, and the escutcheon of the Palaeologi.[3]

Two fragments of a large slab of white marble were discovered by R.
Loeper in 1913 on Mankup and a third fragment of the same slab was
brought by M. Skubetov to the Museum of the Tauric Archive Commission.   They were put together and studied by Latyshev.   He says the
fragments are so small that it is impossible to form any idea of the content of the inscription.   But we have the date, 1403, and according to
Latyshev, the character of the letters and all internal evidence are very
similar to the inscriptions of 1425 and 1427 just discussed, so that we may
at least connect this inscription with Alexis or his family.   We may conclude, as Malitski says, that in 1403 Mankup was already in the possession of the family in which we are interested, most probably in the person
of Alexis.[4]   Two more monograms of Alexis were discovered on Mankup.
The first, set in a circle on a fragment of a limestone slab, was found in
1926 in a wall of the fortress of Inkerman;[5] the other is engraved on a
fragment of a slab found by Loeper in 1912.[6]   In 1837 N. Murzakevich
wrote that he had seen on Mankup a stone with a Gothic (?) inscription,
barely legible, at the corners of which were three hearts; in one of them
was a cross.[7]   This inscription has disappeared.   Another inscription, or,
more correctly, a slab with the remains of an inscription and a monogram, was copied at the close of the eighteenth century and published
by Pallas;[8] it has been several times reprinted from his reproduction.   He

---

[1] Malitzki, *op. cit.*, p. 27.

[2] *Martini Broniovii Tartariae Descriptio* (Cologne, 1595), p. 7: 'Templum Graecum S. Constantini
et alterum S. Georgii humile admodum nunc reliquum est.'   A Russian translation by J. Shershenevich, with notes by J. Murzakevich, in the *Zapiski* of the Odessa Society of History and Antiquities,
VI (1867), 343–344.   [3] See Malitzki, *op. cit.*, p. 29.

[4] Latyshev, 'Epigraphic Novelties from South Russia,' *Izvestiya* of the Archaeological Commission, LXV, 19 (reproduction No. 7); Malitzki, *op. cit.*, pp. 25–26 (reproduction No. 7, p. 25).

[5] Malitzki, *op. cit.*, p. 32 (reproduction No. 9, p. 32).

[6] Malitzki, *op. cit.*, p. 35.

[7] See N. Murzakevich, *History of the Genoese Settlements in the Crimea*, (Odessa, 1837), pp. 85–86,
note; Latyshev, *Collection of Greek Inscriptions of Christian Times*, p. 58 (No. 49); Malitzki, *op. cit.*,
pp. 35–36.   All three in Russian.

[8] P. S. Pallas, *Bemerkungen auf einer Reise in die südlichen Statthalterschaften des Russischen
Reichs in den Jahren 1793 und 1794*, II (Leipzig, 1801), 54.

discovered it in the ruins of Chersonesus; it contains three heart-like shields, a monogram which reminds us slightly of Alexis' monogram, and a fragment of an inscription which mentions 'τὸ κάστρον τῆς Χερσῶνος,' which belonged to Alexis.[1]   As Malitzki remarks: 'It is possible that this inscription is somehow connected with Alexis' general political activity and his attempts to establish himself on the Crimean "coastland" (παραθαλασσία).'[2]

This epigraphic material from Gothia informs us that Alexis' official title at the beginning of the fifteenth century was 'Alexis, prince of the city of Theodoro and the maritime region.'   This title shows that Alexis, ruler of mountainous Gothia, was also in possession of a coastland, certainly along the western shore of the Crimea, where he constructed a port at Calamita.   But perhaps in his imagination the term 'prince of the maritime region' had a larger meaning.   Anxious to establish himself on the southern shore, especially at Balaklava, Alexis might have laid claim to the Genoese coastline, just as after the treaties of 1381–1387 the Genoese regarded the whole territory of Gothia as their vassal state and Alexis as a rebel.

In connection with this should be considered the Genoese escutcheon in the form of a lengthened Greek cross upon an oval shield, which is found, as we have seen, on three slabs with inscriptions.   This emblem, though found in Gothia, is no evidence of the vassalage of that principality to Genoa, Gothia being in reality absolutely independent of Caffa; this escutcheon in my opinion may be explained only by the imperialistic tendencies of Alexis, who continued to regard as his own the Genoese possessions along the south coast which had formerly belonged to Gothia. The escutcheon was a survival of former political relations, and the Genoese authorities of Caffa were no doubt very much irritated at this symbol of Alexis' political ambitions, ambitions which, till the year 1427 at least, Genoa could not force Alexis to surrender.

Alexis' monogram was deciphered for the first time by G. Millet in 1900, and his interpretation has been accepted by Russian scholars.[3]   The escutcheon of the Paleologi on these monuments in Gothia is not to be explained by direct relationship with the Palaeologi of Byzantium[4] or

---

[1] Latyshev, *op. cit.*, pp. 19–20 (No. 9); Malitzki, *op. cit.*, pp. 36–37.

[2] Malitzki, *op. cit.*, p. 37.

[3] G. Millet, in his review of Latyshev's *Collection of Greek Inscriptions of Christian Times from South Russia*, in the *Bulletin Critique*, 21 année, No. 28, Oct. 5, 1900.   See Latyshev, 'Notes on Christian Inscriptions of the Crimea, IV,' in the *Zapiski* of the Odessa Society, XXIII (1901), 76; Malitzki, *op. cit.*, p. 28.

[4] I do not believe that Alexis' conflict with Manuel II Palaeologus, of which we know so little and which ended in Alexis' failure, could have led to the enforced introduction of the Palaeologian emblem into the principality of Gothia; the monogram of the Palaeologi was used in 1476–1477 on the pall of

the Great Comnenes of Trebizond, who were connected with the Constantinopolitan Palaeologi,[1] but by Maria, wife of John, one of Alexis' sons, who was related, as we have noted above, on her father's side to the Palaeologi, and on her mother's side to the family of Tzamblakon, who were also related to the Palaeologi.

In the memory of his people the name of Alexis left a deep impression, so that after his death the capital of Gothia, Theodoro, was sometimes called Alexa. In the spoken language the people sometimes changed the name of Theodoro to Thodoreza (Thodoriza), i.e., Θεοδωρίτσι, little Theodoro.[2]

The year of Alexis' death has not been so far discovered in our sources, so that opinions differ. Bruun remarked in passing that Alexis died in 1456.[3] Braun states that Alexis died in Balaklava in 1428.[4] This dating is probably to be explained by a misprint, for Braun knows well that in 1433–1434 Alexis took and lost Cembalo-Balaklava.[5] The statement that Alexis died in Balaklava is found, as we have noted above, in a prayer inserted in the so-called *synodica*, old lists of the members of the Golovin family, where we read, 'Remember . . . Prince Stephan, called when he assumed the cowl Simon, and his children, Gregory, and Alexis who was killed in Balaklava.'[6] Spiridonov wrote recently that Alexis died between 1 January and 14 May 1455.[7] In this statement he refers to the

Maria, Princess of Mankup, who married the Prince of Moldavia, Stephen the Great, and died in Moldavia at the end of 1477. On Maria see below. In 1477 neither the Byzantine Empire nor the Empire of Trebizond existed, so that there could be no question whatever of Gothia's political dependence. On the conflict with Manuel II see above.

[1] Cf. Köppen, *Krymsky Sbornik*, p. 221: 'Perhaps Alexis himself was a member of the family reigning in Constantinople or was married to a Palaeologian princess?' (in Russian); G. Bratianu, *Recherches sur le commerce génois dans la Mer Noire au XIIIe siècle* (Paris, 1929), p. 204: 'On suppose que les princes de Théodoros ou de Mangoup . . . étaient des Paléologues apparentés à la dynastie de Trébizonde'; Malitzki, *op. cit.*, pp. 29–32. Referring to the epitaph by John Eugenikos, Malitzki conjectures that the marriage of John, Alexis' son, with a Palaeologina may have been performed before the inscription of 1425, where we find the two-headed eagle for the first time, so that this marriage may have given a reason for placing the escutcheon on the inscription. But Malitzki adds that this is a mere hypothesis, and matters may have fallen out quite differently (p. 32).

[2] Report of the Rector and Council of Ragusa to the Doge of Venice, Pietro Mocenigo, on the Fall of Caffa and Theodoro: '(Turci) devicerunt quandam communitatem Alexam, que urbem natura loci inexpugnabilem et industria munitum habebat, quam vulgo Thodorezam (Thodorizam) vocant,' *Monumenta Hungariae Historica, Acta Extera*, v (*Magyar diplomacziai emlékek, Mátyás Király korából*), 1458–1490, II (Budapest, 1877), 346; *Atti della Società Ligure*, VII, ii (1879), 488. The document is dated 18 February 1476.

[3] Bruun, *Chernomorye*, II (Odessa, 1880), 230 (in Russian). Bruun gives no reason for his statement.

[4] Braun *Die letzten Schicksale*, p. 41.   [5] Braun, *op. cit.*, pp. 29–30.

[6] N. Golovin, *Some Words on the Family of the Greek Princes Comneni* (Moscow, 1854), pp. 11–12. See also Malitzki, *op. cit.*, p. 25, n. 1, 38–39. Both in Russian. Cf. above.

[7] D. Spiridonov, 'Notes on the History of Hellenism in the Crimea, I: On the Family History of the House of Mangup,' *Izvestiya* of the Tauric Society of History, Archaeology and Ethnography, II (Simferopol, 1928), 4 (in Russian).

Genoese document of 14 May 1455, where Alexis is mentioned as deceased;[1] but I cannot make out on what evidence he asserts that Alexis died after 1 January.

All these attempts are now to be discarded. We have already noted that in November, 1441, when peace was concluded between Caffa and Alexis, Alexis was still alive. But from a later document, 2 May 1447, we learn that in this year at Calamita and Theodoro Olobei and other sons of the late Alexis were ruling.[2] Therefore, Alexis died between November 1441 and April 1447. If we recall that a document of 13 January 1444 mentions the raid of a galley of Caffa 'in territorio Alexii,' which occurred in 1438, we may conclude with probability that in 1444 Alexis was still living, because in this document Alexis' name is not accompanied by *quondam* as in that of 1447. Therefore Alexis died between 1444 and 1447. It is rather surprising that his death has not been noted in our sources; but we must not forget that only a part of the archive documents on the Genoese Crimea have been published, and we are almost certain that Genoese, Venetian, and other Italian archives will throw new light on this subject and help us to fix the exact date of the death of the ruler who played so important a rôle in the life of the Crimea in the first half of the fifteenth century. Perhaps in 1444–1447 new trouble may have arisen in Balaklava of which we are not yet aware, trouble in which Alexis was killed, as the old *synodica* of the Golovin family, a source not absolutely reliable, assert.

During Alexis' rule in Gothia two West-European travellers visited Tana and Caffa, and their accounts are worthy of consideration. In 1436–1437 an Italian traveller, Iosafat (Giosafat) Barbaro visited Tana, at the mouth of the Don, and after sixteen years of travel in Tartary returned to Venice; after many other journeys in the Near East he died at Venice in 1494. He says a few words concerning the Crimea, which he calls 'the Island of Caffa' ('isola de Capha'), mentions Gothia, and makes the very interesting statement that in his time the Goths spoke German ('in Tedesco'). Barbaro's description follows: 'Behind the island of Capha, which stands on the Major Sea, is Gothia [la Gotthia], and after that Alania, which runs parallel with the island towards Moncastro, as I have said before. The Goths speak German [in Tedesco], which I know by a German, my servant [un fameglio Tedesco], that was with me there: for they understood one another well enough, as we understand a Furlane [of the city of Forli] and a Florentine. From this neighborhood of the Goths and Alani, I suppose the name of Gotitalani to be derived, for the

[1] Report of Carlo Cicala, Consul of Soldaia, to the Protectors on the Condition of this Colony: 'Ego vero hiis proximis diebus aliquas litteras scripsi duobus ex filijs q(uondam) Alexij,' in the *Atti della Società Ligure*, VI, 304 (Doc. 119).

[2] Iorga, *Notes et extraits*, III, 216: 'cum Olobei et ceteris filiis condam Alexii.'

Alani were first in this place. But then came the Goths and conquered these countries, mingling their name with the Alani.'[1] In my judgment, this statement of the survival of the German tongue in the Crimea in the fifteenth century is more important than the other records discussed above and can not be ignored. Barbaro's German servant made himself understood by, and even conversed with, another man of German descent living in the Crimea. Of course, this can not serve as proof that the Crimean Goths continued to speak German. We are well informed that at that time they were hellenized and tartarized. But Barbaro's account proves that among the population of Gothia there were some individuals who had not yet forgotten their mother tongue, unless — and this seems more probable — the man of whom Barbaro wrote was a newcomer from Western Europe.[2] We must admit that some of Barbaro's data on the Crimea are misleading. For instance he remarks: 'Capha, Soldaia, Grasui (Gurzuf), Cymbalo, Sarsona (Cherson), and Calamita — all at this present time under the Great Turk.'[3] We know that the first four places had been ceded by the Tartars to Genoa in 1380–1387, and that Cherson and Calamita belonged to the principality of Theodoro. But under Hadji-Girei, the founder of the independent dynasty of the Gireis in the Crimea, circumstances changed. He did not feel himself bound by the treaties of his predecessors in the fourteenth century, and as we know declared himself the sworn enemy of the Genoese and the friendly suzerain of Gothia. His plan, no doubt, was to unify the Peninsula under his own power. Then also the term 'Great Turk' is rather misleading, because it usually applies not to the Tartar Khan, but to the

---

[1] 'Dietro dell'isola de Capha d'intorno ch'è sul mar maggiore, si trova la Gotthia, e poi la Alania, la qual va per la isola verso Moncastro come habbiamo detto disopra. Gotthi parlano in Tedesco; e so questo, perchè havendo un fameglio Tedesco con me, parlavano insieme, et intendevansi assai ragionevolmente, cosi come s'intenderiano un furlano ed un fiorentino,' *Viaggi fatti da Vinetia alla Tana, in Persia, in India, et in Costantinopoli: con la descrittione particolare di Città, Luoghi, Siti, Costumi, e della Porta del grand Turco* . . . (Venice, 1545), p. 18ᵛ; J. Barbaro, *Viaggio alla Tana*, ed. Ramusio (Venice, 1583), p. 97ᵛ; an English translation: *Travels to Tana and Persia by Iosafa Barbaro and Ambrogio Contarini* (London, 1873), p. 30; a Russian translation by V. Semenov, in the *Library (Biblioteka) of Foreign Writers on Russia*, I (St Petersburg, 1836), 55–56. See Niccolò di Lenna, 'Giosafat Barbaro (1413–1494) e i suoi viaggi nella regione russa (1436–51) e nella Persia (1474–78),' *Nuovo Archivo Veneto*, nuova serie, anno XIV, XXVIII, i (1914), p. 24. This is the best study on Barbaro (the whole article, pp. 5–105; bibliography, pp. 92–93). On the Crimean Goths see p. 24, n. 3, where some information is inexact. See also *Enciclopedia Italiana*, VI (1930), 133. In the sixteenth century Barbaro's data on the Goths and Alans were used in Western Europe by the famous scholar Konrad Gesner (Gessner), *Mithridates Gesneri, exprimens differentias linguarum, tum veterum, tum quae hodie, per totum terrarum orbem, in usu sunt, editio altera* (Zürich, 1610), p. 48.

[2] Braun, (*Die letzten Schicksale*, p. 54) considers Barbaro's account highly important; he writes, 'The Gothic language was in full strength in the fifteenth century in the Tauric Peninsula. We have no ground whatever to doubt Barbaro's account, and the circumstances under which the Venetian traveller learned the tongue of the Goths confirm the truth of his relation.'

[3] J. Barbaro, *Travels to Tana* (London, 1873), pp. 27–28.

Sultan of the Ottoman Turks, whose influence in Barbaro's time was not yet strong in the Crimea.

Almost in the same year that Barbaro visted Tana, a Spanish traveller, Pero Tafur, visited Caffa (1437–1438). He wrote: 'The city is very large as large as Seville, or larger, with twice as many inhabitants, Catholic Christians [Cristianos Catolicos] as well as Greeks, and all the nations of the world.' In another place he remarks: 'So great is the multitude of men [in Caffa] and so many are the different nationalities, that it is a marvel that Caffa is free from plague.'[1] We see that one of the characteristic features of Caffa which struck Pero Tafur was the heterogeneous composition of its population; but Tafur mentions the Goths neither in Caffa nor in the Crimea in general. We may also give the statement of a grammarian, Alberto Alfieri, who lived in Caffa in the first half of the fifteenth century. He writes, '[Caffa] has an excellent harbor, is situated on arid soil . . . where the languages of different people are used. There live Greeks, Armenians, Jews, Nabathaeans; all peoples are represented in the city.'[2] Alfieri also makes no mention of the Gothic tongue.

6. OLOBEI, PRINCE OF GOTHIA. THE STATUTE OF CAFFA (1449). THE FALL OF CONSTANTINOPLE

As we have pointed out, Alexis died in 1444–1447. His successor was his son Olobei, whose name, as we have noted, is given for the first time in an official Genoese document dated 2 May 1447.[3] Olobei is a proper name, not the Tartar title meaning 'Grand Prince' as Spiridonov asserts; Spiridonov declares that in *Genoese Document 34* Alexis himself is called not by his name but by his title Olobei.[4] The document referred to, dated 11 September 1454, states that the Prince of Theodoro, Olobei, notified the Caffian authorities of imminent Turkish danger.[5] But we know now that Alexis died between 1444 and 1447, so that this document can not refer to him. Malitzki has overlooked the document of 2 May 1447, quoted above, which plainly says that Olobei was Alexis' son, and accordingly he hesitates to recognize him as such; Malitzki conjectures that if Olobei (in Malitzki Olubei) was Alexis' son, he may also have

---

[1] *Andanças é viajes de Pero Tafur por diversas partes del mundo avidos* (1435–1439), ed. D. M· Jiménez de la Espada, in the *Coleccion de libros españoles raros ó curiosos*, VIII (Madrid, 1874), 160–161, 164; *Pero Tafur, Travels and Adventures*, translated by Malcolm Letts (New York and London, 1926), pp. 132, 134–135.

[2] 'L'Ogdoas di Alberto Alfieri, Episodii di storia genovese nei primordii del secolo XV,' ed. Antonio Ceruti, in the *Atti della Società Ligure di Storia Patria*, XVII (1885), 314; on the author, pp. 260–263. See E. Skrzinska, 'Inscriptions latines des colonies génoises en Crimée,' *ibid.*, LVI (1928), 7.

[3] Iorga, *Notes et extraits*, III, 216: 'cum Olobei et ceteris filiis condam Alexii.'

[4] Spiridonov, *op. cit.*, p. 4 and n. 2 (in Russian). Malitzki (*op. cit.*, p. 41) also disagrees with Spiridonov in this respect.

[5] *Atti della Società Ligure*, VI, 113. We shall discuss this document later.

borne the name Alexis; the second half of the name Olobei (Olubei), *bei* means chief or prince; could the first half *Olo* (*Olu*) be the contracted Turkish form of Alexis?[1] Of course this hypothesis can not be seriously considered. Olobei is a Tartar proper name, and Olobei himself was a Greek, which is proved by a reliable source.[2] We have already noted that some Christians in the Crimea bore Tartar names, and in the fifteenth century, especially in Gothia where the Tartar influence under Hadji-Girei was very strong, it was almost impossible to tell by the name alone whether a person was Greek or Tartar. If the Italian traveller quoted above, Giosafat Barbaro, had been correct in writing that Hadji-Girei had a son Ulubei,[3] it might have been supposed that Alexis christened his son in honor of Hadji-Girei's son. But as far as I know, no son of Hadji-Girei bore this name.[4]

Olobei was not Alexis' eldest son; from the epitaph discussed above we learn that his eldest son was John. So far, except for the epitaph, the name of John has not been mentioned in any source, and in 1447 shortly after Alexis' death, John's brother Olobei ruled over Gothia. What happened to John and why has his name disappeared from our sources? We know nothing of this enigma; some new archival material may throw light on this personage, who as Alexis' eldest son should have played an important part in the history of Gothia. In my judgment two possible hypotheses may more or less explain this obscure question. I agree with Spiridonov that John and his wife Maria reached Trebizond, where their child Alexis was born and died. John Eugenikos, himself a native of Trebizond, composed the child's epitaph there. In my discussion of this source, I tried to show that in the epitaph Alexis the Elder was regarded as deceased and his eldest son John as ruler of Gothia. If this is the case, John immediately after his father's death left Gothia for Trebizond for good. This would explain the stubborn silence of our sources as to John; he disappeared from Gothia and ended his days in Trebizond. Possibly he left his principality reluctantly, because of some troubles with Hadji-Girei, who for some reason or other supported his brother Olobei. This

---

[1] Malitzki, *op. cit.*, pp. 40–41.

[2] N. Bănescu, 'Vechi legături ale tărilor noastre cu Genovezii,' *Inchinare lui N. Iorga cu prilejul împlinarii vârstei de 60 de ani* (Cluj, 1931), p. 35: 'Novene datte Agutaree (Hadji-Girei), Imperatori Tartarorum, de acordio in Tedoro Olobei Greci,' Doc. 25 June 1455, from *Massaria Caffe*. In his note on Miss Vasiliu's study N. Iorga writes that Olobei is a Tartar name, and refers to a Roumanian family name, Hulubein, *Revue historique du sud-est européen*, VII (1930), 254.

[3] 'Ulubi, son of Azicharai,' J. Barbaro, *Travels to Tana* (London, 1873), p. 27; N. di Lenna, 'Giosafat Barbaro (1413–94) e i suoi viaggi nella regione Russa (1436–51) e nella Persia (1474–78),' in the *Nuovo Archivio Veneto*, XXVIII (1914), 23.

[4] See Bertier Delagarde, 'Kalamita and Theodoro,' p. 35, n. 3. The names of Hadji-Girei's sons are not definitely established, Veliaminov-Zernov, *Izsledovanie o Kasimovskikh Tsariakh*, I (St Petersburg, 1863), 98; H. Howorth, *History of the Mongols*, II (London, 1888), 626.

may perhaps explain to some extent a very obscure official record, dated 17 August 1446, of the expenses of Caffa.   Four hundred and fifty-nine aspers were spent for a present to Usdemoroch, who had *once* been ruler (*dominus*) of the Goths, when he came to a place called 'tres montaniolae.'[1]   Taken alone this record is completely obscure.   But if we assume that after Alexis' death troubles arose in Gothia in connection with his successor which resulted in John's forced departure for Trebizond, Usdemoroch[2] as Hadji-Girei's deputy might have governed in Gothia until the troubles were over and Olobei with the Khan's consent was made Prince of Gothia.   After having completed his task, on his way back to Solkhat through Caffa in August 1446 Usdemoroch was welcomed by the Caffian authorities and given a present.[3]   This is one possible hypothesis to account for the disappearance of John's name from our sources.

Another hypothesis may be advanced regarding this question.   John may have been that son of Alexis who was taken captive by Lomellino at the regaining of Cembalo-Balaklava by the Genoese in 1434.   The name of this son is not given in our source.   We know that after the conclusion of the peace between Alexis and Caffa in 1441 an exchange of captives took place, but among the captives from Gothia who returned to their own country Alexis' son is not mentioned.   Perhaps he did not return to Gothia but went to Trebizond with his wife, with the permission of the Genoese, from Pera, where no doubt the Gothic captives were detained.   John Eugenikos, writing the epitaph in Trebizond after Alexis the Elder's death, proclaimed John 'lord of Khazaria' ('αὐθέντης Χαζαρίας') and called him 'the Great John, who reached the highest glory'; we must assume that Eugenikos wrote as if John had inherited his father's position, though in reality he never did.

I quite understand that these speculations are mere hypotheses not yet capable of proof.   But we must remember that Alexis' eldest son John existed; his existence cannot be denied, because the testimony of the epitaph is plain and trustworthy.   Moreover the silence of our other sources, especially Genoese official documents, may be explained only by the fact that John left Gothia permanently and played no part in the political life of the Crimea.

---

[1] N. Iorga, *Notes et extraits*, I, 38: 'Exenium unum factum Usdemoroch, olim domino Gethicorum, quando venit ad tres montaniolas . . . asp. 459.'   Iorga remarks (*ibid.*): 'C'est un chef des Goths, inconnu par ailleurs.'   The place 'tres montaniolae' is mentioned in another document, 6 June 1442: 'prope tres monticulos' (*ibid.*, p. 36).   This name may be compared with the 'Three Fountains' ('li trey pozi'), a place between Caffa and the mountain Sachim, where the preliminary treaty between the Tartars and Caffa was drawn up in November, 1380.   See above.

[2] I do not yet know the real name hidden in this no doubt distorted form.

[3] In connection with this hypothesis we might conclude that Alexis the Elder died before 1446, so that for the date of his death we should have not the years 1444–1447, as has been suggested above, but 1444–1445.

Olobei inherited and pursued his father's policy in the Crimea: friendship, more or less enforced, towards Hadji-Girei, and enmity towards the Genoese.　Olobei and his brothers, according to a Genoese document, 'boasted openly that they fear nobody as long as their father and the emperor of the Tartars live.'[1]　Now the father was dead; but the other protector, Hadji-Girei, was in power, so that Olobei's policy was in submissive harmony with his.

Probably at the outset of Olobei's rule, in 1446–1447, the Ottoman Turks made their first appearance on the shores of Gothia.　The Turkish sultan Murad II (1421–1451) sent galleys to ravage Trebizond.　After touching its coast, the fleet sailed northward for the Crimea, pillaged Gothia, and took a considerable number of prisoners; but on their return a storm arose and drove the fleet ashore on Asia Minor at Pontic Heraclaea with the loss of several vessels.[2]　This was the first warning in the Crimea of the Ottoman danger which a few years later entirely changed the correlation of political forces in the Peninsula.

In 1447 a conflict arose between Caffa and Trebizond, where at that time John IV Comnenus was reigning.　Contrary to the treaties and agreements concluded with Caffa, John IV sent his brother and heir, the Despot David, with several vessels to the shores of the Crimea.　The fleet reached the neighborhood of Caffa and thence turned to the shores of Gothia, to Calamita.　David, whose first wife was Maria, daughter of Alexis and consequently Olobei's sister, visited Calamita and Theodoro and spent some time with his brothers-in-law.[3]　Unfortunately our document does not say anything on the real purpose of so unusual a visit or its result.　Some other princes on the Black Sea also manifested a hostile policy against Caffa, so that finally the government of Genoa, after having examined letters written by Leonardo de Grimaldi and Giovanni Navone, consul and *massarii* of Caffa, as well as the letter of Dorino Gattilusio, suzerain of Mitylene, directed a commission to make a report

---

[1] *Atti della Società Ligure*, VI (1868), 361.

[2] Laonicus Chalcocondylas, Bk. v, p. 261: 'αἱ τριήρεις προσέσχον ἐς γῆν τε τὴν Κολχίδα, καὶ ἐπὶ τοὺς Γότθους ἀφικόμενοι ἐληλάτουν τὴν χώραν, ἀνδραποδισάμενοι οὐκ ὀλίγην. ἐπανιόντι δὲ τῷ στόλῳ χειμὼν ἐγένετο ἰσχυρός, καὶ ἄνεμος ἀπαρκτίας ἐπιβαλὼν ἐξήνεγκεν ἐς τὴν 'Ασιάν κατὰ τὴν Ποντοηράκλειαν, καὶ φερόμεναι αὐτοῦ ἔνιαι τῶν τριηρῶν διεφθείροντο καὶ ἐν ξυμφορᾷ ἔσχοντο τοιαύτῃ.'　Tomaschek (*Die Goten in Taurien*, p. 53) attributes this raid on Gothia to the year 1446; W. Miller (*Trebizond*, p. 85) to 1442, i.e., to the period of Alexis.　We must admit the dating of this raid is not well established.

[3] Iorga, *Notes et extraits*, III, 216: 'graves injurie, innovationes cabellarum, damna aliaque multiplicia discrimina a certo tempore citra illata nostratibus de Caffa per imperatorem Trapezundarum et per despotum suum, quo cum galeis et fustis contra pacta et deveta Caffe descendit et navigavit per Mare Majus usque ad confinia Caphe et inde declinavit Calamitam et Tedorum ac moram traxit cum Olobei et ceteris filiis condam Alexii, etc. (*sic*).'　According to the editor's '*sic*,' the document unfortunately gives no details of David's visit to Gothia; 'etc.' belongs to the manuscript.　Doc. 2 May 1447.

on this matter. Many letters and energetic protests were dispatched to various places on the Black Sea where the Genoese interests had been damaged and treaties violated. A particularly threatening note was sent to the Emperor of Trebizond to the effect that if he did not accept the conditions Genoa had dictated to him, she would sent a fleet against him and other hostile regions. In spite of this warning news reached Genoa that hostile actions against the Genoese had been committed by the Emperor of Trebizond, the Prince of Kastemuni, and the *sonbachi* (ruler) of Sinope, as well as by Olobei, *dominus Tedori*. Genoa decided to tolerate no longer such behavior from those 'who in the past had usually paid respect to the Genoese and held the latter nearly as their masters.'[1] New measures must be taken against the offenders. It was decided that the new consul of Caffa would bring instructions concerning Olobei and the Emperor of the Tartars.[2] We do not know what sort of instructions these were. No open conflict, however, broke out between Olobei and Genoa.

In August, 1447, a very well-known Byzantine diplomat, a confidential counsellor of the last Byzantine emperor, and a talented historian, George Phrantzes, went to Constantinople to discuss several problems, among them, according to his account, that of Trebizond and Gothia as well as that of the marriage of the Emperor.[3] But here Gothia is erroneously mentioned by Phrantzes for Iberia,[4] i.e. Georgia.

On 28 March 1448 Battisto Marchexano was appointed by Genoa *capitaneus* of all Genoese Gothia.[5] In May, 1449, there is a rather strange coming to light of the seizure of Cembalo-Balaklava by Alexis. In a document dated 26 May 1449 the Republic of Genoa wrote to the consul of Cembalo concerning recompense for the damage he had suffered at the time when 'Alexis had taken possession of Cembalo by force for some time.'[6] The length of time from Alexis' taking of Cembalo in 1433, a well-known date, up to 1449, when the consul of this place was indemnified, is amazingly great. This might possibly serve as confirmation of the

---

[1] *Ibid.*, p. 218: 'illi qui temporibus preteritis solebant Januenses colli ac venerari et fere in dominos habere.' I do not understand the word 'colli'; perhaps 'colere' or 'coli'?

[2] *Ibid.*, pp. 217–218. See Vasiliu, *op. cit.*, pp. 324–325.

[3] Phrantzes, II, 19 (Bonn, ed., p. 203): 'καὶ τῷ Αὐγούστῳ μηνὶ τοῦ αὐτοῦ ἔτους πάλιν ἐγὼ εἰς τὴν Κωνσταντινούπολιν ὑπὲρ πολλῶν τινῶν ὑποθέσεων καὶ περὶ τῆς Τραπεζοῦντος καὶ τῆς Γοτθίας καὶ περί τινος συνοικεσίου διὰ τὸν αὐθέντην μου, ἐπεὶ ἀπ' ἐκεῖσε προεσύντυχον.'

[4] G. Destunis, 'Biography of George Phrantzes,' *Journal of the Ministry of Public Instruction*, CCLXXXVII (June, 1893), 471 (in Russian).

[5] Iorga, *Notes et extraits*, III, 235: '(Battisto Marchexano is appointed) in capitaneum et pro capitaneo totius Gotie.'

[6] *Ibid.*, p. 245: 'pro aliqua recompensacione damnorum per eum passorum tempore quo Alexius locum Cimbali per aliquod tempus vi potitus est.'

not very reliable statement of the *synodica* of the Golovin family, i.e., that towards the end of his rule, between 1444 and 1447, Alexis attacked Balaklava again, pillaged it, and was killed.

On 28 February 1449 was issued a most remarkable mediaeval document, the Statute of Caffa (*Statutum Caphe*), depicting in detail the methods and system of Genoese organization and administration in the Crimea. This Statute has the greatest importance not only for the history of the Crimea but also for the general colonial history of the Middle Ages. The Statute contains ninety-six chapters and embraces all sides of the complicated organization of the Genoese possessions in the Crimea.[1] I shall be concerned here only with the chapters which directly or indirectly refer to Gothia.

Genoese officials, called consuls, were stationed in the cities of that part of Gothia which had been ceded to Genoa by the Tartars according to the treaties of 1381–1387 — in Gurzuf (Gorzonii), Parthenit (Pertinice), Yalta (Jalite), and Alushta (Luste).[2] For relations with various nationalities in the Crimea special bureaus of interpreters were established not only in Caffa, but also in Soldaia and Cembalo-Balaklava. In Caffa there were three interpreters and clerks who, besides Italian, knew and wrote Greek and Saracen,[3] i.e. Tartar. In Soldaia (Sudak) the consul had an interpreter acquainted with Latin, i.e. Italian, Greek, and Tartar.[4] Especially interesting for our subject is the provision concerning Cembalo-Balaklava, which speaks of one interpreter familiar with three languages: Latin, i.e., Italian, Greek, and Tartar; he received a salary of 150 aspers a month.[5] Cembalo, as we know, was a city bordering on the territory of the principality of Gothia, and intercourse between them was extremely frequent and important. In spite of this, there is no mention of the Gothic tongue; an interpreter acquainted with German was not

---

[1] There are two editions of the Statute: 'The Statute for the Genoese Colonies in the Black Sea, issued in Genoa in 1449,' ed. V. Yurguevich, *Zapiski* of the Odessa Society of History and Antiquities, v (1863), 629–815 (Latin text with a Russian translation) and notes, pp. 816–837 (in Russian); 'Statutum Caphe,' ed. P. Amedeo Vigna, *Codice Diplomatico delle Colonie Tauro-Liguri*, ii, ii, in the *Atti della Società Ligure di Storia Patria*, vii, ii (1879), 575–680. For the most recent study on this Statute see E. Skrzinska, 'Le colonie genovesi in Crimea, Teodosia (Caffa),' *L'Europa Orientale*, xiv (Rome, 1934), 113–151.

[2] Yurguevich, pp. 675–676; Vigna, p. 598 (Ch. vi).

[3] See Ch. xv, *De interpretibus curie Caphae et eorum salario*, and Ch. xvi, *De scribis in litteris grecis et saracenis*, Yurguevich, pp. 694, 695; Vigna, pp. 608–609.

[4] Ch. lxxvii. *De ordine Soldaie:* 'Interpres unus sciens linguam latinam grecam et tartaricam,' Yurguevich, p. 771; Vigna, p. 655.

[5] Ch. lxxxi, § 552, *De ordine Cimbaldi:* 'Idem debeat in dicto loco interpres unus seu torcimannius sciens linguam latinam grecam et tartaricam, qui habere debeat pro suo salario singulo mense asperos centum quinquaginta,' Yurguevich, pp. 787–788; Vigna, p. 664. *Torcimannius* is a Turco-Tartar word meaning 'interpreter' (*terdjuman*). See also Doc. cxlvi (6 August 1455): 'averan cosi bonna pratica de lo parlar gregesco e tartaresco,' in the *Atti*, vi, 351.

needed.   This clearly shows once more that although several travellers asserted, practically by hearsay, that in the fifteenth century Gothic was spoken in the Crimea, this was not the case. Extremely interesting is Chapter xxxiv, *De capitaneatu Gotie*, which runs as follows: 'We decree and order that the *capitaneus* of Gothia or a consul of the district of Gothia just mentioned shall not fine any person for a quarrel accompanied with injurious words more than forty aspers.   If a man is condemned to a larger fine, he shall be sent to Caffa, to the consul or his vicar.'[1] Then Chapter xxxv is entitled *On Refraining from Lending (Money) to the Communes of Gothia (De non mutuando comunitatibus Gotie)* and reads thus: 'We decree and order that no Genoese may, dare, or presume to, lend any amount of money to the communes of the places and villages (cazalium) of Gothia, or place these communes in debt by means of the sale of wares or in any other way, under threat of punishment (sub pena audientie denegande), as has been said before in regard to the barons and princes of Ghazaria.'[2]   The last words refer to Chapter xxxiii, according to which 'no merchant or any other Genoese may strike a bargain of any sort or sell any thing or any ware to any prince or baron or dealer (*comerchiario*) of all Gazaria and the Major Sea (Black Sea).'[3]   Book ii of the Statute entitled *On the Administration of the Places Subject to the City of Caffa*[4] gives special provisions for Soldaia and Cembalo, and for the consulates established in the cities outside the Crimea, such as Trebizond, Coppa, Tana, Sinope, Sevastopol (Savastopolis, on the eastern shore of the Black Sea), Samastris (Amastris, in Asia Minor);[5] no mention whatever of Theodoro or Gothia can be discovered.

Four years after the promulgation of the Statute of 1449, in 1453, Constantinople was taken by the Turks.   A new page opened in the history

---

[1] Ch. xxxiv, § 348: 'Statuimus et ordinamus quod capitaneus Gotie seu aliquis consul dicti loci Gotie pro aliqua rixa, specialiter verborum injuriosorum, non possit condemnare aliquam personam ultra asperos quadraginta'; § 349: 'Si quis autem veniret abinde supra condemnandus remittat eum in Capha ad dominum consulem et ejus vicarium,' Yurguevich, p. 726; Vigna, p. 628.

[2] Ch. xxxv, § 350: 'Statuimus et ordinamus quod nullus januensis possit audeat vel presumat mutuare aliquam quantitatem pecunie comunitatibus locorum et cazalium Gotie, vel ipsas comunitates in aliquo obligare per viam venditionis mercium vel alio modo, sub pena audientie denegande ut supra dictum est de dominis baronibus et principibus Gazarie,' Yurguevich, p. 726; Vigna, p. 628.

[3] Ch. xxxiii: 'Quod nullus mercator vel aliqua alia persona januensis possit contrahere aliquo modo vel vendere res aliquas seu merces alicui principi domino vel baroni seu comerchiario totius imperii Gazarie et Maris Majoris,' Yurguevich, p. 725, Vigna, p. 627.

[4] Ch. lxxvii: 'Incipit liber secundus: de ordinibus locorum subditorum civitati Caphe,' Yurguevich, p. 766; Vigna, p. 652.

[5] Yurguevich, pp. 766–810; Vigna, pp. 652–677.   See also 'Disposizioni della Signoria di Genova concernanti la giurisdizione del Consolato di Caffa: A. 1398,' in the *Atti della Società Ligure*, xiv (1878), 101–110: 'officia consulatuum Caffae, Simisci, Cymbali, Trapesondae et Samastri ac Massariae Caffae, quae in Janua concedantur et elligantur' (p. 103); 'consulatus — Symissi, Cimbali, Soldayae, Trapezundae et Samastri' (p. 110).

of the world. This event had a striking repercussion in the Crimea and decided the future destinies of the Peninsula.

In order to avert the imminent Turkish danger from its Crimean colony the government of Genoa made an agreement with the Bank of St George (Uffizio or Banca di San Giorgio), which possessed enormous amounts of money and had almost unlimited credit in the commercial and political circles of that epoch. On 15 November 1453 the government of Genoa ceded all its rights over Caffa and its other colonies on the shores of the Black Sea to the Bank; from that time onward the Bank had to make laws for the colonies, appoint officials, and administer justice.[1] In the text of the act of transfer the following places are mentioned: Caffa, Soldaia, Samastra, Symbolum (Balaklava) and 'other towns and lands that the Grand Commune of Genoa possesses in various regions of the Black Sea.'[2] By this act a new page was turned in the history of the Crimea, and relations between the Bank and Gothia became very active. It is to be emphasized that Gothia with Theodoro was not inserted in this act.

We have an almost complete list of the *capitani* of Gothia elected and appointed by the Bank of St George during the period of its administration, up to 6 June 1475, when Caffa capitulated to the Turks.[3] Apparently the first *capitano* of Gothia under the Bank of St George, Baldassare Andora (Badasar de Andora), was chosen on 22 August 1454, i.e., nine months after the rights of Genoa over her colonies in the Black Sea had been ceded to the Bank. Perhaps he declined the nomination. Later Tommaso Voltaggio (Thomas de Vultabio) and Desserino Canneto (Dexerinus de Caneto) were elected. It is also doubtful whether they took office.[4] For the period from 1454 to 1459 our list is blank. On 9 May 1459 the Protectors of the Bank of St George granted a patent for the *capitaneatus* of Gothia to Girolamo Gherardi for two years. In the document conferring the administration of Gothia on Girolamo Gherardi we read the following interesting lines: 'As we have chosen and constituted our beloved Jeronimum de Guirardis *capitanus* of Gothia for two years . . . we command all of you that after you have seen this document

---

[1] Ag. Giustiniani, *Annali della Repubblica di Genova*, 3rd Genoese ed., II (Genoa, 1854), 383 (*s.a.* 1453): 'E del mese poi di novembre la Repubblica trasferì il dominio della città di Caffa e dell' altre città, e terre che possedeva nel mar maggiore . . . in l'Ufficio di S. Giorgio.'

[2] The text of the act is printed by P. M. Vigna, in the *Atti della Società Ligure*, VI, 32–43; our quotation refers to p. 33: 'capham, soldaiam, samastram, symbolum aliasque urbes ac terras quas excelsum comune Janue ditione tenet in diversis regionibus ponti.' In the special chapter on the Bank of St George in his history of the Republic of Genoa, F. Donaver does not mention the important fact of the transfer of power over the Genoese colonies to the Bank, F. Donaver, *La storia della Repubblica di Genova*, II (Genoa, 1913), 27–33.

[3] 'Serie dei capitani della Gozia,' *Atti della Società Ligure*, VII, ii (1879), 983–986. For an erroneous statement as to the identification of Theodoro with Inkerman, *ibid.*, pp. 981–982.

[4] *Ibid.*, p. 983.

you shall hold and accept him as *capitanus* of Gothia and yield him this office, even if it has been sold to or conferred on somebody else.'[1]   The last words suggest that the office was put up to auction.   On 10 April 1461 Francesco de Mari was elected from among many competitors; the credentials nominating him *capitanus* of Gothia for two years and two months were handed to him on 27 May; he succeeded Girolamo Gherardi.[2] On 28 September 1463 Anfreone Cattaneo (Anfreonus Cataneus) was elected; the patent, for thirteen months only, was delivered to him as Mari's successor on 21 October.[3]   Cristoforo de Franchi-Sacco (Christoferus de Francis Saccus), elected on 19 February 1466 with a patent dated 23 May for twenty-six months, governed Gothia in 1466–1467.[4] Manfredo Promontorio (Manfredus de Prementorio), elected 16 February 1467, with a patent dated 26 May for twenty-six months, governed in 1467–1468.[5]   In 1470–1471 the *capitanus* was Desserino Canneto (Dexerinus de Caneto), elected for twenty-six months 3 July 1470, with a patent dated 14 August.[6]   The *capitanus* of Gothia in 1471–1472 was Giorgio Lazzarini.   Lazzarini had come from Caffa to Genoa with important messages, making the long journey at his own expense, without any subsidy from the government.   To reward his zeal the Protectors of the Bank on 26 October 1470 nominated him *capitanus* of Gothia for twenty-six months, so that he might take office just after the expiration of the term of his predecessor, Desserino Canneto; his patent was issued 15 January 1471.[7]   By a special decree of the Protectors, Nicolò Maffei was declared *capitanus* of Gothia 14 February 1472 and his patent issued 18 February, on condition that he should arrive in Caffa within eight months and not leave Caffa or the other Genoese colonies of the Black Sea, including Pera, until the time of entering on his office should arrive.[8] Maffei's successor should have been Lazzaro Calvi, elected 1 June 1472;[9] but between that date and 11 May 1473, Lazzaro changed his mind and

---

[1] *Ibid.*, p. 983: 'Mandamus vobis omnibus *etc.* quatenus statim visis presentibus eundem Jeronimum in capitaneum et pro capitaneo Gotie habeatis recipiatis *etc.* sibique resignari faciatis dictum officium visis presentibus, non obstante quod alii fuisset venditum vel collatum.'   [2] *Ibid.*

[3] *Ibid.*, pp. 983–984.   [4] *Ibid.*, p. 984.

[5] *Ibid.*, p. 984.   [6] *Ibid.*, p. 984.   Cf. Desserino Canneto in 1454.

[7] *Ibid.*, p. 985: '(Lazzarini venuto da Caffa, latore d'importanti messaggi), sine ullo mercede, et propriis sumptibus tam longum iter (avea divorato).   (Il perchè i Protettori), intelligentes equum et conveniens esse aliqualiter sibi tanti laboris retributionem facere, (il 26 ottobre 1470 lo nominarono capitano della Gozia per mesi ventisei), incipiendis statim finito tempore pro quo id officium ultimate collatum fuit Dexerino de Canneto.'

[8] *Ibid.*, p. 985: 'non discedendo ex Capha vel aliis locis Maris Majoris, Pera comprehensa, donec advenit tempus, quo exercere debebit dictum officium.'   See Doc. MX, in the *Atti della Società Ligure*, VII, i, 839; also Doc. MXI, 840.

[9] *Ibid.*, p. 985.   Doc. MXIX, in the *Atti*, VII, i, 851: 'ad capitaneatum Gotie pro mensibus viginti sex Lazarum Calvum q.Joh.'

declared that for legitimate cause he could not take office; he asked to be replaced by his own brother, Antonio Calvi. Complying with this request, the Protectors appointed Antonio and on 18 May 1473 signed his credentials for twenty-six months.[1] The last *capitanus* of Gothia was Gianagostino Cattaneo, in 1474–1475. Owing to the penury of our documentation for the year 1474 we do not know when he was nominated the act of the regular assembly for the election of all Crimean officials for this year being lacking. His credentials are dated 10 September 1474.[2] As we shall see later, in 1475 the Genoese possessions in the Crimea and Gothia proper were conquered by the Turks.

Thus in 1453, under the imminent Turkish danger, the Genoese colonies in the Crimea were handed over to the Bank of St George, which became responsible for their administration and safety. For the first time after the fall of Constantinople, the Turkish danger made itself felt in 1454. Under the new political circumstances the general situation in the Crimea changed. Caffa regarded the Prince of Theodoro as her most important ally against the Turks, the more so since the Tartar Khan proved friendly to the Turkish Sultan, supported him in his military undertakings against the Crimea, and threatened Caffa from the north. The Prince of Gothia was forced to arrange his policy according to the new correlation of political forces and under the Turkish menace to hold the balance as best he could between the Genoese and the Tartars.

Not only Caffa realized the importance of friendly relations with the Prince of Gothia; the Turkish Sultan, also, realized their value for his own aggressive policy against the Crimea. Genoa with its commercial and political significance throughout the Black Sea, including Pera, was in those regions the chief enemy of Muhammed II, and he was eager to harm Caffa not only politically but also economically. In an official report of the Consul of Caffa to the Protectors dated 11 September 1454, we read that wares from Turkey to the Crimea were carried not, as usual, to Caffa, but to Calamita, which as we have seen above had been constructed by Alexis of Gothia and potentially might become an economic rival to Caffa.[3] But apparently the prince of Gothia did not side with Muhammed II, for the latter's military aggressions in the Crimea were not limited to Caffa and its dependencies but also included Gothia.

---

[1] *Ibid.*, pp. 985–986: 'se propter legittimas causas accedere non posse . . . subrogari loco ejus Antonium Calvum, fratrem suum.'

[2] *Ibid.*, p. 986. See Alb. M. Condioti, *Historia de la institución consular en la antigüedad y en la edad Media*, I (Madrid, Berlin, Buenos-Aires, Mexico, 1925), 546–547 (on Genoese consuls in Gothia, the Statute of 1449, and the *capitani* of Gothia).

[3] *Atti*, VI, 111: '(quae) ex Turchia veniunt ad Calamitam conducuntur.' For the construction of Calamita by Alexis see above.

On 14 July 1454 a Turkish fleet attacked Caffa. The Tartar Khan, Hadji-Girei, was acting against Caffa in alliance with the admiral of the Turkish fleet. This time Caffa was not taken, but before the siege was raised undertook to pay an annual tribute to the Turkish Sultan.[1] In view of the Turkish menace Caffa did her best to reach a satisfactory agreement with Hadji-Girei and the Prince of Gothia for common defense, but without result, because as we know Hadji-Girei fought on the Turkish side.[2] The day after the conclusion of the agreement with Caffa the Turkish vessels left that harbor and sailed westwards to the shores of Gothia, which at that time was unprepared for war. Without meeting any resistance the Turkish vessels mercilessly devastated the Gothic coast and then returned to Constantinople.[3] The common danger temporarily connected Gothia with Caffa, so that in the same year, 1454, the Prince of Theodoro, Olobei, aware through a Turkish spy of the Turkish plans against Caffa, immediately notified her authorities of the danger.[4]

But on the border between these two powers friction was felt from time to time. In May 1455 the consul of Soldaia (Sudak), Carlo Cicala, reporting to the Protectors on the situation of his city, wrote as follows: 'A few days ago I wrote to two sons of the late Alexis, our neighbors, concerning some of their subjects who had maltreated the people of Soldaia, persuading the princes to punish them and henceforth to live peaceably; in this respect they will always find me well disposed.'[5] As we have noted above, this document gives us the very interesting information that in 1455 Alexis' two sons were ruling in Gothia; one of them, as we know, was Olobei. At the same time some of the Genoese in the Crimea cher-

---

[1] For a detailed relation of the siege of Caffa by the Turks in 1454 and the imposition of annua tribute, consult the report of the officials of Caffa to the Protectors of the Bank, in the *Atti della Società Ligure*, vi (1868), 102–112 (Doc. xxxiii). See M. Volkov, 'Four Years of the City of Caffa (1453, 1454, 1455, and 1456),' *Zapiski* of the Odessa Society of History and Antiquities, viii (1872), 109–144 (in Russian); Heyd, *op. cit.*, ii, 382–383; Braun, *Die letzten Schicksale*, p. 30; N. Iorga, *Studiĭ istorice asupra Chiliei și Cetăţiĭ-Albe* (Bucarest, 1900), p. 114.

[2] *Atti*, vi, 102–103 (11 September 1454): 'Propter quod omnino oportebat cum Agicharei Tartarorum imperatore intelligentiam prehabere nec non cum . . . Gotie domino, et ut hoca dipisceremur varijs diversisque semitis id tentavimus obtinere.'

[3] *Atti*, vi, 104: '[After the siege of Caffa] demum sequenti die versus Gotiam navigantes venerunt, ubi plura in maximum illarum dedecus dampna intulerunt, cum nullam fecerint obstaculi . . . sionem, deinde Constantinopoli navigarunt.' Heyd, *op. cit.*, ii, 383; Iorga, *Studiĭ*, p. 114.

[4] *Atti*, vi, 113 (Doc. 11 September 1454): 'Percepimus ex pluribus avisationibus et presertim ex litteris Olobei de Lothedoro, qui in adventu cujusdam fuste Theucrorum ad terras suas modum habuit secreto retinere quendam Theucrum qui Theucrorum dispositionem sibi confessus est.'

[5] Doc. cxix (14 May 1455): 'Ego vero hiis proximis diebus aliquas litteras scripsi duobus ex filijs q. Alexij nobis vicinis pro aliquibus eorum subditis non se bene habentibus cum hominibus istius loci, eos hortando ut illos corrigant et quod de cetero velint pacifice vivere. Ad quod me semper bene dispositum invenient,' *Atti*, vi, 304.

ished the idea of the annexation of the Princedom of Theodoro. In the same year, 1455, the Genoese authorities were occupied in putting in order the castles and fortifications of St George and St Nicholas at Cembalo (Balaklava).[1] In this year also, Olobei, or, as he is called in the document, 'Olobei, the Greek of Theodoro,' with the authorities of Caffa gave Hadji-Girei a present, which, if I understand the text correctly, cost 31,000 aspers.[2] This fact may be explained by the new situation in the Crimea after the fall of Constantinople, when both Olobei and Caffa, outwardly forgetting their former rivalry and enmity, became particularly interested in drawing the Crimean Khan to their side in view of his tendency to act with Muhammed II.

In the same year, 1455, an engineer, Giovanni Piccinino (Johannes Piceninus), notifying the Protectors of the fortification of Caffa and asking for the reward promised him, mentioned the possibility of taking the castle of Theodoro, and added that, if the Protectors would entrust the authorities of Caffa with a body of a hundred men and one galley which Piccinino might command on an expedition to Cembalo, he would without doubt conquer the whole of Gothia for the Genoese.[3] But this rather adventurous suggestion found no favor with the Protectors, who realized that in view of the Turkish danger to the Genoese colonies in the Crimea the Prince of Theodoro was too important an element to be ignored or irritated. In this year (1455) a present was sent by Caffa to Olobei.[4] Therefore on 27 November 1456, the Protectors of the Bank of St George sent a very flattering letter to the Prince of Theodoro, Olobei, as their 'most beloved brother,' who 'in his mind and disposition might be called a Genoese citizen.' They expressed their trust in God that strong forces of all Christians, on sea as well as on land, might soon

---

[1] See Doc. xcvii (28 January 1455), *Atti*, vi, 279–280. For information about fortifications in Cembalo see also Chapters lxxxi–lxxxv in the Statute of 1449 (*De ordine Cimbaldi*), *Atti*, vii, ii (1879), 661–668; Yurguevich, pp. 783–796.

[2] N. Bănescu, 'Vechi legături ale tărilor noastre cu Genovezii,' in the *Inchinare lui N. Iorga* (Cluj, 1931), p. 35: 'Novene datte Agutaree [Hadji-Girei], Imperatori Tartarorum, de acordio in Tedoro Olobei Greci per s. d. Damianum de Leone massarium, etc. pro anno elapso de 1455, tempore consulatus magnifici d. Tome de Domoculta debet pro Teodorcha de Telicha Velacho asperos 31,000' (Doc. 15 June 1455). On Theodorca de Telicha see *ibid.*, p. 34. The first word of the text, *novena*, means presents in grain, barley, etc. See Iorga, *Notes et extraits*, i, 38 and n. 4.

[3] Doc. cliii (6 September 1455): Per piu siade sono comparsudo davanti a meser lo consolo e massari offeriandomi che cum pocha provixione de homini di prendere lo castello de lo Thedoro, fin a chi non me acurdaito le orege. Perchè vi conforto che voatili dare balia ai supradicti meser lo consolo e massari che me volin dare saltem homini centum chi me accompagnan cum la galea fin alo Cembalo, che non o dubii che cum mia arte lo dicto castello prendero, e se mi sera daito li dicti homini centum, non dubito che tuta la Gotia serebe soto la segnoria vostra,' *Atti*, vi, 370. See Vasiliu, *op. cit.*, p. 327; Malitzki, *op. cit.*, p. 41.

[4] 'Exenum factum per dominum Olobei dominum Thodori,' Bănescu, 'Contribution . . . ,' *Byz. Zeitschrift*, xxxv (1935), 35, n. 1; he refers to Mass. Caffe 1455, fol. 55ᵛ.

be ready against the enemies of Christ, and that Caffa and Theodoro might be reinstated in their former security. 'If we can do anything for the profit of Your Magnificence,' the Protectors conclude, 'we shall always be eager and ready.'[1] In connection with this letter, the Protectors wrote also to the consul and *massari* of Caffa (27 and 29 November 1456): 'As we understand that the favorable attitude of the magnificent prince of Theodoro towards your efforts is of the greatest importance, we are writing a letter to him which you will find in this message; and we suggest that you deliver it to the prince of Theodoro or keep it [yourself], according to your judgment based on consideration of the general situation. But we suggest that you strive to be on friendly and peaceful terms with the prince of Theodoro, because in the opinion of all the experienced men of Caffa at this time his friendship is most useful to this city.'[2] From these documents we learn that the Protectors of the Bank of St George regarded very highly the support and friendship of the Prince of Gothia, and reflected the hope of European states of that time for the organization of a general crusade against the Turks. In this year Olobei dispatched Phocas, a Greek, as ambassador to Caffa, where he was entertained by the Caffian authorities.[3] In the same year (1456) the Pope ordered his legate in Hungary, Cardinal Carvajal, to support the Genoese colonies. The Pope accorded subsidies to Caffa, and the Prince of Theodoro, Olobei, approved of this action.[4] In 1457 two envoys of Olobei, Caraihibi and Bicsi, appeared in Caffa and were entertained there.[5]

Although the Protectors realized the importance of friendship with the Prince of Theodoro, they were not pleased to discover that he had learned

---

[1] Doc. cccxii (27 November 1456): 'Magnifico et potenti domino Olobei, Tedori domino . . . tanquam fratri nostro dilectissimo . . . Confidimus in Domino quod intra breve tempus parabuntur contra hostes nominis christiani tam validi exercitus omnium christianorum maritimi ac terrestres, ex quibus civitas nostra Caphe ac magnificentia vestra pristinam securitatem recuperabunt. Si quid autem est aut erit in quo possimus pro commodis vestre magnificentie laborare, inveniemur semper cupidissimi parati,' *Atti*, vi, 655–656. See Braun, *Die letzten Schicksale*, p. 33; Vasiliu, *op. cit.*, p. 328.

[2] Doc. cccxiv (27 and 29 November 1456): 'Quoniam etiam maximi momenti fore intelligimus ut pari modo magnificus dominus Tedori conatibus vestris faveat. Scribimus si litteras quarum exemplum inclusum invenietis, monentes vos ut ipsi domino Tedori eas litteras vel presentetis vel retineatis prout prudentie vestre consyderatis rerum ac temporum condictionibus utilius judicaverint. Illud etiam vos monemus ut studeatis cum eodem Tedori domino amice pacificeque vos habere. Quin omnium peritorum rerum caphensium judicio ejus amicitia hoc tempore illi civitati utillissima est,' *Atti*, vi, 660. See M. Volkov, 'Four Years of the City of Caffa (1453, 1454, 1455, and 1456),' *Zapiski* of the Odessa Society of History and Antiquities, viii (1872), 144 (in Russian).

[3] 'Expense facte pro Focha greco de Theodoro misso parte Olobei domini Teodori,' Bănescu, *op. cit.*, 35, n. 1, with reference to Mass. Caffe 1456, fol. 41ʳ.

[4] See N. Iorga, *Studiĭ istorice* (Bucarest, 1900), p. 119.

[5] Bănescu, *op. cit.*, 35, n. 1; 'pro alapha Caraihibi de lo Tedoro misso per Olobei dominum Thedori' (Mass. Caffe 1457, fol. 69ᵛ); 'pro Bicsi Noncio Olobi d(omini) Theodori' (Mass. Caffe 1457, fol. 75ʳ).

of some secret instructions given to the authorities of Caffa.   On 8 February 1458, the Protectors wrote: 'As we have learned that the prince of Theodoro had information about some paragraphs in the instructions given your predecessors, we urge you to take great pains that this ignominy may not befall you.   You must keep all your deliberations absolutely secret, so that no one may get any knowledge of them, or even form any plausible conjecture.'[1]   In the same document we have a very important statement about the commercial relations of Caffa and other places subject to Genoa, the weakness of Caffa, and the tremendous power of the Turkish Sultan.   There were in the basin of the Black Sea four potentates who were trading actively with Caffa and its Crimean dependencies: the Emperor of the Tartars, the Emperor of Trebizond, the Prince of Theodoro with his brothers, and the Prince of Moncastro.[2] Taking into consideration the Turkish danger, the Protectors urgently recommended Caffa by any means to live in peace with all these powers and to avoid 'any discords and scandals,' because Caffa at that time was considerably weakened and in view of the tremendous power of the Sultan it would be extremely dangerous to have a conflict with even one of the countries mentioned.[3]   The Protectors then express the point of view mentioned above, that the Prince of Theodoro and his brothers were wrongfully occupying Gothia which really belonged to Caffa; and that 'against the rights and privileges of Caffa' they were building a port in Calamita and there loading and unloading vessels, which considerably decreased the taxes paid to Caffa.   'If matters in Caffa,' the Protectors conclude, 'seem to you so prosperous that you may by force or com-

---

[1] Doc. ccclxxvii (8 February 1458): 'quoniam significatum nobis est dominum Tedori habuisse notitiam de quibusdam articulis appositis in instructionibus precessorum vestrorum, oneramus vos diligenter animadvertatis ne ejusmodi dedecus vobis accidere possit. Immo omnia consilia vestra adeo secreta intra vos retineatis, ut de eis non modo aliquis ullam notitiam habere non possit, sed etiam ullam conjecturam veram concipere nequeat,' *Atti*, vi, 811.

[2] Moncastro, the ancient Greek colony Tyras, now Akkerman, at the mouth of the Dniester.   At this time the fortress was under the power of the prince of Moldavia, Stephen the Great, whose second wife was, as we shall note later, Maria, a princess of Mankup.   In Roumanian Moncastro is Cetatea-Albă (Civitas Alba; cf. the Turkish name Akkerman, *ak* meaning *white*).   Roumanian scholars, especially N. Iorga, have cast new light on the rather obscure history of Moncastro in the fifteenth century.   See also G. Brătianu, *Recherches sur Vicina et Cetatea Albă* (Bucarest, 1935), pp. 119–126.

[3] 'Ut scitis, sunt in illo mari pontico he quatuor dominationes, videlicet imperator Tartarorum, imperator Trapezundarum, dominus Tedori et fratres ejus, ac dominus sive communitas Mocastri, quarum dominationum subditi magnum commercium habent cum Caphensibus et reliquis populis ditioni nostre subjectis.   Propter quod salvis iis que singillatim de eis inferius dicemus, volumus ac vos majorem in modum oneramus ut omnibus artibus ac formis studeatis cum ipsis omnibus pacifice vivere, omnesque discordiarum et scandalorum occasiones cum eis devitare.   Quemadmodum enim intelligitis Caphensis civitas haud mediocriter attenuata est, et propter tremendam potentiam domini regis Turchorum nimis periculosum esset hoc tempore cum aliqua dictarum dominationum armis certare,' *Atti*, vi, 815; Iorga, *Studii*, p. 121; Virginie Vasiliu, *op. cit.*, p. 302.

promise stop this damage, it seems to us suitable that you try the way which is more fitting from your point of view. But if circumstances suggest that you should rather conceal your feelings without encroaching upon our rights, we leave this also to your discretion.'[1]

In all likelihood, Olobei's rule ended in 1458, because after this year his name does not occur in Genoese documents; for several years our sources say 'dominus Tedori et fratres ejus' without particularizing the chief ruler. In a cipher (*alphabetum ziffratum*) sent by the Protectors to Caffa on 24 March 1458 Olobei, *dominus Thedori*, is characterized as *dubius*, the Turkish Sultan as *acer*, the Emperor of Trebizond as *discors*, and the Tartar Khan as *timor*.[2] If Olobei really ceased to rule in 1458, we do not know the name of the chief ruler of Gothia until 1471.

From a document of 7 November 1465 we learn that Gothia dealt in slaves. A certain Michael Bals, probably a Wallachian, owed 700 aspers for two slaves, a man and a woman, from Gothia.[3]

7. The Fall of Caffa (June 1475) and of Maritime Gothia

Meanwhile the Turks were progressing in their conquests of various Christian centers. In 1456 Muhammed conquered Athens from the Franks; shortly after all Greece with the Peloponnesus submitted to him. In 1461 Trebizond, capital of the once independent Empire which had been closely connected, politically and economically, with the Crimea, passed into the hands of the Turks. When in 1467 the Protectors of the Bank of St George reiterated their urgent suggestion to the authorities of Caffa to live in peace and concord with various dominions of the Black Sea, they specified the Emperor of the Tartars, the Prince of Theodoro, and 'all other dominions of the Pontic Sea.'[4] Trebizond of course was

---

[1] 'Idem dicimus quantum respicit dominum Tedori et fratres ejus qui indebite occupant Gotiam ad urbem Caphe pertinentem, contraque jura et privilegia Caphe portum in Calamita publice fieri faciunt, et ibidem navigia onerare et exonerare in gravem jacturam vectigaluum Caphe. Si res Caphenses adeo prospere vobis viderentur ut possetis vel vi vel compositione evitationi ejusmodi damnorum providere, utile nobis videretur eam viam tentare quam commodiorem prudentie vestre judicarent. Si vero conditiones temporum vobis suaderent ut potius dissimularetis sine prejudicio jurium nostrorum, id quoque judicio prudentie vestre relinquimus,' *Atti*, vi, 815–816. See Braun, *Die letzten Schicksale*, p. 34; Vasiliu, *op. cit.*, pp. 328–329.

[2] *Atti della Società Ligure*, vi, between pp. 832–833. See Braun, *Die letzten Schicksale*, p. 34; Malitzki, *op. cit.*, p. 42; Vasiliu, *op. cit.*, p. 328. All speculations by R. Loewe (*Die Reste der Germanen am Schwarzen Meere*, p. 222) on four brothers, the eldest Alexis, the second (Olobey?) who was killed by Muhammed ii, the third Saichos, and the fourth co-regent with him, are to be ignored.

[3] N. Bănescu, *Vechi legături ale tărilor noastre cu Genovezii*, p. 34 and note 2: 'Michael Balsi Ungarus debet pro consteo unius sclavi et sclave Goticorum emptis per ipsum — asperos 700.' On the meaning of *Ungarus* in the sense of 'a Roman from Ungro-Vlachia' or 'a Wallachian (Velachus)' see *ibid.*, p. 33.

[4] Doc. dcclxxvi (16 June 1467): 'Circa receptionem fratris imperatoris, de quo scribitis, et intelligentiam habitam cum domino Tedori, nihil aliud dicendum videtur nisi quod nos generaliter semper

not mentioned.   At that time the new Crimean Khan Mengli-Girei(about 1469–1474) opened a policy of friendly understanding with Caffa, which could not last long because most of the influential Tartar magnates sympathized with Muhammed II.   In 1470 in their new instructions to the authorities of Caffa the Protectors give their approval to the measures taken by Caffa to conclude agreements and treaties with the Emperor of the Tartars, who in this document is called the Emperor of the Scythes, and with the Prince of Theodoro.   For this purpose the brother of the Emperor of the Tartars had even come to Caffa.[1]   No doubt one of the conditions of the treaty made with the Khan of the Tartars was that Caffa should pay him yearly tribute.   In their message of 21 January 1471, the Protectors wrote to the authorities of Caffa: 'We are pleased to know that you sent an embassy to the King of the Tartars with the tribute at the proper time, and we wish you to do this every year.   In addition we approve that you persuade the prince of Gothia to do the same.   And if he has not yet accepted the proposition, he ought finally to accept it because above all we judge it useful that you and he try to live in peace with that king.'[2]   Caffa was forced to accept these humiliating conditions in hopes that the Khan of the Tartars might thus be prevented from acting with the Sultan against the Crimea.   Whether or not the Prince of Gothia also paid annual tribute to the Tartars, I do not know.   But the tribute did not save Caffa.

In 1465 a new prince appears in Gothia whose name is given in both Italian and Russian sources; the Italian documents call him Saichus or Saicus, the Russian Isaïko.   His name of course was Isaac.   He was probably Olobei's son.[3]   In 1465 the Caffian authorities sent a certain Nic-

---

laudamus omnes illas vias ac formas ex quibus civitas illa Caphensis in pace et concordia conservari possit, tam cum dictis domino imperatore et domino Tedori quam etiam cum quibuscumque aliis dominationibus Maris Pontici.   Circa quod iterum atque iterum oneramus vos ita vos contineatis, ut omnino sequatur semper ejusmodi concordie et quietis effectus,' *Atti*, VII, i, 490.

[1] Doc. DCCCCIV (28 April 1470): 'Ex (letteris vestris) cognovimus inter cetera ea que intervenerant circa tractatus et conclusiones compositionum serenissimi domini imperatoris Scitarum et domini Thodori ac fratres ejusdem domini imperatoris in Capham transmissos, que omnia nobis admodum placuerunt et visa sunt prudenter gubernata fuisse,' *ibid.*, p. 674.

[2] Doc. DCCCCXXXV (21 January 1471): 'Placuit nobis quod legationem cum tributo tempore debito miseritis domino regi Turcorum, et sic de cetero per vos singulis annis fieri volumus.   Laudantes insuper quod persuadeatis domino Gotie idem faciat, et si adhuc compositionem non accepisset omnino eam accipere studeat, quoniam super omnia utile judicamus quod vos et ipse cum eodem domino rege pacifice vivere studeatis,' *Atti*, VII, i, 731.   See Vasiliu, *op. cit.*, p. 329.

[3] See V. I. Ogorodnikov, 'Ivan III and the Jews Living out of Russia (Khozya Kokos and Zacharias Gooil-Goorsis),' *Essays Presented to D. A. Korsakov (Mélanges Korsakoff)*, Kazan, 1913, p. 61, n. 1 (in Russian): 'If Isaïko is not the same person as Olobeï, he is probably his son, or a very close relative. We know nothing definite about the personality of Isaïko.'   See also Braun, *Die letzten Schicksale*, p. 41.

colò de Turrilia to Isaac (Saicus), the prince of Theodoro.[1]   In the same
year (1465) another Caffian official (orguxius), Vartabet, apparently of
Armenian origin, was sent to Alushta, Cembalo (Balaklava), and thence
to Calamita (Inkerman), the port of Theodoro.[2]   This shows that under the new prince negotiations between Caffa and Theodoro continued.
We do not know when Isaac began to rule over Gothia, but since he was
probably, as I believe, Olobei's son, he must have succeeded him about
1458, when Olobei died.   On 26 April 1471 the Protectors of the Bank of
St George sent a letter to 'our magnificent and dearest friend, Saichus,
Prince of Theodoro.'   From this letter we learn that Saichus came to
Caffa in person to discuss the very important problem of that period —
the defense of Caffa and Gothia against the Turks.   The Protectors were
very much pleased with Saichus' visit to Caffa, once more emphasized
their conviction that in view of the common danger it was best 'to live
together in sincere and fraternal love and understanding,' and declared
themselves always ready to defend 'His magnificence,' i.e. Saichus.[3]   Apparently in connection with such spirit, in the same year (1471), if I correctly understand the text, two chests of projectiles, which cost the Caffian authorities 400 aspers, were sent for Saichus from Caffa, via Cembalo-
Balaklava, to Calamita.[4]   In the instructions given by the Protectors
to the consul of Caffa, Antonietto Cabella, on 16 June 1472, they urge
him again to live by any means in peace and quiet with the three dominions of the Pontic Sea whose subjects carried on active trade (magnum commercium) with Caffa and other places under its control, i.e. with

---

[1] Bǎnescu, 'Contribution . . . ,' *Byz. Zeitschrift*, xxxv (1935), 35, n. 1: 'pro panibus duobus
zuchari datis Nicolao de Turrilia misso ad dominum Saicum d(ominum) Tedori' (reference to Mass.
Caffe 1465, t. ɪɪ, fol. 71ᵛ).

[2] 'Pro Vartabet orguxio misso ad magnificum dominum consulem usque Cimbalum et de inde
Calamitam Teodori et Lustam,' Bǎnescu, *op. cit.*, 33, n. 2 (with reference to Mass. Caffe 1465, t. ɪ,
fol. 66ᵛ).

[3] Doc. ᴅᴄᴄᴄᴄʟxᴠɪɪ (26 April 1471): 'Magnifico amico nostro carissimo domino Saicho, domino
Tedori etc.   Magnifice amice noster carissime, a noi e molto piaciuto che secondo siamo advisati da
li nostri de Capha, vostra magnificentia se sia transferta personaliter in quella cita et fermato cum
quella nove intelligentie et confederatione per defensione de li stati de tute doe le parte, circa la ob-
servantia de le quale, benche non bizogne, havemo confortato et molto incarrigato li dicti nostri de
Capha et pari modo confortiamo la vostra magnificentia, la quale crediamo intenda che non solamenti
molte altre legitime rasone sed etiam lo respecto de lo timore doveti continuamente haveire et voi et
loro de lo comune inimicho vi debemo tuti persuadeire a vivere insieme cum sincero e fraternale amore
et intelligentia, e cosi confortiamo la vostra magnificentia, per honore e defensione de la quale se
offeriamo semper prompti et apparegiati,' *Atti*, ᴠɪɪ, i, 769.   This letter was sent to Caffa with a document also dated 26 April 1471, giving instructions to the authorities of the city; it contains these
lines: 'Mittimus annexas litteras duas, alteras directas domino imperatori tartarorum, reliquas vero
domino tedori, quas reddi facere poteritis, si eas utiles judicabitis, et non aliter,' *ibid.*, p. 766.

[4] 400 aspers 'pro capsiis duabus veretonorum . . . missis in Cimbalo domini Saicho pro Calamitta
Bǎnescu, *op. cit.*, 33 (with reference to Mass. Caffe 1471, t. ɪ, fol. 157ᵛ).

the Emperor of the Tartars, the Prince of Theodoro and his brothers, and the commune of Moncastro, with whom all discords or scandals should be avoided.[1]   After speaking of the extreme importance of maintaining friendship with the Khan of the Tartars, the Protectors write: 'We wish you to have the same attitude towards the prince of Theodoro and his brothers. You will realize that this prince, contrary to past habit, personally came to Caffa and formed a true friendship with us. We wish you to endeavor not only to keep it in the future but also to do your best to increase it; we hope that on his side he will do his part, because mutual and sincere goodwill between the Capheans and himself will be of no less profit to his magnificence than to us.'[2]

In the cipher (*alphabetum ziffratum*) appended to these instructions and directed to Antonietto Cabella, 'the designated consul of Caffa,' we find that *dominus Tedori*, instead of being called *dubius*, as in the cipher of 24 March 1458 (see above), is characterized as *vigilans*.[3]   To a certain extent the ciphers of 1458 and 1472 well reflect the change in the attitude of the Genoese authorities towards the Prince of Theodoro, who, because of ever-growing danger from the Turks, became extremely important to Caffa.

But in spite of the apparent friendship between Caffa and the Prince of Theodoro, as described in this message, the same document notes that there were in Caffa people who were secretly receiving money from the Emperor of the Tartars and the Prince of Theodoro or his brothers, and for this 'shameful gain' they communicated many things to those rulers 'to the grave injury and ruin of this city; so that forgetting God and their own honor and honesty they betrayed the fatherland.'[4]   A serious investigation should therefore be undertaken and severe punishment inflicted on the traitors.

Isaac was well known not only among his neighbors but even in the far north, at the court of the Grand Prince of Moscow. Isaac's sister

---

[1] Doc. MXXXI (16 June 1472), *Atti*, VII, i, p. 867. Also *Actes et fragments relatifs à l'histoire des Roumains, ressamblés par N. Iorga*, III, part I (Bucarest, 1897), 50. See N. Iorga, 'La politique vénitienne dans les eaux de la Mer Noire,' in the *Bulletin de la section historique de l'Académie Roumaine*, II (1 Oct. 1914, Nos. 2–4), 355 (Antoniotto de Gabella).

[2] 'Pari modo volumus vos habeatis erga dominum Tedori et fratres ejus. Quem dominum invenietis preter consuetudinem superiorum temporum Capham personaliter se transtulisse et cum nostris veram amicitiam contraxisse, quam volumus in dies non solum conservare sed etiam quantum in vobis erit augere studeatis. Quod et ipsum pro parte sua etiam curaturum speramus, quoniam mutua et sincera inter Caphenses et ipsum benivolentia non minorem magnificentie sue quam nostris utilitatem paritura est,' *Atti della Società Ligure*, VII, i, 868.   [3] *Atti*, VII, i, 873; see also n. 1.

[4] 'Verum quoniam significatum nobis est . . . esse preterea nonnullos alios qui provisiones pecuniarias aliquando perceperunt ab ipso imperatore Tartarorum seu domino Tedori vel fratribus ejus, et propter ejusmodi turpem questum multa ipsis dominis significarunt in grave damnum et perniciem illius civitatis, et obliti Dei et proprii honoris et honestatis patriam prodiderunt . . . ,' *ibid.*, p. 868.

Maria married Stephen the Great (1457–1504), a *voevode* (prince) of Moldavia,[1] 'who was to exhibit for nearly half a century exceptional powers of endurance, courage, and political wisdom,' 'one of the greatest princes of his time,' and 'Athlete of Christ,' as Pope Sixtus IV characterized him. At that time he held in his power the castle and port at the mouth of the Dniester, the ancient Maurocastron of the Byzantines, Moncastro of the Genoese, Belgrad of the Slavs, Cetatea Alba of the Roumanians (later Akkerman).[2] Through his marriage with Maria, whose family as we know was related to the Palaeologi and the Comneni of Trebizond, Stephen the Great might have conceived the idea of pretending to the throne of Byzantium if the Turks should be defeated and driven back out of Europe.[3]

Maria's fate in her new home is not without both political and romantic interest. She arrived at the court of Stephen the Great on 4 September 1472,[4] and the marriage was celebrated on 14 September.[5] Maria was

[1] For the English reader who wishes to be acquainted with the significance and activities of Stephen the Great of Moldavia, the best references are N. Iorga, *A History of Roumania*, translated by J. McCabe (London, 1925), pp. 80–94; N. Bănescu, *Historical Survey of the Roumanian People* (Bucarest, 1926), pp. 22–24; R. W. Seton-Watson, *A History of the Roumanians from Roman Times to the Completion of Unity* (Cambridge, 1934), p. 41–49. In Roumanian, the special monograph by N. Iorga, *Istoria lui Ştefan-cel-Mare* (Bucarest, 1904); on Maria of Mankup (Mangup), pp. 138–140.

[2] N. Iorga, *A History*, pp. 80 and 88; Bănescu, *op. cit.*, pp. 22.

[3] O. Tafrali, *Le trésor byzantin et roumain du Monastère de Poutna* (Paris, 1925), p. 54.

[4] Ureche, *Letopiseţul tării Moldovei până la Aron Vodă* (1359–1595), ed. G. Giurescu (Bucarest, 1916), p. 52: 'In 6980 [=1472], September 4, Stephen the Voevode [Prince] brought Maria of Magop [*sic*] in order to take her to wife' (in Roumanian). Gregory Ureche wrote one of the oldest Moldavian chronicles; he lived during the reign of Basil Lupu (1634–1653) and translated into Roumanian with critical discussions the contents of the ancient Slavonic annals. Not having at Madison the Roumanian editions of Ureche and Şincai, I asked Professor N. Bănescu of the University of Cluj (in Roumania) to send me the passages in which I am interested; I express here my cordial gratitude to him.

[5] *Vechile cronice moldovensci până la Urechia, Texte slave cu studiu, traduceri şi note de Joan Bogdan* (Bucarest, 1891), p. 146 (A Brief Tale of the Moldavian Princes; in old Slavonic): 'In the year 6980 [=1472], the voevode Stephen took to wife Maria, a princess of Mangova,' p. 176 (*Cronica moldopolona;* in Polish): 'Anno Domini 6980 [=1472], Septembris 14, wziąt z Mangopa; czarstwo tam bylo z Przekopskim czarzem krzescianscy.' A Roumanian translation of these two passages on pp. 195 and 225–226.   In this edition the year 6980 is reckoned as 1471 of our era, K. W. Wojcicki, *Bibljoteka staroźytna pisarzy polskich*, VI (Warsaw, 1844), 56 (*Spisanie Kroniki o ziemi Woloskiej, także o Hospodarach*): 'A Dni 6980 septembris 14 wziąt sobie Steffan Wojewoda żonę Maryą Zmangopo [of course=z Mangopu — from Mangup], Czarstwo tam bylo z Przekopskim Czarem Krześciańcsy.' Przekopsci Czar — the Perekopian Tsar — is the Tartar Tsar. Professor K. Chyliński of Lwów (Poland) calls my attention to the fact that in Polish the word *carstwo* (*tsarstwo*) signifies 'a kingdom,' 'a kingly couple,' or 'a kingly family'; as in our text the adjective *krześciańscy* is plural, he believes that *carstwo* means here 'a kingly couple' or 'family,' so that the translation of this text runs as follows: 'The Voevode Stephen took to wife Maria from Mangup; there was a princely Christian family under the Tartar emperor.' The last words correctly represent the principality of Theodoro as a vassal state under the protection of the Crimean Khan. N. Iorga accepts 14 September (1472) as the date of Stephen's wedding, N. Iorga, *Istoria lui Ştefan-cel-Mare* (Bucarest, 1904), pp. 138–139. See also N. Bănescu, 'Contribution . . . ,' *Byz. Zeitschrift*, XXXV (1935), 22.

Stephen's second wife. In a recently published source Maria of Mankup is called a Circassian.[1] Her Circassian origin is nowhere else mentioned and at first glance this reference seems completely obscure. If I am not mistaken we have no information whatever so far on the relations of the principality of Gothia with the Caucasian peoples to whom the Circassians belong. But I will try to show how this allusion may have appeared. We have a very interesting letter dated 12 August 1482 addressed by Zachariah, prince of Matrega (Taman, in old Russian sources Tmutarakan), to the Protectors of the Bank of St George. In it he tells how, after the taking of his castle Matrega by the Turks in 1482, he decided to leave his country for Genoa by land, and how during his journey the Veovode Stephan robbed him and let him go 'almost naked' so that he could not continue his journey. He writes that the Gothic princes ('signori Gotici') who sought refuge at Matrega so ruined him that he was forced to ask the Protectors of the Bank to send him a thousand gold coins (ducats).[2] Zachariah of Matrega (Taman) is well known in Russian documents of that time, because the Russian Grand Prince Ivan III Vasilyevich (1462–1505) several times asked him to come to Moscow and stay there. In the letters from the Russian Grand Prince, Zachariah, who of course should be identified with Zacharias de Guizolfi Prince of Matrega mentioned in Genoese documents, is usually called a Jew; but on one occasion he is referred to as 'Zachariah the Circassian.'[3] I shall set aside here the question of the identity of Zachariah the Jew and Zachariah de Guizolfi, a theory some scholars refute, as well as the question of his rôle in the history of the heresy of the Judaizers under Ivan III in Russia;[4] I wish

---

[1] *Kronika czasów Stefana Wielkiego Moldawskiego*, ed. Olgierd Górka (Kraków, 1931), p. 97 (*s.a.* 6979): 'In dem selbygen jar in dem menet Septembry an dem 14 tag bracht man dem Stephan voyvoda dye furstyn auss Maйgop [*sic!*] myt dem namen Marya; sy was ein Zerkassin und hat 2 tochter myt yr.' The editor of the *Chronicle*, the Polish scholar Olgierd Górka, discovered its manuscript in Munich; this is now the oldest Roumanian chronicle we have, or to be more precise, a partial German version embracing the period from 1457 to 1499. According to the Chronicle, Maria was a Circassian and had two daughters. I am greatly indebted to my old friend, Professor K. Chyliński, of Lwów (Poland), who called my attention to this chronicle and sent me the necessary text.

[2] *Atti della Società Ligure*, IV, cclvii: 'in quelo locho sono stato derobato de lo segnor Stefano Vaivoda yta et taliter che vegandome cossì nudo no avi deliberacione de seguire lo mio viagio . . questi signori gotici continue me mangiano . . .' Cf. the message of the Jew Zachariah of Taman to the Russian Grand Prince Ivan Vasilyevich, in 1487–1488, where Zacharias writes, 'On my journey the Voevode Stepan robbed me and tortured me almost to the end [death], and then let me go naked' (in Russian), in the *Sbornik* of the Imperial Russian Historical Society, XLI (St Petersburg, 1884), 72.

[3] *Sbornik*, XLI, 114: 'Zachariah Cherkasin'; see also p. 309 (April, 1500): 'Zachariah is called the Fryazin [=Italian, Frank], and lived in Cherkasy.'

[4] On this subject see J. Brutzkus, 'Zachariah, Prince of Taman,' *Evreyskaya Starina*, X (Leningrad, 1918), 132–143; on the Gothic princes at Matrega, p. 140 (in Russian; earlier literature is indicated in this article); G. Vernadsky, 'The Heresy of the Judaizers and Ivan III,' SPECULUM, VIII (1933), 436–454 (on Zachariah of Matrega, pp. 450–451). See also V. Ogorodnikov, 'Ivan III and the Jews Living Abroad, II, Zachariah — Gooil — Goorsis,' in the *Essays presented to D. A. Korsakov* (*Mélanges Korsakoff*), Kazan, 1913, pp. 64–67 (in Russian).

only to emphasize the fact that in our literary tradition 'the Gothic princes' took refuge at Matrega, the prince of which is sometimes called 'a Circassian.' In my opinion this tradition is not very reliable; it is hardly to be supposed that the Gothic princes mentioned in the Genoese document written in 1482 were Princes of Theodoro or Crimean Gothia, unless they were Princes of Gothia under the Turkish power, of whose existence we know, and had fled to Matrega before it was taken by the Turks in 1482.[1] I have noted this tradition only in the hope that it may show why in the excerpt quoted above Maria of Mankup was called 'a Circassian.'

Maria's new home in Moldavia proved inhospitable to her, and her marriage was unhappy. After the fall of Caffa and Theodoro-Mankup which were taken by the Turks in 1475, Stephen lost hope of gaining the Princedom of Theodoro. Soon after his marriage he abandoned Maria, and fell in love with another Maria, Maria-Voichita, daughter of Radu the Handsome (Radoul cel Froumos), a prince of Wallachia (1462–1474).[2] The unfortunate Maria of Mankup died on 19 December 1477, and was buried in the monastery of Putna.[3] The inscription on her tomb runs as follows: 'In the year 6985 on December 19 there breathed her last the pious servant of God, Maria, spouse of the pious Stephen the Voevode, the reigning prince of Moldavia, son of Bogdan the Voevode.'[4] After her death Stephen married Maria-Voichita, who became his third wife.[5] The magnificent pall from Maria's tomb has been preserved in the Roumanian monastery Putna, where she was buried. The pall is of red silk now faded to brick color, and is adorned with fine embroideries of silk thread; it has a portrait of the princess arrayed in a ceremonial blue-grey

---

[1] See *Excursus*, at the end of this book.

[2] G. Şincai, *Cronica Românilor*, II, 91: '(Under the year 1473) au luat pre Doamna Radului Vodă, şi pre Voichita, fata lui, au luat-o şie Doamna, că-i murise Doamna ce au avut.' G. Şincai lived in the eighteenth century; his statement is erroneous, because in 1473 Maria of Mankup was still alive.

[3] Ureche, *Letopiseţul*, ed. Giurescu, p. 64 (under the year 6985); Şincai, *Cronica Românilor*, II, 111; he erroneously states that Maria of Mankup succeeded Maria-Voichita; also p. 203 (the same confusion). *Vechile cronice moldovenesci până la Urechia* (Bucarest, 1891), p. 146 (in old Slavonic); p. 196 (Roumanian translation); p. 261, n. 35. Tafrali refers Maria's death to 19 December 1476, O. Tafrali, *Le trésor byzantin et roumain du Monastère du Poutna* (Paris, 1925), pp. 54, 64. In his earlier popular article 'Maria of Mangup and the Pall of the Monastery of Putna,' which appeared in a periodical of Bucarest, *Viitorul*, 26 December 1923, Tafrali gives the same year (1476) and remarks at the close of his article: '(Maria died) in 1476, and not in 1477, as certain historians have asserted.' I am greatly indebted to Professor O. Tafrali, who was so kind as to send me a French translation of his article. Iorga, *Istoria lui Ştefan-cel-Mare*, p. 189 (1477); A. Xenopol, *Istoria Romînilor*, IV (Jassy, 1896), 109–110 (1477); V. Vasiliu, *op. cit.*, p. 331, n. 3.

[4] N. Iorga, *Viaţă femeilor in trecutul românesc* (Vălenii-de-Munte, 1910), p. 15; also in Tafrali's writings.

[5] N. Iorga, *Istoria lui Ştefan-cel-Mare*, p. 202. Ph. Bruun confounds the two Marias when he says that in 1476 Stephen the Great of Moldavia married 'Maria de Magop,' Ph. Bruun, *Notices historiques*, p. 93.

garment very similar to the costume of Helen, wife of the Byzantine Emperor Manuel II, represented in a miniature of an illuminated manuscript of Dionysius the Areopagite which is now preserved in the Louvre in Paris. At the two extremities of the pall is the monogram of the Palaeologi.[1]

Towards the close of the fifteenth century relations between Stephen of Moldavia and Isaac of Theodoro grew very hostile. On 10 January 1475, Stephen won a brilliant victory over the Turks, who suffered a complete defeat and lost the greater part of their troops. Elated, he decided to begin a new policy in the Crimea; and soon after the battle, at the end of January, through his envoy opened interesting negotiations with the Genoese authorities in Caffa. He proposed to make peace with the Genoese and pay 1300 Venetian ducats for all damages inflicted by him upon them on condition that Caffa should support him in his aggressive policy against the Tartar Khan and Isaac, Prince of Theodoro and Gothia. This meant a defensive and offensive alliance against two forces in the Peninsula whose friendship was exceedingly important to the Genoese in view of the Turkish danger, and Caffa declined Stephen's overtures.[2]

As has been noted above, the name of Maria's brother, Isaac, was known at the court of the far-off Grand Prince of Russia, Ivan III Vasilyevich (John III), who ruled from 1462 to 1505. He opened negotiations with Isaac (Isaicus). In 1472 or 1473 a Jew of Caffa, Khozya Kokos (Kokos Jidovin), in the Jewish form (*Jidovskim pismom*) wrote a message to Moscow asking if Ivan III wished to marry his sixteen-year old son to the princess of Mankup. The Grand Prince was pleased to accept this plan. At that time active and important relations existed between Ivan III and the Tartar Khan, Mengli-Girei. In the spring of 1474 the

---

[1] For the description of the pall and Maria's costume see O. Tafrali, *op. cit.*, pp. 51–52; *Idem*, 'Le trésor byzantin et roumain du Monastère de Poutna,' in the *Comptes Rendus de l'Académie des inscriptions et belles-lettres* (1923), p. 370; N. Iorga, 'Une source négligée de la prise de Constantinople,' in the *Bulletin de la section historique de l'Académie Roumaine*, XIII (Bucarest, 1927), 68 and n. 4; *Idem*, 'Les grandes familles byzantines et l'idée byzantine en Roumanie,' *ibid.*, XVIII (1931), 2; G. Brătianu, *Recherches sur le commerce génois dans la Mer Noire au XIIIe siècle* (Paris, 1929), p. 204. The miniature of the manuscript of Dionysius the Areopagite has been often reproduced. Some references are given in my *History of the Byzantine Empire*, II (Madison, 1929), 273, n. 18; the latest reproduction in my *Histoire de l'Empire Byzantin*, II (Paris, 1932), between pp. 322–323.

[2] *Atti della Società Ligure*, VII, ii, 195 (Doc. MCXVII, 10 February 1475): 'Dictus voivoda missit his superioribus diebus huc oratorem suum ad componendam pacem nobiscum, offerens se de omnibus damnis per ipsum contra nostros illatis restituere ducatos MCCC venetos. Quos acceptare noluimus, quia requirebat devenire ad dictam pacem sub conditionibus, ex quibus opus esset nos restare inimicos domini regis teucrorum ac domini Saici domini Theodori et Gottie.' I believe that this proposal was made by Stephen after the Turkish defeat on 10 January, because this letter written on 10 February says that Stephen's envoy had come to Caffa only a few days before this date ('his superioribus diebus'). Miss Vasiliu believes that Stephen's proposal preceded his victory on 10 January (Vasiliu, *op. cit.*, p. 333).

boyar (noble) Nikita Vasilyevich Beklemishev was ordered by Ivan III, on his way to Baghchesarai, the residence of the Khan in the Crimea, to pay a visit to Mankup and call on Isaicus. It is to be supposed that the latter had already been properly informed by Khozya Kokos of the proposed match. Beklemishev visited Isaicus, who extended his friendship to the Grand Prince and professed his wish to carry out the marriage. We read in a Russian document, 'My *boyar* Mikita (i.e., Nikita Beklemishev) visited Prince Isaicus and saw the girl.' In the spring of the following year, 1475, Ivan III sent another ambassador to the Khan, the *boyar* Aleksei (Alexis) Ivanovich Starkov, giving him instructions, a special 'note to Oleksei (i.e., Alexis Starkov) of the Mankup affair.' According to these instructions Starkov was to go first to Caffa to visit the Jew Kokos and tell him, 'I have presents from my master, the Grand Prince, to Prince Isaicus, and in addition I have to tell him something. Go with me to Isaicus.' The Jew Khozya Kokos was to be interpreter and intermediary between Isaicus and Starkov. According to the same instructions, 'when Oleksei (Starkov) sees Prince Isaicus, he shall give the Prince and his Princess (i.e. wife) the Grand Prince's greetings, deliver the Grand Prince's presents to them as well as to their daughter, and inquire after their health. Then Oleksei shall tell Prince Isaicus from the Grand Prince: "My master, the Grand Prince Ivan Vasilyevich, notifies you: our *boyar* Mikita (Beklemishev) told us that you offered us your friendship and that on our account you had honored him, and we express our gratitude to you for this and your friendship".' Kokos was instructed by Starkov in the name of the Grand Prince to speak as follows to Prince Isaicus: 'You sent me your message saying that you having a daughter asked me to honor you and take your daughter as wife to my son. My other *boyar* Mikita (Beklemishev) visited you and saw the girl. And you said to my *boyar* Mikita that you wished that I might honor you and marry your daughter to my son.' Starkov was further instructed to notify the Grand Prince how many thousand gold coins was the dowry of the girl. He was also to draw up a list [of the items of the dowry] and send it to Ivan.[1] But these negotiations broke off abruptly[2]

---

[1] The instructions of Ivan III to Beklemishev and Starkov are published in the *Sbornik* of the Imperial Russian Historical Society, XLI (St Petersburg, 1884), under the title *Documents (Pamiatniki) of Diplomatic Relations of the State of Moscow with the Crimean and Nogai Hordes and Turkey*, I, 1–9, 12–13. The instructions to Beklemishev are dated March, 1474, and those to Starkov 23 March 1475. On the Jew Kokos (*Kokos Jidovin*), p. 50. See also A. Malinovski, 'Historical and Diplomatic Collection (Sobraniye) of Affairs between the Russian Grand Princes and the Tartar Tsars in the Crimea, from 1462 to 1533,' *Zapiski* of the Odessa Society of History and Antiquities, v (1863), 184–187. V. Ogorodnikov, 'Ivan III and the Jews Living out of Russia (Khozya Kokos and Zacharias Gooil-Goorsis),' in the *Essays Presented to D. A. Korsakov (Mélanges Korsakoff)*, Kazan, 1913, pp. 59–62; N. M. Karamzin, *A History of the Russian State*, 2nd ed., VI (St Petersburg, 1819), 87–89, and

because Isaicus died in the same year, 1475, as Starkov's and Kokos' visit. In 1475 Isaicus, whose friendly policy towards the Turks[1] probably aroused discontent among his subjects, was overthrown by his own brother Alexander, who at that time with his sister Maria, the second wife of Stephen the Great, was living at Moncastro. An Italian vessel took Alexander on board in Moncastro and brought him to Gothia.[2] Evidently Stephen the Great played a very important rôle in Alexander's undertaking, because the Hungarian ambassadors at his court in their report to their king, Matthew Corvinus, dated June, 1475 state that 'some time before that the Voevode Stephen had sent Alexander, his wife's own brother, to the Principality which is called Mango,' i.e. Mankup.[3] This proves once more that through his marriage to Maria of Mankup Stephen the Great had ambitious plans of exercising exceptional influence on Gothia and finally perhaps even of taking possession of the Crimean Principality.

Alexander was very successful in his expedition. On the third day after he had landed in the Crimea, he overthrew and killed his own brother Isaicus and took possession of Mankup, his 'paternal heritage.'[4]

---

n. 125 (pp. 40–41). Karamzin used the manuscript of these documents from the Archives of the Foreign College in Moscow, *Crimean Affairs*. All these books in Russian. Köppen, *Krymsky Sbornik* (St Petersburg, 1837), pp. 96–97, 282–283 (in Russian); Ph. Bruun, *Notices historiques*, pp. 72–73, 93; *idem*, in his review of an Italian publication *Atlante idrografico del medio evo*, ed. C. Desimoni and L. Belgrano, in the *Zapiski* of the Odessa Society, VIII (1872), 296 (in Russian); Braun, *Die letzten Schicksale*, p. 35. See also the Russian edition of my essay, 'The Goths in the Crimea,' in the *Izvestiya* of the Russian Academy for the History of Material Culture, I (1921), 50–51 (pagination of an offprint); in this English edition, above, pp. 48–49; G. Vernadsky, 'The Heresy of the Judaizers and Ivan III,' SPECULUM, VIII (1933), 449–450.

² On Starkov's embassy see the recent article by N. L. Ernst, 'Ivan III's Conflict with Genoese Caffa,' *Izvestiya* of the Tauric Society of History, Archaeology, and Ethnography, I (Simferopol, 1927), 167 ff.; Malitzki, *Notes on the Epigraphy of Mangup*, pp. 42–43.

¹ See Iorga, *Studiĭ istorice*, p. 142: 'prietinul Turcilor,' i.e., 'a friend of the Turks.'

² From a letter of Stephen the Great to his own envoys to King Matthew Corvinus of Hungary (20 June 1475): 'aplicuit ad Albam (i.e. Moncastro) una navis Italorum de Pangopa (i.e. Mankup), illa navis, que aportaverat compatrem nostrum Alexandrum,' *Monumenta Hungariae Historica, Acta extera*, VI = *Magyar Diplomacziai Emlékek, Mátyás Király korából (1458–1490)*, IV (Budapest, 1878), *Toldalék* (Supplement), 308 (Doc. 13); *Atti della Società Ligure*, VII, ii, 479 (Doc. XXI).

³ 'Quomodo preteritis diebus ipse Vajvoda Stefanus misisset Alexandrum fratrem carnalem consortis sue in Regnum, quod dicitur Mango,' *Mon. Hung. Hist.*, ibid., p. 306 (Doc. 12); *Atti*, VII, ii, 477 (Doc. XX). The document is dated: 'die Domenica post festum nativitatis Beati Joannis Baptiste.'

⁴ 'et solus nuntius naravit nobis ore proprio, narando nobis sic, quod frater Dominationis uxoris mei, Alexander venit ad locum ... et die tertia lucratus est dictum locum Mangop hereditatem paternam et. ... ipse pronunc in Mangop et non est aliter,' *Mon. Hung. Hist.*, ibid., p. 308 (Doc. 13). *Atti*, vol. VII, ii, 479 (Doc. XXI). The printed text of this letter of Stephen quoted above is rather incomplete. See also Spandugino, *op. cit.*, in Sathas, *Bibliotheca Graeca Medii aevi*, IX, 155: 'vedendo Mehemeth che il principe di Gothia [i.e. Alexander] havea amazzato il suo fratel maggiore [i.e. Isaicus] et usurpatosi lo stato.' On Isaicus' violent death see Iorga, *Studiĭ*, p. 142: 'ucigênd pe propriul sĕŭ frate, Isac'; O. Tafrali, *Le trésor byzantin et roumain du Monastère de Poutna* (Paris, 1925), p. 54.

According to the report quoted above of the Hungarian ambassadors at the court of Moldavia in Moncastro to Matthew Corvinus, 'he energetically took this (principality) and brought all the *majores et minores* in the principality of Mango under his power.'[1] The violent death of Isaicus and the occupation of Gothia by Alexander took place before the fall of Caffa, which was captured by the Turks on 6 June 1475, that is, early in the spring of this year.

In 1474, with the Turkish danger impending, Caffa once more was very anxious to live at peace with the Princes of Gothia. Two official documents dated in this year describe some damage done to Gothic landowners and farmers, stealing of cattle and horses or burning of buildings in the border district of Alushta and Cembalo (Balaklava). The Princes of Gothia presented a formal complaint to the Genoese authorities who were afraid lest such 'scandals' might involve Caffa in war with the princes of Gothia.[2]

In 1472 Mankup is mentioned in a very different connection, and this mention has not yet been satisfactorily clarified. In the train of Sophia Palaeologina, the niece of the last Emperor of Constantinople, who in 1472 was brought to Moscow and married to the Russian Grand Prince Ivan (John) III Vasilyevich, was a certain Constantine. According to a Russian hagiographic source, he was from Italy, from Amoriya, of a princely family of the city of Mavnuk ('Mavnukskago grada'). In Russia Constantine took refuge in the cowl, received the name of Cassian, and retired to the Therapontov monastery; later he build his own monastery on the banks of the river of Uchma and there ended his days. He died, a very old man, on 2 October 1506.[3] This monastery stood until 1764. In the nineteenth century, when Bruun wrote his essays, there were two stone churches on the site of the former monastery; close to the

---

[1] 'quomodo . . . illud (Regnum) potentia sua . . . soliciter optinuisset et universos majores et minores in illo Regno Mango dominio suo subegisset,' *Monum. Hung. Hist., ibid.*, p. 306 (Doc. xii); *Atti*, vii, ii, 477 (Doc. xx). Malitzki, (*op. cit.*, p. 43) remarks that it is not known 'whether Alexander was Isaac's son or his nephew.' Alexander was neither Isaac's son nor his nephew, but his brother. Miss Vasiliu says that according to Moldavian sources Alexander can be none other than Olobei's son (*op. cit.*, p. 331).

[2] *Atti*, vii, ii, 412 (Doc. 19 August 1474): 'Si furta fiunt per illos gottos equorum et bestiarum tartarorum.' *Ibid.*, p. 319 (Doc. probably of the same year): 'Noviter presumpserunt comburi facere certas mandrias domini Iuste in maximum ejus dampnum et villipendium dominorum Gotie. . . . Ex quibus dubitandum est ne orientur scandala que possent nos facere intrare in guerram cum dictis dominis Gotie.' These two documents when mentioning Gothia and its prince always say 'domini Gotie,' i.e., in the plural.

[3] See Philaret, *The Russian Saints*, 2nd ed., Section iii (Kiev, 1861–1865), p. 188; D. M. Strukov, *The Holy Constantine, Prince of Mangup, in the Cowl Cassian* (St Petersburg, 1874); Bruun, *Chernomorye*, ii, 230; I. Brilliantov, *The Therapontov Belozerski Monastery* (St Petersburg, 1891), pp. 55–60 (in this book a bibliography is given). All four books in Russian. A very brief statement on Constantine-Cassian in Le P. Pierling, *La Russie et le Saint-Siège*, i (Paris, 1896), 161.

door of one of them, on an outer wall, was a plate with a relief representing a two-headed eagle with drooping wings, without a crown; this eagle
recalls the escutcheon of Prince Alexis of Gothia which we find engraved
on the slabs bearing the inscriptions of 1425 and 1427 which we have discussed above.[1] It is almost certain that in the name Mavnuk we may
recognize Mankup, so that Constantine (Cassian), who accompanied
Sophia to Moscow, may have been a close relative of Olobei, Isaac,
Alexander, and Maria. I believe Bruun was right is supposing that
Constantine was of the family of the Princes of Mangup (Mankup) in
the Crimea. According to Bruun, Constantine in his youth may have
been sent to Constantinople and after the capture of that city by the
Turks may have sought refuge in Italy like the last Emperor's brother
Thomas Palaeologus, Sophia's father, Despot of Morea (*Amoriya*).[2] Finally, a Prince of Mankup might reasonably have been deemed worthy of
the honor of accompanying the daughter of the Despot of Morea to Russia, partly for the reason that some members of his family were there
already. For in 1391 or 1403 as we have noted above, a Greek prince,
Stepan Vasilyevich Khovra (Khomra or Komra), who possessed the
cities of Sudak, Mangup, and Balaklava, had left the Crimea for
Moscow, where he became the founder of the well-known Russian family
of Golovini.[3]

Meanwhile events in the Crimea were developing very rapidly. Discord arose between the Crimean Tartars and their Khan Mengli-Girei.
He was forced to take refuge in Caffa, where the Genoese were ready to
support him. The Tartars appealed to Muhammed II, who wanted
nothing better than a pretext for intervention; he had long been anxious
to get hold of the Crimea and now had an excellent excuse for interfering.
On 31 May 1475 a strong Turkish fleet under the command of the Grand
Vizier, Kedyk-Akhmet Pasha, appeared before Caffa; on 1 June, the
troops were landed, and after five days of siege the city opened its gates
and surrendered (on 6 June). According to an official report, 'the terrible
dragon,' i.e., the Sultan, ordered five hundred Genoese and 'other Latin
families to migrate to Constantinople.'[4] By the fall of Caffa the destiny
of all Genoese possessions in the Crimea was sealed.[5]

---

[1] See Bruun, *Chernomorye*, II, 231–232.

[2] Thomas Palaeologus reached Rome on 7 March 1461, D. Zakythinos, *Le Despotat Grec de Morée*,
I (Paris, 1932), 288.   [3] On Stepan Vasilyevich see above.

[4] 'Quingentas Januensium et aliorum latinorum familias Capha Constantinopolim migrare jussit
truculentus drago,' *Atti*, VII, ii, 488, Doc. XXV, 'A Report of the Rector and the Council of Ragusa to
the Doge of Venice, Pietro Mocenigo, February 18, 1476.'

[5] A detailed account of the fall of Caffa was written by an eyewitness in Constantinople, where he
was sent from Caffa with other captives. It is published by M. G. Canale, *Della Crimea: del suo
commercio e dei suoi dominatori*, III (Genoa, 1856), 346–354; the manuscript of this account is to be

Shortly after, in the same year, 1475, Soldaia-Sudak, a flourishing city of Maritime Gothia, which as we know belonged to the Genoese after the treaties of 1381 and 1387, was also taken by the Turkish fleet after a heroic defence by the inhabitants. Before turning to our chief source on the fall of Soldaia, Martin Bronevski, who wrote in the second half of the sixteenth century, I wish to give here a few words of the report of a contemporary, Jörg of Nuremberg, whose statement has never been used. In his *History of Turkey* he writes: '[In 1475 after the taking of Caffa the Turk] marched and won the castle Sodoya, where three sons of the King of the Tartars were taken; he released them and made the eldest son King in Tartary.'[1] As has been said, our chief evidence on the fall of Soldaia comes from the description of *Tartaria* by the ambassador of the Polish-Lithuanian King Stephen Batory (1576–1586), Martin Bronevski, to the Crimean Khan, Muhammed-Girei. Bronevski was in the Crimea in 1578–1579 and visited Soldaia. There he met a Greek Metropolitan, 'an honest man,' who had come to the Crimea from the Greek islands to visit the local clergy, evidently by the order of the Patriarch. The Metropolitan offered Bronevski hospitality, and Bronevski accepted his invitation and stayed with him. The Metropolitan told Bronevski the pathetic story of the fall of Soldaia. After a strong Turkish fleet had arrived and

---

found at Florence, in the *Archivi di Corte e Stato di Firenze*, in the *Carte Strozziane*, Filza 304, 1–25. A report of the Hungarian ambassadors to Matthew Corvinus, in the *Atti*, VII, ii, 477–478. A very interesting report of 'Praepositi Ecclesiae Albensis annunciantis amissam esse Caffam,' in L. de Hurmuzaki, *Documente privatóre in Istoria Românilor*, II, i (Bucarest, 1891), 12–13 (Doc. xv, 1475). 'Lettera di Laudivio de Nobili di Vezzano sulla caduta di Caffa,' ed. A. Neri, *Giornale Ligustico*, II (Genoa, 1875), 137–153; the text of the letter on pp. 144–146. Also Ag. Giustiniani, *Annali della Repubblica di Genova*, 3rd ed., II (Genoa, 1854), 472–479. See J. W. Zinkeisen, *Geschichte des osmanischen Reiches in Europa*, II (Gotha, 1854), 385–387 (he quotes Laudivius Vezanensis' *Letter*, p. 385, n. 3); Ph. Bruun, *Notices historiques*, pp. 71–72; W. Heyd, *Histoire du commerce du Levant*, II, 402–404; V. Smirnov, *The Crimean Khanate under the Power of the Ottoman Porte to the Beginning of the Eighteenth Century* (St Petersburg, 1887), pp. 275–276 (in Russian); Braun, *Die letzten Schicksale*, pp. 35–36; N. Iorga, *Studiĭ istorice asupra Chiliĭ şi Cetăţiĭ-Albe* (Bucarest, 1900), p. 142. Xenopol incorrectly says that Caffa was taken in July, A. Xenopol, *Istoria Românilor*, IV (Jassy, 1896), 110. F. Donaver writes that the Turks occupied Caffa on 24 August, F. Donaver, *La storia della Repubblica di Genova*, II (Genoa, 1913), 97; L. Kolli, 'The Fall of Caffa,' *Izvestiya* of the Tauric Learned Archive Commission, LV (1918), 145–174 (unfinished because of the author's death; in Russian). The Russian chronicles also mention the fall of Caffa, *Simeonovskaya Lietopis*, under the year 6983–6984 (1475), in the *Complete Collection of Russian Chronicles*, XVIII (1913), 250: 'In the same year the Turkish Sultan sent an army on ships (korablyakh) and vessels (katergakh) against Caffa; and they came and took it in the month of June' (in old Russian). Also *Stepennaya Kniga*, *ibid.*, XXI (1908), 580. The *Stepennaya Kniga* is the *Rank Book of the Tsar Genealogy* compiled in the sixties of the sixteenth century. See P. Vasenko, *The Kniga Stepennaya of the Tsar Genealogy and Its Significance in Old Russian Historical Literature*, I (St Petersburg, 1904).

[1] Jörg of Nuremberg, *Geschichte von der Türkey* (Memmingen, *s.d.*), fol. 6ʳ.: 'Darnach zog er (der Turck) und gewan das slos Sodoya darin gefangen waren drey son des Tartarischenskonigs [*sic*], die erlost er und mact den eltesten son zu einem Konig in Tartaria.' This edition came out before 1496. On Jörg of Nuremberg see below.

the infantry had landed, the Turks saw that Soldaia was energetically and stubbornly defended by the Genoese; but as a result of the long siege and famine, being unable to hold out, several hundreds, or as the Metropolitan asserted, a thousand choice men retreated into a big church, which is still standing, in the lower fortress and sold dearly their lives. The Turks burst into the fortress where the Genoese made a desperate resistance and inflicted severe losses on them. Then the Turks blocked the doors and windows of the church where the Genoese had found their last refuge, so that all of them perished there and the Turks left their bodies in the church unburied. According to the Metropolitan's story, the bodies of the dead Genoese were still in his time lying within the church. Bronevski was not allowed to enter.[1]

After the fall of Caffa Stephen the Great at once felt immediate danger to his own country. In his letter of 20 June 1475, he mentioned the allied actions of the Crimean Tartars with the Turks, and expressed the opinion that the Turks were then 'proceeding against us and our country by sea and by land.'[2] In a letter dated June, 1475, the ambassadors of the King of Hungary, Matthew Corvinus, to Stephen the Great report also that the Voevode Stephen realizing imminent danger, through his *boyars* (nobles), asked the ambassadors to hand the letter over to Matthew Corvinus as soon as possible; in this letter Stephen begged the King of Hungary to turn his attention to Stephen's menaced country, hoping that if Corvinus moved to support him the Turkish Sultan would less readily take the field against Moldavia and Hungary.[3]

---

[1] *Martini Broniovii Tartariae descriptio* (Cologne, 1595), p. 10: 'A Metropolita quodam viro Graeco et honesto, qui ex insulis Graecis ad visitandos presbyteros illos tum eo advenerat et hospitio me exceperat accepi. Quod cum immanissima gens Turcarum eam civitatem ingenti maritimo exercitu oppugnasset, a Genuensibus fortiter et animose illa defenderetur, verum cum obsidionem diuturnam ac famem Genuenses diutius ferre, nec impetum tam numerosi exercitus Turcarum sustinere amplius possent, in maximum templum illud, quod adhuc ibi integrum est, centeni aliquot, vel, ut ille asserebat, mille fere viri egregii sese receperunt, et per dies aliquot in arce inferiori, in quam Turcae irruperant, fortiter et animose sese defendentes, insigni et memorabili Turcarum strage edita tandem in templo illo universi concidere, templi illius portae et fenestrae a Turcis muro impletae caesorum cadavera in eum usque diem insepulta jacent. In id templum ne accederem, a Caphensi Seniaco quondam Turca, quem in ea arce perpetuum ille habet, ego prohibitus sum.' A Russian translation by J. Shershenevich with notes by J. Murzakevich in the *Zapiski* of the Odessa Society, vi (1867), 347. See also V. Vasilievski, *Works*, iii (Petrograd, 1915), ccv–ccvi (in Russian).

[2] 'Et de Turcis ita sciatis . . . ipsi Turci prevaluerunt et expugnaverunt Caffam . . . uniti sunt Tartari cum Turcis . . . percipimus . . . quod veniunt ad nos contra nos et contra terram nostram et per aquam et per terram,' etc., *Mon. Hung. Hist., ibid.*, p. 308 (Doc. xiii); *Atti*, vii, ii, 479 (Doc. xxi).

[3] 'ipse Stefanus Vajvoda intelligit sibi iminere periculum, petit nos medio horum Bujoronum Suorum, quatenus literas nostras ad Majestatem Vestram velocissime daremus, ut Majestas Vestra dignaretur convertere faces suas ad partes Regni sui inferiores, et in dies festinaret discedendo. Quoniam sperat idem Vajvoda, quod postquam Majestas Vestra moverit se, Turcus ipse non ita facile proficiscetur vel contra Regnum Moldavie vel Majestatis Vestre,' *Mon. Hung. Hist., ibid.*, p. 307 (Doc. xii); *Atti*, vii, ii, 478 (Doc. xx).

8. The Fall of Theodoro (December 1475)

After the fall of Caffa, Soldaia, and Maritime Gothia in general, came the turn of Mountain Gothia and its capital Theodoro. The fall of this almost impregnable stronghold made a strong impression in various countries, so that our evidence regarding this event both contemporary and subsequent, is much more detailed and substantial than might be expected. Let us glance at the sources for the fall of Theodoro.

Our most reliable contemporary sources are two: the account given by an anonymous witness of the fall of Caffa in his letter mentioned above, and the official report of the Rector (Rettore) and the Council of Ragusa to the Doge of Venice, Pietro Mocenigo 18 February 1476.[1] These give a concise and exact presentation of the taking of Theodoro by the Turks, emphasizing the heroic defense of the stronghold by the local prince and his subjects.

Among Western writers contemporary with the fall of Theodoro who noted this event in their writings is to be mentioned Laudivius da Vezzano, *eques Hierosolimitanus*, quoted above in connection with the fall of Caffa. In his letter on the fall of the latter city he writes as follows: '(After the capture of Caffa the Turk) fought the Goths, who dwell beyond the Danube, in order to take their fortified stronghold; and he brought an army near it. The inhabitants of the city however resisted every day more and more vigorously, so that it was uncertain who would be victorious. Now you know the result of the unlucky war that recently took place in the Tauric Peninsula.'[2]

Another contemporary writer, Jörg (Joerg) of Nuremberg, a German, author of a *History of Turkey* (*Geschichte der Türkey*), is so little known that I wish to devote a few lines to him and his story. As far as I know, no one dealing with the history of Turkey, not even N. Iorga in his recent *History of the Ottoman State* (*Geschichte des Osmanischen Reiches*), has used Jörg of Nuremberg. In 1896, in his book *Die Reste der Germanen am Schwarzen Meere*, R. Loewe first quoted this book and gave Jörg's passage

---

[1] The Anonymus in M. Canale, *Della Crimea*, iii, 354. The report in the *Monumenta Hung. Hist., Acta Extera*, v = *Magyar Diplomacziai Emlékek, Mátyás Király Korából (1458–1490)*, ii (Budapest, 1877), 345–346, and in the *Atti della Società Ligure*, vii, ii, 488–489.

[2] 'Lettera di Laudivio da Vezzano sulla caduta di Caffa,' *Giornale Ligustico*, ii (Genoa, 1875), 146: 'Hinc ad Getas qui trans Danubium incolunt arma convertit, ut arcem eorum munitissimam expugnaret, et jam castra admovit. Huic tamen ab oppidanis in dies acrius resistitur, ut incertum sit, ad quos potius victoria declinet. Habes igitur infelicis belli exitum, quod nuper in Taurica Chersoneso gestum.' Sometimes this letter has been published with the letters of Cardinal Jacopo (Jacob) Piccolomini (1422–1479), the friend of students and scholars, who compiled a continuation of the *Commentarii* of Pope Pius ii. See *Iacobi Piccolomini Epistolae* (Milan, 1521), p. 310 v.; cf. also p. 310r. Therefore some scholars attribute Laudivius' letter to Jacopo Piccolomini; see R. Loewe, *Die Reste der Germanen am Schwarzen Meere* (Halle, 1896), p. 221.

on the fall of Theodoro, which is called by Jörg *Sandtodero* (i.e., Saint Theodoro). Loewe referred to a very old edition, Memmingen, 1496.[1] There is no copy of this book in the United States of America. In 1932 I could find no copy of it in the Bibliothèque Nationale of Paris. From the Catalogue of Printed Books in the British Museum I knew that the Museum possesses a copy in the edition of 1500.[2] Jörg has apparently been ignored and forgotten by all historians interested in the history of Turkey. I then wrote to the best authority in Turcology now in Europe, Professor Franz Babinger of Berlin, asking him to give me more information on Jörg. In two letters he gave me exhaustive information on this subject which I make use of here, and for which I am very happy to express my most cordial gratitude to him.

There are three editions of Jörg's *History of Turkey*. The original text is given in Jörg of Nuremberg, *Geschichte von der Türkey*, printed in Memmingen by Albrecht Kunne without date; the text contains eight sheets and a wood engraving. This edition is very rare and is found in Germany only in Munich (Bayerische Staatsbibliothek) and in Tübingen (Wilhelmsstift). This text was reprinted in the Memmingen edition in 1496, which contains thirty sheets; the much larger size of this edition is explained by the fact that there were added various items which have no reference whatever to Jörg's writing. The third edition came out in Nuremberg (printed by Hans Mair) in 1500; it contains seventy-eight sheets and a wood engraving different from that in the first edition. This edition reproduces the original text, word for word, and contains other data on Turkey the origin of which has not yet been established.

We know of the author's life only what he tells us himself at the beginning of his book. In 1456 he was sent to Stephen, Duke of Bosnia, where he worked casting guns; from his work he was called 'Büchsenmeister' (master gunsmith). In 1460 with his wife and child he was captured by the Turks. The Sultan, learning that Jörg was a 'Büchsenmeister,' spared his life and gave him a good salary to follow his trade. He spent over twenty years in captivity.[3] In 1480 the Sultan sent him

---

[1] R. Loewe, *op. cit.*, pp. 221–222. Jörg of Nuremberg has been mentioned neither in Franz Babinger, 'Die türkischen Studien in Europa bis zum Auftreten Joseph von Hammer-Purgstalls,' in *Die Welt des Islams*, VII (Berlin, 1919), 103–129, nor in the list of Western writers on the Ottoman Empire before 1600, in H. A. Gibbons, *The Foundation of the Ottoman Empire* (New York, 1916), p. 322, nor in W. L. Langer and R. P. Blake, 'The Rise of the Ottoman Turks and Its Historical Background,' *American Historical Review*, XXXVII (1932), 468–505.

[2] British Museum, *Catalogue of Printed Books*, Vol. Joan-John (London, 1889), fol. 90. See L. Hain, *Repertorium bibliographicum in quo libri omnes ab arte typographica inventa usque ad annum M.D. typis expressi*, II, ii (1831), 156 (Nos. *9380, 9381, 9379). *Supplementum to Hain's Repertorium Bibliographicum*, by W. A. Copinger, part I (London, 1895), 277 (No. 9381 with reference to the British Museum).

[3] R. Loewe (*op. cit.*, p. 221) erroneously says that Jörg spent three years in Turkey.

to Alexandria, where he met some Franciscan monks who with some merchants helped him to reach Venice. From this city he went to Pope Sixtus IV and became his 'Büchsenmeister.' Although he stayed many years in Turkey, he gives very little information on his own experiences in this country. His information as far as the history of Turkey is concerned is very brief and, according to Professor Babinger, second-hand. It is unexpectedly strange that Jörg and his *History* have escaped the attention of all specialists in the history of Turkey.

In his history Jörg gives a brief account of the fall of Theodoro. After mentioning the capture of Caffa and Soldaia (Sodoya) by the Turks he relates: 'Afterwards (the Turk) marched to the city with the name of Sandtodero, where there were three kings and fifteen thousand men, young and old; but he could not take it and was compelled to withdraw with loss. Then three months later [the inhabitants of the city] surrendered voluntarily. [The Turk] killed the kings with all the folk.'[1]

There are several West European writers of the sixteenth century who also mention the fact of the fall of Theodoro-Mankup. Matthias of Miechow, a Polish *canonicus* from Krakow, who in 1517 wrote *A Description of Asiatic and European Sarmatias*, mentions that at that time 'the dukes of Mankup who were Goths in their origin and language retained only the fortress of Mankup.' Matthias continues: '[After the capture of Caffa, Muhammed] smote with the sword two dukes and brothers of Mankup, the only survivors of the Gothic race and language, the hope of the continuation of the family of the Goths, and took possession of the fortress of Mankup. Thus the Goths have been completely exterminated, nor does their genealogy appear any longer.'[2] This passage was

---

[1] Jörg of Nuremberg, *Geschichte von der Türkey* (Memmingen, *s.d.*)fol. 6r: 'Darnach zog er fur ein stat mit namen Sandtodero dar inn waren drey konig und xv. tausendt menschen iung und alt, er mocht der mit gewynnen sunder mit schanten must er dar von. Darnach aber drew monat do ergaben sie sich mit willen. Er ertodt die konig mit allem volck.' This text, after the edition of 1496, is also given in R. Loewe, *op. cit.*, pp. 221–222. In January, 1934, Babinger published an article on Jörg in the German newspaper of Zagreb (Agram, in Croatia) *Morgenblatt* (28 January 1934): 'Eine unverwertete Quelle zur bosnischen Geschichte.' In this article Babinger refers to our correspondence. See A. Vasiliev, 'Jörg of Nuremberg, a Writer Contemporaneous with the Fall of Constantinople,' *Byzantion*, x (1935), 205–209.

[2] 'duces de Mankup qui generis et linguae Gothorum fuerunt, dumtaxat castrum Mankup retinentibus . . . (Muhammed) binos quoque duces et fratres de Mankup, unicos Gothici generis ac linguagii superstites ad spem gregis Gothorum prolificandorum, gladio percussit et castrum Mankup possedit. Sicque Gothi penitus . . . extincti sunt, nec eorum genealogia amplius comparet,' *Descriptio Sarmatiarum Asianae et Europianae, auctore Matthia a Miechow, Historiarum Poloniae et Magni Ducatus Lithuaniae Scriptorum . . . Collectio Magna*, ed. Laur. Mizlerus de Kolof, I (Warsaw, 1761), 192. See Tomaschek, *Die Goten in Taurien*, p. 55; Braun, *Die letzten Schicksale*, p. 37; F. Elie de la Primandaie, *Etudes sur le commerce du moyen-âge, Histoire du commerce de la Mer Noire et des colonies génoises de la Krimée* (Paris, 1848), p. 206, n. 3.

used by the famous sixteenth-century scholar Konrad Gesner (1516–1565)
who was born at Zurich, in his book *Mithridates*.[1]

Theodore Spandugino, 'Constantinopolitan patrician,' who has been
mentioned above as our earliest evidence on independent Gothia, was
born about 1453, in all likelihood not in Greece but in Italy, probably in
Rome. By nobility of birth, by his diplomatic and military talents, by
his ardent patriotism, and especially by his profound knowledge of oriental affairs, he became well known at various European courts, where he
was highly esteemed. He lived in Venice, France, Rome, and Constantinople. Mastering the Turkish language, he used the early Ottoman
chronicles and the late Byzantine chronicles which have not come down
to us. The year of his death is unknown; after 1538 we lose track of
him. There are three versions of his book on the Ottoman Sultans, of
which the third, edited by C. Sathas, is most important. Spandugino,
who wrote in Italian, entitled his history or memoirs *On the origin of the
Ottoman Emperors, Their Court Ceremonial, the Form of Their Warfare,
Their Religion, Rites, and the Customs of the Nation*, and dedicated the
book to Henry, Dauphin of France.[2] His report on the fall of Theodoro
follows: 'Then seeing that the prince of Gothia had killed his elder brother
and usurped the state, Muhammed sent his *biglierbei*, i.e., one of the
governors-general, and the latter besieged the prince who surrendered to
him on condition that property and lives should be spared. But Muhammed bringing him to Constantinople ordered him to be beheaded,
saying to him, "The pledge which my officer promised to you, let him
keep it." And [Muhammed] made his little son become a Turk, whom
I saw still alive, when I was last in Constantinople.'[3]

In 1578, as we know, Martin Bronevski (Broniovius), ambassador

---

[1] 'superfuere et ad aetatem usque nostram duces Gothorum nobilissimi de Mancup, qui castrum
Mancup semper a Tartarorum vi defenderunt, donec Machumet Turcorum Imperator Caffam
expugnavit Tartarosque ac peninsulam suo subjecit imperio; tum et castrum Mancup cepit ac duos
fratres de Mancup gladio percussit, in quibus et tota Gothorum illorum nobilitas cessavit. Gothi
vero qui adhuc in montibus supersunt, ut plurimum vineas colunt, et inde vitam sustentant,' *Mithridates Gesneri, exprimens differentias linguarum, tum veterum, tum quae hodie, per totum terrarum orbem,
in usu sunt, Casper Waserus recensuit et libello commentario illustravit, Editio altera* (Zürich, 1610),
p. 48 r. and v. See Tomaschek, *op. cit.*, p. 56; Braun, *op. cit.*, p. 37. 'Gessner' is the modern form of
'Gesner.'

[2] Theodoro Spandugino, patritio Constantinopolitano, *De la origine deli imperatori Ottomani,
ordini de la corte, forma del guerreggiare loro, religione, rito, et costumi de la natione*, C. Sathas, *Documents inédits relatifs à l'histoire de la Grèce au moyen-âge*, ix (Paris, 1890), 133–261; Spandugino's
biography in the preface, pp. iii–xxxi. Henry, Dauphin of France, was to be King Henry ii
(1547–1559).

[3] Sathas, p. 155: 'Dapoi adunque vedendo Mehemeth che il principe di Gothia havea amazzato
il suo fratel maggiore et usurpatosi lo stato, mandò lo suo biglierbei, civè uno di capitani generali di
terraferma, et assediò detto principe, il quale se li rese d'accordo, salvo tamen ho havere et le persone;
ma conducendolo fino a Costantinopoli, Mehemeth lo fece decapitare, dicendoli: Li patti che lo
mio capitano ti ha promesso lui te li osservi; e fece Turco uno suo figliolo piccolo, elquale viddi
l'ultima volta che io fui a Costantinopoli esser anchora vivo.'

of the King of Poland, Stephen Batory, to the Crimean Khan Muhammed-Girei II (1577–1584), visited Mankup and from an aged Greek
presbyter who was 'not ignorant' ('non rudis') learned the following information. 'Just before the city (Mankup) was besieged by the Turks,
two Greek princes (duces), uncle and nephew, who apparently were
related to the Constantinopolitan or Trepezuntine emperors, resided
there. The Christian Greeks, however, had not inhabited the city for
many years, and, shortly after, this city was snatched by the infidel and
most cruel people of the Turks, after an assurance of impunity had been
granted and violated. Those princes were taken away alive to Constantinople by the most cruel and wicked emperor of the Turks, Selim, one
hundred and ten years ago and cruelly slain.'[1] The Greek presbyter
makes two errors in his report. The Sultan to whom Mankup fell was
Muhammed II, not his grandson Selim I (1512–1520),[2] and one hundred
and ten years before the year in which Bronevski visited Mankup,
1578, would be 1468, while we know that Mankup-Theodoro fell in 1475.

The Greek chroniclers of the fifteenth century concentrated all their
interest on the fundamental fact of the fall of Constantinople, though
they paid some attention also to the Turkish conquest of Greece and Trebizond. The far-off Crimea was of course out of reach of their records.
As far as I know, only one later anonymous Greek chronicler, of the end
of the sixteenth century, who briefly recorded events from 1391 to 1578,
says a few words on the conquest of the Crimea by the Turks, and mentions the names of Caffa, Theodoro, and Gothia. The text of the chronicle runs as follows: 'Soon afterwards [the Turk] marched and took
without any war Caffa, Theodoro, Gothia, and all the country round
about.'[3]

[1] 'Veruntamen a Presbytero quodam Graeco homine jam annoso, probo, et non rudi, quem ibi
vidi, accepi, quod paulo ante civitatis ejus a Turcis obsidionem Duces quidam duo Graeci, quos
Constantinopolitanorum vel Trapezuntii Imperatorum sanguinis fuisse certe apparet, patruus et
nepos ibi mansissent. Graeci vero Christiani non multis tamen annis eam inhabitavere, ac paulo
post ab infideli et immanissima Turcorum gente civitas illa fide eis data et violata erepta fuit. Duces
illi Constantinopolim vivi abducti a crudelissimo et sceleratissimo Turcarum imperatore Selimo ab
annis centum et decem crudeliter contrucidati sunt,' *Martini Broniovii Tartariae Descriptio* (Cologne,
1595), pp. 7–8. A Russian translation by J. Shershenevich, in the *Zapiski* of the Odessa Society of
History and Antiquities, VI (1867), 344 ('patruus et nepos' is wrongly translated 'grandfather and
grandson').

[2] Selim I was related to the Tartar Khan in the Crimea and even took refuge in the Peninsula.
See N. Iorga, *Geschichte des osmanischen Reiches*, II (Gotha, 1909), 310–311. This fact may perhaps
explain to a certain extent the presbyter's mistake. Bronevski himself of course was not familiar
enough with the past history of the Crimea to be able to rectify the error.

[3] 'μετ' οὐ πολὺ δὲ πορευθεὶς ἔλαβε τὸν Καφᾶν, τοὺς Θεοδώρους, τὴν Γοτθίαν καὶ πᾶσαν τὴν περίχωρον ἄνευ
πολέμου τινός,' *Historia politica et patriarchica Constantinopoleos* (Bonn ed., 1849), p. 45. In new
editions of this chronicle instead of 'τὴν περίχωρον' is printed 'πᾶσαν τὴν Περατίαν,' i.e., the oversea
land, 'Ἀνωνύμου Ἔκθεσις χρονική, in Sathas, *Bibliotheca graeca medii aevi*, VII (Paris, 1894), 585;
Ecthesis Chronica, ed. S. Lambros (London, 1902), p. 33 (here instead of 'μετ' ὀλίγον' is printed
the 'μετ' ὀλίγων.'

We have also a group of Turkish sources.   Turcology is not my field, so that my data on Turkish sources will be incomplete and casual.   The question of the so-called early Ottoman chronicles is very debatable and complicated, and, according to F. Babinger, every investigator who deals with the Turkish domination in Europe in the fourteenth and even in the fifteenth century is painfully struck by the complete unreliability of the Ottoman chronicles for this period.   They are full of confusion and contradictions so serious that even the most unbridled imagination can not reconcile them.[1]   Some Turkish chronicles have not yet been published and may be used only in manuscript in various European libraries.

The old anonymous Ottoman chronicles mention the fact of the taking of Caffa and Mankup by the Turks.[2]   Among these is the chronicle of Ashiq-Pasha-Zadé, who was born in 1400 and died soon after 1484.   His historical work describing events up to 1478 was copied by later Turkish historians, especially by Neshri.[3]   Ashiq-Pasha-Zadé relates the taking of Caffa and Mankup; I shall give here his account of the fall of Mankup, which is related to the version of Saʻd ed-Din.[4]   The story runs as follows:

[After the taking of Caffa and some other castles and regions] the Turks proceeded (sailed) and arrived in front of Mankup.   They landed and aimed their guns at the fortress.   The Tekur (= Tekfur, prince) of Mankup saw that those who had conquered the region of Caffa had come against him.   And the Tekur came to Akmet Pasha in order to surrender this fortress.   The Tekur had a rival who was also in this stronghold and who did not want to surrender it.   The latter shut the gates and began to fight.   The fighting lasted long.   The Tekur came near [the fortress] several times and called upon it to surrender; but no one heeded his words.   The [Turkish] warriors endeavored to break in at weak points but realized that they could not take the fortress by force.   [The Turks] added more troops, and Akhmet Pasha arrived himself.   Some days later the troops which were stationed near the fortress, moved; in one place they saw a passage, and many men burst into the interior of the fortress.   When [the in-

---

[1] F. Babinger, 'Byzantinisch-osmanische Grenzstudien,' *Byzantinische Zeitschrift*, xxx (1929–30), 413.   See also W. L. Langer and R. P. Blake, 'The Rise of the Ottoman Turks and Its Historical Background,' *American Historical Review*, xxxvii (1932), 472.

[2] F. Giese, 'Die altosmanischen anonymen Chroniken in Text und Uebersetzung,' *Abhandlungen für die Kunde des Morgenlandes*, xvii, i (Leipzig, 1925), p. 153.   See also N. Iorga, 'Cronicele turzeşti ca izvor pentru istoria Românilor,' in the *Academia Romana, Memoriile secţiunii istorice*, 3rd Series, ix (Bucarest, 1928–1929), 14.   The Turkish text of these chronicles is published by F. Giese (Breslau, 1922).   The chronological end of the chronicles is given differently in various manuscripts, F. Giese, 'Einleitung zu meiner Textausgabe der altosmanischen anonymen Chroniken,' in the *Mitteilungen zur Osmanischen Geschichte*, i (Vienna, 1921), 61.

[3] F. Babinger, *Die Geschichtsschreiber der Osmanen und ihre Werke* (Leipzig, 1927), pp. 35–38.

[4] The Turkish text is published by Friedrich Giese, *Die Altosmanische Chronik des ʻAšik-paša-zāde* (Leipzig, 1929), pp. 177–178.   For the translation of the text I express my cordial thanks to Professor N. Martinovich of New York.

habitants of the city] saw the movement of the Turkish troops, they began to come out of the fortress. And the troops of Islam who were at the passage attacked the infidels from the fortress and drove them back into the fortress. By means of this manoeuvre [the Turks] took possession of Mankup. Then after taking Mankup they treated Mankup in the same way as they had treated Caffa. They took the chiefs of each conquered region and brought them to Stambul, and handed over their treasures to the Sultan; they gave the wives and daughters of the chiefs as presents to the Sultan's officials. Those chiefs were executed. At his own pleasure the Sultan appointed a governor of Mankup. In the name of the Sultans the prayer of Islam was recited [in Mankup]; so that the house of the infidel became the house of Islam. . . . The date of this victory was 880 after the Hegira [1475], and the victory occured by the hand of Akhmet Pasha, a servant of Sultan Muhammed.

I have unfortunately so far been unable to use *The History of Muhammed the Conqueror* by Tursun Beg, who had a personal share in the taking of Constantinople and in the campaign against Belgrad, and who died probably soon after 1499. His *History* deals with the period of Muhammed II and the first six years of the reign of Bayazid II, i.e., it goes down to the year 1487.[1] More than a century ago Hammer-Purgstall, in his *History of the Ottoman Empire*, reported on the taking of Mankup by the Turks and referred to nine Turkish historians whose manuscripts he had used who mention the fact of the fall of Mankup (Menkub).[2] I shall speak briefly of these historians.

1. Mehmed Neshri, who died at Brussa in 1520, wrote a history of the world in six parts; the sixth part only, dealing with the history of the house of Othman, is a contemporary source, reaching the year 1485. For a long time Neshri's *History* was very highly regarded.[3] He strongly affected the whole of later Turkish historical writing, and his name has been often referred to as a source.[4] Neshri himself, as I have noted above, used the chronicle of Ashiq-Pasha-Zadé. As far as I know, the Turkish text of his *History* has not yet been published; copious extracts from it given in German by Th. Nöldeke and P. Wittek do not include the fact of the fall of Mankup.[5]

[1] F. Babinger, *Die Geschichtsschreiber*, pp. 26–27. The Turkish text of Tursun Beg's *History* was published in Constantinople by Mehmed 'Arif Bey in 1914–1916. I am greatly indebted to Professor N. Martinovich, of New York, who called my attention to Tursun Beg's *History*.

[2] J. von Hammer, *Geschichte des osmanischen Reiches*, 2nd ed., I (Pesth, 1834), 525; *idem, Histoire de l'Empire Ottoman*, III (Paris, 1836), 197–198.

[3] Th. Nöldeke, 'Auszüge aus Neśri's Geschichte des osmanischen Hauses,' *Zeitschrift der Morgenländischen Gesellschaft*, XIII (1859), 177: 'Der Werth dieser Geschichte ist höchst bedeutend.'

[4] Babinger, *Die Geschichtsschreiber*, pp. 38–39.

[5] Th. Nöldeke, *op. cit.*, XIII (1859), 176–218, xv, 333–380; Paul Wittek, 'Zum Quellenproblem der ältesten osmanischen Chroniken (mit Auszügen aus Neśrī),' *Mitteilungen zur Osmanischen Geschichte*, I (1921), 77–150.

2. Saʻd ed-Din (1536–1599) lived in Constantinople and was the author of a very famous history of the Ottoman Empire which embraces the period from the origin of the Ottoman house to the death of Sultan Selim I (1520).[1]   Saʻd ed-Din gives a rather detailed relation of the siege and fall of Mankup.   His narrative runs as follows:[2]

The taking of the city of Menkub.   Ahmed Pasha Gheduk had subjugated the whole region of Caffa and Asach (Azov) and then planned to conquer also the region of Menkub; he laid siege to this very strong city and after some fighting destroyed its walls.   The prince (Techiur)[3] was so frightened that he could find neither calm nor rest; and in order to save his own life and that of his family he left the city, immediately went to meet the Pasha, and declared to him his own obedience and homage to the King (Sultan).   But within the city was one of his relatives who was very persistent and obstinate in his purpose and tenaciously held the city.   Therefore the Techiur, who was disgusted and offended, tried to persuade him to give up his tenacious resistance; but whenever the Techiur came to the city and tried to persuade him to surrender, crying and saying to him, 'The end of this obstinacy will be very bad!', the other paid no attention to this, continued the contest, and did not cease to fight and defend the city.   Seeing that it would take a long time to seize the city by force, the Pasha pretended to abandon the city; he departed with the major part of his troops and left a small part of his soldiers for the siege of the city; he went feigning to wish to return home, but he hid his men in an ambush and stayed there waiting for an opportunity.   The defenders of the city seeing that the Pasha had retreated with sad and melancholy countenance, and being confident in the fortress of this city and the strength of their own hands, as well as believing that the expression of his visage which they had seen was true and genuine (in reality being a mere fiction), they despised those who remained for the siege, and went many times out of the city. They began to fight against the besiegers; but when they were fighting against them, the besiegers retreating separated them from the city and pretending to take to flight withdrew them from the city and caught them in a trap.   Then the noble lion-hearted soliders and valorous warriors who had stayed in ambush came out and attacked the unfortunate men with sabers; while they were fighting, the Pasha caught them from behind, cut off their retreat, and struck with sabers those who fled towards the city.   Those valorous warriors, zealous for the honor of the faith, attacked their enemies on all sides with sabers, poured out a rain of a thousand evils, woe to them, upon their heads, making them swim

[1] Babinger, *Die Geschichtsschreiber*, pp. 123–126.   The Turkish text was published in Constantinople (see p. 126).

[2] I am greatly indebted to Professor N. Martinovich, of New York, for the translation of this account from its Turkish original.   See also *Chronica dell'origine e progressi della casa ottomana composta da Saidino Turco, Parte seconda tradotta da Vincenzo Bratutti Raguseo* (Madrid, 1652), pp. 295–297 (an Italian version).

[3] Tekur = Tekfur, i.e., a ruler, tsar, prince.   I believe here Tekur means a brother of Alexander, the last Prince of Mankup.   The episode given by Saʻd ed-Din shows that there was disagreement between the brothers as to the defence of the city.

in a sea of blood and rending the garment of their lives. Thus the defenders of Menkub were defeated and destroyed by the wise stratagem and great valor of the Pasha; and the banners of fidelity were planted and raised on the highest walls and bastions of this city, and the celestial globe was filled with the sound of cymbals of joy and jubilation. With the divine aid, in this war of Caffa, many very strong cities were taken and incorporated in the Ottoman countries; and the faithful soldiers by the grandeur and excellence of the faith enriched themselves with enemy spoils, as is fitting. These acquisitions occurred in the year 880 = 1475.

3. Idris of Bitlis (Bitlisi, in Kurdistan), who died in Constantinople in 1520, was the author of a long history of the Ottoman Empire written in the Persian tongue comprising the period from 1310 to 1506. His work is no doubt an extremely important mine of as yet unexploited information. The original text has not yet been published, and its editing is one of the most urgent problems of Turkish historical study.[1]

4. Mustafa-ben-Ahmed, often called Ali (1541–1599), a very trustworthy and reliable historian, author of more than thirty writings, compiled a detailed Ottoman history from the founding of the Ottoman Empire to the reign of Mehmed III (1595–1603). His history, of which the most important part has not yet been published, is a rich source of historical information.[2]

5. Mehmed Solaqzadé, who died in Constantinople in 1657, wrote a condensed history of the Ottoman Empire which is original only for the period of Murad IV (1623–1640).[3]

6. Abd ul-Aziz, called Qara Chelebi-Zadé (1591–1658), was a very fruitful writer in many different branches. His chief work is a history in four parts entitled *Rawdet ül-ebrar*; it covers the period from the creation to the year 1646; the fourth part only deals with Ottoman history.[4]

7. Husein Hezarfenn, who died in Constantinople in 1691, a highly educated man, wrote a history of the world, including Greece and Rome as well as Byzantium; he was the first Ottoman historian to use Western sources. His history stops at the year 1672.[5]

8. Mustafa ben-'Abdullah, usually known as Hadji Khalfa (Khalifa), often also called Katib Chelebi (1609–1657), was the greatest *polyhistor*[6] among the Ottomans, and his knowledge embraced all branches of the human mind and civilization. In one of his numerous writings, the

---

[1] Babinger, *Geschichtsschreiber*, pp. 45–49.

[2] *Ibid.*, pp. 126–134.   [3] *Ibid.*, pp. 203–204.

[4] *Ibid.*, pp. 204–206. The text *Rawdet ül-ebrar* was published in Bulaq in 1832.

[5] *Ibid.*, pp. 228–230. A detailed table of contents of this history is found in J. von Hammer, *Geschichte des Osmanischen Reiches*, ed. in ten volumes (Pesth, 1827–1835), IX (1833), 184–185.

[6] *Polyhistor* is the name given to learned men acquainted with several different realms of knowledge.

Chronological Tables, written in Persian (introduction and some additions in Turkish), Hadji Khalfa mentions the fall of Mankup.[1]

9. 'Abdullah-Chelebi, called Ridwan Pasha-Zadé, who lived in the seventeenth century, wrote a sort of world history. In addition he compiled a short history of the Crimean Khans.[2]

The names only of these nine Turkish historians were mentioned by Hammer in his *History of the Ottoman Empire*, when he spoke of the fall of Caffa and Mankup.

The Turkish historian Djennebi writes: 'In 1475 [after the taking of Caffa] Kedyk-Akhmet Pasha decided to take possession of the fortress of Mankup. This is a large fortress on the top of a high and barely accessible mountain. The Greeks had taken possession of it and established themselves therein. And Akhmet Pasha mentioned above began this hard task; and he established himself in the fortress and took it.'[3]

The Russian annals (*letopisi*) also mention the fact of the taking of Caffa and Mankup by the Turks and express the hope that the Russians may not endure such harm and cruelty from the Turks as many other Christian countries, among them Caffa and Mankup, have endured.[4]

Let us now on the basis of all this material draw a picture of the fall of Theodoro-Mankup.

After the capture of Caffa, 6 June 1475, the speedy subjugation of Maritime Genoese Gothia, and the establishment of a new order there under the Turkish régime, the Turkish troops, led probably by an infantry general under the supreme command of the Grand Vizier Kedyk-Akhmet Pasha,[5] in the autumn of the same year (1475) entered the territory of the principality of Gothia and drew near Theodoro. According to the report of the Rector and the Council of Ragusa, at that time the

---

[1] *Ibid.*, pp. 195–203. But as far as I know, the two translations of the *Chronological Tables* of Hadji Khalfa fail to mention Mankup. See *Cronologia historica scritta in lingua Turca, Persiana, e Araba, da Hazi Halifé Mustafá*, tradotta nell'Idioma Italiano da Gio. Rinaldo (Venice, 1697), p. 134: 'Da Yedich Ahmet Passà furono espugnate le Città di Caffà, e Assach.' The other translation, in French, has not been published; its manuscript is to be found in the Bibliothèque Nationale of Paris: *Bibl. Nat. Fonds français, no. 5587*. The title follows: *Chronologie Mahometane depuis la création du monde jusques à l'année 1079 de l'Hégire c'est à dire jusques à l'année 1670 de la naissance de Jésus-Christ par Mustapha Hadgi Khalifeh autrement dit Kiatib Zadeh*, traduit par Antoine Galland, p. 147: 'Kedek Ahmed Pascha se rend maistre de Keffè et d'Azak.'   [2] *Ibid.*, pp. 176–177.

[3] V. Smirnov, *The Crimean Khanate under the Domination of the Ottoman Porte up to the Beginning of the Eighteenth Century* (St Petersburg, 1887), p. 281 (in Russian). Smirnov used a manuscript text of this history. The part of Djennebi's narrative concerning the taking of Caffa and Mankup had been previously published by Veliaminov-Zernov, *Izsledovanie o Kasimovskikh Tsariakh*, I (St Petersburg, 1863), 103–105 (original text) and in Russian translation, 100–103.

[4] These Russian annals are published in the *Polnoye Sobraniye Rooskikh Letopisei* (Complete Collection of Russian Annals): *Voskresenskaya*, VIII (1859), 207; *Nikonovskaya*, XII (1901), 202; *Lvovskaya*, XX (1910), 347; *Ermolinskaya*, XXIII (1910), 182; *Tipografskaya*, XXIV (1921), 201.

[5] Spandugino (p. 155): 'mandò lo suo bigliebei, civè uno di capitani generali di terraferma.' Our best source is the report of an anonymous eyewitness in Canale, *Della Crimea*, III, 354.

population of the city of Theodoro and of Gothia in general consisted of thirty thousand 'homes,' i.e. probably families,[1] and the city of Theodoro alone, as Jörg of Nuremberg asserts, contained 15,000 men 'young and old' who lived through the horrors of the Turkish attacks and siege.[2] The stronghold, almost impregnable by its natural location and adequately fortified for the occasion, was defended not only by nature but also by the heroic resistance of Prince Alexander and his three hundred Wallachs (Valacchi).[3] Five attacks on the stronghold by the Turks were of no avail, and the only road which led to the city could not be forced. Then the Pasha decided to blockade Theodoro and cut off the food supply. The siege lasted over three months.[4] Famine began to rage among the congested population of the city. Finally, at the end of December 1475, Theodoro-Mankup, or as the report of the authorities of Ragusa says, 'the community Alexa which in common speech was called Thodoreza (Thodoriza),' surrendered,[5] on condition that the lives of the Prince and his people, as well as their property, should be spared.[6] The pretended departure of the Grand Vizier Kedyk-Akhmet Pasha with the bulk of his army from the city and their ambush, related by Sa'd ed-Din, may have really occurred, and led to the final victory of the Turks.[7] After the fall of Theodoro the Turks occupied the rest of Gothia without difficulty. Of course the late Greek chronicler was wrong in asserting that Caffa, Theodoro, and Gothia were taken by the Turks without resistance.[8]

After the fall of Theodoro-Mankup Sultan Muhammed II appointed a governor there. A prayer for the Sultan was recited in one of the churches converted into a mosque, and, according to a Turkish chronicler, 'the house of the infidel became the house of Islam.'[9]

---

[1] 'Hic comes inter urbem et comitatum suum possidebat, ut ferunt, domos 30 mille,' *Mon. Hung. Hist., Acta extera*, v = *Magyar Diplomacziai Emlékek, Mátyás Király Korából (1458–1490)*, II (Budapest, 1877), 346; *Atti della Società Ligure*, VII, ii, 488.

[2] Jörg of Nuremberg (fol. 6ʳ): 'xv. tausendt menschen iung und alt (in Sandtodero).' See also R. Loewe, *op. cit.*, p. 222.   [3] I shall speak later of these three hundred Wallachs.

[4] Jörg of Nuremberg (fol. 6ʳ): 'Darnach aber drew monat do ergaben sie sich mitwillen.' Loewe, *op. cit.*, p. 222.

[5] 'Decembri vero prope exacto ipsorum turcorum gentes in ipso mari majori devicerunt quandam communitatem Alexam, que urbem natura loci inexpugnabilem et industria munitam habebat, quam vulgo thodorezam (thodorizam) vocant,' *Mon. Hung. Hist., ibid.*, p. 346 ('Thodorizam'). *Atti*, VII, ii, 488 ('thodorezam').

[6] Spandugino (p. 155): 'il quale [the Prince] se li rese d'accordo, salvo tamen ho havere et le persone.' Jörg of Nuremberg (fol. 6ʳ): 'do ergaben sie sich mit willen.' Loewe, *op. cit.*, p. 222.

[7] V. Bratutti, *Chronica dell'origine e progresso della casa ottomana composta da Saidino Turco* (Madrid, 1652), pp. 296–297.

[8] *Historia politica* (Bonn ed., 1849), p. 45; ed. Sathas, in the *Bibliotheca graeca medii aevi*, III, 585; ed. S. Lambros (London, 1902), p. 33. See J. W. Zinkeisen, *Geschichte des osmanischen Reichs in Europa*, II (Gotha, 1854), 387: 'Menkub und Tana ergaben sich ohne Widerstand.'

[9] Fr. Giese, *Die Altosmanische Chronik des 'Ašik-paša-zäde* (Leipzig, 1929), p. 178. See also *idem*, 'Die altosmanischen anonymen Chroniken,' *Abh. für die Kunde des Morgenlandes*, XVII, i (1925), 153.

Our sources for the fall of Theodoro are so reliable that we can be sure that the Prince of Gothia in whose reign Theodoro was taken by the Turks was Alexander, who after killing his elder brother Isaac had taken possession of the principality.   It is important to emphasize this point, because some scholars believe that the last Prince of pre-Turkish Gothia was Isaac.[1]

Apparently after Isaac's violent death and Alexander's establishment in Gothia there were some other brothers alive, or at least one brother. A document of 6 June 1472 mentions 'Dominus Tedori et fratres ejus.' In this year Isaac was ruling over Gothia; in the same year, in September, his sister Maria reached Moldavia from Gothia; and their brother Alexander also went to Moldavia, either with Maria or soon afterwards.   Thus 'fratres ejus' includes certainly one brother of Isaac besides Alexander, possibly two or more.   Mathias of Miechov says that at the time of the siege and taking of Mankup by the Turks there were in the city 'two princes and brothers' ('binos quoque duces et fratres de Mankup').   I believe therefore that it is probable that after Isaac's death there were two brothers in Theodoro, Alexander and another prince whose name is unknown.[2]   Alexander was married and had a son and daughters.[3]

The account of an anonymous eyewitness published by Canale[4] relates that a body of 300 Wallachs was fighting with the prince of Theodoro against the Turks in 1475.   Who were these 300 Wallachs?   Bruun mentions them but gives no explanation of their presence.[5]   Tomaschek calls them 'shepherds' ('Hirten'),[6] a puzzling epithet, and Braun in one pas-

---

[1] 'Alexander, the last prince of pre-Turkish Gothia,' in Heyd, *Histoire du commerce du Levant*, II, 405; Iorga, *Studiĭ*, pp. 142–143; *idem*, *Geschichte des osmanischen Reiches*, II, 175; Tafrali, *Le trésor byzantin et roumain du Monastère de Poutna*, p. 54; Malitzki, *op. cit.*, p. 43; Vasiliu, *op. cit.*, p. 331.   In his note to the document of 6 June 1472, Iorga incorrectly says that at that time Alexander was 'dominus Tedori'; Alexander seized Theodoro in 1475: *Actes et fragments relatifs à l'histoire des Roumains*, III, i, 50, n. 2.   Neither Braun (*Die letzten Schicksale*) nor Loewe (*op. cit.*) mentions the name of Alexander.   Bertier Delagarde believes that Alexander was Isaac's son, not brother ('Kalamita and Theodoro,' p. 19, n. 2).   Many scholars do not know of Alexander and consider Isaac the last Prince of Gothia: Köppen, *Krymsky Sbornik*, pp. 282–283; Braun, *Die letzten Schicksale*, p. 38 (genealogical table) and p. 80; Tomaschek, *Die Goten in Taurien*, p. 54; Ogorodnikov, *Ivan III and the Jews Living Abroad*, p. 62 (in Russian); Kulakovski, *The Past of the Tauris*, 2nd ed., p. 120 (in Russian).   I do not know why Bănescu calls the last prince of Theodoro not Alexander but Alexis: Bănescu, 'Contribution . . . ,' *Byz. Zeitschrift*. XXXV (1935), 22, 33–34.

[2] Jörg of Nuremberg says that there were 'three kings' ('drey konig'; in Loewe, *op. cit.*, p. 222: 'dry künig') when the Turks took Theodoro; I believe these were the two brothers and Alexander's son, who is mentioned in Spandugino (p. 155).   Bronevski gives 'an uncle and a nephew.'   See also Loewe, *op. cit.*, p. 222: 'two brothers and the son of one of them.'

[3] *The Report of the Rector and the Council of Ragusa*, 18 February 1476: 'Captum eum tota familia, et Constantinopolim traductum jugularunt, exceptis uxore et filiabus, quas tyrannus in usum suum, sive in abusum, retinuit,' *Mon. Hung. Hist.*, *Acta extera*, II, 345; *Atti della Società Ligure*, VII, ii, 488. Alexander's son is mentioned in Spandugino (p. 155); see preceding note.

[4] Canale, *Della Crimea*, III, 354.   [5] Ph. Bruun, *Notices historiques*, p. 72.

[6] Tomaschek, *Die Goten in Taurien*, p. 54.

sage quoting Tomaschek also calls them 'Hirten'; but in the addenda to his study Braun writes: 'Are the 300 Wallachs who helped Isaico to defend his residence against the Turks perhaps not shepherds as Tomaschek believes, but the auxiliaries (Hilfstruppen) which Stephen sent Isaico, his father-in-law?'[1] As we know now, when Stephen sent Alexander, his brother-in-law, to Gothia to take possession of the principality and to depose his brother Isaac, he gave him 300 Wallachs as a sort of bodyguard.[2] They fought valiantly in Theodoro against the Turks and probably all perished on the field of battle.

In this connection I shall give some passages from an interesting letter sent in 1475, i.e., the year of the fall of Theodoro, by the King of Hungary, Matthew Corvinus, to one of his nobles, Michael Fancsy. After a severe reproach for infidelity, the King writes: 'By such rumors and troubles you have endeavored to hold back from their obedience to us the Sicilians (Siculos) who were ready to enlist in our service . . . . Therefore we order you on your fidelity and firmly enjoin you if you ever wish to deserve our favor that you go to Stephen, Moldavian Voevode, our faithful and beloved friend, together with 300 Sicilians and assist and support us there sincerely and at the time when he [Stephen] needs help . . . if you fulfil our command and show herein your service to us, we shall not recall your evil deeds any longer but shall receive you into our favor.'[3]

If we compare this document with the anonymous account published by Canale, we may come to very interesting conclusions. Both documents belong to the year 1475, at the close of which Theodoro-Mankup was taken by the Turks; both documents mention a body of troops of 300 men; this detachment is at the disposal of Stephen, who may use it in case of need. Thus we may be almost certain that the 300 Wallachs who fought heroically in Theodoro as Alexander's bodyguard were the 300 'Siculi' who were sent by Matthew Corvinus to his 'faithful and beloved' Stephen the Great, and in turn sent by Stephen to the Crimea with his brother-in-law Alexander. The Hungarian noble Michael Fancsy to whom Corvinus addressed the letter may either have perished during the siege and fall of Theodoro or have been taken prisoner and sent to Constantinople.

Another debatable question is connected with the fall of Caffa and

---

[1] Braun, *Die letzten Schicksale*, p. 36, and Addendum, p. 80. Of course he is wrong in believing that Isaac was the last Prince of Gothia. See above.

[2] See Iorga, *Geschichte des Osmanischen Reiches*, II (Gotha, 1909), 175; Iorga, *Istoria lui Ştefan-cel-Mare* (Bucarest, 1904), p. 164: 'with Moldavian soldiers'; Malitzki, *op. cit.*, p. 43; Vasiliu, *op. cit.*, p. 331.

[3] L. de Hurmuzaki, *Documente privatóre in Istoria Românilor*, II, i (Bucarest, 1891), 11 (Doc. XIII): 'tibi firmiter injungimus, quod si unquam gratiam nostram promereri cupis, in continenti cum 300 Siculis ad Stephanum Voivodam Moldaviensem, fidelem nostrum dilectum proficisci, ibique Nobis sincere et hoc tempore cum ipse auxiliis indigeat, assistere et auxiliari debeas . . .'

Theodoro.   When the Crimean Khan, Mengli-Girei, was forced by a revolt to flee from his possessions, he found refuge in Caffa with the Genoese, and in 1475 was taken prisoner by the Turks, either in Caffa or in Theodoro.[1] Turkish sources disagree on this subject.   The anonymous author of a brief Turkish history says that 'although some histories assert that Mengli-Girei was taken prisoner at the conquest of Mankup, it is clear from their presentation of this statement that it is groundless.'[2] Another Turkish historian, Djennebi, plainly writes that at the surrender of Mankup the Vizier Akhmet-Pasha took several Christian princes and sent them to the Sultan Porte; among them was Mengli-Girei, the former ruler of the Tartars.   'His brothers had overcome him and forced him to shut himself up in the fortress of Mankup.'[3]   According to another Turkish manuscript, which was brought by A. Jaubert from the Crimea in 1819, Kedyk-Akhmet Pasha took possession of the fortresses of Caffa and Menkub in 880 (= 1475); and 'Mengli-Girei Khan who had been taken prisoner by the Venetians (?) and shut up in Mankup, fell also into the power of the Pasha, who immediately sent him to Constantinople.'[4]   It is possible that Mengli-Girei first took refuge from his own countrymen in Caffa and later under the Turkish menace left Caffa for Mankup-Theodoro, where he was taken by the Turks.[5]

The final fate of Alexander and his family is known.   They were brought to Constantinople, and there Alexander was beheaded, his son was forced to become a Turk, i.e., a Muhammedan, and the lives of his wife and daughters were spared that they might enter the Sultan's harem.[6]   Apparently Alexander was not killed immediately after arriving in Constantinople.   We have a letter dated 20 May 1476 sent from Pera by a certain Genoese, Antonio Bonfilio, to his countryman Azius

---

[1] V. Smirnov, *The Crimean Khanate under the Domination of the Ottoman Porte up to the Beginning of the Eighteenth Century* (St Petersburg, 1887), p. 275 (in Russian); Hammer-Purgstall, *Geschichte der Chane der Krim* (Vienna, 1856), p. 33.

[2] *Ibid.*, p. 276. Smirnov used a manuscript text of this *History*. See also A. Negri, 'Excerpts from a Turkish Manuscript of the Odessa Society Containing a History of the Crimean Khans,' in the *Zapiski* of the Odessa Society of History and Antiquities, I (1844), 382.

[3] Smirnov, *op. cit.*, p. 281.

[4] 'Précis de l'histoire des Khans de Crimée, depuis l'an 880 jusqu'à l'an 1198 de l'hégire, traduit du turc par M. Kazimirski, revu par M. Amédée Jaubert,' in the *Nouveau Journal Asiatique*, XII (Paris, 1833), 349–351.   The Venetians mentioned in the text of course should be the Genoese.

[5] Bruun writes that after his father's death Mengli-Girei must have taken refuge in Mankup, which at that time belonged like Caffa to the Genoese, and that Mengli-Girei was taken prisoner in Mankup, Bruun, *Notices historiques*, p. 72 and 93.   On p. 72 Bruun uses the Turkish text translated by Kazimirski (see preceding note).

[6] *The Report of the Rector and the Council of Ragusa*: 'iugularunt, exceptis uxore et filiabus, quas tyrannus in usum suum, sive in abusum, retinuit,' *Mon. Hung. Hist., Acta Extera*, II, 345; *Atti*, VII, ii, 488; Spandugino (p. 155): 'et fece Turco uno suo figliolo piccolo.' Spandugino saw Alexander's son when he was in Constantinople. See Iorga, *Studiĭ istorice*, p. 145.

Gentile. If I correctly interpret its text, Bonfilio writes that recently a Moldavian ambassador had been in Constantinople to arrange terms of peace with the Sultan. Evidently one of the conditions of peace was the liberation of Alexander, who was a relative of the Moldavian Prince, and of the other *signori* of Gothia. The ambassador was told that the Goths must all die, but that for the time being they were still alive in prison. He went to the prison to inquire for them.[1] His intercession did not help, and Alexander was executed as well as other eminent people from Gothia, perhaps including his own brother.

When the chief Genoese authorities, the last *capitanus* of Gothia, Gianagostino Cattaneo, the last consul of Caffa, Antoniotto Cabella, and his opponent and rival the *massarius* Oberto Squarciafico, realized the unavoidable surrender of Caffa, in all likelihood they also left their city with Mengli-Girei and took shelter in the impregnable stronghold of Theodoro-Mankup. We may not accordingly flatly deny the theory of the active participation of the Genoese in the heroic defense of Theo-doro-Mankup against the Grand Vizier, which was emphasized by Canale and reproduced by P. Amadeo Vigna.[2] That Mengli-Girei and the Genoese authorities fled from Caffa to Theodoro is very probable. All of them, unless some of them perished during the siege and final attack, were taken prisoners and sent to Constantinople. Mengli-Girei's life was spared, and he was granted by the Sultan a governorship in the Crimea.

In another passage Vigna, filled with patriotic enthusiasm, writes that he wishes to award to Gianagostino Cattaneo, as the last *capitano* of the place,[3] the merit of the heroic resistance to the Grand Vizier in Mankup, where 'had taken refuge, as in a secure shelter, the small remnant of the Genoese who had escaped general massacre, and where were the petty

---

[1] *Actes et fragments relatifs à l'histoire des Roumains, rassamblés par N. Iorga*, III, i (1897), 55: 'De novo, qui è stato lo ambassatore de' Valachi per fare la pace et dicto ambassatore hà dimandato in la pace lo signore de lo Tedoro che era parente del Vlacho, et altri signori de Gutia; dico li hà facti morire tuti et hà da intendere allo ambassatore de' Vlachi i dicti essere in prexone et fexe fentizamente andare lo ambassatore de' Vlachi alle prexoni de fora ad parlare con le altre persone, che erano in prexone, digando erano essi . . . ' Bronevski says that the princes of Gothia were ex-ecuted not under Muhammed II but under Selim (1512–1520), M. Broniovius, *Tartariae Descriptio* (Cologne, 1595), pp. 7–8.

[2] Canale, *Della Crimea*, II, 147; Vigna, in the *Atti della Società Ligure*, VII, ii, 178–179. Cf. Heyd, *Histoire du Commerce du Levant*, II, 405. Heyd says there are no sources for the participation of the refugees from the Genoese territory in the defense of Theodoro-Mankup. On the general situation in Caffa just before its fall, see L. Kolli, 'The Fall of Caffa,' in the *Izvestiya* of the Tauric Learned Archive Commission, LV (Simferopol, 1918), 145–147 (on the basis of Vigna's study and Genoese documents; in Russian).

[3] Vigna calls Gianagostino Cattaneo 'ultimo capitano del luogo' (*Atti*, VII, ii, 986), which is rather misleading; Cattaneo was never the *capitanus* of Mankup.

Greco-Christian sovereigns of that country having their residence on Mankup. Misfortune made them friends and the same religion cemented even more strongly the bonds between them, so that one of the Genoese, possibly Gianagostino Cattaneo mentioned above, was appointed commander and defender of the castle. It is a pity that imprudence, not very easily pardonable in the commander of the blockaded fortress, has in great part stripped his noble wreath of its leaves.'[1] The last words refer to an episode given by Canale. The castellan (*castellanus*) who commanded the fortress and who according to Vigna was a Genoese went out of the city on a hunting expedition and was captured by the Turks; this was the cause of the fall of the stronghold.[2]

In my opinion, Canale's account, which is based on manuscript material, should now be verified by the study of this material; but this has not yet been done. Only when it is shall we be able to express a definite judgment on this question. So far we are only able to say that Alexander, the last Prince of pre-Turkish Gothia, his brother, his 300 'Wallachs,' the local troops and population of Theodoro and Gothia in general who no doubt crowded into the stronghold from the neighboring mountains and valleys, and probably the Genoese authorities from Caffa and maritime Genoese Gothia, heroically defended the residence of the Princes of Gothia and finally failed in the unequal struggle against the Grand Vizier and his powerful army.[3]

The fall of Caffa and Mankup is mentioned in various Russian chronicles. After the last traces of the subjection of Russia to the Tartars were effaced in 1480, the Russian chronicles are filled with joy and jubilation on account of this most significant achievement in the history of Russia at the close of the fifteenth century. In connection with this, under the year 1481 (6989) we find a very interesting prayer in which the names of Caffa and Mankup are given. The prayer follows: 'Oh, brave and valiant sons of Russia! Endeavor to preserve your country, the Russian

[1] Vigna, *ibid.*, pp. 986–987.   [2] *Ibid.*, p. 178.

[3] All writings dealing with the Goths in the Crimea devote more or less attention to the siege and fall of Theodoro: Köppen, *op. cit.*, pp. 282–283; Bruun, *Notices historiques*, p. 72; Tomaschek, *Die Goten in Taurien*, p. 54; Braun, *Die letzten Schicksale*, p. 36; Heyd, *op. cit.*, II, 405; Loewe, *op. cit.*, pp. 221–222; a few words in Kulakovski, *The Past of the Tauris*, p. 120; a mere mention of the fall of Caffa, Cembalo, Inkerman, Gothia, and Cherson, in F. Donaver, *La storia della Repubblica di Genova*, II (Genoa, 1913), 97–98; Bănescu, 'Contribution . . . ,' *Byz. Zeitschrift*, XXXV (1935), 33–34. The fall of Mankup is mentioned in the histories of the Ottoman Turks: J. Zinkeisen, *Geschichte des Osmanischen Reiches in Europa*, II (Gotha, 1854), 387; J. von Hammer, *Geschichte des Osmanischen Reiches*, 2nd ed., I (Pesth, 1834), 525 (his French edition, III, Paris, 1836, 197–198); V. Smirnov, *The Crimean Khanate under the Domination of the Ottoman Turks up to the Beginning of the Eighteenth Century* (St Petersburg, 1887), pp. 275–281 (in Russian); N. Iorga, *Geschichte des Osmanischen Reiches*, II (Gotha, 1909), 174–175. A. Krymski does not mention the fall of Theodoro-Mankup, *History of Turkey* (Kiev, 1924), pp. 102–103 (in Ukrainian).

land, from the pagans; do not spare your lives! May your eyes never see the destruction of your homes, the slaughter of your children, and the violation of your wives and daughters in the way other great and glorious lands have suffered from the Turks. These lands are called Bulgarians and Serbians, Greeks and Trebizond, Ammorea (Morea), Arbonasy (Albanians), and Khorvaty (Croatians), Bosia (Bosnia), *Mankup and Cafa*, and many others.'[1]

With the fall of Theodoro-Mankup and the occupation of the whole territory of Gothia by the Turks the history of the principality of Gothia in the Crimea comes to a close.

In 1484 after a long and glorious resistance two very important Moldavian ports, Chilia (Kilia) on the Lower Danube and Moncastro (Cetatea Alba, Akkerman) at the mouth of the Dniester, fell into the hands of the Turks. 'I have won,' said the Sultan in his manifesto, 'the key of the door to the whole of Moldavia, and also to Hungary, the whole region of the Danube, Poland, Russia, and Tartary, and the entire coast of the Black Sea.'[2] The imposing ruins of Moncastro-Akkerman are still standing today and strike visitors with awe.[3] After the conquest of the shores of the Black Sea the Turkish Sultan transferred many inhabitants of Caffa, Trebizond, Gothia, Sinope, and Moncastro (Cetatea Alba, Ἀσπρόκαστρον) to Constantinople and settled them there.[4]

---

[1] *Polnoe Sobranie Russkikh Letopisei* (Complete Collection of Russian Chronicles): *Nikonovskaya letopis*, XII (1901), 202 ('Mankuk'); *Voskresenskaya*, VIII (1859), 207 (under the year 6988=1480); *Lvovskaya*, XX (1910), 347; *Ermolinskaya*, XXIII (1910), 182; *Tipografskaya*, XXIV (1921), 201. See Köppen, *Krymsky Sbornik*, p. 266; A. Kunik, 'The Foundation of the Empire of Trebizond in 1204,' in the *Uchenyya Zapiski* of the Imperial Academy of Sciences, II (St Petersburg, 1854), 707. Both in Russian.

[2] N. Iorga, *A History of Roumania*, translated by K. McCabe (London, 1925), pp. 91–92. See a detailed account in N. Iorga, *Studiĭ istorice asupra Chilieĭ şi Cetăţiĭ-Albe* (Bucarest, 1900), pp. 155–164; some documents, pp. 279–281; *idem, Istoria lui Ştefan-cel-Mare* (Bucarest, 1904), pp. 203–211 (Chapter IV: Căderea Chiliei şi Cetăţii-Albe); *idem, Geschichte des Osmanischen Reiches*, II (Gotha, 1909), 268–270. See also the Turkish chronicle by Rustem Pasha (1500–1561) recently published and translated: F. Giese, 'Die altosmanischen anonymen Chroniken,' *Abhandlungen für die Kunde des Morgenlandes*, XVII (1925), 38; 'Die osmanische Chronik des Rustem Pascha,' by Ludwig Forrer, in the *Türkische Bibliothek*, XXI (Leipzig, 1923), p. 17; N. Iorga, 'Cronicele turceşti ca izvor pentru istoria Românilor,' in the *Academia Romana, Memoriile sectiunii istorice*, 3rd Series, IX (Bucarest, 1928–1929), 15. On Rustem Pasha see F. Babinger, *Die Geschichtsschreiber der Osmanen und ihre Werke* (Leipzig, 1927), pp. 81–82.

[3] Among other reproductions of the ruins of Moncastro see some beautiful plates in E. Skrzinska, 'Iscrizioni Genovesi in Crimea ed in Costantinopoli,' *Atti della Società Ligure*, LVI (1928), Nos. 54, 55, and 56.

[4] Phrantzes, III, 11 (Bonn ed., p. 308): '(After the capture of Constantinople the Sultan) μετ' ὀλίγον δὲ καί τινας ἀποίκους εἰσήνεγκε, καὶ ἐκείνην τὴν διάλεκτον λεγομένους σουργούνιδες, ἔκ τε τοῦ Καφᾶ, Τραπεζοῦντος καὶ Σινωπίου καὶ Ἀσπροκάστρου. καὶ οὕτως τὴν πόλιν ἐκατῴκησε'; *Historia Politica et Patriarchica Constantinopoleos*, Bonn ed., p. 45= Ἀνωνύμου Ἔκθεσις Χρονική, in Sathas, *Bibliotheca Graeca Medii aevi*, VII (Paris, 1894), 585,= *Ecthesis Chronica*, ed. S. Lambros (London, 1902), p. 33:

In the second half of the fifteenth century Stephen the Great of Moldavia played a considerable part in the history of Gothia. As we have said, he married Maria of Mankup and helped her brother Alexander to overthrow his brother Isaac and to become the last Prince of pre-Turkish Gothia. I think Miss Vasiliu is well advised to compare Stephen with Alexis of Gothia. Of course the two men belonged to two different periods, because Alexis died between 1444 and 1447 and Stephen in 1504. But they have many points in common. Both enjoyed long reigns during which they never ceased to fight their enemies. They both erected many buildings in their countries. They looked for allies and friends in the West and were informed of the events of Western Europe. Both, though for different motives, availed themselves of the good offices of Venice. By their merits they exceeded the narrow limits of their countries. Though petty princes of the East, they deserve a place in the history of European civilization.[1]

In connection with Turkish danger Stephen's plan was to organize a Christian league in order to reconquer the Crimea and force the Ottoman blockade of the Black Sea. But, as G. Brătianu says, 'It was too late for such ambitious projects; the Turkish domination was not to be shaken in those regions till the wars of Catherine the Great.'[2]

'μετ' οὐ πολὺ δὲ πορευθεὶς ἔλαβε τὸν Καφᾶν, τοὺς Θεοδώρους τὴν Γοτθίαν καὶ πᾶσαν τὴν περίχωρον ἄνευ πολέμου τινὸς καὶ ἔφερεν αὐτοὺς σουργοίνιδας.' The word 'σουργοίνιδες' means 'colonists -coloni.' See Lambros' *Index graecitatis*, p. 110.

[1] V. Vasiliu, 'Sur la seigneurie de "Tedoro" en Crimée au XVe siècle,' in the *Mélanges de l'École Roumaine en France*, 1929, I, 333–334.

[2] G. Brătianu, *Recherches sur Vicina et Cetatea Alba* (Bucarest, 1935), p. 126.

CHAPTER VI

GOTHIA UNDER THE TURKISH SWAY
(FROM 1475 TO THE END OF THE EIGHTEENTH CENTURY)

1. GOTHIA UNDER TURKEY

THE Gothic Princes are several times mentioned under the Turkish power, so apparently the Sultans did not abolish this title; but of course the Princes were Turkish officials, sometimes Christian and sometimes Muhammedan, and Gothia was a Turkish province. Our information on this later period is of course even scantier and more scattered than that on the previous epoch.

According to Bronevski, who heard this story from the Crimean Greeks, eighteen years after the fall of Mankup, i.e., in 1493, a terrible fire burst out in Mankup which almost entirely demolished the city; only the upper castle was spared. This latter possessed a gate adorned with marble and bearing a Greek inscription, and a large stone building. This building was the prison into which the infuriated Khans threw the envoys of the Grand Princes of Moscow, and the prisoners were sometimes very severely treated.[1]

In 1901 a dated Greek inscription was discovered on Mankup which reads as follows: 'In the days of the governor (ὑποτηρητής) Tzula this wall was restored'; then follow the words 'Τζουλα βητη . . . ὑπολετα' and the year, 'αφγ' (1503). This inscription is very interesting because it shows that in 1503, i.e., twenty-eight years after the Turkish conquest, the inhabitants of Mankup still spoke Greek and were taking care to restore the walls of their city, which had probably been destroyed during the Turkish siege. From the inscription we learn that the population of Mankup was under the power of a Turkish governor, whom they called in his own tongue 'ὑποτηρητής' and whose name was Tzula.[2] In all likelihood the words 'Τζουλα βη' are the governor's name Tzoula accompanied

---

[1] 'Postquam vero a Turcis ea (Mancopia) capta esset, postmodum vero anno decimo octavo, ut Christiani Greci perhibent, subitaneo et horribili incendio orto funditus fere demolita est. Idcirco nihil quicquam insignius praeter superiorem arcem, in qua porta insignis cum Graecis textibus multo marmore ornata, et domus alta lapidea est. In eam domum Moscorum nuncii Canorum barbarico furore nonnumquam detruduntur, ac durius ibi asservantur,' *Martini Broniovii Tartariae Descriptio* (Cologne, 1595), p. 7. A Russian translation by Shershenevich, in the *Zapiski* of the Odessa Society of History and Antiquities, VI (1867), 343.

[2] V. Latyshev, 'Greek and Latin Inscriptions Found in Southern Russia in 1901,' *Izvestiya* of the Archaeological Commission, III (St Petersburg, 1902), 31–33. The text of the inscription follows: 'ἐκτίσθη ὁ τεῖχος τὸ ὑπὸ ἡμερῶν ὑποτηρητοῦ Τζουλα . . . Τζουλαβητη . . . ν πολετα . . . ἔτος, αφγ.'

by the Turkish title *bi* or *bei* (cf. Kemal-bi, of whom we shall speak below), and perhaps the letters 'πολετα' denote his surname or family name, which in this apparently distorted form can not be identified.

In 1504 in a letter to the Russian Grand Prince, Ivan III (1462–1505), the Crimean Khan Mengli-Girei notified him that the Sultan Bayazid II (1481–1512) had assigned for fortifications in the Crimea a thousand men as well as a number of workers from the cities of Caffa and Mankup.[1]

At the end of 1512 the Russian Grand Prince, Vasili III (1505–1533), sent a *boyar* (noble), Alekseyev, as his envoy to the Sultan Selim I (1512–1520). Graciously received by Selim, he returned to Moscow in 1514 accompanied by the Sultan's envoy, a prince of Mankup, Kemalbi. In his letter to a Russian official in Moscow, Georgius Trakhaniotes, whom he had known before, Kemalbi mentioned that he had formerly been called Theodorites, and that he had sent his nephew Manuel to Trakhaniotes.[2] The envoy's Turkish name, Kemalbi, consists of the Turkish (Arabic) word *kemal*, 'perfection,' and the Turkish title *bei* or *bey*, sometimes *bek*, 'lord,' 'master.' Bruun says that Kemalbi would not have had the right to the name of Theodoretes (in Bruun, Theodorite), unless he himself or his ancestors had belonged to the family of the Princes of Theodoro or Theodori.[3] Tomaschek says also that Theodoretes (Θεοδωρίτης) means '*originating* from Theodoroi,'[4] and Loewe follows him.[5] Braun doubts Tomaschek's statement; he believes that the envoy was a Christian named Theodoretes (Theodoret), who accepted the Turkish name Kemal-bi in Constantinople.[6] It is quite possible that Kemalbi-Theodoretes may be traced back to the statement given by Spandugino, who during his stay in Constantinople saw a little son of Alexander, Prince of Gothia. Alexander, as we know, was executed, but his child became a Turk, i.e., a Muhammedan. Perhaps Kemalbi was Alexander's son, and in this case Theodoretes could be interpreted as Kemalbi of

---

[1] A. Malinovski, 'Historical and Diplomatic Collection (Sobraniye) of Affairs between the Russian Grand Princes and the Tartar Tzars in the Crimea from 1462 to 1533,' in the *Zapiski* of the Odessa Society of History and Antiquities, V (1863), 173; *Sbornik* of the Imperial Russian Historical Society, XLI (St Petersburg, 1884), 540. Both in Russian.

[2] N. Karamzin, *History of the Russian State*, 2nd ed. (St Petersburg, 1819), VII, 60 and n. 105 (pp. 27–28) with reference to unpublished materials in Russian; *Nikonovskaya Letopis*, *s.a.* 7022=1514, in the *Complete Collection (Sobraniye) of Russian Chronicles*, XIII, i (St Petersburg, 1904), 17 (in Old Russian).

[3] Bruun, *Notices historiques*, pp. 76 and 93; *idem*, *Chernomorye*, II (Odessa, 1880), 235–236 (in Russian).

[4] Tomaschek, *Die Goten in Taurien*, p. 54.   [5] Loewe, *Die Reste der Germanen*, p. 223.

[6] Braun, *Die letzten Schicksale*, pp. 37–38. Ogorodnikov calls the envoy Theodoret-Kemal, prince of Mangup, V. Ogorodnikov, 'Ivan III and the Jews Living Outside Russia,' in *Essays Presented to D. A. Korsakov* (Kazan, 1913), p. 61, n. 1 (in Russian).

Theodoro-Mankup.[1]   We do not know the outcome of Kemalbi's diplomatic career.[2]

In 1522 another Prince of Mankup, Skinder (Alexander), appeared in Moscow.   He was sent by the Sultan Suleiman II (1520–1566) not on a diplomatic mission but on business, to purchase Russian furs.   His behavior in Moscow was so rough and scandalous that the Russian Grand Prince Vasily III through his ambassador, Morozov, presented a complaint to the Sultan asking him henceforth to send a man more familiar with his business and not exclusively interested in his own profit.   Skinder was in Moscow also in 1524, and he died there in 1530.[3]   According to Tomaschek, whom Loewe follows, Skinder was probably not of Greek origin but a full-blooded Turk ('ein Vollblut-Türke'), like *Mahmut aga Mangupski*, under the Crimean Khan, Dewlet-Girei I (1551–1577).[4] With no basis for his opinion Ogorodnikov remarks that perhaps Theodoret-Kemalbi and Skinder were the sons of the Prince of Theodoro, Isaicus, and later became Turks.[5]   Skinder is the last Prince of Mankup mentioned in our sources.

In one of the later Russian chronicles is a rather obscure story to the effect that in 1540 the envoy of the Russian Grand Prince to the Crimean Khan, Gavrilo (Gabriel) Yanov, came from the Crimea to Moscow accompanied by the Khan's envoy, Azirthegad, who brought a message from his sovereign.   As far as I am able to understand the text of the Chronicle, the *Amanguitskiye* princes persuaded the Khan's son, without the Khan's knowledge, to raid the Grand Prince's territory; in his message the Khan expressed the hope that this incident would not break his friendship with the Grand Prince.[6]   In the adjective *Amanguitskiye* the editor of the Chronicle recognizes Mangup,[7] so that we have to deal here with the Princes of Mankup.   But the passage is obscure and the editor's interpretation very tentative.

In 1554 Ogier Ghislain de Busbecq (1522–1592) came to Constantinople as ambassador of Emperor Ferdinand I at the Ottoman Porte.   This

---

[1] Spandugino, *op. cit.*, p. 155. See Malitzki, *op. cit.*, p. 44.

[2] Bruun conjectures that the uncle and nephew mentioned by Bronevski who were supposed to be the Princes of Mankup captured by the Turks in 1475 were Kemalbi and his nephew Manuel; they were later beheaded by the Sultan Selim, Bruun, *Notices historiques*, p. 77.   I do not see any plausible reason for this conjecture, particularly since Bronevski, as we have shown above, was incorrect in his information.   See Köppen, *Krymsky Sbornik*, p. 284, n. 420.

[3] Karamzin, *op. cit.*, VII, 115–116, 148, and notes 233, 235, 236, 298. See Bruun, *Notices historiques*, pp. 77, 93; Braun, *Die letzten Schicksale*, p. 38.

[4] Karamzin, *op. cit.*, IX, n. 252; Tomaschek, *op. cit.*, p. 54; Loewe, *op. cit.*, p. 223; Soloviev, *History of Russia*, V, 384 ff. (in Russian).   [5] Ogorodnikov, *op. cit.*, p. 61, n. 1 (in Russian).

[6] *Nikonovskaya Letopis*, in the *Complete Collection* (*Sobraniye*) *of Russian Chronicles*, XIII, i (St Petersburg, 1904), 131, *s.a.* 7048=1540 (in Old Russian).

[7] See geographic index to the *Nikonovskaya Letopis*, *ibid.*, XIV, ii (St Petersburg, 1918), 174.

Flemish noble was more than a diplomat; he was a widely educated man. He collected Greek manuscripts, which are now in the National-bibliothek at Vienna, as well as coins and Greek inscriptions discovered at Angora in Asia Minor, including the famous *Monumentum Ancyranum*. He was deeply interested in the Turkish language, so that one of the eminent orientalists of our day calls him 'the founder of Turkish studies.[1] For our purpose his *Four Turkish Letters*, especially the fourth, is extremely interesting.[2] He met two Crimeans in Constantinople who asserted that in the Crimea there were still at that time many people who used the Germanic (Gothic) tongue; and they gave Busbecq a list of vocables supposed to be Germanic. Busbecq mentions two principal cities in Crimean Gothia, Mankup and Sciuarin (now the village Suiren). In his fourth letter occurs the following passage:

Here I cannot pass over in silence what I have learned about the people who now still inhabit the Tauric peninsula; I have very often heard that by their tongue, customs, appearance, and carriage of body they remind us of their Germanic origin. Therefore I have long been anxious to see some one of that people, and if it were possible, to get from him something written in that language; but I could not succeed in this. An incident however satisfied my desire. When two delegates from that country were here who in the name of that people pre-sented to the Sultan (ad principem) some complaints, and when my interpreters met them, the latter remembering my commission brought them to my home for luncheon. One was more distinguished than his companion, showing in his face a certain inborn simplicity, and he looked like a Fleming or Batavian; the other was shorter, with well-set body, or brown complexion, a Greek by origin and tongue, but who through his frequent intercourse knew that language (Germanic) well; owing to propinquity, as often happens with the Greeks, he had imbibed their language so thoroughly that he had forgotten his own. Asked about the character and customs of those peoples he answered aptly. He said that the people are bellicose, and they even today dwell in many villages; from them the prince of the Tartars when he goes on an expedition enrolls eight hun-

[1] Franz Babinger, 'Die türkischen Studien in Europa bis zum Auftreten Josef von Hammer-Purgstalls,' in *Die Welt des Islams*, VII (Berlin, 1919), 108. He calls Busbecq a man of genius ('der geniale A. G. van Busbeck').

[2] I have used the edition *Augerii Gislenii Busbequii D. Legationis turcicae Epistolae IV* (Hanover, 1629). Many other editions are given in Tomaschek, *Die Goten in Taurien*, p. 57. In 1919 Babinger (see the preceding note) deplored the fact that these letters had not been translated into any modern European language. I think Babinger is not exact in his statement. Before 1919 the *Turkish Letters* had already twice appeared in English; first, in an anonymous version, published in London in 1694; and secondly in C. T. Foster and F. H. B. Daniell, *The Life and Letters of Ogier Ghiselin de Busbecq*, 2 vols. (London, 1881). We have now two recent translations, German and English: *Vier Briefe aus der Türkei von Ogier Ghiselin von Busbeck, aus dem Lateinischen übertragen, eingeleitet und mit Anmerkungen versehen von Wolfram von den Steinen* (Erlangen, 1926); *The Turkish Letters of Ogier Ghiselin de Busbecq, Imperial Ambassador at Constantinople 1554–1562*, newly translated from the Latin of the Elzevir edition of 1633 by E. S. Forster (Oxford, 1927).

dred foot-soldiers, the chief strength of his troops. Their principal cities are two, the one *Mancup* and the other *Sciuarin* .... Now I have written down a few vocables among many which sounded German; for the form of many words was plainly different from ours.[1]

Then Busbecq gives a list of Germanic words.[2]

Busbecq's report, at first sight, is so exact and reasonable that apparently the conclusion admits of no doubt that in the sixteenth century German was spoken in some parts of Gothia. It is surprising that Bronevski (Broniovius) who visited Mankup in 1578, only a few years after Busbecq had received and written down his information, made no mention whatever of the existence of the Goths there. As Braun says, 'His silence on this point is really a riddle which is not easy of solution.'[3] At the beginning of the seventeenth century Busbecq's account had already been reproduced by a German scholar, Caspar Waserus, in his commentary on Gesner's book *Mithridates* mentioned above.[4]

It must be left to philologists with a wide historical background to elucidate the obscure but tantalizing problem of the survival of the Gothic tongue in the Crimea during the Middle Ages. We know that from time to time in our sources scattered, brief, and vague information on this subject appears, and these data have been given and discussed in the pages of this book; most of them, in my judgment, fail of being reliable. But if in the middle of the sixteenth century Busbceq, a highly educated man and scholar, after a thorough investigation of the question through two men from the Crimea, considers it possible to make so positive a statement, the problem cannot be discarded. A new objective study of the survival of the German tongue in the Crimea requires to be undertaken by philologists well acquainted with the history of the Goths in the Crimea.[5]

In 1578 the ambassador of Stephen Batory, King of Poland, Martin Bronevski, whose name and writings have been often mentioned above,

[1] *A. Busbeqii Legationis turcicae Epistolae IV* (Hanover, 1629), pp. 242–243; E. S. Forster, *The Turkish Letters of Ogier Ghiselin de Busbecq* (Oxford, 1927), pp. 201–202.

[2] Busbecq, pp. 244–245; Forster, pp. 203–204. The German words are also given in Braun, *Die letzten Schicksale*, pp. 57–60; Tomaschek, *Die Goten in Taurien*, pp. 58–67 (with a commentary). In connection with this problem, on Busbecq see A. Kunik, 'On the Report of a Gothic Toparch,' *Zapiski* of the Academy of Sciences of St Petersburg, xxiv (1874), 141–142 (in Russian); Braun, *op. cit.*, pp. 55–56, 64–66; Loewe, *Die Reste der Germanen*, pp. 127–179; R. Much, in *Anzeiger für indogermanische Sprach- und Altertumskunde*, 1897, pp. 193–209, esp. p. 196 (this is a review of Loewe's book).   [3] Braun, *op. cit.*, p. 65.

[4] *Gesneri Mithridates* ... , *Caspar Waserus recensuit et libello commentario illustravit*, 2nd ed. (Zürich, 1610), 'Ad Mithridatem Commentarius,' pp. 109–111.

[5] Recently some doubt concerning the correctness of Busbecq's information has been expressed. See, for example, M. H. Jellinek, *Geschichte der gotischen Sprache* (Berlin and Leipzig, 1926), pp. 17–18.

visited Mankup-Theodoro.[1] His description leaves a sad impression.
In Mangup, or according to Bronevski, in 'Mancopia seu Mangutum, ut
Turcae vocant arx et oppidum,' lived only one Greek priest (presbyter)
and a few Turks and Jews; the rest of the city lay in ruins and was con-
signed to oblivion. After the destructive fire in 1493 only the upper
castle, as has been noted above, was left, with its marble gate with a
Greek inscription and a high stone house where the envoys from Moscow
were imprisoned by the Sultan's orders. Two churches, those of St Constantine and of St George, still stood almost intact, and on their walls
Bronevski saw pictures of the Emperors and Empresses to whom the
princes of Mankup had been related.[2] The broken marble columns of
a temple lay on the ground and testified 'that once this place was famous
and important.'[3] In the rocks of the mountain upon which the city was
situated were cut many cave dwellings in a good state of preservation.
The mountain abounded in streams of limpid water. There was no trace
of the Goths nor any inscription in their tongue.

Travellers of later times mention Mankup and list the peoples dwelling
there, but make no mention of the Goths. I shall give only a few examples. In 1634 the Dominican Emiddio Dortelli d'Ascoli, Prefect of
Caffa, Tartary, and so forth, wrote a description of the Black Sea and
Tartary. He stayed in the Crimea over ten years. He says that a Turkish pasha governed Caffa, Balaklava, 'Mancopa,' Bospro, Taman, etc.;
that Mankup was one of the most important places in Tartary. He spe-
cifically notes that 'Mancopa,' a castle between Balaklava and Baghchesarai, was impregnable on account of its natural position; that it was
the last fortress which surrendered to the Turks; and that it abounded
in clear streams. There resided a *kadi*, i.e., a judge, appointed from Constantinople. The city was almost totally ruined and sparsely populated;
its inhabitants were Greeks, Turks, and Jews, but mostly Jews who dealt
in leather.[4] It is very important to notice that although d'Ascoli spent
over ten years in the Crimea, and visited many places there, he heard
nothing of the Goths.

[1] *Martini Broniovii Tartariae Descriptio* (Cologne, 1595), pp. 7–8. A Russian translation by
Shershenevich, in the *Zapiski* of the Odessa Society of History and Antiquities, vi (1867), pp.
343–344.

[2] 'In templis illis Graecis in parietibus effigies et habitus adornati Imperatorum et Imperatricum
earum, ex quorum sanguine eas ortas et prognatas fuisse apparent.'

[3] 'Phanum marmoreis et serpentinis columnis ornatum humi jam prostratum et corruptum in-
signem et clarum quondam eum locum extitisse testatur' (p. 8).

[4] 'Descrittione del Mar Negro e della Tartaria per Il. D. Emiddio Dortelli d'Ascoli, lett. Dom.
Prefetto del Caffa, Tartaria, etc. 1634,' ed. N. Dashkevich, in the *Chteniya* of the Historical Society
of the Annalist Nestor, v (Kiev, 1891), iii, Materials, p. 23 (Mancopa); 27 (Mancupra), and 31–32
(Mancopa). A Russian translation by N. Pimenov with notes by A. Bertier Delagarde, in the
Zapiski of the Odessa Society of History and Antiquities, xxiv (1902), 113, 117, 121.

D'Ascoli's friend and companion, another Dominican, John de Luca, who in 1625 wrote a description of the Perekop and Nogai Tartars, Circassians, Mingrelians, and Iberians (Georgians), also mentions Mangup-kalé among seven other cities in the Crimea. In another place he writes that an impregnable city called Mangup is built on a mountain and inhabited by the Jews. 'A Tartar governs there. There all the Khans' treasures are kept; there also they take shelter during some troubles in their possessions, which happens rather often, for the Turkish Sultan takes away from the Khans the greater part of their land and keeps it at his own disposal.'[1]

Other travellers in the Crimea, G. Beauplan in the first half ot the seventeenth century, Mortroye at the outset, and Charles Peyssonel in the middle of the eighteenth century, say that Mankup was inhabited by Jews, and Peyssonel adds, 'and by some Muhammedans.'[2]

Referring to Busbecq's account, P. S. Pallas, who made a very interesting journey through South Russia in 1793–1794, writes as follows: 'No smallest trace of Gothic is to be discovered in any Tartar dialect; and the story published by Busbecq of a remnant of the old Goths among the Crimean Tartars, can have arisen only from the Germans, Swedes, or Livonians captured by the Tartars . . . . In the whole of the Crimea there is no trace of the Gothic language in the names of rivers, valleys, mountains, or regions.'[3]

At the end of the eighteenth century the Metropolitan of the Roman Catholic churches in Russia, Siestrzencewicz de Bohusz, also visted the Crimea, described Mankup, and mentioned the name of the Crimean Goths.[4]

The Crimean Goths interested not only the travellers who visited the Crimea or, like Busbecq, lived in the East, but also West European scholars who never travelled in the Crimea. A German scholar of the sixteenth century, Joachim Cureus (Curäus; 1542–1573), in his *Gentis Silesiae Annales*, says that according to widespread opinion descendants of

---

[1] John (Jean) de Luca, 'Description of the Perekop and Nogaï Tartars, Circassians, Mingrelians, and Iberians (Georgians, Gruzins),' in the *Zapiski* of the Odessa Society of History and Antiquities, xi (1879), 475, 484 (a Russian translation by P. Yurguenko). I have used also an old Dutch translation, *De Landschappen der Percoptize en Nogaize Tartars, Circassen, Mingrelianen, en Georgianen beneffens die van de Crim . . . in't Yaar 1633 Jan de Luca* (Leyden, *s.d.*), col. 7. I have not seen the edition of Luca's description in the *Recueil des voyages au nord* (Amsterdam, 1725), vii, 100 (according to Loewe, *op. cit.*, pp. 183, 185). [2] See Loewe, *op. cit.*, p. 183.

[3] P. S. Pallas, *Bemerkungen auf einer Reise in die südlichen Statthalterschaften des Russischen Reichs in den Jahren 1793 und 1794*, ii (Leipzig, 1801), 363–364, or another edition, ii (Leipzig, 1803), 318. See also Braun, *op. cit.*, p. 68.

[4] Siestrzencewicz de Bohusz, *Histoire du royaume de la Chersonèse Taurique* (Brunswick, 1800), pp. 252 ff.; *Idem, History of the Tauris* (St Petersburg, 1806), pp. 283 ff. (in Russian). There is a second French revised edition (St Petersburg, 1824). See Braun, *op. cit.*, pp. 68–69.

the Goths have survived who still spoke their own language; he recalls that Philip Melanchthon often recited a story told by a German humanist, Wilibald Pirckheimer (Pirchamerus; 1470–1530), of Nürnberg: how merchants of this city sailing with the Venetians to Crete and Cyprus were cast by a storm on the shores of the Aegean Sea, not far from the Bosphorus; how they met there a man singing in German, and asked him from what country he came; and how he told them that his own country was situated not far away, where lived his people who were Goths.[1]   The text makes no mention of the Crimea, but at least it proves the existence of a widespread tradition that Gothic was still spoken in the near East.

Another German theologian and humanist of that epoch, Johannes Cochleus (1479–1552), in his *Vita Theodorici regis Ostrogothorum et Italiae*, asserts that a very dependable and well-educated man, Nicholaus Spatharius, a Moldo-Wallachian, who as an interpreter, spent many years in Constantinople at the Ottoman court, stated that in the Crimea there were about three hundred villages with a population of Gothic origin; these people used a peculiar Teutonic language and were Christians. They had a Gothic bishop whose residence was in Caffa or Theodosiopolis (Theodosia); and they called their language Gothic.   A later editor of the *Vita Theoderici* and commentator, a Swedish archaeologist, Johannes Peringskiöld (1654–1720), remarks that the Swedish scholar, Johan Sparfvenfeldt (Sparfvenfelt; 1655–1727) was convinced of the authenticity of this story.[2]

Another German theologian and historian of the sixteenth century, Georgius Torquatus (1513–1575), in his *Annales Lipsiae et Quidlinburgi* gives a very distorted tradition.   After mentioning that the remnants of the Goths are in Transylvania, he says: 'In the mountains of the Tauric peninsula, near the Bosphorus, not far from Constantinople, and in Asia as far as Northern Armenia, they use at home among themselves their own language, i.e., Germanic very similar to the tongue of the Saxons; but outside and dealing with foreigners they use Greek, Tartar, or Hun garian.'[3]

A German traveller in the East, in Russia, Persia, and especially Japan, Engelbert Kämpfer (1631–1716), writes that 'the language spoken in the

---

[1] *Gentis Silesiae Annales a Joachimo Cureo Freistadiensi* (Wittenberg, 1571), p. 14: 'non procul inde suam abesse patriam, in eaque habitare suam gentem, quae esset Gotthica.'   This text is also given in Loewe, *op. cit.*, pp. 116–117 (with incorrect reference to p. 13 for p. 14); see pp. 116–121.

[2] *Vita Theoderici regis Ostrogothorum et Italiae auctore Joanne Cochleo Germano, cum additamentis et annotationibus . . . opera Johannis Peringskiöld* (Stockholm, 1699), p. 348.   See Loewe, *op. cit.*, pp. 187–191, especially p. 191.

[3] *Monumenta inedita rerum germanicarum praecipue Magdeburgicarum et Halberstadiensium*, ed. Fr. E. Boysen, *T. I. qui Georgii Torquati Annales continet* (Leipzig and Quedlinburg, *s.d.*), pp. 89–90. G. Torquatus compiled his Annals in 1561–1574 (Boysen, I, 89).   See Loewe, *op. cit.*, pp. 47–48, 125.

peninsula of the Crimea, or *Taurica Chersonesus*, in Asia, still retains many German words, brought thither, as is supposed, by a colony of Goths, who went to settle there about eight hundred and fifty years after the Deluge. The late Mr Busbecq, who was Imperial ambassador at the Ottoman Porte, collected and published a great number of these words in his fourth letter; and in my own travels through that country I took notice of many more.'[1] As Kämpfer's manuscripts are preserved in the British Museum this material has been carefully investigated; and we know now that Kämpfer himself never visited the Crimea and that he obtained his information by hearsay only.[2]

Finally Johann Beckmann (1739–1811), a German scholar and traveller, advanced the theory that the Crimean Goths mentioned by Busbecq were merely Jews (Juden). He writes: 'No one recently has been able to discover there [in the Crimea] any trace of the Goths. In December 1796 my learned friend, Professor Hacquet of Lemberg, wrote me information which I wish to insert here. "I can assure you," he wrote, "that many Jews, who are everywhere *am Pontus*, have been taken for old Germans or Goths. If Busbecq says that he spoke German with the Goths in Constantinople, these were no other than exiled Polish or Hungarian Jews. . . . Certainly Pallas will give information of these Jews, the supposed Goths, in his description of the Crimea".' Beckmann continues, 'Alas! I do not find this information in the excellent notes on his journey through the southern governments of the Russian Empire.'[3] Beckmann's theory was not without results; in 1884 at the Fourth Archaeological Congress at Odessa, a Russian scholar raised the question whether or not Busbecq's Goths were Jews.[4]

The question of what finally became of the Crimean Goths presents no difficulties. As I have already pointed out in this book, they were gradually hellenized and afterwards tartarized; but in spite of centuries of Tartar and Turkish domination most of them preserved their Greek-Orthodox faith. In 1778 a number of Crimean Christians who spoke Tartar emigrated from the Peninsula to Russia. 'In those emigrants, and especially in those who came from the heart of old Gothia, we must see the last descendants of our Crimean Goths.' In their veins 'perhaps flowed some drops of Gothic blood.'[5]

---

[1] *Historia Imperii Japonici Germanice scripta ab Engelberto Kaempfero, Anglice vertit — Johannes Casparus Scheuchzer* (London, 1727), I, i, Ch. VI, p. 84. Neither Braun (*op. cit.*, p. 67) nor Loewe (*op. cit.*, p. 93) was able to use Kämpfer's book itself.   [2] See Braun, *op. cit.*, p. 67.

[3] Johann Beckmann, *Litteratur der älteren Reisenbeschreibungen*, I (Göttingen, 1807), 179–180.

[4] See Braun, *op. cit.*, p. 68.

[5] Braun, *op. cit.*, pp. 69, 75. On the Goths in the Crimea after the fall of Gothia see also Loewe, *op. cit.*, pp. 221–227.

2. Church Life in Gothia from the Thirteenth to the End of the Eighteenth Century

For a period of six centuries, from the thirteenth century to the close of the eighteenth, for church life in the Crimea our sources give us a fairly long list of names of the hierarchs of Gothia, often with brief statements on their activities. No continuous picture, of course, can be drawn on the basis of this material.[1]

As previously, there were four Greek Orthodox eparchies in the Crimea: those of Cherson, Gothia, Sugdaia and Phullae, and Bosporus. The hierarchs of these eparchies were appointed and consecrated by the Patriarch of Constantinople; relations between the Patriarch and the Crimean church were active, and the Crimean hierarchs often took part in the meetings of the synods at Constantinople.

In the thirteenth century the Archbishop of Gothia, Arsenius, was raised to the rank of Metropolitan.[2] In 1292 the Metropolitan of Gothia, Sophronius, took part in a council at Constantinople.[3] In 1317 a litigation between the Metropolitans of Gothia and Sugdaia was examined by the Patriarch. Some villages which belonged to the eparchy of Sugdaia were abandoned because of a Tartar incursion; on the villagers' return to their homes they came under the jurisdiction of the Metropolitan of Gothia, who levied from them a canonical tax. The Metropolitan of Sugdaia complained to the Patriarch.[4] In September of 1347 the Metropolitans of Sugdaia and Gothia attended the meetings of a council in Constantinople.[5] In October, 1368, the Patriarch entrusted the Metropolitan of Gothia with the supervision of the Church of Cherson.[6]

Beginning with the end of the fourteenth century there are several documents on disputes between the Metropolitan of Cherson on one side and the Metropolitans of Gothia and Sugdaia on the other; the subject of dispute was a village, Elissos. In 1382 it was assigned to the Metropolitan of Sugdaia. The synod convoked at Constantinople in that year was attended, among other members, by a Metropolitan of Gothia.[7] In

---

[1] For the order of the Metropolitans of Gothia I follow in general two Russian works: Arch. Arsenius, 'The Gothic Eparchy in the Crimea,' *Journal of the Ministry of Public Instruction*, CLXV (1873), 60–86, and Bishop Hermogenes, *The Tauric Eparchy* (Pskov, 1887).

[2] Arsenius, p. 69; Hermogenes, p. 149. Cf. Kulakovski, *The Past of the Tauris*, 2nd ed. (Kiev, 1914), p. 114 (in the fourteenth century).

[3] Arsenius, p. 69; Hermogenes, p. 149; Tomaschek, *op. cit.*, p. 46; Braun, *op. cit.*, p. 51.

[4] Miklosich and Müller, *Acta et diplomata graeca medii aevi*, I, No. 41, pp. 75–76; Archimandrite Antonin, 'Ancient Acts of the Constantinopolitan Patriarchate Referring to Novorossiya,' *Zapiski* of the Odessa Society of History and Antiquities, VI (1867), 445–446 (a Russian translation of the documents published by Miklosich and Müller).

[5] Miklosich and Müller, I, No. 120, p. 270; Antonin, p. 472.

[6] Miklosich and Müller, I, No. 240, pp. 500–501; Antonin, pp. 457–458.

[7] Miklosich and Müller, II, pp. 42–44; Antonin, p. 472.

the following year (1383) a Metropolitan of Gothia was again in Constantinople.[1] At the same time there was a long dispute between the Metropolitans of Gothia and Cherson for the possession of Sikita (Nikita), Parthenit, Lampas, Alusta, Phunae, and Alanica. Both Metropolitans were summoned to Constantinople by the Patriarch, where their dispute was settled. But on their return to the Crimea the clergy of their churches and lay officials resumed the struggle, and matters came to such a pass that several men were killed. By order of the Patriarch, in 1384 the Metropolitan of Sugdaia and Phullae, and a monk, Isidorus, were entrusted with the careful examination and settlement of this case.[2] In 1385 the village Kinsanus (Κινσάνους), the object of a dispute between the Metropolitans of Cherson and Gothia, was finally assigned by the Patriarch to the Metropolitan of Gothia, Theodosius.[3] But this measure failed to settle the dispute; the Metropolitan of Cherson was not satisfied with the decision, and bitterly complained everywhere of having been unjustly treated. Finally Patriarch Nilus reconsidered the matter and, with the consent of the Metropolitan of Gothia, assigned Kinsanus with its neighboring villages to the eparchy of Cherson. At that time the Metropolitan Theodosius died, and the new Metropolitan, Antonius, was consecrated. Before he left Constantinople for the Crimea it had been once more decided that the Metropolitan of Cherson should have Kinsanus with the neighboring villages only: 'all other territory whatsoever shall belong to the Metropolitan of Gothia; if the Metropolitan of Cherson is content, so be it; if not, he shall lose what he possesses now.' This arrangement, signed by Patriarch Nilus, is dated March, 1386.[4] In the same month the Patriarch gave Yalita, a well-known city on the coast of the Crimea, into the supervision of the Metropolitan of Gothia.[5] Antonius was Metropolitan of Gothia three years, from 1386 to 1389,[6] and in the latter year he was at Constantinople where he took part in several synods convoked by the Patriarch, in February, March (March 17), and April.[7] In August, 1390, Patriarch Macarius, supported by the Emperor himself, restored to the Metropolitan of Cherson all the places which had formerly belonged to him: Kinsanus again with all its neighboring villages, Phunae, Alania, Alusta, Lampado-Parthenit, and Sikita (Nikita) with Khrikhari (Χρίχαρι).[8] At the synod in Constantinople,

---

[1] Miklosich and Müller, ɪɪ, pp. 48–51; Antonin, p. 472.

[2] Miklosich and Müller, ɪɪ, pp. 67–68; Antonin, pp. 460–461.

[3] Arsenius, p. 69; Hermogenes, p. 149; Miklosich and Müller, ɪɪ, pp. 69–70; Antonin, pp. 461–462.

[4] Miklosich and Müller, ɪɪ, pp. 71–74; Antonin, pp. 464–466.

[5] Miklosich and Müller, ɪɪ, pp. 74–75; Antonin, pp. 466–467.

[6] Arsenius, p. 149; Hermogenes, p. 70.

[7] Miklosich and Müller, ɪɪ, pp. 115–133; Antonin, p. 473.

[8] Miklosich and Müller, ɪɪ, pp. 148–150; Antonin, pp. 467–469.

6 November 1396, an examination was made of an official complaint of the Metropolitan of Gothia against the Metropolitan of Cherson, who for a considerable sum of money had sanctioned a fifth marriage, against church law.[1] In October, 1399, the former great *chartophylax*, John Holobolus, was mentioned as Metropolitan of Gothia.[2] In July, 1401, he was present at a synod in Constantinople.[3] John Holobolus in all likelihood died in 1410.[4]

In 1427 'the Metropolitan of the city Theodoro and of all Gothia,' Damianus, restored the church of the Apostles Peter and Paul at Parthenit, which had been erected late in the eighth century by the Archbishop of the city Theodoro and of all Gothia, John, of whom we have spoken at length above. From N. Repnikov's excavations in Parthenit, we know that this church, restored by Damianus at the outset of the fifteenth century, was destroyed for the second time late in that century by the Turks, and was probably restored once more in the sixteenth century on a more modest scale.[5] Under the years 1424 and 1428–1429 an *Episcopus de Tedoro* is mentioned in the accounts of Caffa.[6] The name of the Bishop (or the Bishops) is not given.

After the capture of Constantinople in 1453 and of Theodoro and Gothia in 1475, the Turks preserved the religion and religious institutions of the Greeks, as well as the Greek ecclesiastical organization. Therefore the eparchy of Gothia continued to exist, and many names of Gothic Metropolitans have survived from the epoch of Turkish sway.

According to an inscription, in 1587 the Metropolitan of Gothia, Constantius, built and adorned the church of John the Precursor and Baptist.

---

[1] Miklosich and Müller, ii, p. 270; Antonin, p. 470.

[2] Miklosich and Müller, ii, p. 304; Antonin, p. 473. An undated document signed by Patriarch Antonius also mentions the Metropolitan of Gothia, Miklosich and Müller, ii, p. 198; Antonin, p. 473. Patriarch Antonius ruled for the first time from 1389 to 1390 and for the second time from 1391 to 1397.　　　　　　　　　　　　　[3] Miklosich and Müller, ii, p. 519; Antonin, p. 473.

[4] Arsenius, p. 71; Hermogenes, p. 149 (1399–1400). See also Köppen, *Krymsky Sbornik,* p. 69; Kulakovski, *The Past of the Tauris,* p. 131. Both in Russian.

[5] The inscription is dated 10 September 6936=A.D. 1427, V. Latyshev, 'A New Inscription from Parthenit,' in the *Zapiski* of the Odessa Society of History and Antiquities, xiv (1886), 64; *Idem, Collection of Greek Inscriptions of Christian Times from South Russia* (St Petersburg, 1896), No. 70, pp. 77–79. Greek text and a Russian commentary. Hermogenes, p. 150 (year 1428). The year of this inscription is given incorrectly in Karatilov, 'A Recent Archaeological Find in the Crimea,' in the *Zapiski* of the Odessa Society, viii (1872), 308–309 (1422), and in Vasilievski, *The Life of John of Gothia, Works,* ii, ii, 422 (1425); Kulakovski, *The Past of the Tauris,* p. 131. Some information on the church conditions in Gothia in the fifteenth century is to be found in *Cod. 18298 Lat. Munich.* See S. Lambros, "Ὑπόμνημα περὶ τῶν Ἑλληνικῶν χωρῶν καὶ ἐκκλησιῶν κατὰ τὸν δέκατον πέμπτον αἰῶνα,' in Νέος Ἑλληνομνήμων, vii (1910), 360–371; on p. 365: 'Item in Cothia [*sic!*] alter archiepiscopus, quod genus per se diversis linguis distinguitur et subditur in parte Thartaris et in parte Januensibus.' Cf. p. 371.

[6] N. Bănescu, 'Contribution . . . ,' *Byz. Zeitschrift,* xxxv (1935), p. 35 (reference to Mass. Caffe 1424, fol. 123ʳ; 1428–29, fol. 67ᵛ).

It is interesting to note that Constantius was supported by the zeal and means of a certain Binata, son of Temirke, evidently a Christian of Tartar descent, as his father's Tartar name proves.[1] We know the name of the Metropolitan of Gothia in 1635, Seraphimus, who presented a formal complaint to the Tsar of Russia, Michael Feodorovich (1613–1645) on the oppression of his church by the Tartars.[2] In 1639 a new Metropolitan of Gothia, Anthymus, arrived in the Crimea;[3] in 1652 he was deposed and replaced by Daniel; under the same year David is also mentioned as Metropolitan of Gothia.[4] In 1673 after David's death Methodius was consecrated Metropolitan of Gothia.[5] In July, 1678, the Metropoly of Gothia was united with that of Caffa.[6] In 1680 the Metropolitan of Gothia was Neophytus and in 1707 Macarius.[7] From 1710 to 1721 the Metropolitan of Gothia and Caffa was Parthenius. This title of the hierarchs of Gothia survived down to the end of their eparchy.[8] From 1725 to 1769 the Metropolitan of Gothia was Gedeon, whose seat was in Mariampol, a suburb of Baghchesarai, the residence of the Crimean Khans.[9] His unusually lengthy rule was interrupted in 1750, when for some reason, probably political, he was exiled by Patriarch Cyril v to the Barlaam monastery, one of the Meteora monasteries in Thessaly; but after ten years of exile, in 1760, he returned to the Crimea and again became Metropolitan of Gothia.[10] A special decree (*firman*) was issued by the Sultan Mustafa iii (1757–1773), dated 1759, in which he commands that Gedeon shall rule as Metropolitan 'over the Christians dwelling in Caffa, Mankup, Balaklava, and Azov, according to former examples, old customs, and their law.'[11] It is very probable that during

[1] This inscription, discovered in the Crimean village Bia-Sala, was published in 1837 by Köppen in his *Krymsky Sbornik* (pp. 40–41). Since no trace of the inscription has been preserved, Latyshev in his *Collection of Christian Inscriptions* (No. 62, pp. 67–68) reproduced its text from Köppen's edition; Arsenius, p. 73; Hermogenes, p. 150; Braun, *Die letzten Schicksale*, p. 65; Kulakovski, *op. cit.*, pp. 124, 131.

[2] Arsenius, p. 74; Braun, *op. cit.*, p. 66. [3] Hermogenes, p. 150.

[4] Sathas, *Bibl. graeca. medii aevi*, iii, 587: '(In 1652) κατ' ὀκτώβριον, καθαίρεσις Γοτθίας 'Ανθίμου καὶ ὑπόμνημα Γοτθίας Δανιήλ. (ἄνευ ἡμερομηνίας) περὶ τοῦ κατ' ἀποκοπὴν διδόναι τὸν Γοτθίας Δαβὶδ τῇ Μ. ἐκκλησίᾳ τὸ ἐτήσιον χαράτσιον γρόσια 75 καὶ ἄσπρα 8 χιλιάδας, ἀντὶ πάσης ἄλλης δόσεως.' See Braun, *op. cit.*, p. 66; Vasilievski, *Works*, ii, ii, 427, n. 2. Kulakovski (*op. cit.*, p. 131) gives the incorrect year 1657.

[5] Sathas, iii, 599: '(In 1673) κατ' αὔγουστον, ὑπόμνημα Γοτθίας Μεθοδίου, ἀντὶ τοῦ ἀποθανόντος Δαυίδ.' Hermogenes, p. 150; Braun, *op. cit.*, p. 66; Vasilievski, *Works*, ii, ii, 427, n. 2.

[6] Sathas, iii, 604, Vasilievski, *ibid.*; Kulakovski, *op. cit.*, p. 130. [7] Hermogenes, p. 150.

[8] Arsenius, p. 74; Hermogenes, p. 150; Köppen, *op. cit.*, p. 69; Braun, *op. cit.*, p. 66.

[9] Arsenius, pp. 74–81; Hermogenes, p. 150; Braun, *op. cit.*, p. 66; Kulakovski, p. 131.

[10] On this episode see D. Spiridonov, 'Notes on the History of Hellenism in the Crimea, ii: Gervasius of Soumela,' in the *Izvestiya* of the Tauric Society of History, Archaeology, and Ethnography, ii (Simferopol, 1928), 9–10 (in Russian). I use the pagination of a reprint. Spiridonov gives sources.

[11] A. Negri, 'The Firman Given by the Turkish Sultan Mustafa, at the Request of the Constantinopolitan Patriarch Seraphimus, to the Metropolitan Gedeon for the Crimean Eparchy (a Russian translation from the Turkish),' in the *Zapiski* of the Odessa Society of History and Antiquities, ii (1850), 680–684, especially 680.

his exile Gedeon was replaced in the Crimea by Gervasius, *hieromonachus* of Soumela, who belonged to the widely known monastery of Soumela, close to Trebizond.[1]

The last Metropolitan of Gothia and Caffa was Ignatius, who ruled from 1771 to 1786 and was destined to organize and execute the migration of 31,280 Christians, Greeks, and Armenians, from the Crimea, including of course the territory of former Gothia, to the city Mariupol on the northern coast of the Sea of Azov. A special ukase (decree) of Empress Catherine the Great, issued in 1779, brought about this emigration from the Crimea into the Christian territory of the Russian Empire. Ignatius, the real founder of the city Mariupol, established his seat there and in his new country continued to bear the title of Metropolitan of Gothia and Caffa. The Armenian emigrants settled in the city of Nakhichevan, in the Caucasus. The list presented by Ignatius in 1783 enumerated sixty villages and six towns whence the people of his flock had emigrated. It is interesting to note that in Ignatius' list the names of Sugdaia, Mankup-Kalé, where in the fifteenth century the see of the Gothic eparchy was located, and Cherson (in Turkish *Sary-Kermen*), are missing. Evidently at that time these cities were in a state of complete ruin. After the death of Ignatius, on 16 February 1786, the eparchy of Gothia and Caffa ceased to exist. The community of Crimean emigrants was ascribed to the 'Slavonic' eparchy of that time, which later took the name of Ekaterinoslav.[2] In the Greek *Ecclesiastical History* of Sergios Makraios, which covers the period from 1750 to 1800, we read that in 1783 the Gothic eparchy became subject to the supervision of the Holy Synod established by Peter the Great in St Petersburg.[3] With the death of Ignatius died also the last memory of the existence of the Goths in the Crimea.[4]

[1] Spiridonov, *op. cit.*, p. 10 (in Russian; pagination of a reprint).

[2] Arsenius, pp. 82–84; Hermogenes, p. 151; Gavriil, 'The Emigration of the Greeks from the Crimea to the Guberniya (Government) of Azov and the Foundation of the Eparchy of Gothia and Caffa,' in the *Zapiski* of the Odessa Society of History and Antiquities, ɪ (1844), 197–204, especially 203; S. Serafimov, 'Notes from the Archive of the Eparchy of Gothia in the Crimea,' *ibid.*, vɪ (1867), 591–595; Kulakovski, *The Past of the Tauris*, p. 131, and especially 134–135; Braun, *op. cit.*, pp. 66–67, 75.

[3] Sathas, *Bibl. graeca medii aevi*, ɪɪɪ (Venice, 1872), 334: 'ὁ μητροπολίτης Γοτθίας προσηνώθη τῇ ἐκκλησιαστικῇ ἱερᾷ διοικήσει τῆς ἐν Πετρουπόλει ἁγιωτάτης συνόδου προσνεμηθείς.' Sergios Makraios died in 1819, Sathas, ɪɪɪ, Introduction, p. 81.

[4] Braun, *Die letzten Schicksale*, p. 75.

EXCURSUS

The 'Goths' in the Letter of David of Trebizond

DAVID, the last Emperor of Trebizond, wrote a letter dated 22 April 1459 to Philip, Duke of Burgundy, relating his recent exertions to form an anti-Turkish league. This project was the consolidation of various Caucasian peoples against the Turks. According to the letter David was himself prepared to take steps with thirty galleys and 20,000 men, his relative Hassan 'with 50,000,' 'George VIII, King of Georgia, with 60,000,' the Duke of Cherchere in Georgia 'with 20,000 cavalry,' Dadian Liparit, Prince of Mingrelia, and his son 'with 60,000,' 'Rabia (Prince of Abkhazia) with his brother and his barons with 30,000 men.' Besides these, 'the nation of the *Githi* and *Arani*' had promised to fight under the standard of 'King George of the Persians.'[1]

Two recent historians of Trebizond, W. Miller and Th. Uspenski, without any comment identify the 'Githi' of the letter with the Goths,[2] that is the Crimean Goths. Of course George King of the Persians is George King of Georgia. We are well informed as to the position of Gothia in the middle of the fifteenth century, her relations with the Tartars and Genoese, her external policy limited by these relations, and her quite insignificant military forces, so that it is absolutely impossible for us to admit that the Crimean Goths could have taken part in the anti-Turkish coalition David was attempting to form from the Caucasian peoples.

In his letter the 'Githi' must be the Caucasian tribe *Djik* or Circassians, and the 'Arani' the Alans or Ossetins, both located northwest of the Caucasian mountains.[3]

David's letter of 22 April 1459 has no reference whatever to the Crimean Goths.

In connection with this letter I believe that the Gothic princes ('signori Gotici') who are mentioned in the letter dated 12 August 1482 addressed by Zachariah, Prince of Matrega, to the Protectors of the Bank of St George, and discussed above, were not the Gothic Princes of Theodoro but also were the 'Githi,' from the Caucasus.

---

[1] David's letter in *Baronii-Raynaldi Annales Ecclesiastici*, xxix, 200–201: 'Githorum et Aranorum principes' (p. 200); 'natio Githorum et Aranorum promittunt militare sub vexillo regis Persarum' (p. 201); 'Georgius rex Persarum promptus est cúm sexaginta (*or* quadraginta) millibus hominum' (p. 201). Cf. *Epistola Gorgorae Georgianae ducis*: 'tum Githiarum et Sasoni populi' (*ibid.*, p. 202).

[2] W. Miller, *Trebizond, The Last Greek Empire* (London, 1926), p. 98; Th. Uspenski, *Outlines on the History of the Empire of Trebizond* (Leningrad, 1929), p. 135.

[3] See M. Brosset, *Additions et éclaircissements à l'Histoire de la Géorgie* (St Petersburg, 1851), pp. 408–409. Brosset also refers to the compound form *Githiarani*, i.e., *Djik* and *Alans*. Cf. the name *Gothalani*. In connection with the project of this anti-Turkish league several oriental envoys from the Caucasus, including an envoy from David, Emperor of Trebizond, arrived in Rome. See Georg Voigt, *Enea Silvio de' Piccolomini, als Papst Pius der Zweite, und sein Zeitalter*, iii (Berlin, 1863), 645–646.

GENEALOGICAL TABLE OF THE PRINCES
OF GOTHIA

THIS table is entirely tentative. Our material is too fragmentary and incomplete for any authentic reconstruction of the ruling line in Gothia.

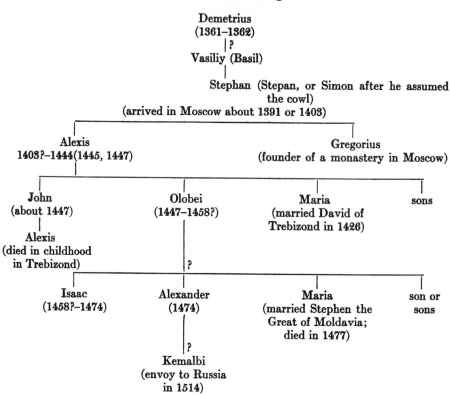

Demetrius
(1361–1362)
| ?
Vasiliy (Basil)

Stephan (Stepan, or Simon after he assumed
the cowl)
(arrived in Moscow about 1391 or 1403)

Alexis
1403?–1444(1445, 1447)

Gregorius
(founder of a monastery in Moscow)

John
(about 1447)

Olobei
(1447–1458?)

Maria
(married David of
Trebizond in 1426)

sons

Alexis
(died in childhood
in Trebizond)

?

Isaac
(1458?–1474)

Alexander
(1474)

Maria
(married Stephen the
Great of Moldavia;
died in 1477)

son or
sons

?

Kemalbi
(envoy to Russia
in 1514)

INDEX

In this index the notes to the text have not been taken into account. Besides this, references to the following names are not given because of their very large number: Crimea, Europe, and Goths.